The Festival of Brigit
Celtic Goddess and Holy Woman

This book is dedicated to the memory of my grandmother, Bridget, who told of the strawboys who danced at her wedding,

and it is also dedicated to Maj, to Sorcha and Ger, Luke, Féilim and Dualta, and to Pádraig and Justin.

Frontispiece: Girls Selling their St Brigit's Crosses at St Brigid's Well *(Daigh Bhríde)*, Liscannor, Co. Clare, 1983

[National Folklore Collection, University College Dublin]

THE FESTIVAL OF BRIGIT

Celtic Goddess and Holy Woman

by

Séamas Ó Catháin

PHAETON PUBLISHING LTD.
Dublin

The Festival of Brigit
Celtic Goddess and Holy Woman

[FIRST PUBLISHED IN IRELAND & U.K. 1995]
THIS SECOND EDITION PUBLISHED 2023
by Phaeton Publishing Limited, Dublin

Copyright © Séamas Ó Catháin 1995 & 2023

Séamas Ó Catháin has asserted his right to be identified as the author of this work

Cover & book design copyright © O'Dwyer & Jones Design Partnership, 2023

British Library Cataloguing In Publication Data: a catalogue record for this book is available from the British Library

ISBN: 978-1-908420-32-9   PAPERBACK
ISBN: 978-1-908420-31-2   HARDBACK

All rights reserved. No part of this publication may be reproduced, stored in, or introduced into a retrieval system, or transmitted, in any form or by any means (electronic, mechanical, photocopying, recording, or otherwise) without the prior written permission of the publisher.

This book is sold subject to the condition that it shall not, by way of trade or otherwise, be lent, re-sold, hired out, or otherwise circulated, without the publisher's prior consent, in any form of binding or cover other than that in which it is published, and with a similar condition imposed on all subsequent purchasers.

Contents

	page
LIST OF ILLUSTRATIONS	vii
INTRODUCTION (to the 1995 edition)	viii
INTRODUCTION (to this 2023 edition)	xiii
CHAPTER 1 *Oíche Fhéile Bríde...*	1
Notes to Chapter 1	34
CHAPTER 2 *Vita enim mortuorum...*	49
Notes to Chapter 2	74
CHAPTER 3 *An ghrian sa ló...*	89
Notes to Chapter 3	127
CHAPTER 4 *Booley and Baile*	144
Notes to Chapter 4	167
CHAPTER 5 *Weave a circle round him thrice...*	175
Notes to Chapter 5	225
REFERENCES & BIBLIOGRAPHY	239
INDEX OF NAMES	258
INDEX OF SUBJECTS	263
ACKNOWLEDGEMENTS	273

Illustrations

Figure no.   page

Frontispiece: Girls selling Brigit's Crosses, Liscannor, 1983   ii
1. Brideswell *(Tobar Bhríde)*, Co. Roscommon   5
2. St Brigid's Well *(Daigh Bhríde)*, Liscannor, Co. Clare   5
3. *Brídeoga* (younger Biddy Boys), Co. Kerry, 1974   17
4. *Brídeoga* (older Biddy Boys), Co. Kerry, 1974   17
5. *Brídeog* – effigy of Brigit   19
6. *Crios Bríde* girdle   19
7. Brigit's Crosses   23
8. Weaving St Brigit's Cross, Co. Antrim, 1905   25
9. Weaving St Brigit's Cross, Co. Donegal, 1975   25
10. Churn and Staff, Co. Donegal   29
11. Churn and Staff, Co. Kerry   29
12. Churn and Staff, Co. Galway   29
13. Wild Angelica, Co. Mayo   29
14. Cross Slab, St Brigit's Well, Cliffoney   31
15. Drawing of Cliffoney Cross Slab, Co. Sligo   31
16. Bust of Celtic Deity *Cerrunnos*   31
17. *Lucia* with crown of lighted candles, Sweden   31
18. Sámi shaman drum   32
19. Cross detail from a Sámi shaman drum   33
20. Bronze group: *dea Artio*, Bern   51
21. Pre-Christian bear sculptures, Armagh   51
22. *Drunnur* (tailbone), Faroe Islands   62
23. St Brigid's Well, Inishowen, Co. Donegal   73
24. *Tarvos trigaranus* Celtic monument, Paris   108
25. *Esus* (woodcutter) face of *Tarvos* monument   108
26. Papil Stone slab, West Burra, Shetland   111
27. Detail of Papil Stone, Scotland   111
28. Sámi Turf Dwelling, Finnmark, Norway   126
29. View of *Sliabh Liag*, Teelin, Co. Donegal   181
30. View of *Sliabh Liag* (Slieve League), Teelin   181
31. *Tobar na mBan Naomh*, Teelin, Co. Donegal   185
32. Seán Ó hEochaidh at *Tobar na mBan Naomh*   185
33. *Emegender* dolls, Siberia   211
34. St Brigid's Well, Clondalkin, Co. Dublin   224
35. Irish Folklore Commission Questionnaire, 1942   257

Back cover: St Brigit's Well & Cross Slab at Cliffoney

Introduction

IN GAELIC TRADITION, the Festival of Brigit gives its name to the month of February (*Mí na Féile Bríde* etc., 'The Month of the Festival of Brigit') and is celebrated as one of the so-called 'Quarter Days' which divide the year into four three-month periods. As such, it marked the beginning of the spring season just as the other landmark days, *Bealtaine* (1 May), *Lúnasa* (last Sunday in July or first Sunday in August), and *Samhain* or Hallowe'en (eve of 1 November) in turn signalled the start of the summer, harvest, and winter seasons respectively.

Today, the Festival of Brigit incorporates the name of the one of three great saints who ranks in the roll of honour of early Irish Christianity alongside Patrick, the patron saint of Ireland, and Colm Cille (Columba), Irish colonizer of Scotland and founder of Iona. According to tradition, festivals of this kind were usually celebrated over a period extending from the eve of the feast until the evening of the following day, in other words twenty-four hours made up of a night and a day in that order. This ancient, fundamental concept is enshrined in the designations *Oíche Fhéile Bríde* (St Brigit's Eve) and *Lá Fhéile Bríde* (St Brigit's Day) – 31 January and 1 February respectively. However, these are not the oldest names associated with this festival in Irish tradition, for in earlier times it was called *Imbolc* – a word whose basic meaning has much to do with the notion of milking and milk-production.

There was too an earlier Brigit who preceded Brigit Abbess of Kildare, who lived in the fifth and sixth centuries and who was the subject of no less than three early *Lives*. These accounts are repositories of a body of lore which reveals as much about her pagan predecessor as it does about the shadowy figure of the Christian saint herself, certain aspects of whose character, as James Kenney tells us, 'must be based on the myth or the ritual of a goddess, probably a goddess associated with a fire cult.' The triplicated form of the earlier Brigit is emphasized by the ninth-century Irish glossator,

Introduction

Cormac mac Cuilleanáin who notes the existence of –

> 'Brigit i.e. a learned woman, daughter of the Dagda. That is Brigit, woman of learning, i.e. a goddess whom *filid* worshipped. For her protecting care was very great and very wonderful. So they call her goddess of poets. Her sisters were Brigit, woman of healing, and Brigit, woman of smith-work, daughters of the Dagda, from whose names among all the Irish a goddess used to be called Brigit.'

Cormac's Brigit in turn harks back to the eponymous goddess of the *Brigantiae*, one of the great Celtic tribes of Ireland, Britain and mainland Europe.

Procreation and regeneration, both vegetable and animal, are factors basic to the continuity of human kind. Small wonder, therefore, that Brigit, whose very name embodies the concept of growth, should powerfully symbolize these, and that down the ages she should have remained such a constant icon of veneration for heathen and Christian Celt alike. Christian devotion to the saint was imbued with the spirit of the goddess, as is vividly demonstrated by the fact that attributes of her divine character are still distinguishable in modern Irish and Scottish folk tradition surrounding the Feast of St Brigit. In effect, the cult of St Brigit, powered by many of the traditions associated with pagan Brigit, may be said to have functioned as a vehicle for transmitting ancient elements of the culture of the prehistoric era down to our own time.

The arrival of Brigit's feastday – 1st February – betokened a turning point in the year: the worst rigours of winter had been left behind and the onset of spring weather and the coming of new growth could now be confidently expected. The displacement of dark winter, withered and dead, by spring – bright, young and bursting with the promise of new life – is the age-old background and fundamental consideration against which both Brigit, the pagan goddess of the Celts, and the development of the Christian cult of St Brigit, as well as the complex of folk tradition associated with it, should be seen. Regarding the manner in which the festival of Brigit was actually conducted, as is by and large the case with its sister festival *Lúnasa*, the early literature is silent. Consequently, in striving to conceive a picture of it, we are forced to depend heavily on the documentation provided in the folklore record. Fortunately, this source proves capable of elucidating the nature of the festival in an amazing variety of ways.

The task of structuring the sequence of events and activities associated with Brigit's festival in modern times, is relatively straightforward. A meaningful assessment of this material compels the adoption of a more ambitious approach, however, and a widening of the focus to include not only folkloristic but also literary, archaeological and other sources. The aggregation of this material and the interpretation of the evidence which it yields, together with the insights achieved through etymological analysis, uncovers something of the deeper significance of the rich symbolism associated with many features of the festival and also raises a raft of intriguing questions about them. Extension of the ambit of the exercise to include non-Celtic materials introduces a valuable dimension which enables us to place the basic complex in an even wider perspective. The fundamental value of the evidence offered by the folklore record is strengthened rather than weakened by this approach.

To begin with, the course of questing and quarrying in search of relevant parallels carries us backwards in time to the realms of classical tradition on the one hand, and to an exploration of the ancient Germanic culture on the other, and further beyond these again to the oldest levels of European culture as a whole. In this connection, the history of the Celts and their likely origins, the various patterns of interchange and borrowing between them and their neighbours, and the whole panorama of cultural goods common to the Celts and their fellow Indo-Europeans, renders fairly predictable the appearance of Artemis, Cybele, Hera, Hestia and Juno and many other figures of Greek tradition as well as their Roman counterparts, all clamouring for our attention no less insistently than Thórr and Óðinn and numerous other notables of Norse mythology.

Less expected, perhaps, is the emergence of a clear possibility of finding in Scandinavian and Celtic sources, similar if not altogether identical reflexes of pre-Indo-European culture. The extent to which the culture of the various circumpolar peoples, particularly that of the Sámi and the Finns, may have impacted upon the Germanic populations of Scandinavia is currently a lively subject of debate and also a topic of utmost relevance here. The discovery that aspects of the traditional celebration of the coming of spring in Ireland and Scotland may be linked with that virtual lynchpin of circumpolar culture – the bear cult – adds enormous weight to the arguments favouring recognition of the importance of elements of Finno-Ugrian culture as an underlying influence on Scandinavian tradition as a whole. More importantly for us, the establishment of this connection opens a challenging new perspective on the traditions of the Celtic peoples, both ancient and modern, insular and continental, not least with regard to contemporary Gaelic folklore and the interpretation of many aspects of early Irish literature and Celtic archaeology.

The bear's singular habit of hibernating resulted in it being looked upon as a kind of *zeitgeber* in respect of the shifting seasons. In northern climes, the emergence of the bear from its slumbers in springtime marked a turning point in the year. The animal was thus effectively cast in a similar role to Brigit who manifests herself in a parallel situation within the context of the festival held in her honour. Behind this lies a good deal more than meets the eye, however, for, as with numerous other population groups, the bear cult struck deep roots among the Celtic peoples within whose culture etymological, archaeological, and, to some extent, literary evidence indicates a long-standing and intimate interest in and at least some knowledge of this extraordinary animal and its habits.

This is a circumstance which appears distinctly out of step with ecological reality, at least as far as Ireland is concerned, for, unlike, say, parts of the Nordic world where the bear roams free to the present day and where a concomitant intensity of comment about it in contemporary folklore was much in evidence, Ireland has been bear-free, so to speak, for four thousand years or thereabouts. In spite of this fact, aspects of the bear feast as celebrated by the Sámi people, the Finns and others, and other elements such as the story of the Bear Wife of Sámi and Icelandic tradition, can be traced to Celtic soil and run to ground in the context of Brigit and her festival.

Nor is the bear the only creature with which we have to contend: the dog (from which it is descended), the primordial cow, the bee whose behaviour so baffled Aristotle, the humble winkle and barnacle and the enigmatic oyster-catcher, the storied crane and other long-beaked birds also turn up. Plant-life also features, with reference to angelica, rushes, straw, flax, various kinds of trees (especially alder, birch, oak, pine, and willow), and mushrooms most prominent, while acorns, honey, milk and milk products and foods (principally butter), the crafts of spinning and weaving, and the practice of transhumance are strongly represented too. Delicately reposing within a sophisticated web of sexual and fertility symbolism, these and a variety of other elements and images cry back in one way or another to the basic issue of procreation and productiveness.

Not unexpectedly for one whose nuns 'after the manner of the Vestal Virgins tended 'a perpetual ashless fire ... blown by fans or bellows only, and surrounded by a hedge within which no male could enter', the Abbess of Kildare boasted strong fire associations, and on a less exotic note, like many another Irish saint, a string of holy wells dedicated to her name, the waters of some of the latter being credited with the power to combat barrenness or sterility. Other wells harbour reference to triplicated figures sporting characteristics appropriate to fate goddesses such as the Norns, and to other groups with strong childbirth associations with which Brigit can also be shown to be connected.

Some of the material presented in this study appears here in English for the first time. In the case of the Irish language, it is drawn largely from the resources of the manuscript archive of the former Irish Folklore Commission, now the Department of Irish Folklore at University College Dublin. Also making its first appearance here is a range of source material which has been available to this point in a variety of Nordic languages only.

From the relatively narrow base provided by accounts of the festival of Brigit as widely celebrated in Ireland and Scotland in recent times there springs a series of associations and parallels which has inexorably extended the scope of this study. The broad dimensions of this canvas render futile the best efforts of one individual to cover it completely. Nothing daunted, my attempts to discern a pattern of meaning within this picture have caused me to stray in many directions. In some respects, at least, I believe it may be claimed that this joyful pursuit has not been entirely in vain. Some issues have been clarified and others made to appear in a new light, beckoning ultimate resolution by those better qualified than I to grapple with them. Much, however, still lies awaiting discovery in the lap of the goddess.

S. Ó C.

Introduction to the Second Edition

A REFERENCE IN THE OPENING LINES of Chapter 1 of the first edition of *The Festival of Brigit – Celtic Goddess and Holy Woman [FOB]* typifies Brigit and her Festival as being 'a popular and constant target among folklore collectors over the years.' Footnote 5 to Chapter 1 of *FOB* cites the existence of the Irish Folklore Commission's 1942 Questionnaire on 'The Feast of Brigid', the replies to which run to 2,435 manuscript pages and advert to the response to other Questionnaires also containing references to Brigit – 'Local Saints' and 'Holy Wells', issued around the same time. These statements convey little about the status of the collection to which these sources belong and where they abide today. Thankfully, the re-publication of *FOB* affords an opportunity to enlarge on the genesis and development of this famous collection and to describe its importance in greater detail.

The termination of the Commission and the transfer of its staff and holdings to University College Dublin (UCD) was completed in 1970. Thereafter, the collection and the substantial augmentations to it became known as the Irish Folklore Collection, and, latterly, the National Folklore Collection (NFC). UCD now houses the premier collection of materials for the study of the widest imaginable spectrum of Irish folk tradition, latterly recognised by UNESCO as being of 'world significance' and 'outstanding universal value to culture.'

The bulk of these vast holdings was assembled under the auspices of the Irish Folklore Commission (IFC) from 1935 to 1970, whose inspirational Honorary Director, Séamus Ó Duilearga (1900-1980), together with three key colleagues – Seán Ó Súilleabháin (1903-1996), Máire McNeill (1904-1987), and Caoimhín Ó Danachair (1913-2002) – laid the foundation of a national collection of which Ireland can be justly proud. They were ably assisted by a team of full-time and part-time collectors operating in the field across the island of Ireland; the Commission's endeavour also extended in a small but vitally important measure to Scotland, and, to a lesser degree, the Isle of Man.

The efforts of the Commission's collectors were bolstered by the contributions of a network of highly motivated questionnaire correspondents located all over the country, and also by the mustering of an army of schoolchildren and their teachers during the operation of the Schools' Collection scheme conducted during an eighteen-month period in 1937-1938, immediately prior to the commencement of the second World War (1939-1945). The work of the Commission continued under the auspices of the Department of Irish Folklore and its successors at UCD, resulting in substantial additions to the original holdings across the board.

While the salvage of objects of ethnological interest did not form part of the Commission's brief, their documentation constituted an important element of the Commission's multifaceted range of enquiry, not only in terms of word pictures but also in pictorial and photographic form.

All in all it may be claimed that the scope and quality of these collections propelled Ireland to the forefront in terms of research potential in folklore and ethnology and kindred disciplines, a circumstance frequently acknowledged by foreign scholars who readily understood its significance for the study of wider European folk tradition.

I have felt obliged to apprize readers in greater detail of the background to the creation of the single most important source of folklore material central to this study, namely the National Folklore Collection and have included remarks to that effect in this new introduction. This edition has afforded me an opportunity to make a number of minor adjustments to the presentation and layout of the main text and footnotes – mainly in order to make them more reader-friendly. Apart from the rectification of typographical and spelling errors, adjustment of punctuation and paragraphing, and limited re-arrangement of occasional infelicitous phraseology, the text and footnotes remain broadly in line with the first edition.

* * *

I was introduced to this celebrated collection by those who created and planned it, including the above-mentioned trio, and members of the phalanx of full-time and part-time collectors who reaped the harvest and brought the plan of action to fruition. The latter group were instructed (and, in large measure recruited) by Ó Duilearga, and followed guidelines supplied by him and by

Ó Súilleabháin through various publications, principal among them *A Handbook of Irish Folklore* (first published by the Folklore of Ireland Society in 1942).

Ó Duilearga in his foreword to the *Handbook* described this seminally important publication as 'an encyclopedia of Irish, and, indeed, of West-European tradition.' It was, Ó Duilearga said, 'a treasure-house of fact and fancy, of ritual and observance, custom and belief', in which lies mirrored 'the routine of rural life of our ancestors, a source of inestimable value to the student of European ethnology and ... social history of the Irish countryman.' Or as Delargy's successor in the Chair of Irish Folklore at UCD (Swedish-born Bo Almqvist, 1932-2013) had it – 'thanks to this book we are in a position to say, whenever we are asked: "What do you mean by Irish folklore?" that our definition is: 'all such things as are mentioned and enquired about in *A Handbook of Irish Folklore*.'

Seán Ó Súilleabháin's appointment as Archivist marked a key moment in the implementation of the plan of campaign launched by the Commission in 1935. Shortly after his appointment, he was despatched to Sweden where he studied first with Carl Wilhelm von Sydow in Lund, and then in Uppsala, where he met members of staff at *Landsmålsarkivet*, one of the great Swedish folklore archives.

They initiated him into the workings of the system for the classification of Swedish folklore materials that had been developed and actively applied there. In the space of a few months, Ó Súilleabháin quickly absorbed the basic structure and contents of the Uppsala index, succeeded in positioning himself for attuning them to Irish needs, and thus laid the foundation for his *Handbook*.

Ó Súilleabháin followed the layout and content of the Swedish model closely, but did not cleave slavishly to its configuration. Instead, he strove to bring the Uppsala index – its contents and the order of their presentation – into line with the existing Irish materials with which he was already so well acquainted. In this process, he applied not only his unrivalled familiarity with the body of material that had been assembled by the Commission to that point, but also the folk tradition of his native place and other parts of Ireland with which he was intimately acquainted.

On his return to Ireland, the *Handbook*, gradually began to assume the form in which we know it today, its compilation being completed in 1940, and its publication achieved in 1942. Apart from minor changes 'necessary to cope with the various types of tradition found in Ireland ... the Swedish system stands unaltered,' Ó Súilleabháin wrote; he also noted that his work provided the added benefit of rendering available 'the detailed scheme for folklore collection worked out at Uppsala' for the first time in English.

Bo Almqvist described it as '... one of the finest gifts that the Swedish people ever received from Ireland, because the system has never been laid down in print in Sweden, and it was through the *Handbook* more than anything else that it came to be known and imitated internationally.' Since 2014, it has been available in a Kindle ebook edition (*Scríbhinní Béaloidis* / Folklore Studies 22, *Comhairle Bhéaloideas Éireann* / The Folklore of Ireland Council 2014), to which I had the privilege of contributing a new introduction in honour of my old friend and teacher.

The *Handbook* satisfied the need 'for a comprehensive guide to assist the eight full-time and forty or so part-time collectors in their work,' as Ó Súilleabháin put it, adding that the collectors received it 'with joy, and field-work improved out of all recognition.' He concluded that the 'the content of this huge collection would have been much poorer and more restricted had not the *Handbook* been available.' In short, it is no exaggeration to say that this landmark publication shaped the future of folklore research in Ireland.

* * *

Ó Súilleabháin was careful to clarify the motivation for the changes wrought by him, and they are easily identifiable. Nowhere is that circumstance more obvious than in his Chapter 12, entitled 'RELIGIOUS TRADITIONS', in which domain the rich folk culture of Post-Reformation Sweden – the 'Great Protestant Nation of the North' – ran a poor second to 'Catholic Ireland.'

Four pages of Chapter 12 (551-554) are devoted to 'SAINTS', major and minor, including 'Saint Brigid' who – in Ó Súilleabháin's words – occupied 'a prominent place in Irish oral tradition.' Some of the information about her, he noted 'has come from manuscript or printed sources, but it is evident that a great deal of it is traditional and has been preserved orally for centuries.'

Further particulars of the roadmap for the pursuit of field-work enquiries into the web of tradition concerning Brigit is set out in two further chapters of the *Handbook* – Chapter 8 'TIME', and Chapter 14 'SPORTS AND PASTIMES'. The broad detail there is presented in sub-sections entitled – 'Festivals of the Year', 'The Saints' and 'Festival Amusements and Games' and the finer detail is presented under the following sub-headings: 'St Brigid's Feast', 'The Vigil of St Brigid's Feast', 'St Brigid's Day' (Chapter 8); 'Saint Brigid' (Chapter 12); and 'St Brigid's Eve Amusements' (Chapter 14).

The Questionnaire entitled 'The Feast of St Brigid' was drafted by Ó Súilleabháin and adroitly deployed by the Commission to arrive in the hands of correspondents in January 1942, taking full advantage of the upcoming Quarter Day on 1 February and the marking of the festival period centred upon Brigit. The *Handbook* would be published towards the end of that same year. This study draws heavily on the concentrated body of material engendered by this Questionnaire, a copy of which is included on page 257 at the end of this new edition.

In this book I have attempted to uncover (in a wider international context) aspects of the motivation of previous generations in sustaining and preserving ancient practices and beliefs, and at least vouch the hope that I may have succeeded in promoting a wider appreciation of the important role of folk culture as an essential component of seeking to gain a deeper understanding of the past.

S. Ó C. December 2022

—*Chapter I*—

Oíche Fhéile Bríde agus Lá Lúnasa
The Eve of the Feast of Brigit and *Lúnasa* Day

IN THE COURSE OF MY ENGAGEMENT with field-work I managed to catch glimpses of traditions regarding Brigit and the celebration of her Feast in action and in popular memory at various locations in Ireland, and am glad to be able to feature some of that material here. The making of crosses on St Brigit's Eve was ubiquitous, as also, to a lesser extent, the *Brídeoga* or Biddy-Boys doing the rounds in her honour. The time-honoured injunction for a household to bid Brigit welcome on her night was less common by far, surviving only (sporadically) in Irish-speaking districts.

The wording of this intriguing formula, as I heard it, goes as follows: *'Gabhaigí ar bhur nglúna, fosclaigí bhur súile agus ligigí isteach Bríd!'* ['Get on your knees and open your eyes and let Brigit in!'], which drew the enthusiastic response from those within: *'Is é beatha! Is é beatha! Is é beatha na mná uaisle!'* ['Welcome! Welcome! Welcome to the noble woman!']. This formula has a venerable ring to it, as evidenced in the categorizing of a great deal of the material relating to Brigit as being 'traditional', having been 'preserved orally for centuries'.

That this extraordinary exchange failed to survive the disruption caused by language loss is not unexpected. Yet, when I asked someone about the detail of Brigit's reception on the eve of her feast in her English-speaking area, I was dismayed to meet with the following astonishingly meagre reflex of the Irish-language collocution appropriate to the occasion: 'They just said 'Here's wee Brigit!' I was told.

In another setting, it was delightful to hear the recital of the hearthside prayer for 'raking the ashes', commonly delivered as the last glowing embers were in the process of being covered to preserve the fire overnight. In this instance, the honours are evenly divided between Brigit and the Virgin Mary (see pp. 91, 124 ff.). The nightly custom of 'raking the ashes' remained extant as long as hearth-fires existed and continued to be attended in this fashion, but the accompanying prayer was destined to disappear with the language in which it was made and found no counterpart in the new dispensation.

These examples underline the importance of the priority accorded to the Irish-language field-work undertaken by the Irish Folklore Commission (and its successor organisations – the Department of Irish Folklore and the National Folklore Collection at University College Dublin) and my own good fortune in being in a position to supply a modest contribution to the record in this regard.

The most important calendar festivals of the year in Ireland received considerable attention from collectors and provide a wealth of material for study and analysis. Comprehensive treatments such as *The Festival of Lughnasa* (1962) by Máire MacNeill (the folklorist daughter of Eoin MacNeill, Irish scholar and 1916 revolutionary), or *Blood Rite: The Feast of St Martin in Ireland* by the brilliant young scholar Billy Mag Fhloinn (published 2016 in Helsinki in the prestigious Folklore Fellows Communications series [no. 310]), provide yardsticks for future investigations. – My imagination was fired by Máire MacNeill's supposition in relation to the festival of *Lúnasa* that there is 'a folk-logic identifying human fertility with the fertility of the crops' and I embarked on an exploration of the folklore materials pertaining to the Feast of Brigit, pursuing the trail of what MacNeill called 'magical reasons for mating' rather than engaging with NFC (and other) materials on a broader scale.

I followed MacNeill in other ways too in speculating about what may be learned from 'the practice of the festival-celebration [of *Lúnasa*]', by incorporating folk legends and other narrative genres (as in her chapter 'The Associated Legend-Types'), and in introducing readers to relevant tradition material relating to other Irish saints, principal among them being Colm Cille.

Brigit's story is set in the context of the rural economy, diet, and daily life of earlier centuries – reflecting interaction with creatures big and small in field, farm, and forest, some like the bear and wolf long extinct in Ireland, others more durable like the birds of the air, and the humble cow providing vital nourishment for human kind.

The approach I chose to take has led me in many unexpected directions far distant from twentyfirst-century Ireland and far back in time, on a pathway of discovery and wonder.

* * *

Chapter 1

Starting from *Oíche Fhéile Bríde agus Lá Lúnasa*[1] [The Eve of the Feast of Brigit and *Lúnasa* Day], this first chapter gives an account of a range of customs and beliefs associated with the saint and her unseen presence during the celebration of her Festival (covering the twenty-four hour period from the evening of 31st January until the following evening) in family and wider community settings. Elements such as fertility, fate, fire, and light, Brigit's folk status as coeval and coequal with the Blessed Virgin Mary, her intimate connection with milk and butter production, and her healing and protective powers are highlighted.

In her monumental *The Festival of Lughnasa*, Máire MacNeill writes:

> Fuller understanding of the old goddess's part in the harvest festival must wait on studies, still to be made, of the local legends of the myth of the mythological old woman known as the *Cailleach Bhéara* and also of the cults of St Brigid and St Ann... Brigid must have been closely connected—at least two important Lughnasa sites were dedicated to her, and she is named at several others. Still she hardly appears in the festival legends. She has only a passive part in the Lughnasa complex.[2]

Just as was the case for MacNeill's brilliant exposé of *Lúnasa*, so also much of the raw material which would form the basis for the kind of studies mentioned by her above is to be found in rich abundance in the manuscript holdings of the National Folklore Collection.[3]

The Feast of Saint Brigit, in common with the other Quarter Days of Irish tradition,[4] was the target of particular attention being the topic for an Irish Folklore Commission Questionnaire[5] and also a popular and constant subject of enquiry among folklore collectors over the years. The purpose of this study is to attempt to isolate and highlight certain hitherto largely ignored or, at best, badly understood aspects of the cult of Brigit which feature prominently in Irish folk tradition and which cast her in the role of a fertility figure comparable to her harvest counterpart Lugh. In essaying this task, I could do no better than follow the trail blazed by Máire MacNeill when she wrote:

> Lughnasa is not a marrying time... If one presupposes a folk-logic identifying human fertility with the fertility of the crops, there is no magical reason for mating at reaping time. If the incentive (to help

the crops) were thought of in terms of human pregnancy, the union should be made at Samhain; if in terms of the growth of the crops, it should be made at the beginning of spring, about St Brigid's Day.[6]

I am in complete agreement with MacNeill's supposition that there is a 'folk-logic identifying human fertility with the fertility of the crops'. The correctness of this approach will be further substantiated by material I will adduce below. I will also try to show that her 'magical reason for mating' is, as she indeed hints, directly associated with the beginning of spring and the Feast of Saint Brigit.

One of the two important Lúnasa sites linking 'the old goddess' and the harvest festival, to which MacNeill refers, is Brideswell or *Tobar Bhríde* in County Roscommon (Fig. 1).[7] Like *Daigh Bhríde* (Saint Brigid's Well) at Liscannor, County Clare (Fig. 2)[8] and the St Brigid's Well in the parish of Ballinakill, County Galway,[9] it is a *Lúnasa* site which bears the name of the saint whose feast day is celebrated, not in harvest time, but on the first of February, traditionally the first day of spring in Ireland.[10] In common with a number of other wells dedicated to Saint Brigit, Brideswell also exhibits some highly significant connections with what may be broadly described as 'fertility' as is made clear by the following:

> In 1604 Randal MacDonnell, son of Sorley Boy, and afterwards first Earl of Antrim (1620), married Ailis, daughter of the great Hugh O'Neill, and they were for a while childless. They made the pilgrimage to Tobar Bhríde and later, in gratitude, for answered prayer, Randal, now Earl of Antrim, erected a gateway leading to the well, bearing his arms and date 1625.[11]

Kilbride *(Cill Bhríde)* near Ballycastle, County Mayo also boasts a 'St Bridget's Well' which 'is supposed to possess a cure for sterility' and which also happens to lie in close proximity to yet another major *Lúnasa* site.[12] The potential to 'cure sterility' was a feature of the healing powers of a number of holy wells here and there throughout the country.[13] Devotion to Saint Brigit was, indeed, widespread among the ordinary people, finding in later years its most elaborate surviving expression in the Irish-speaking or recently Irish-speaking parts. Seán Ó hEochaidh, former full-time folklore collector in Donegal noted:

Fig. 1 *(above)*: Brideswell *(Tobar Bhríde)* County Roscommon.

Fig. 2:
St Brigid's Well
(Daigh Bhríde)
Liscannor,
County Clare.

According to tradition, the old people had great belief in *Bríd* in this district and any time they would be in danger or in difficulty they would place themselves under her protection and patronage. This was also the case with regard to their children as can be heard in some of their lullabies to the present day:

Huis-a-bá, a lil ghil, ó huis-a-bá hí,
Beannacht Naomh Bríd ar leanbh mo chroí.[14]
(...'Oh the blessing of Brigit on the child of my heart.')

Another Donegal collector, Aodh Ó Domhnaill of Rannafast, writing in or around the same time, declares:

I used often hear when an old woman would ask the name of a child and when she would be told that her name was *Bríd*. I often heard that old woman remark in a kindly way while, perhaps, at the same time placing her hand reverently on the child's head – 'Oh, *Bríd*, the Holy Woman or blessed'![15]

Devotion to the saint as we shall see, often directly involved children or young adults and was frequently directed in particular towards the welfare of children and of females, both younger and older. One popular practice associated with the devotion to Brigit that is highly relevant in the context of the present discussion was that involving an object called the *Brat Bríde*, described by an informant from County Cork in the following terms:

This was a custom that was confined solely to the women and girls of the house. A piece of any kind of unwashed cloth in the house was taken out on the day before the first of February and placed on a bush. This was left there all day for it was supposed that when the night came Saint Brigid used pass by and touch this cloth. It was then brought in after dark and was torn in pieces and a piece was given to every female in the house. This was to have Saint Brigid protect them wherever they went.[16]

An informant from Kerry is more specific:

Pieces of the *brat* was sewn into young girls' clothes. This was supposed to guard them against any misfortune during the year and especially to preserve their virginity.[17]

Chapter 1

Uniting the twin concerns of providing an antidote to barrenness or sterility and securing a safe delivery at the end of a pregnancy, we have the following dramatic account from Donegal in which the crucial role played by the *Brat Bríde* is outlined:

> There was a poor old woman going around this place long ago and she had a shawl which was a *Bratach Bríde* of fourteen-years' standing and any request she made in the name of the shawl, she was granted it. She went into one of the houses here once. There was a cow tethered at the lower end of the house, about to calve, but the calf wasn't coming and appeared unlikely to do so and the cow seemed doomed. The poor woman enquired – 'Are you not doing any good?' They said they weren't. 'Well, go down again', says she, 'and try her once more.' The men went down and tackled the cow again. And the old woman shook the shawl over the cow and went down on her two knees there and began to pray to Brigit the Holy Woman. It wasn't ten minutes till the cow was all right. There was another woman in this place, long married, unable to have a family and not looking like she was ever going to have one either. This old woman came in to visit her one day. She told the poor woman how things were and how she would like to have a family. The poor woman removed her shawl and shook it three times over her in the name of God and Mary and Brigit the Holy Woman. She had her family after that.[18]

The normal method of utilizing the *Brat Bríd* in maternity cases was generally a much less flamboyant affair; it was by no means an unusual stratagem resorted to by country midwives or 'handy women' when attending at a birth. This account from Kerry provides us with a first-hand description of the precise manner in which the *Brat Bríde* was deployed:

> N... had one of those *brait*... She was a handy woman and she used to place it on the head of any woman sick in childbed. I was very bad when I was having my first child and N... placed the *Cochall Bríde* on my head and I got relief...[19]

The *Brat Bríde* was applied to parturient and postpartum cows in somewhat similar fashion:

> *Brat Bríde* was supposed to be an infallible cure for cows after calving that had kept what they call here 'the clanins'... They mean the

afterbirth. They placed it on the hindquarters of the cow and it got alright.[20] Always when a cow calves on that particular farm, the *brat* is spread over the cow's back. This brings good luck and the cow will have abundance of milk and the calf will thrive marvellous.[21]

As we have seen above, the protection and preservation of virginity or, what is, in effect, its antithesis – the elimination and relief of sterility and barrenness – clearly forms an important part of the picture along with the adoption of various measures designed to guarantee a successful pregnancy and a safe delivery. Of equal if not even greater importance were the measures taken subsequent to the birth in order to safeguard the new-born, be it human or beast, from evil forces, together with the steps taken to provide for its nourishment and sustenance in the early stages of its existence. The latter consideration concentrated mainly upon the necessity to secure and maintain an adequate supply of milk. This was something which was by no means guaranteed to be found readily to hand in the generally unproductive period that straddled the end of the winter season and the commencement of the spring proper, the period characterized, on the one hand, by the description *Na Faoilligh*, an Irish name for the month of February, a word which may have been perceived as meaning 'the leavings of the year'[22] and, on the other, by the designation *mí sílta*, 'the month of sowing'.[23]

* * *

> The country people always regarded and do still the advent of *Féile Bríde* as marking the end of nature's sleep during winter and her re-awakening to a fresh activity of life. This is of course exemplified in numerous ways in the animal and vegetable worlds. The mating instincts of animals (beasts and birds) are aroused even to the fishes of the sea. In the vegetable kingdom, signs of budding life are evident, and there is altogether a general re-birth, so to speak, of the natural order in the world.[24]

The folk tradition can, in fact, be quite detailed and explicit about such matters:

> Jackdaws and crows and other birds mate on that day.[25] Eggs were put down to hatch on St Brigid's Day if there was a broody hen to

be got as tradition had it that anything that started its growth on that day would prove 100% fertile.[26] There is nothing in the water or in the ground that is not thinking of propagating by the Feast of *Bríd*.[27]

By the same token, a definite connection seems to have existed in popular imagination between the instigation of the initial phase of the fertility cycle in beasts and also, perhaps, as we shall see, in human kind, on the one hand, and the preparation of the ground for the propagation of crops, on the other. The generation of new human life must always have been of paramount importance – since, without having sought to guarantee the perpetuation of his own species in the first place, there would be little point in man continuing to devote himself to breeding animals and cultivating crops so as to provide for the physical welfare and further survival of the species. But, the management of livestock and the tilling of the soil in order to produce a reliable supply of food was also a vital consideration and, accordingly, demanded and received its due measure of attention.

> New life is infused into the earth on Brigid's Day and a token to commence manual labour on the farm.[28] People always made an effort to start ploughing on St Bridget's Day. They said that if [you] had not your name written on [the] ground before that day you were late.[29] Men planted something on St Bridget's Day in order to 'redden' the soil.[30]

The timing of the commencement of agricultural activity might vary according to the climatic conditions prevailing in different parts of the country. In Cape Clear, in the far south of Ireland, for example, it was a case of not only getting the ploughing season under way but also actually starting to sow the crops:

> ...in this island wheat was always sown immediately after St Brigit's Day and potatoes likewise.[31]

By contrast in the far north of Donegal, however:

> There was little or no connection between planting and the Feast of *Bríd*... except that people liked to plant sally for making baskets for they feel there is no better or luckier time for this than the dark days around the Feast.[32]

But whether the act of sowing seed or carrying out other planting took place on or about the actual feast day – around which time, at the very least, preparation for such activity was generally expected to have begun – ultimately Brigit was called upon to impart her blessing to the work:

> On the night of the first of February the family rosary was always offered by the old people to Saint Brigid to bring blessing on the crops for the year.[33] A small sheaf of oats and potato used to be left on the doorstep until bed-time and stuck on a *scolb* ['scollop'] and put up behind a rafter on St Bridget's Eve. When the spring came, the oats would be rubbed between the hands and the seed would be put with the oats for sowing. The potato used to be cut and put with the rest of the 'slits'. While this was being done, St Brigid was being invoked to protect the crops from diseases.[34]

With the end of winter and the coming of spring which brought the prospect of new growth and better grazing, it was confidently expected that the milk supply would improve, a process, it was widely believed, not likely to be left unaided by Brigit:

> It is still said here that the milk has gone up into the cows' horns from Christmas until after the Feast of St Brigid. This means that there is a scarcity of milk during this time.[35] Usually milk is very scarce in January but the old people used to say during the month when they heard anyone complaining of the scarcity of milk – 'It won't be scarce very long now as *Bríd* and her white cow will be coming round soon.'[36] I heard that some of the older women of the Parish take a blessed candle to the cow's stall on Brigid's Eve and singe the long hair on the upper part of the cow's udder so as to bring a blessing on her milk.[37]

A cow would normally be expected to calve once a year and a newly-calved cow with a good supply of milk was a blessing indeed at this time of year. As A.T. Lucas points out, people were anxious to see to it that their cows would calve at this time:

> ...it was entirely logical to control breeding so that the birth of the calf coincided with the spring renewal of herbage so that the cow would benefit from the improving grazing thus enabling her to produce abundant milk for the sustenance of the calf during its first

weeks of life. As the calf grew able to graze for itself, more and more milk became available for human use.[38]

Protection of this milk supply was of crucial concern to man and beast alike:

> The new calved cow is put under the protection of St Brigid. The candles blessed on the day following her feast day are used in blessing the cow previous to milking after calving. St Brigid is believed to have every interest in farming life at heart, especially the milch cow.[39] The new springer was always put under St Bridget's protection. After she calved and before being put out on grass a sort of ceremony was performed by the man and woman of the house. One stood each side of the cow and then passed a tongs of coal round over [her] kidneys and under her udder three times and repeating prayers to Saint Bridget as they did so. Then the coals were quenched by throwing them in the drain in the cowhouse and a red rag containing a cinder and a grain of salt was tied on the tail, a drop of holy water was sprinkled on the cow and she was driven with great ceremony to join the herd. The spancel and the tongs were flung after her and then picked up and put away. How the tongs fell, foretold how lucky the milker would be and being touched with her old spancel protected her from fairies or spells of any kind. *Faraoir!* This custom has now died out.[40]

If for some reason or other, the cow was unable to give milk, once again recourse was had to Brigit:

> In a prayer or charm called the *Buarach Tháil*, there is a special petition to St Brigid where a cow is unable to yield or rather secrete her milk... For the purpose of this charm a *buarach* for the affected animal has to be made from rushes cut from one clump, and preferably growing in or on the bank of a river forming the mearing between two townlands. The *buarach* is tied around the cow's hind legs and the prayer *Buarach Tháil* then said. The spell is then broken and the cow gives the milk. This exercise or charm is still practised.[41]

Spring calving as Lucas tells us:

> ...meant that the cows had gone dry by the end of the autumn but a very limited supply of milk could be maintained over the winter

months if a few autumn calvers received special fodder and shared the warmth and shelter of the dwelling house.[42]

The 'stripper' (Irish *gamhnach*)[43] was a kind of cow which was capable of providing another kind of answer to this problem, as this account from County Mayo succinctly explains:

> This is a cow which did not calve at the usual time. From the time that a cow has her first calf, she should calve once a year. For about three seasons of that year she should be giving milk. She would be dry for about a season (three months) before calving. If that cow were to miscarry before she became dry, she would then have extra milk. In places where the land was poor and especially where little manuring was being carried out, it was very frequently the case that cows got a bad rearing so that they did not take the bull as they normally should. They might even continue without a while to a household which had no milk (six months or so). It would be said that they had got the cow for her milk. Such cows received better feeding in those places and after a short while they would take the bull again.[44]

The system of controlled breeding with all its vagaries fitted comfortably within an annual cycle running from spring to spring with the commencement of the process of insemination at one end and the delivery of new life at the other. The successful timing of the initial stages of this process could only be approximate and it was not, of course, totally under human control, no more than, say, the choice of date for the sowing of seeds or the planting of crops was capable of being determined in advance with exactness and precision from year to year. Sowing/insemination might well occur within a limited period of time the exercise being repeated as necessary until such times as germination/conception occurred, in order for crops to come to maturity at harvest time and, of particular interest to us here, parturition to take place and a new supply of milk to arrive in or around the time expected – in other words, at the beginning of spring, the very time when it was most needed and likely to be of most benefit.[45]

It is the beginning and the end of this process, insemination and parturition, that concerns us most here, not only in terms of cattle breeding, but also with regard to the cycle of human fertility itself. As Máire MacNeill says, 'folk-logic' was, indeed, capable of 'identifying human fertility with the fertility of the crops', a perception which was likely to have been particularly acute, it would seem on the evidence, in the case of human sexual congress that happened to occur from spring time onwards rather than at any other time.[46] The mating of animals also readily fitted into this same picture and, with reference to cows and women, generated, in at least one instance, a degree of interchangeable terminology that is not without its own special interest: in Kerry, a *maighdean bhuaile*, literally 'a booley[47] maiden', was the name given to a cow which would not take the bull[48] the same description was also applied to a wife who had failed to conceive.[49]

As we have seen, tradition is fairly explicit with regard to the animal world (birds and beasts) and to the vegetable kingdom. As is evident from the folklore of childbirth, for example,[50] it has also proved relatively forthcoming about certain matters pertaining to human sexuality. Comparatively speaking, however, comment muted to the point of reticence is the hallmark of the folklore record in matters pertaining to sexual intercourse between humans.[51] When touched upon, this was a subject which, naturally, tended to be handled with the utmost discretion; it was also a topic which is capable of being treated, as we shall now see, with a considerable degree of sophistication.

* * *

Imbolc/óimelc the ancient name for the festival of Brigit is defined thus in the ninth-century *Cormac's Glossary:* '*is [i] aimsir andsin tic as cáirach. melg. .i. ass arinní mblegar*'[52] 'that is the time the sheep's milk comes. milking i.e. milk that is milked'). Though condemned as 'a fanciful etymological explanation'[53] this statement has, nevertheless, inspired oft-repeated assertions that the pagan name of our feast, as *imbolc/óimelc* is said to be, has something to do with the period of the coming into lactation of sheep.[54] Eric Hamp, characterizing Cormac's gloss as being 'overdrawn and imprecise', has shown that the word simply means 'milking', conceding that the earlier interpretation was not entirely misdirected since it still managed to point in the general direction of the true meaning of the word, in so far as it showed that 'we are dealing with a name based on an old pastoral or husbandman's term'.[55] 'We are not told', complains Hamp, however, 'what the role of milk(ing) was in connection with the feast'.[56] Hamp goes on to show that there is a clear possibility of semantic development to a meaning 'clean/purge' from the original Indo-European root whose basic meaning, in turn, he argues, is 'purification'. The latter meaning he establishes partly by association with various Roman institutions, particularly the Lupercalia, and partly by making a connection with the goddess Juno, one of whose many epithets is *februa*, a word which Hamp suggests may be ultimately derived from *februus* meaning 'purifying'.[57]

Hamp's identification of *imbolc/óimelc* as 'a word based on an old pastoral or husbandman's term' is vindicated by Seán Ó Súilleabháin's earlier advocation of food-production as the chief line of study for understanding the meaning underlying the body of tradition associated with St Brigit's Day.[58] Food-production is, indeed, a key element: the production of food, however, is not by nature a one-off kind of affair, but rather a systematic, continuous process, involving, certainly in the case of livestock, the successful scheduling of reproduction of animals from year to year. In so far as that is implied by Ó Súilleabháin when he states: 'Every manifestation of the cult of the saint (or of the deity she replaced) is bound up in some way with food production'[59] he still finds himself on safe ground. The concept of reproduction as it affects mankind, however, does not seem to have been a factor considered by Ó Súilleabháin or to have entered Hamp's calculations. Ironically, it is reproduction – human reproduction – which provides the key to the puzzle of what Hamp called 'the role of milk(ing)… in connection with the feast'. It is Hamp's reference to Juno and to the Lupercalia, however, that provides us with an important clue leading us further along the road to a better understanding of what the festival of Brigit was really about. *Februa* was but one of many significant epithets borne by Juno – 'first and foremost the goddess of marriage and protector of married women'[60] and 'a special object of worship by women at all the critical moments of life'.[61] It is her oldest titles, Lucetia and Lucina, that principally concern us here. Juno Lucetia was the feminine principle of the celestial light (of which Jupiter was the masculine principle). Goddess of light, she was by derivation the goddess of childbirth, Juno Lucina, for the new-born baby was brought into the light and as such Juno Lucina was invoked by wives who were barren.[62]

To the best of my knowledge, Alexander Carmichael was the first to reflect upon the relationship between Juno and Brigit, on the one hand ('she is... the Juno of the Gael')⁶³ and Brigit and Mary (*'ban-chuideachaidh Moire'* – the aid-woman of Mary'),⁶⁴ on the other. Carmichael explains her soubriquet – '*Bride boillsge*, Bride of brightness' (she is also described as *'lasair dhealrach oir, muime chorr Chriosda'* ⁶⁵ 'radiant flame of gold, noble foster-mother of Christ')⁶⁶ – by reference to an Irish legend of which he quotes a rather curious version.⁶⁷ This legend is of a type common enough in Irish tradition,⁶⁸ the following County Galway example being a fairly typical representative of it:

> The Blessed Virgin was about to be 'churched' and as she was going to the church, she met St Brigid. Our Blessed Lady was very shy in going to the altar rails before the whole congregation and she told Brigid how she felt. 'Never mind,' says Brigid, 'I'll manage that part all right'. She got a harrow and put it on her head turning the points upwards. They went into the church and no sooner had St Brigid entered than every point of the harrow turned into a lighted candle. The whole congregation turned their eyes on St Brigid and her crown of lighted candles and the Blessed Virgin proceeded to the altar rails and not an eye was turned on her until the ceremony was over. The Blessed Virgin was so delighted with St Brigid that she gave her her day before her own and that is the reason that St Brigid's Day is before the feast of the Purification.⁶⁹

By the spectacular assumption of a harrow candelabrum on her head, Brigit is, in effect, cast as 'light mother' to Mary, a position which confers upon her the honoured status of midwife *par excellence* making her the perfect role model for any ordinary country midwife or 'handy woman'.⁷⁰ 'Light mother', indeed, is what the country midwife was called in the Nordic countries as we learn from the following account from Wilhelmina in northern Sweden:

> The lying-in woman was not allowed to lie in bed, but a straw bed was prepared for her on the floor. There she rolled herself to and fro and turned round according as the pains affected her, and what seemed to be most convenient for the arrival of the foetus. During the delivery, she knelt down, her legs being fairly spread and the upper part of the body leaning against the seat of a chair. It was supposed that the very best position for her was to lean against her husband or grasp him firmly. This was believed to ease the delivery. When the lying-in woman had taken up this position, it was time for the light-mother

to take charge. She knelt down behind the lying-in woman 'to catch the child' and this appeared from behind the mother – just as a female quadruped brings forth its offspring while standing.[71]

With this we may compare the following Irish account from County Mayo:

> The expectant mother was transferred from the kitchen bed which was her usual sleeping place, to the straw-littered floor. She put on her husband's sleeved waistcoat or *'báinín'* which was an outside flannel garment worn by men in those days. As the great event drew near, the husband stood at his wife's back, and placed his hands on her shoulders while she was in a kneeling position on the floor. With words of faith, hope and encouragement, he buoyed and morally supported her during her ordeal, the midwife being simultaneously engaged in the great task of bringing a new human life to the world – the long story of mankind. In the absence of the husband he was usually represented by some man, if possible a neighbour or friend of the woman... To the present day one hears among the country people expressions such as 'Paddy Moloney's wife is in the *sop*', 'It is time she was in the sop', "She was hardly out of the *sop* etc.' These sayings are derived from the time when childbirth took place not in a bed but in straw on the floor, as already described. Sop is the Irish word for a wisp of straw. Similarly there are also old Irish expressions such as *'Ón oíche a tháinig mo mhullach ar an tsop'* – 'From the night my 'top' (head) came on the ground', *'Ón oíche a tháinig mé ar an tsop'* – 'Since the night I came to the straw', which are the equivalents of saying 'Since the night I was born'.[72]

The country midwives of Scandinavia were also called 'strawmothers' and 'earthmothers'.[73] but neither of these terms, nor the term 'light-mother' seem to have been applied to their Irish counterparts. Nevertheless, they could have quite aptly been used of Brigit. As we shall see, the associations between light and straw (and rushes) are emphasized in a number of ways in the context of the body of tradition surrounding Brigit and the ceremony enacted in her honour on the eve of her feast. This ceremony is divided into three parts each of which, in turn, will now be subjected to a brief examination.[74]

* * *

Chapter 1

The following account from County Mayo provides us with a good description of the first of the three constituent elements of the programme of activities customarily carried out on St Brigit's Eve:

> Before nightfall, usually the man of the house procured a garment for the *Brat Bríde*... The man took out this article of clothing into the haggard, drew a good long sheaf of straw out of the stack, and wrapped the garment around the sheaf in a manner giving it as far as possible the rough outline in appearance of a human body. He then reverentially carried the object between his arms, in the manner one carries a child, and deposits it outside at the back door. He leaves it there and comes into the house... Then when the supper is laid on the table, and the inmates are ready to sit in, the man of the house announces that he is now going out to bring in Brigid, as she too must be present at the festive board. The man goes out and round to the back door where he kneels, and then in a loud voice says to the people inside who are expectant and waiting for the coming request: *Téigí ar bhur nglúna agus fosclaígí bhur súile agus ligigí isteach Bríd.* Response from within: *Is é beatha, is é beatha, is é beatha...* On the third response *Is é beatha* from the people within he takes up the bundle, gets up off his knees, and comes around to the open door, while the people within continue repeating the *Is é beatha*, as he is coming round, and when he enters the door they finish the response with *Maise, is é beatha agus sláinte.* Then the object (the sheaf of straw and *brat*) is laid carefully and respectfully against the leg or rail of the table, and under the table. The family then sit down to the supper preceded by a short prayer or invocation such as: *A Bhríd Bheannaithe, go gcuire tú an teach seo thar anachain na bliana* ['Blessed Brigit, may you protect this house from harm during the (coming) year']. When supper is finished there was the ejaculatory prayer – the usual one – of *Deo gratias le Dia agus cumhdach Dé ar lucht shaothrú na beatha*[75] ['*Deo Gratias* to God and God's protection on those earning a livelihood'].

The ritual here described was of a kind repeated with variations on this festive evening in many parts of Ireland.[76] At its heart is the demand for entry in the name of Brigit, a demand which is immediately and joyously conceded. Brigit is represented by the straw out of which a rough image of her has been fashioned and out of which same materials, later in the proceedings, crosses, cow-tyings and various other emblems and artefacts were manufactured in her honour and named after her.[77] In some cases the unused remainder of the straw was used to make up a rough and ready bed, a *sráideog* or 'shakedown', in which the holy woman was welcome to spend the night.[78] While the close communal nature and intimate family character of the circumstances in which a welcome was extended to Brigit rather tended to dominate the character of the evening, this did not exclude the possibility for the circle to be widened in order to accommodate the wider community: by means of the institution called the *Brídeog* (Figs. 3, 4), Brigit's arrival in the locality was announced and news of it carried from house to house.[79]

> The *Brídeog* procession from house to house was and still is held on the eve of the feast. Both boys and girls took part and there are sometimes two or three (or more) groups, each group out for itself in an area of a square mile according as the district is thickly populated or not. Sometime during the last week in January the young people who may be of any age up to twenty years, gather at a certain house in the kitchen or barn of which the rehearsals take place. Boys dress in girls' clothes as a rule and vice versa. Long ago a peeled turnip was used to represent the head of the *brídeog* which was draped like a baby being brought to the Chapel to be baptised. The places for eyes, nose, and mouth were cut out and coloured with soot or any other colouring available. A stick was inserted in the turnip to lend body to the *brídeog* and to make it easy to carry. Each participant prepared some item of entertainment to be performed on entering the houses. These items took the form of songs, music on flute or violin (later accordion), rhymes etc. When Irish was still the language, there were prayers in which the players interceded to St Brigid for blessings and favours for the members of the house, who were then asked to contribute something for the *brídeog*. This took the form of bread or butter: it is only in very recent times that money has been given and accepted. Early in the evening of Jan. 31, the *Brídeogs*, as they are called, commence their rounds. They are all disguised and are led by the one carrying the *brídeog* who is first to enter a house... The *Brídeogs*, are always welcome as it would be regarded as unlucky to be uncivil or inhospitable where they are concerned... Long ago when what was received was in kind, it was all collected in bags and afterwards a 'feast' (as is said) was held in some of the neighbour's houses... Priests were always against girls taking part in the processions and whenever they met them, they were sure to take the disguises off the *Brídeogs* to find out if there were girls among

Chapter 1

Figs. 3 & 4: *Brídeoga* (Biddy Boys, Biddies), Cill Ghobnait, County Kerry, 1974

them. Should a girl be found she was severely reprimanded by the priest and sent home. Boys were allowed to carry on.[80] Occasionally the company might be entirely female, restricted to girls not older than fourteen years of age, who made their rounds on the morning of the feast day, rather than on the eve of the feast. The welcome was as warm as ever, however, with the woman of the house addressing the doll image of Brigit thus:

> *Móire is dachad ar maidin duit, is a Chríostaí óig, tá an bhliain caite agus tánn tú tagaithe aris inár dtreo.*[81] 'A very good morning to you and, young Christian, this year is spent and you have come to us once again'.

'Then', this account continues, 'the woman of the house would take the *brídeog* in her arms and kiss it'.[82] Frequently, the *brídeog* consisted of clothes arranged on a churn dash[83] surrounded by stuffing and padding,[84] thus creating a 'figure which could stand by itself when placed on the ground' (Fig. 5).[85] In some parts, the *brídeog*, while still maintaining a prominent role as part of the procession, seems, nevertheless, to have been eclipsed in importance by the *Crios Bríde*, around which a somewhat complicated ceremony involving 'passing through' was enacted (Fig. 6).[86]

> The *Crios Bríde* was made from a straw rope (*súgán* whose two ends were attached to the bottom of the cross. The *crios* was about twelve feet long. Some of the people would go through the ceremony, that is, pass through the *crios* three times, kissing it and then emerging from it right foot foremost...[87]

The following prayer usually accompanied the presentation of the *crios*:

Crios, Crios Bríde mo chrios,	The Girdle, the girdle of Brigit, my Girdle,
Crios na gceithre gcros;	The Girdle of the four crosses,
Muire a chuaigh ann,	Mary entered it,
Agus Bríd a tháinig as;	Brigit emerged from it;
Más fearr sibh inniu,	If you be improved today,
Go mba seacht fearr a bheas sibh	May you be seven times better,
Bliain ó inniu.[88]	A year from today.

* * *

Fig. 5:
Brídeog
('Biddy') –
Effigy of Brigit.

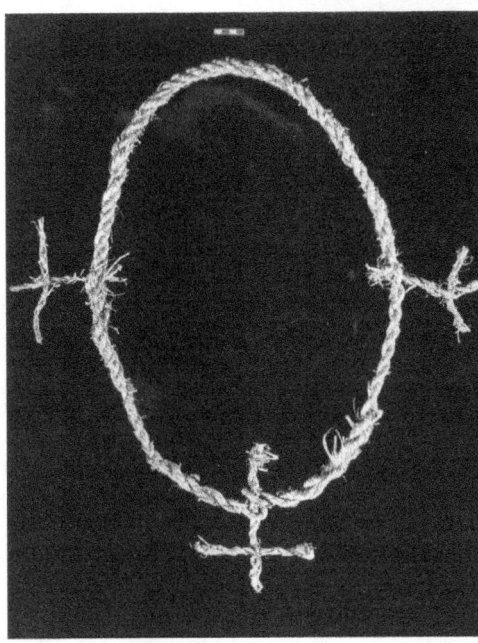

Fig. 6:
Crios Bríde
('Brigit's Girdle') –
A rope, 2-3m in length, usually of straw, spliced or woven into a loop and decorated with three or four crosses.

> | | |
> |---|---|
> | Oíche Shamhna gan bia, | Samhain Eve without food, |
> | Oíche Nollag Mór gan arán, | Christmas Night without bread, |
> | Oíche Fhéile Bríde gan im, | St Brigit's Eve without butter, |
> | Is é sin an gearán tinn.[89] | That is a sorry complaint. |

Her welcome and reception into the house complete, Brigit proceeded to be further incorporated into the family circle by means of a ceremonial meal held in her honour during which, it was believed, she took her place at table and partook of the food. This 'feast' generally consisted of little more than extra generous helpings of the normal daily fare and, as such, it revealed a strong bias towards milk foods and milk products, principally butter.[90]

> In order to give the festival a fitting celebration, the woman of the house for a week or ten days before Bridget's night, was, as they called it 'gathering a drop' that is collecting milk for churning on the eve of [the feast of] St Bridget. Generally, milk was scarce at this season but the housewife, if at all possible, put some by for a bit of butter for this particular night, as the feast was considered to be a poor one if butter was absent from the supper table. If there was a neighbour who had but very little, or no milk, a can of the freshly made buttermilk with a lump of butter was sent to such a person by the more fortunate or better off neighbour or neighbours, in order that the needy one would also be able to do justice to his or her celebration of the night in question.[91]

In certain parts of the country, special emphasis was laid on the making of *brúitín* or 'poundies',[92] whose manufacture and consumption customarily involved the addition of massive portions of butter:

> In the evening on the eve of the Feast of *Bríd*, a potful of potatoes suitable for making *brúitín* is brought in and peeled. Every house makes sure they have a bit of butter available for that night. Indeed, very few houses you would enter that day would not show the mark of the churn still visible on the floor, or, just as likely find the man of the house caught with his apron on him, helping his wife at the churning, if she was short of help. Anyway, no house is without butter... At nightfall, the potatoes are put on to boil. A sheaf of scutched straw is brought in when the potatoes are boiled – well on in the night – they are removed from the fire and drained of water.

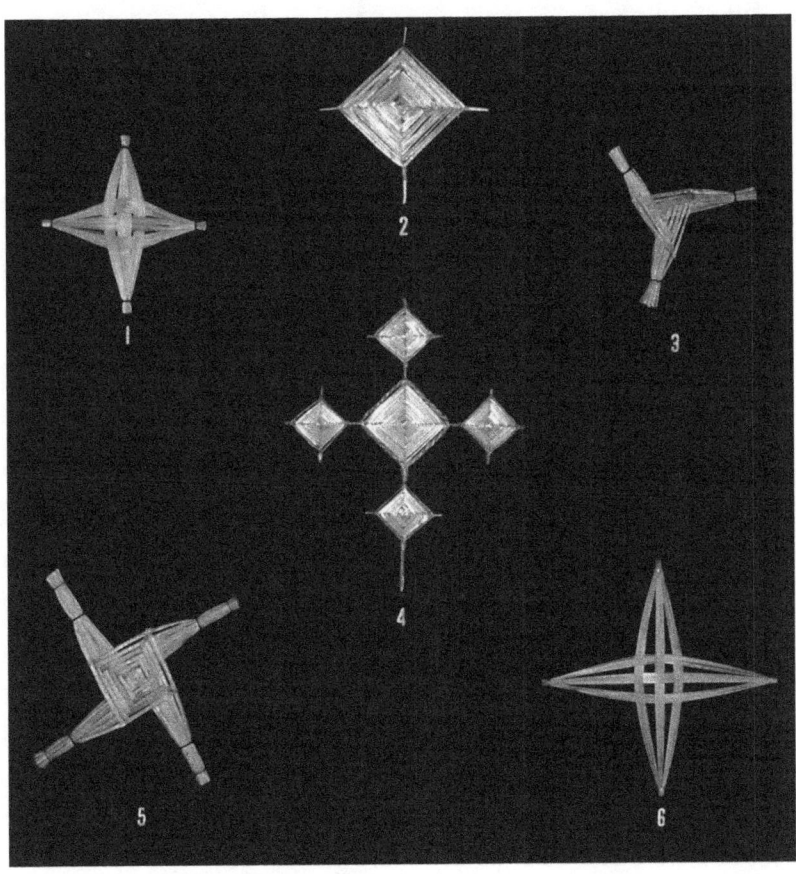

Fig. 7: Brigit's Crosses –
various regional styles woven in straw, reeds, and rushes.

> The sheaf of straw is then placed on the floor underneath the pot and the potatoes are mashed. That sheaf of straw is called *Leaba Bhríde* and that is the straw with which the crosses are subsequently made... I should add that it is customary for everyone within – big and small, young and old – to take a turn at the beetle, at the making of the *brúitín* that night.[93]

Another account from a neighbouring part of Donegal adds a number of interesting details:

> The pot is taken off the fire, the water is carefully drained away and the pot is placed on the middle of the kitchen floor. The woman of the house gets the pounder, saying: 'Thanks be to Brigid for what she sends us' – and begins to pound the potatoes. The man of the house tries his hand and so on until the poundies are ready. A large dish is then filled up for the grown-up men and placed on the table. A large hole is made in the centre in which is placed a lump of butter. The butter soon melts. The men sit round, each with a spoon in his hand. A short prayer is said and they fall to and it is marvellous how quickly the dish of poundies disappear. The women folk and the smaller children just eat out of the pot, butter being put in just as in the dish.[94]

The third and final phase of the festive ceremonial is that which concerns itself with the weaving of crosses (Fig. 7) and other artefacts from straw or rushes (Figs. 8 & 9). Whereas this particular occupation was prescribed as an essential part of the festival, significantly weaving, spinning, or the turning of wheels, was otherwise strictly forbidden.[95]

> I remember hearing that no wheel should be turned. So carts, spinning wheels; etc were idle.[96] On St Brigid's Day, the old women would spin no wool. They would not turn the spinning wheel that day.[97]... In the evening, everyone ceased whatever they were doing. The old women stopped spinning and they washed and cleaned themselves up as well as if they were going to Mass and they donned whatever good clothes they had.[98]

The remainder of the evening was given over to the weaving of tyings and straw or rush crosses, the latter made according to a variety of designs and patterns. This sometimes involved a

Fig. 8 *(above)*:
Weaving St Brigit's
Cross, Toome,
County Antrim, 1905

Fig. 9:
Weaving St Brigit's
Cross, Croaghs,
County Donegal, 1975

division of labour as between the sexes and between the different generations within the household:

> They would have their supper then and the young folk would start making the crosses. The man of the house did not start with the crosses, but rather, if he happened to have a few sheep, he would begin by making tyings from the first of the rushes for the lambs which were due to be born. When he judged that he had sufficient made, he would place them carefully behind the crib and then, when the lambing season commenced, he would place these tyings round the necks of the lambs when they were born. People were of the opinion that this would bring all kinds of luck and prosperity with the lambs. Then when he had finished making the tyings, he would start on the crosses and make his own share of them. They would all be left in a heap there until the morning of *Bríd's* Day.[99]

The unused portion of the straw or rushes might serve to make up a rough bed for Brigit or be left to be strewn in the byre on the morrow, as bedding for the cattle: it was never simply thrown out or otherwise carelessly disposed-of.[100] On Saint Brigit's Day itself, the crosses (Fig. 7) were placed in position in the dwelling house and in the various outhouses.[101] As was the case with the *Brat Bríde*, which stood ready to be requisitioned and pressed into service, in the manner already described,[102] the crosses could also serve the needs of the family which had fashioned them in ways which might necessitate their removal from their customary location for example, a cross might be placed in a basket of seed potatoes and carried into the fields to lend its blessing to the business of planting the new season's crops.[103] It is also the case that crosses were employed to promote human fertility, as is revealed by an account from County Mayo, which speaks of a specially woven cross, in the style of a Saint Brigit's cross, being used, with some modifications, to this very end:

> When a couple were married the mother or mother-in-law as the case may be makes a cross of straw and singes a bit of each of the four ends of the cross. She then places the cross under the tick in the bed in which the couple are going to sleep. This is done to make sure that there will be a family.[104]

* * *

'The most striking thing about the folk-tradition of the Lughnasa assemblies', writes Máire MacNeill, 'is the absence of Lugh'.[105] In the festival legends, he tends to be replaced by St Patrick and also sometimes by St Brendan.[106] Evidence for the association of Brendan with Brigit comes from the ninth-century *Bethu Brigte*;[107] the coupling of these two names also occurs, in a verse composed by a thirteenth-century critic of the Irish monks of the monastery of St Jakob in Regensburg. Outraged at the blatantly partisan Irish advocacy of both Brendan and Brigit's close kinship with members of the Holy Family, he exclaimed:

> *Sunt et ibi Scoti qui cum fuerint bene poti*
> *Sanctum Brandanum proclamant esse decanum*
> *In grege sanctorum, vel quod Deus ipse deorum*
> *Brandani frater sit et eius Brigida mater.*[108]

That Brigit should be regarded as being Our Lord's mother and Brendan his brother was clearly too much for the local 'ordinary poor Christians', who, this critic declared, 'do not believe that this is true, but rather reckon the Irish to be crazy and irreverent'.[109] Relevant in this context also is the existence of holy wells dedicated to Brendan and Brigit located in close proximity to one another at a number of Lúnasa sites.[110] We stand in prospect, therefore, it would seem reasonable to suggest, of matching the 'passive part in the Lúnasa complex', played by Brigit and alluded to by Máire MacNeill, with the shadowy presence of Lugh, lurking in the background of Brigit's festival celebrations. Lugh is not adverted to or named except, perhaps, in so far as the words *luachair* 'rushes' (an all-important ingredient of the festival) and *dubluachair* 'midwinter' – a compound which means literally 'black brightness' – may be etymologically connected with him and thus embracing the central element and meaning of his name.[111] In the context of the two Quarter Days named after them – *Lá Lúnasa* and *Lá Fhéile Bríde* – Lugh and Brigit stand in relationship to one another in much the same way as did the Great Goddess and her youthful male partner, the Young God – Brigit the embodiment of generation and procreation in perpetuity, the mistress of fecundity and the protector and giver of life exercising her regenerative function in union with her male partner.[112]

Union and regeneration are symbolic themes which dominate the three central phases of the festival celebrations in honour of Brigit. The chain of symbolic actions begins with the male partner, the man of the house, seeking admission to his home in the name of Brigit. He orders those within to get on their knees, open their eyes and admit Brigit,[113] in other words to be prepared to submit themselves to the notion of insemination and possible impregnation through the good offices of the goddess who rules over such matters. The commencement of this process is gladly welcomed by those within.

The second phase consists of feasting, the centrepiece of which is butter, the product of churning (Figs. 10, 11, 12). The action of churning, which might be seen as imitating the act of sexual intercourse, represents creation. The appearance of the butter may be taken to stand for the arrival of the much hoped for product of that sexual union.[114] The implements used for churning also carry their own obvious sexual message: the churn and churn dash representing the female and male sexual organs respectively. The etymologies of the words *cuinneóc* and *muide* both meaning 'churn', and the word *loinid*, 'churn dash', would seem to further enhance the correctness of this interpretation: *cuinneóc* may be related to Old Irish *cuiniu*, 'a woman'[115] and it may also be connected in some way to the Indo-European root *kṷendh-ro-*, the basis for a number of words for Angelica Silvestris or wild angelica.[116] This plant has an umbelliferous flower and a hollow stem and as such may also be thought of as symbolizing the vulva and phallus (Fig. 13).[117]

Interestingly, the wild angelica is called *lus an lonaid*[118] in Scottish Gaelic and its Irish name *an chuinneog mhidhe*,[119] it will be readily understood, is no less pertinent to the matter here under discussion. The word *muide* seems to possess definite sexual connotations: it comes from the Latin *modius*[120] a word meaning 'a vessel', hence 'a measure (called a peck), that which fills the vessel'; 'to peck' is, in turn, a verb which means 'to churn' and it would also seem to be related to German *ficken* and to English *fuck*.[121] Finally, there is the intriguing possibility that *loinid* 'a churn dash' may be related to *linga*, the main object of worship of the Hindu deity Śiva.[122] *Linga* means 'a sign', here a sign in the shape of a cylinder with a rounded top; it also means 'phallus'.[123] The phallic qualities of the *loinid* are also highlighted in a setting other than churning (but still connected with the celebration of the feast of Brigit) namely its function as the central axis around which the doll image of Brigit, the *brídeog* (a word which also means 'a bride')[124] is constructed. We may also note that the act

Chapter 1

Figs. 10, 11, 12 *(above)*:
Churn and Staff –
at Gleneely, County Donegal
(above top left);
at Rinnín County Kerry
(above right);
at Gorumna, County Galway
(above left).

Fig. 13: Wild Angelica
County Mayo.

of calling for admission in Brigit's name, while this decorated shaft is thrust through the door opening,[125] functions within the tradition as an alternative to the action of the man of the house in seeking entry, armed with a sheaf of straw his *brídeog* as it were —and it must be seen as an exact parallel to it.

The third and final phase of the festival celebrations, that which centres upon the weaving of crosses in honour of Brigit, is dominated by the symbolism of the cross, an object which, as we have seen, was plainly perceived in folk tradition as possessing the potential to promote fertility. The symbolism of the cross is a multivalent complex of great antiquity.[126] The swastika, basically a Greek cross with its arms bent at right angles, is one of the oldest types of cross and it is also found among the variety of cross types in honour of Brigit. We find remarkable evidence of an early association between Brigit and the swastika on an inscribed stone from the early Christian period located near St Brigid's Well at Cliffoney, County Sligo (Figs. 14 & 15).[127]

This stone is described by W.F. Wakeman as presenting 'the appearance of an early Christian cross', but possessing, nevertheless, 'the savour of a pagan origin'.[128] Wakeman also noted that, surmounting what he called 'the Mithraic symbol or *Swastica*, in the head of the cross occurs a canopy of not ungraceful design which is not like... anything found elsewhere in these countries.'[129] This 'canopy' seems to bear a remarkable resemblance to the curving decoration of the horned head of the 'Cernunnos' deity, the 'striking analogy between which' in his role as the Lord of the Animals and the god Śiva in his aspect as Pashupati 'Lord of the Beasts" is stressed by Proinsias Mac Cana (Fig. 16).[130] If the Cliffoney swastika stone proves to have an association with the cult of horned deities, then, perhaps, it may be claimed that we see united on this Christian cross, the symbols of the same two potent fertility figures that continued to be remembered in the folklore associated with *Lá Lúnasa* and *Oíche Fhéile Bríde*, down to our own time. We may also discern in Wakeman's 'canopy of not ungraceful design' and what lies behind it an explanation for Brigit's bizarre harrow head-dress.

Perhaps, the best-known parallel to the latter is manifested in the Lucia tradition of Sweden and other Scandinavian countries where a girl, dressed in white, appears at the time of the winter solstice bearing a crown of lighted candles on her head (Fig. 17). The Akkas of Sámi tradition are also pictured with headgear which

Figs. 14 & 15: Early Christian cross slab at St Brigit's Well, Cliffoney, Co. Sligo.

Fig. 16: Bust of figure likened to Celtic 'Cernunnos' deity (*'the horned one'*); Germany, 4th cent. BC.

Fig. 17: *Lucia* – girl dressed in white with a crown of lighted candles, offering food & drink on 13th December morning in Sweden.

might be construed as representing a crown of candles, sharply contrasting with an accompanying depiction of Sámi male deities who sport rounded, curving head-pieces (*as in* Fig. 18, *opposite*) similar to that shown on the Cliffoney swastika stone.

Among the many interesting aspects of the symbolism associated with crosses, we may single out but four for special mention – the tree, the number four, navigation and weaving.[131] First, the cross represents the *tree of life*, the *axis mundi*; it evokes verticality and achieves communication between three levels of the cosmos – subterranean space, earth and sky (Fig. 19).[132] The tree provides access to the invisible world and in many cultures a particular species or a single tree was designated for this purpose. For the Celts, it seems to have been the oak[133] and, significantly, this happens to be the tree commemorated in the placename *Cill Dara* marking the spot where Saint Brigit was said to have 'founded a church... beside an ancient oak-tree which existed till the tenth century'.[134] The number four symbolizes the totality of space and time: among its many cosmological aspects are the four cardinal points, the four elements, the four celestial beings (sky, sun, moon and stars) and the four divisions of time (day, night, month, year).[135] The image of the mast and the yard that crosses it is reproduced in the cross which thereby signifies navigation[136] while the process of weaving,[137] one of man's oldest activities, is closely bound up with attempts to determine what the future held and with fate.[138] The most basic element of weaving is the crossing of two threads at a centre involving the formation of a vertical line (warp) through which a horizontal line (woof) passes, creating a cross at the central meeting point. Spinning the thread of fate for the new-born was an activity commonly associated with goddesses of fate.[139]

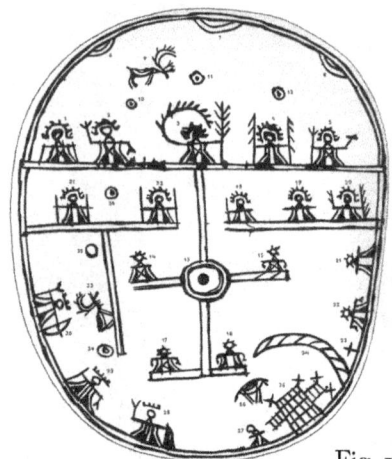

Fig. 18

* * *

Thus far I have attempted to widen the base for the further investigation and consideration of the true nature of Brigit and her festival. I have sought to develop the strictly 'agricultural' interpretation of the festival to encompass the implications of regeneration and reproduction, particularly as it affects humans, touching briefly on such subjects as sterility and barrenness, mating, birth, fate and future prospects. As the sample material from the archived inventory of Irish folklore exposed here amply indicates, this is a worthy part of a rich Irish heritage which promises to reward closer study.

Though subject to a process of censorship and reshaping from the beginning of the Christian era, the old traditions of Brigit's festival survived and ultimately found a life-line among the lower orders of society.[140] The Irish country people, to use Máire MacNeill's phrase, 'became its recorders'.[141] They promoted the tradition with dignity, piety and pride, assimilating it seamlessly into the deep Christian faith of Ireland, without allowing it to become totally submerged. It must have been something of a balancing act and a conscious one at that, if the testimony of one Donegal *seanchaí* is anything to go by: *Bhí dhá Naomh Bríd ann. Bhí Naomh Bríd thuas i gCill Dara, ach seo Naomh Bríd as an áit seo...*[142] 'There were two saints [called] *Bríd*. There was a *Bríd* up in Kildare, but this is the *Bríd* from this place...' The compromise between these two continued until, already in decline, the traditions of Brigit, the old goddess and the Holy Woman, were swept to oblivion by the new culture of the twentieth century.

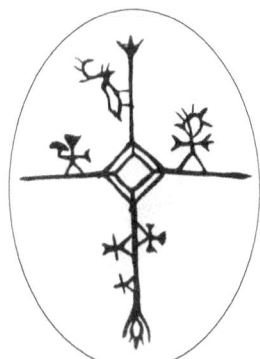

Fig. 19: Cross detail from Sámi shaman drum

Notes to Chapter 1

NFC = National Folklore Collection [+ MS. volume number + page number(s)].
Quotations from the National Folklore Collection are by kind permission of Professor Bo Almqvist, Head of the Department of Irish Folklore, University College Dublin.

1   NFC 90:224. This is glossed by the informant – *Is é sin, is ionann fad daofa* ['That is to say they are of equal length']. For a discussion relevant to the binary pair *oíche* and *lá*, cf. note 111 below.
2   MacNeill, Máire. *The Festival of Lughnasa*. Oxford: 1962 (412-3). This was republished by the Folklore of Ireland Council, University College Dublin in 1982, which edition contains 'additions and corrections, by the author' (p. 671-80).
3   A brief account of the Department of Irish Folklore, its holdings and the relationship between it and the former Irish Folklore Commission is given in *Celtic Cultures Newsletter* 5 (1987), 28–32. For the Irish Folklore Commission, see Briody, Michael, *The Irish Folklore Commission 1935-1970. History, Ideology, Methodology*, Helsinki 2007.
4   *Imbolc* (February 1st), *Bealtaine* (May 1st), *Lughnasa* (Sunday closest to August 1st), *Samhain* (November 1st). Cf. Ó Danachair, C. *The Quarter Days in Irish Tradition*. 1959 (47–55).
5   Various forms of the name Brigit occur in quotations (Brigid, Bridget, *Bríd* etc.), but the form Brigit has been preferred elsewhere. *See also* IFC [/NFC] Questionnaire Form of 1942 at Fig.35 on page 257 below.
6   MacNeill 1962 (424).
7   MacNeill 1962 (633-4).
8   MacNeill 1962 (275-86).
9   MacNeill 1962 (633-4).
10 MacNeill 1962 (Chapter 12 *passim*, 260–86 and Appendix II, 601-51) contains reference to some such sites.
11 Quoted in MacNeill 1962 (633-4). For a description of the ceremonies and other activities associated with this well, cf. Delaney (56–9). Ó Muirgheasa 1937a (174) in noting the existence of this well and the McDonnell association with it, comments: '...wells with such a reputation must have been scarce when these pilgrims could find none nearer to North Antrim than that of Athlone...'
12 NFC 903:199. Downpatrick Head *(Dún Briste)* and its *Lúnasa* connections is described in MacNeill 1962 (107-12 *et passim*).
13 Cf., for example, Ó Muirgheasa 1936 (158), and also NFC 903:98, which latter source refers to a lake into which people used to drive cattle to be cured, perhaps of sterility, though this is not specifically stated. Hall (21), categorically identifies such a well in Dublin: 'At St Patrick's well, in a corner within the cathedral, which is an old Gothic building, notwithstanding that superstition and ignorance are fast decreasing, even yet many who have weak eyes and head-aches, wash their eyes and head, and think themselves

cured. They also believe that the water of this well prevents retching, &c. &c and I observed a woman who had come more than forty miles to drink of, as it is believed also to cure barrenness' (Cf. note 11 above). According to MacKinlay (112) wells such as those of St Fillan at Comrie, and of St Mary at Whitekirk, and in the Isle of May were visited by wives 'anxious to become mothers'. Cf. in reference to *Tobar na mBan Naomh*, Chapter 5, pp. 184ff. and also note 127(p. 46) below. Moe (23-82 [English summary 273-81]), mentions – in the course of his discussion of the role of the Nordic rulers of fate, the *nornir*, female deities who appeared at the birth of children (cf. note 139 below) – 'several holy wells, in Germany, patronized by women wishing to have children, who invoke 'the three Maries' (274)'. For treatments of a number of tale types relevant to this and other themes dealt with in this article, cf. Moe (28=33); Laurent (73–9); Delarue (254-64); Belmont, (185-96 [for which reference I am grateful to Fionnuala Williams]); cf. also Lövkrona, note 72 below. The relevance of one of these tale types is noted thus by Ross 1967 (217): 'The possibility that one of the Ribchester goddesses has horns has also been noted. In one Irish folktale supernatural women spin and weave for a lazy wife. According to the Tipperary version of the tale, they are horned'. For a brief survey if Irish holy wells, cf. Ó Danachair 1958, (35-42). For further discussion relevant to this subject, cf. p. 30 above and notes 127, 130 and 140 below.

14 NFC 904:131. Translated from the Irish. The spelling of Irish-language NFC manuscript material has been modified to bring it more into line with modern usage and occasionally the punctuation in these and other quotations from NFC manuscript material has been adjusted for the sake of clarity. Longer quotations from original Irish-language NFC material are rendered here in English translation only. For a full Donegal version of this lullaby, cf. *An Stoc* 2, 1, Samhain 1924, 2.

15 NFC 904:59. Translated from the Irish. The blessing is given in the original as – *Bríd bhan-naomh nó bheannuigh*, the final element of which I take to be *bheannaithe* in reference to *Bríd*. Noteworthy is the frequency with which the saint is referred to in the 'Feast of St Brigid' NFC Questionnaire replies – especially those from Donegal – as *Bríd Bhan-naomh* rather than *Naomh Bríd*. 'Are girls named after the Saint in your district?' – one of the questions posed in the NFC Questionnaire 'The Feast of St Brigid' – drew a positive response from all parts of Ireland. A reply to the NFC Questionnaire on 'Patron Saints' sums up the popular attitude to the name: 'There is a custom held by numerous families in South Longford to christen the first female child Brigid or 'Bridie' and you find a lot of girls having that name' (NFC 946:302).

16 NFC 900:53-4. Cf. note 19 below.
17 NFC 899:169.
18 NFC 904: 67-9. Translated from the Irish.
19 NFC 899:108. Translated from the Irish. The *Brat Bríde* – here called *Cochall Bríde* ['Brigit's Mantle'] – was also described as a *ribín* 'ribbon' and, as we see above, a *brat(ach)* ['cloak']. It could, indeed, be any kind of cloth or practically any article of clothing (cf. Danaher 1972, 33 and NFC 900:159, 163; 903:50; 904:160), including men's clothing, especially waistcoats, significantly the

latter also being commonly worn by women in childbed (cf. pp. 16 ff. above). In parts of County Donegal, it was the custom for each member of the family to deposit an article of clothing in a basket which was then left outside for the saint's blessing in the usual manner, the basket being subsequently brought in and their garments then retrieved by the different family members (cf. NFC 904:67, for example).

For some interesting parallels in the Greek classical tradition, cf. *Encyclopaedia of Religion and Ethics*, ed. J. Hastings, Edinburgh 1909 [HENCEFORTH *EORE*], 2. 648, where it is stated: 'When birth had ended happily, the women brought their clothes to Artemis as an offering… Artemis Brauronia also received the clothes of women who had died in childbed'. Cf. note 70 below.

20 NFC 902:245.
21 NFC 902:254.
22 *Contributions to a Dictionary of the Irish Language* [HENCEFORTH *DIL*] F-*fochraic*, 22. In Scotland, we are told: 'The *Faoilleach* corresponded roughly to the present month of February, embracing the last two months of Winter, O[ld] S[tyle] and the first two of Spring. Sometimes the first half was called the '*Faoilleach Geamhraidh*' and the other half the '*Faoilleach Earraich*'' (Nicolson, 411). Black pinpoints what he calls an 'important cosmological fact about the faoilteachan, namely that they lie like a bridge across the spring quarter-day, and can therefore be assumed to have roots in the pre-Christian calendar' (5) and he concludes that 'it is likely… that *na faoilteachan* are in origin 'the leavings' while not excluding 'the possibility of interference by a derivation of *fáel* (later *faol*) 'a wolf' or some other word' (6).
23 Wagner 1972 (80). Quoting from *Críth Gablach* (ed. D. A. Binchy, Dublin 1970), lines 535ff.: '*Acht nammá atáa mí nád n-imthet rí acht cethrur. Cia cethrar? Rí 7 brithem 7 dias a manchuini. Cia mí i(n) n-imthet in tucht sin? Mí sílta(i)*' – which Wagner translates 'there is, however, one month when the king goes around accompanied only by three people. Who are the four? The King, the judge and two in attending. In which month does he go around in this manner? In the month of sowing'. Wagner concludes that the term *mí sílta* 'is an ancient name for the month(s) of Spring'.
24 NFC 903:46. This passage serves as an introduction to the outstanding reply made to the NFC Questionnaire on the 'Feast of St Brigid' by Michael Corduff of Rossport, County Mayo.
25 NFC 902:242.
26 NFC 903:78.
27 NFC 902:57. The Irish text runs: *Níl aon rud dá mbíonn san uisce ná sa talamh nach mbíonn ag síolrú faoi Fhéile Bríde.*
28 NFC 901:129.
29 NFC 906:113.
30 NFC 903:78.
31 NFC 900:40. McManus (195) in his description of life in Connamara, County Galway, in the years immediately prior to the Great Famine, mentions that 'from the time of sowing their potatoes in February, [the people] ate no more food of that root till the new crop'.
32 NFC 904:405. This account was rendered by the famous Donegal *seanchaí*,

Niall Ó Dubhthaigh. Sally [willow] – wound around the churn – was also used as part of a counter charm against butter stealing (NFC 169:404) and as a 'virility herb' which was 'brewed to effect and produce sex virility in a lethargic (presumably!) man' (NFC 1220:56). Cf. Rahner, Chapter 6 'The Willow Branch of the Next World' 286ff.; note117 below; Walde & Pokorny (2. 649).

33 NFC 900:55.
34 NFC 900:82.
35 NFC 900:90. Translated from the Irish. This seems to have been a fairly common notion – cf. *Béaloideas* 11 (1941), 75; *Irisleabhar na Gaedhilge /The Gaelic Journal* 5 (1894), 89 and *ibid.* 15 (1905), 55.
36 NFC 899:258–9. The significance of the colour white in relation to Brigid (cf. *Lá Fhéile Bríde Bán:* [NFC 901:157] and of Brigit's white cow – vis-à-vis *An Glas Ghoibhneann* (Cf. MacNeill 1962, 165) – is discussed on pp. 195 & 217-218 below.
37 NFC 900:120. In Sweden, it was believed that inflammation of the udder in cows and of the breast in women could be cured by the application of an animal penis while in Norway this was achieved by passing a human penis around udder or breast as the case might be (quoted in Matthiessen, 76). Cf. p. 81(note 61) below.
38 Lucas 1989 (41).
39 NFC 900:100.
40 NFC 903: 79–80.
41 NFC 903: 56. *Buarach tháil* means 'spancel of secretion' and is not, as far as I know, the name of a particular folk prayer as such; perhaps, the administration of this charm may have been accompanied by the recitation of one of the many other occasional prayers in which the name of Brigit was invoked, for example, the prayer said when milking a bad-tempered cow (NFC 902:24) or the blessing for a cow after calving (NFC 257:23-4). *Naomh Micheál, Ardaingeal* – St Michael, the Archangel – is referred to in the latter: *'Taraí a Bhríd agus bligh, taraí a Naomh Micheál, ardaingeal agus beannaigh an mart'* ['Come Brigit and milk, come St Michael the Archangel and bless the ox']. This saint, whose feast day is on 29 September, finds frequent mention in traditional prayers to St Brigit. St Michael is also mentioned in connection with a date in May – 'the 8th of May, a day set apart to commemorate a fight between the devil and St Michael' (Courtney [34]) – and this, perhaps, may indicate the possibility of his being connected with the second of the Irish Quarter Days, *Bealtaine*. MacNeill 1962 (207) draws attention to St Michael in the context of a legend which links him to St Fíonán and the Blessed Virgin Mary in connection with a number of holy wells and a West Kerry *Lúnasa* site and she concludes: '...it is pleasing to find the great archangel made a contemporary and equal of the Irish saint. Indeed, we wonder if the Blessed Virgin, the Archangel and the Saint have not moved into the roles and changed the play of three earlier *Dramatis Personae'*. Cf. also notes 110 and 127 below.
42 Lucas 1989 (41). It could be that these autumn calvers and their calves were thought of as being under the special protection of St Michael, the Archangel whose feast day occurs at this time of year and who is frequently mentioned in prayers addressed to St Brigit. Cf. note 41 above.

43 The word *gamhnach* is often replaced in modern spoken Irish by 'stripper', an English word meaning 'A cow not in calf but giving very little milk' (Wright [5. 821]). Wright (820), quotes 'o strip' as meaning *inter alia* 'to draw the last milk from a cow by pressure of the thumb and finger', 'to cleave or wipe by drawing the fingers of the hand along the surface'. It may be that this word bears a similar relationship to Old Irish *gam* 'winter' as that pertaining between *gam* and the word *gamhain*, as postulated by W.J. Watson 1926 (432), who also adds – 'calves became stirks at Hallowmass'. Among the citations given by the *DIL* G, 41, the following three may be of special interest: '*blicht a ngamnachaib* (a sign of evil times to come) *iar ndisca inar ngamnachaib...*' fig. 'of a very productive river' and 'of a tree: *gamhnach dharach duilleadhach ar siubhal go gnáth* – the leafy stirk of an oak swaying ever more' (in respect of the latter of which, cf. note 132 below and Chapter 2, note 91).

Watkins (114) has suggested that *mathgamain* – one of a number of *Noa* names for 'bear' – literally means 'bear calf'. This etymology is of great interest in its own right, but should *mathgamain* prove rather to be a compound of *moth* ('the membrum virile ?)' and 'hence in Irish gram. the masculine gender' [*DIL* M,175] and *gamhain*, then, perhaps – given that the *gamain* in question were female – *mathgamain* might be considered for inclusion with the binary pairs discussed in note 111 below. Male calves were unpopular and tended to be disposed of relatively quickly (cf., for example NFC 171:288-9; 434:408; 463:186-7) whereas female calves were much more prized as the following saying clearly indicates: *Lá Fhéile Pádraig, leath an earraigh thart /Lao breá baineann ag an bhoin /Agus lán meadair fána bhlas* ('St Patrick's Day, half the spring gone by/A fine female calf born to the cow/And a flavoursome churn of milk'). Cf. notes 114, 116 and 119 below.

44 Personal communication from Mr. John P. Burns, Stonefield, County Mayo. Translated from the Irish.

45 I would suggest that the 'limited period of time' in question may be equated with the season running from 1 February to 1 May, the span between the first and second of the two Quarter Days. As distinct from *Lá Fhéile Bríde*, *Bealtaine* was regarded as a highly unlucky time for a birth to take place – 'A child born on May Eve is not supposed to grow at all' NFC 42:202); cf. also NFC 1835:141 and *Irisleabhar na Gaedhilge / The Gaelic Journal* 14 (1905), 845. By the same token, as far as marriage was concerned, harvest time, as MacNeill 1962 (424) has pointed out, was deemed an inauspicious season for marriage: 'It is not lucky to marry in harvest – always poor, always gathering, never having anything" (NFC 96:335). For a survey of Irish traditions relating to luck in marriage, cf. McLaughlin (Conboy).

46 'Underlying the symbolic associations between the earth, its caves, furrows and waters and the vulva is the notion of the transformative powers of female sexuality. In the furrow the seed transforms itself into fruit or grain; in the cave/womb of the earth death transforms itself into life; in the womb of woman, male and female sexual fluids transform themselves into a human being' – Marglin 1987b (533). Cf. also notes 51,112 and 127 below.

47 For a discussion of the practice of booleying (transhumance), cf. Ó Danachair, 1983-4 (39); for older Irish sources, cf. Lucas 1989 (58–67);

an account of the practice as remembered by Donegal *seanchaí*, Niall Ó Dubhthaigh, is rendered by Seán Ó hEochaidh 1943 (130-58): an English translation of this by can be found in Ó Danachair 1983-4 (42-54). Cf. note 48 below.

48 NFC 146:129. Interestingly, *maighdean bhuana* is one of the names given in Scotland to the last handful of corn cut; this is also called 'maiden' and – as in Ireland – *cailleach* (MacLagan, 149-51). For a survey and distribution of the latter and other Irish terms, cf. Gailey 1972 (1-33). MacLagan (153), in resolving what he perceives to be the crisis of identity between the *maighdean* and the *cailleach*, concludes: 'There can be little doubt as to who is the *Cailleach*, and just as little who the Maiden, viz. Bridget'. Cf. note 111 below. Paterson (19) comments: 'The making of straw crosses presents a rather perplexing problem. It suggests that the cult of the saint may have been in some way linked with the harvest in past days… [it] makes one wonder whether Brigid took over some of the attributes of the Calliagh [Cailleach], besides those of her pagan namesake.'

49 NFC 20: 257-8.

50 Cf., for example, the NFC Questionnaire on Childbirth and also O'Connor.

51 'J.M. Synge in his *The Aran Islands* (1907) says of the Aran islanders of the beginning of the twentieth century that they were interested in fertility rather than eroticism, and on the evidence of the extant monuments and literature, his observation could apply to those people who created the mythology of the Celtic goddesses… Their sexuality was merely the instrument of their fertility, whether in terms of progeny or of the fruitfulness of the land with which they were so often identified' – Mac Cana 1987 (160).

52 *DIL* I, 70.

53 *Loc.cit.*

54 Cf., for example, Ross 1976 (126); S. C. Ó Súilleabháin 1982 (242) and Webster (32) who states: '…*Imbolc* or *Oímelg* [was] celebrated on 1st February. It was based on the old pastoral lambing season and therefore had powerful fertility associations. Little is known about it, presumably as it was mainly practised by the women and carried out in secret, away from profane male eyes'.

55 Hamp 1979/80 (106).

56 Hamp, *loc.cit.*

57 Hamp 1979/80 (111). J. de Vries 1961b (80) also indicates a meaning 'purification', relating *imbolc ('imb + folc')* to the Roman *Februa*. The notion of purification (and also feasting, discussed below, pp.92ff, 176ff) is touched upon in the following verse from an early Irish calendar poem dealing with the Quarter Days (Meyer 49 [for which reference I am indebted to Dr Miceál Ross]):

'Tasting every food in order,
This is what behoves at Candlemas *(Imbolc)*;
Washing of hand and foot and head,
It is thus I say.'

58 Mason (164, note 4).

59 Mason, *loc. cit.* A brief account of the customs associated with the festival

can be found in S Ó Súilleabháin 1977 (66-7). An illustrated overview of the festival customs is also contained in Evans (267-70) and in S. C. Ó Súilleabháin 1977 and S. C. Ó Súilleabháin 1982. Cf. note 48 above.
60 Lurker (178).
61 *The Encyclopaedia Britannica*, Cambridge 1911, Eleventh edition [HENCEFORTH *EB*], 15. 560.
62 *New Larousse Encyclopaedia of Mythology*, London 1972, 202. As Juno Populonia, she watched over the multiplication of the race, as Juno Moneta, she advised those about to be married, as Juno Pronuba, she watched over the arrangement of marriages, as Juno Cinxia, she unknotted the bride's girdle, as Juno Ossipago, she strengthened the bones of the infant and as Juno Rumina, she assured the mother's supply of milk (*EB loc.cit.* and *Funk and Wagnalls Standard Dictionary of Folklore Mythology and Legend*, ed. Maria Leach, New York 1950 [HENCEFORTH *FW*] 2. 563 and Warde Fowler Index *sub* Juno, 357). Practically all of the many attributes and epithets of Juno as well as many aspects of the Lupercalia, (the ancient Roman fertility festival held on 15 February and also the Matronalia (held on 1 March) exhibit in a variety of ways strong similarities to traditions of Brigit and the range of customs associated with her feast day.
63 A. Carmichael, *Carmina Gadelica*, Edinburgh and London 1928, [HENCEFORTH *CG*], 1, 164. Carmichael's account of Brigit and her festival in Scottish Gaelic tradition and a detailed comparison of the Scottish with the related Irish material together with the subsequent assessment of both in the context of the older Irish literary tradition as manifest in the various *vitae* of Brigit is given at various junctures below. For assessments of Carmichael's contribution to the collection of Scottish Gaelic folklore materials in general, see MacCurdy; Thompson (1964–6); Robertson; Campbell (1978) and Bruford (1983).
64 *CG* 1. 165.
65 *CG* 1. 169.
66 *CG* 1. 174, 175.
67 *CG* 1. 169.
68 According to information kindly supplied by Dr Pádraig Ó Héalaí, some twenty–eight versions have been identified hitherto.
69 NFC 902:187–8.
70 *Bean ghlún*, the usual Irish name applied to such individuals, would seem to be what is reflected in *CG* 1 160-1: *'Is i Bride mhin chaidh air a glun* – It was Bride fair who went on her knee'. J.-M. Picard (368 and Note 12, p. 374) draws a parallel between the symbolism of the knee in Irish and Finnish tradition with particular reference to the death tale of Guaire mac Áedáin in Adomnán's *Vitae Columbae* and the wounding of Väinämöinen's knee in the Kalevala; the knee, as Picard points out, 'was considered by the ancients as one of the seats of the vital fluid... and the word for knee was used to designate the male sexual organs'.

An account from County Limerick highlights in a matter-of-fact way the casual linking of Brigit and Mary in everyday speech: 'Go into any house in this parish with the usual *'Bail ó Dhia oraibh'* ['God bless all'] and the invariable greeting is *'Bríd is Muire dhuit'* ['Brid and Mary bless you'].

The fact that the name of *Bríd* is put first is no slur on the B.V.M.' (NFC 407:119).

Willetts (180), notes what he calls 'the old familiar relationship of Mother and Maid' is exemplified by the association Britomartis-Diktynna and Diktynna-Artemis, figures of the utmost relevance for an understanding of Brigit. Cf. Green 1989 (189–90) in relation to 'The dual mothers of Celtic tradition' and also Christ (276–9 and sources quoted there.

71 Quoted in Lid, N. *Light-mother and Earth-Mother.* 1946 (13).
72 NFC 1340:418. Michael Corduff (cf. note 24 above), who wrote this account, also draws attention to a Mayo tradition of what he dubs 'male *accoucheurs*' (NFC 1340:431) in which context we may also mention the Icelandic *ljósi* which indicates 'a male obstetric assistant' (cf. Lid 1946, 4–5). Cf. in this context Chapter 5, below *passim* and also Jacobsen (1984), 91-111, and sources quoted there and, for a highly relevant folkloristic analysis, cf. Lövkrona (73-124).

In a recent article, Slotkin argues for an interpretation of the *cess noínden* 'the Ulster debility' which would bring it well within the sphere of what he calls 'an actual ritual assembly associated with human fertility and group integration' (145). Carmichael, with his description of the *banal Bride* (the equivalent of the Irish *Brídeoga* [cp. the accounts given on pp. 18-20 above]), provides us with the connection to Brigit: 'The 'banal Bride', Bride maiden band, are clad in white, and have their hair down, symbolizing purity and youth. They visit every house, and every person is expected to give a gift to Bride and to make obeisance to her. The gift may be a shell, a spar, a crystal, a flower, or a bit of greenery to decorate the person of Bride. Mothers, however, give *'bonnach Bride'*, a Bride bannock, *'cabag Bride'*, a Bride cheese, or *'rolag Bride'*, a Bride roll of butter. Having made the round of the place the girls go to a house to make the *'feis Bride'* Bride feast. They bar the door and secure the windows of the house and set Bride where she may see and be seen of all. Presently the young men of the community come humbly asking permission to honour Bride. After some parleying they are admitted and make obeisance to her. Much dancing and singing, fun and frolic, are indulged in by the young men and maidens during the night' (*CG* 1. 167).

73 Lid 1946 (13ff.,10ff).
74 The analysis of regional distribution patterns associated with the various festival customs pertaining to the Feast of St Brigit has been touched upon sporadically by Danaher 1972 (13-37); in particular, the distribution of *Brídeoga* has been treated by the same author (as Ó Danachair) 1965 (1967), 97-9.
75 NFC 903:51-3. The sequence commencing: *Téigí ar bhur nglúna...* is repeated three times. Elsewhere we are told that the grace before meals normally recited on New Year's Eve was the one recited on this occasion (NFC 904:137-8 where the text is also given and NFC 904:233 where it is stated that this 'was the only occasion when grace was said in my native place').
76 Cf., for example, S. C. Ó Súilleabháin 1977 (3) and 1982 (244) and Danaher 1972 (19–20).

77 Cf. J.C. O'Sullivan 1963 (60-81) and cf. also Gailey 1968 (84–93); Gailey 1969 (85) and Andrews (49–52).
78 'The rushes that were left were formed into a bed and the best clothes that could be got were put on it' (NFC 904:219). Cf. also NFC 904:51 and cp. *CG* 1. 167-8
79 I use *Brídeog* to describe what is usually called in English, 'Biddies' or 'Biddy Boys' (Carmichael's *banal Bride*), i.e. groups of young people going from house to house carrying an effigy of the saint, and *brídeog* is used to describe the effigy itself.
80 NFC 903:231-4. Cf. Danaher 1972 (24–31); S. C. Ó Súilleabháin 1977 (10); Gailey 1969 (85) and cp. Simon (83–8) and cf. note 19 above.
81 NFC 899:154. Gifts offered included eggs and pins (NFC 899:53, 93), the latter being generally associated with childbirth and fertility and, perhaps, symbolically binding and loosing and the avoidance of bonds that represent maladies (cf. note 13 above) – cf. Mac Cana 1986 (328) and sources quoted there.
82 *Loc.cit.* Cp. the *Crios Bríde* ceremony described above (p. 20).
83 NFC 903:95. This is also noted by Carmichael (*CG* 1. 167) as being an Irish custom. For the symbolic significance of the churn dash and churning, cf. p. 28 above.
84 NFC 899:153. Cf. Gailey 1969 (85).
85 NFC 903:95.
86 'Passing through' – *'smöjning, jorddragning'* – is described by Tillhagen 1958 (116) as being one of folk medicine's most frequently employed remedies with a 3,000-year pedigree stretching back to the *Rigveda*.
87 NFC 902:5.
88 NFC 902:4.
89 NFC 904:51. For illustrations of the *Crios Bríde*, descriptions of the *Crios Bríde* ceremony and examples of the *Crios Bríde* rhyme, cf. Danaher 1972 (34–7) and S. C. Ó Súilleabháin 1977 (242–53).
90 Cf. Mahon, 124.
91 NFC 903:48-9.
92 'Potatoes peeled, boiled, mashed with a beetle, mixed with onions and eaten with butter', Traynor, 217.
93 NFC 904:50-1. Danaher 1972 (22), draws attention to the habit of the placing of the straw or rushes underneath the pot, as in this case, or, in some instances underneath the supper while it was being eaten. As is made clear by the account given on p. 17 above, this could easily amount to one and the same thing, since the supper was actually eaten from the pot.
94 NFC 904:161-2. Yet another Donegal account (NFC 904:234) adds further interesting detail emphasizing the notion of Brigit's unseen presence at the feast: 'It has been a custom here to leave a spoon over and above the number required by the members of the household. I think the idea was that the extra spoon was for the saint'. With regard to segregation of the sexes, cf. note 72 above and pp. 196ff. below.
95 For a survey of highly relevant beliefs in Finnish tradition, cf. Enäjärvi-Haavio, especially 'End of the Spinning Season' (49-53).

96 NFC 903:77. Cf. also Danaher 1972 (14-5) where it is stated: 'In some places any kind of work which required the turning of wheels, such as carting, milling and spinning, was carefully avoided. This was especially the case in south County Kerry and west County Cork, from which area we hear of dressmakers refusing to operate their sewing machines, and of men walking long distances rather than use bicycles. In a few localities ploughing and smithwork also came under the ban.' A similar ban marked the vigils of feast-days of the Virgin Mary in the Nordic world (*Kulturhistoriskt lexikon för nordisk medeltid*, Malmö 1956 – [= *KL*], 11. 370).
97 NFC 903:35. Translated from the Irish.
98 NFC 904:134. Translated from the Irish.
99 NFC 900:138–9. Translated from the Irish.
100 Cf., Danaher 1972 (23).
101 Cf., Danaher 1972 (22–3) and S. C. Ó Súilleabháin 1977 (4) and 1982 (244).
102 Cf. p. 7 above.
103 Cf. p. 8 above, and also Danaher 1972 (35).
104 NFC 1234:42. Elsewhere (NFC 70:206), we learn that, for luck, three wisps of straw would be lit in the nest in which a hen was going to clock (for which reference I am grateful to Dr Miceál Ross.).
105 MacNeill 1962 (409). For a wide–ranging discussion of how Lugh 'may have reappeared in the Christian milieu in the persons of various saints', cf. Ó Riain, (38–55).
106 MacNeill 1962 (101 ff, 409ff.).
107 Ó hAodha (§6, p.18 and §6, p.34). Cf. also note 13 above and note 108 below.
108 Hammerich (31–2). From *Carmen satiricum* by Nicholas de Berbera (end 13th cent.), loosely translated as follows:
Here be Gaels who when taking a drop
Brendan they dub the saint at the top
Not only that but God as his brother
While vouching Brigit to be His mother.
109 Hammerich (32).
110 MacNeill 1962 (630). Knott (Introduction, xxi) quotes Eóin MacNeill as stating: 'I have myself proposed to derive *Brénainn* from Cymric *breenhin* < **Bregentinos…*' which would seem to indicate the possibility of the names Brigit and Brendan being derived from the same source. My thanks are due to Professor Próinséas Ní Chatháin for this reference.
111 Cf. *DIL* L, 217 'rushes' and *luacha(i)r* 'brightness, brilliance'. For the etymology of *luachair*, cf. Williams 1989 (454–6). Lugh 'the brilliant young god' (MacNeill 1962, 426) stands in sharp contrast to his opponent Crom Dubh – 'the dark bent one' (MacNeill 1962, 28). In similar fashion, he may be thought of as ithyphallic whereas Crom Dubh's name would probably indicate the opposite condition. MacNeill (1962, 410) was before her time in recognizing this 'concept of a necessary duality, an opposition which is really a collaboration'. The same system of binary opposition finds, in a variety of ways, a ready application to Brigit as well as to Brigit and Lugh. Cf. notes 1 and 43 above and note 125 below and for an exposition of

the theory of binary pairs as applied to aspects of early Irish literature – including reference to Brigit – cf. McCone 1990 (193-4).

112 Gimbutas (1974) develops this theme at length and, elsewhere (1987, 511) sums up the process behind the development of the Great Goddess thus: 'As a consequence of the new agrarian economy, the pregnant goddess of the Paleolithic was transformed into an earth fertility deity in the Neolithic. The fecundity of humans and animals, the fertility of crops and thriving of plants and the processes of growing and fattening became of enormous concern during this period. The drama of seasonal changes intensified, which is manifested in the emergence of a mother–daughter image and of a male god as spirit of rising and dying vegetation'. Treating of 'Agriculture and Sexual Symbolism', and, dealing in particular with the 'invention of agriculture', Bolle (319) comments: 'The acts of a great goddess, the divine character of the earth, the significance of women, the ritual nature of work on the land and its bond with sexual involvement all amount to a new total experience of the everyday world and its ultimate foundation'. Cf. also Rahner (20), James (Chapter 8, "The Goddess and the Young God', 228ff.) and notes 46 and 51 above.

113 The fundamental meaning of the command 'Open your eyes!' I take to be 'Let in the light!' i.e. 'Let Brigit in!', an ultimatum immediately replicated by *'Lig isteach Bríd!'* Viewed in the context of Brigit's role as midwife (Cf. notes 62, 70 and 72 above), the initial injunction in this passage could also be taken to as directly relating to Brigit; therefore, the significance of the sequence is that it may embody a triplicated enunciation of the name Brigit – i.e. 'Brigit! Brigit! Brigit!' – an announcement which in turn is met with the triplicated response 'Hail! Hail! Hail!'. The injunction to 'Open your eyes!' may also be relate to the process of entering a trance – cf. Butterworth where it is argued that 'supernatural vision follows upon the 'opening of the eyes'" (74).

114 This is the kind of reasoning that may lie behind the following passage in Brian Merriman's famous poem, *The Midnight Court:* 'Cuinneog bhainne dhá greadadh le fórsa... Míle moladh le Solas na Soilse' ['A churning of milk being beaten with force... utmost praise to the Light of Brightness'] (Ó Murchú, 33). *'Solas na Soilse'* most likely represents a reference to Brigit. The action of pounding potatoes in a pot (cf. pp. 22-24 above) is the symbolic equivalent of churning.

115 *DIL* C (3), 1974, 596. Hamp's review (1979, 1-7) of a range of scholarly contributions concerning the etymology of Old Irish *bé* (neuter) and *ben* (fem.) 'woman', raises the prospect of identifying *cuinneog* with *bean* and hence with Vedic *jani* (cf. p. 28 above).

116 Pokorny 1959 (1. 631 s.v. *k̑uendh-ro-,-no-*): 'in *Pflanzenbezeichnungen* Lat. *combretum 'eine aromatische Pflanze, wohl eine wermutartige; nir. cuinneog, Angelica silvestris...*'. 'The heavenly deities 'churned' the primordial waters with the world axle, the Polar-star, a (phallic) spear, a high mountain etc. at the time of creation' – A. de Vries 1974 (98, s.v. churning). Cf. notes 115 and 117.

117 'The plant is erect in habit... often as much as 5-6 ft high... [it] was considered especially noisome to witches' – Horwood & Fitch (3, 53).

In Nordic tradition, this plant was credited with being able to cure menstrual problems and problems associated with pregnancy; it was used as an antidote for sicknesses in humans and in animals, believed to have been caused by witches' spells; as a cure for various complaints in poultry and in newly–calved cows and it was put in the churn to prevent butter being stolen by magic means: Brøndegaard (298, 299). de Bhaldraithe 1991 (147–8) concurs with Malone's (160) proposed interpretation of the Irish expression *bainne clabair* as meaning 'churn-dash', adverting to the proverbial saying, *'Nár thaga súiche ar do loine'*, 'May your churn-dash [i.e. *membrum virile*] never grow sooty' (used jocosely in congratulating the father of a new-born child), and to the apposite use of the word *clapar*.
118 Cameron (42). Two Sámi names for this plant – *acan grasie* and *acan bosska* – mean 'grass of the Thunder–god' and 'Angelica–plant umbel of the Thunder-god' respectively (Qvigstad 1901, 305), in which context, cf. p. 120-121 below. A report written by Samuele Rheen around 1670, describes the great liking which Sámi people had for angelica as a vegetable food and as a medicinal herb (Rheen, 21). According to Phebe Fjellström (who is of the opinion that the 'practice of collecting and eating Angelica archangelica probably goes back to an early northern Eurasian stage of food–getting') it was used by the Sámi to curdle (and preserve) reindeer milk and was well–known and, in some instances cultivated in many parts of the Nordic world, in Iceland and in Norway, the gathering of it being undertaken collectively by groups of young people (1971, 539–41). Cf. also in this context, Solheim (530–2). The plant also features in Snorri Sturluson's *Heimskringla* Jónsson (ed., [Chapter 92, p. 419]) where in *Óláfs saga Tryggvasonar* the curious story of Óláfr Tryggvason's presentation of a giant stick of angelica to his queen, Tyri, is told, an anecdote which, according to Alexander Bugge, supports a case for Irish influence. Cf. also Chapter 3, note 19.
119 Hogan (25). For a discussion of other terms relating to churns and churning, cf. Wagner & Keller (277–301).
120 *DIL* M, 184.
121 Skeat (437) lists the following meaning for the verb 'to peck': 'to strike with something pointed'. Wright, *op.cit.*, 4, 450, gives, *s.v.* 'peck…' 4. with *out* or *upon* provides the meaning 'to churn a small quantity of milk'. Danish *pik*, Swedish *pick*, meaning 'a pointed object' are listed by Buck (258) as being 'Among the semantic sources of vulgar terms [for penis]'. Cf. *ibid.*, 279 for *fuck/ficken*. Wentworth & Flexner (380) record the use of 'pecker' for penis.
122 Kramrisch (40).
123 *Loc. cit.*
124 Harrison (307), draws a parallel between the *brídeog* (= 'bride') and the bride from whom strawboys 'claim the favours of the bride (a kiss or permission to dance with her)' and outlines the difficulty of establishing their exact relationship to one another, all against the background of the *crosáns* ['jesters'] who, he warns, we should be careful not to assume to be 'the forerunners of the biddy boys' (304). It may also be appropriate in the light of my findings here to devote further consideration in this context to the role of the Sheela-na-Gigs (cf., in this context, Rynne (1987), 189-202. The *brídeog* is sometimes adverted to in the rhymes recited by the *Brídeoga* in terms of her

inability to speak (Danaher 1972, 29). The folk prayer, *Teagasc Bríde*, would also seem to contain a reference to her speechlessness: '...*Chloiginn úd anall atá gan teangaidh*' *(Irisleabhar na Gaedhilge /The Gaelic Journal* 4 (1893), 214. The nature of the relationship between Brigit 'the Speechless' and *Labraid* 'the Speaker' (also known as *Labraid Moen* 'The Dumb Speaker" is a subject deserving of further examination. Honko (117-31), outlines aspects of the Finno-Ugrian tradition in regard to the passive role of both bride and bridegroom in the marriage ceremony, with its special strictures on the bride to remain silent. For an Irish parallel, cf. Gailey 1969 (92). Irish tradition also required that silence be maintained in the byre the presence of a springer cow. *Handwörterbuch des Deutschen Aberglaubens*, eds. E. Hoffmann-Krayer and H. Bächtold-Stäubli, Berlin and Leipzig 1935/1936 [HENCEFORTH *HDA*], 7. 1468, *s.v. schweigen*, emphasizes the importance of silence in the agricultural context, e.g. when a cow calves, silence is observed in the house; a first-time calver must be milked in silence the first time she is milked after calving so as to ensure that, subsequently, she will be easy to milk; a cow which tends to be unruly when being milked is tethered with a pulley which has been removed from a spinning wheel, while maintaining complete silence. The same source also lists a wide range of other agricultural practices and spring customs for the proper performance of which silence is regarded as being a necessary prerequisite. For a discussion of the significance of silence and noise and the contrast between them, cf. Lévi-Strauss 1970a (327ff.). Cf. note 125 below.

125 'When they arrive at a house, the leader raises the latch and puts in the *brídeog*. All the others follow on' (NFC 907:67). 'Liminal situations cluster round Brigit' as McCone 1990 (187) points out. The application of van Gennep's principles of liminality to the account of the birth of Brigit (as found in section four of her *First Life*) which McCone accomplishes with relative ease, could be even more effortlessly applied to the Brigit of Irish folk tradition and would, of course, be equally apt (cf. pp. 17–18 and note 111 above).

126 Cf. A. de Vries 1974 (118–20); and also Ries (155–66) and sources quoted there.

127 Wakeman (365–84). Professor Michael Herity, to whom I owe this reference, informs me that this stone is unlikely to date later than the seventh century. Along the coastal fringe running from Galway to Tory Island, Herity (95-143) has isolated and examined six pilgrimage sites of special interest at five of which the 'series of art historical dates in the sixth and seventh centuries... seem to date the institution of the *turas*...' (121). At two, probably three, of these sites, holy wells play an important role (120), and at one of these – Rathlin O'Birne Island, County Donegal – there is a '*Chi–Ro* slab' with a 'canopy' not unlike that described by Wakeman. There may be good reason to see a link between *turas* sites, such as those described by Herity, and other sites such as St Brigid's Well at Cliffoney, County Sligo, *Tobar na mBan Naomh* in Teelin, County Donegal and the holy well and the traditions of St Brendan on Inishglora, County Mayo (cf. Chapter 5, note 35 below). It may be claimed that Colm Cille, Brigit, Brendan and a number of other Irish saints – such as Gobnait – all have fertility/fecundity connections, as well as wells and pilgrimages dedicated to them, the full significance of which has yet to be properly examined and

explained (cf. in this context Chapter 5, below). The circumambulation of the monuments of Glencolmcille, for example, in the course of making the *turas* there, might be regarded as originally having been a way of seeking magical protection and as such might be compared with other methods of achieving this aim, such as digging or ploughing a furrow around a settlement, once a common practice. 'In most agricultural societies, the furrow or the seed hole stand for the vulva. The seed stands for semen, and the plough, or digging stick for the phallus' – *EOR* 15. 533. Needless to say, this approach would serve to further enhance and emphasize the potential fertility associations and affinities of *turas* sites such as Glencolmcille. Wakeman ties St Brigid's Well at Cliffoney to an incident said to have occurred during her visit to Connacht when, we are told, it was her wont to seek out a pool of icy water near the monastery in which she would immerse herself, praying and weeping all through the night. By dint of the severity of her self-mortification, God saw to it that the pool ran dry, thus preventing Brigit from continuing with this penance (O'Hanlon [90-1]). Bathing as a means of purification and a method of renewing virginity was practised by, *inter alios*, Hera, the pre-Hellenic Great Goddess and forerunner of Juno (Graves 1. 50-1), and wells 'with trees symbolize[s] the divine marriage (vulva and phallus)' – A. de Vries 1974 (496) and cf. also Lucas 1963 (40–2). Mac Cana 1970 (27) speaking of 'Gaulish "Mercury": Irish Lugh' states that 'he is often associated with a goddess "Maia or Rosmerta... who evidently represents wealth and material abundance", and he later claims that Lugh and the goddess ['the sovereignty of Ireland'] who represents the land and its prosperity can scarcely be dissociated from the Gaulish monuments to Mercury and Rosmerta' (Mac Cana 1970, 29). Mac Cana's description of the relief from Glanum in which 'Mercury equipped with his usual attributes is accompanied by Rosmerta who bears a cornucopia' (25) forbears to make mention of another prominently featured object, grasped by Rosmerta in her right hand. This illustration also occurs in Green (1989, 59) and is there described as being a 'rudder on a globe'. While this may not be altogether out of character, it could well also turn out to represent a churn dash and churn. This interpretation would be supported by Green's Fig. 22 (58) which shows 'Mercury and Rosmerta with sceptre, ladle and bucket', also stating that 'Rosmerta's association with a vessel suggests links with cauldrons of renewal and regeneration'. While this may well be so, if Rosmerta is to be equated with Brigit, as I would suggest, then in view of my findings here, butter–imagery, rather than 'wine–imagery', as Green would have it, is what is likely to be intended (Cf. Chapter 5, note 58 below).

128 Wakeman (381). Descriptions of some 'swastika stones' elsewhere in Ireland – notably in Kerry – and in Scotland can be found in Wakeman (379–82).
129 Wakeman (381).
130 Mac Cana 1970 (38). For further discussion of horned deities in Celtic tradition, cf. Mac Cana 1970 (44–8); Ross 1973 in *Rawson* (ed.), 83ff. and Green 1989 (86–9). Green 1989 (27) also draws attention to instances of horned goddesses, powerful symbols of fecundity, embodying close links with the animal world. Cf. further re Cernunnos, Bober (13–51).
131 Cf. Ries (155–66).

132 Cf. Ries (158); Mac Cana 1970 (50), 134; Mac Cana 1987 (156-7); A. Watson 1981 (165-80), and, with special reference to the monastery of Kildare, Lucas 1963 (32) and Doherty (48). J.L. Campbell 1958-61 (75-6), commenting on the expression *gamnach darach duilleadach* (cf. note 43 above and note 137 below), which is used to describe a type of tree hated by Suibhne, notes: 'the habit of the oak tree of retaining its last year's leaves far into the spring, long after trees like the birch, alder and rowan have started putting out green leaves. Seen at this time, with its old leaves, the oak looks ugly amongst the other trees. In respect of the suggestion... that the phrase may mean 'an infertile leafy oak', it is interesting to note that in MacDonald's Vocabulary (1741) the Oak is included in the list of 'Barren Trees'.
133 Mac Cana 1970 (50).
134 Hyde 1899 (158).
135 MacQueen (131) and A. de Vries 1974 (201-2).
136 Cf. Rahner, Chapter 7, 'Odysseus at the Mast', 328ff.
137 Cf. A. de Vries 1974 (495–6) and note 138 below.
138 Cf. Onians (303ff), 'The Weaving of Fate', 349ff. I owe this important reference to Dr Pádraig Ó Héalaí.
139 'The prehistoric Great Goddess survives still in folklore. She appears as Fate (or sometimes) as the three Fates, who attends the birth of a child and foretells the length of its life', Gimbutas 1987 (511). Cf. note 13 above and Chapter 5 below.
140 'A remarkable continuity stretches from the pagan goddess to her Christian namesake of the early sixth century, the saint Brighid of Kildare whose monastery of *Cell Dara*, 'the church of the [sacred] oak' was doubtless on the site of a pagan sanctuary' (Mac Cana 1987, 154). In reference to 'Gaulish 'Minerva': Irish Brighid', Mac Cana 1970 (34) states that 'dedications [to Minerva] show that her cult was especially strong among the lower orders' and, with regard to the Cernunnos cult (cf. note 127 above), speculates that – 'if in fact the Cernunnos cult did not quickly wither under the pressure of Christianity, then it is not impossible that traces of it survived into recent times in certain areas of popular custom' (48). Horned *Brídeoga* (cf. NFC 903:141) and horned Wrenboys (cf. Gailey 1969, 83) undoubtedly marked part of that survival, a phenomenon also adorned, long after Ireland turned Christian, by Brigit and her festival customs as by Lugh and his. In both instances, we are fortunate to possess in the folklore record an invaluable witness to important aspects of the nature of what 'must once have been a vast body of ritual which fell into disuse at some stage and was noticed only casually in the written record' (Mac Cana 1987, 154).
141 MacNeill 1962 (428).
142 NFC 694:189

— *Chapter 2* —

Vita enim mortuorum in memoria est posita vivorum
'The life of the dead is placed in the memory of the living'—Cicero

THE PREVIOUS CHAPTER has drawn attention to the strong fertility element associated with the name and person of Brigit and the celebration of her feast day in Ireland. The desirability of exploring number of interesting Nordic (including Finno-Ugrian) connections and delving in classical as well as other sources of the ancient world for more information about the background of this powerful fertility figure has also been indicated.

We may commence begin by alluding to a striking feature of the lexis of the Irish language, namely a profusion of names for the bear. There are, in fact, no less than eight of these: *art, math, mathgamain, milchobur, beithir, rustóg, úrsóg,* and *béar*.[1] Three of these names – *art, math(gamain)* and *milchobur* – are of particular interest to us here; the balance, with the possible exception of beithir, derive from less interesting origins.[2] The first of these bear names – *art* – is used as a proper name, most notably, of course, as the name of the father of Cormac mac Airt – 'the ideal king of Irish tradition' – as Ó Cathasaigh calls him 'in whose reign 'Ireland became a Land of Promise'.[3] Old Irish *art* (Welsh *arth*, cognate with Greek άρκτοσ, Latin *ursus*) has a healthy Indo-European pedigree (yielded by the root **(H)rtko-* according to Hamp).[4] Among the zoomorphic divinities of the Celts we may also note the presence of a *Mercurius Artaios* and especially a *dea Artio* whose names connect them with the bear (Fig. 20).[5] Preserved in this wise, we thus find in Celtic culture a vestige of earliest Indo-European civilization. As far as the word for 'bear' is concerned, it is worth noting that this is not something which holds true for a whole range of other northern and western European languages. In the Germanic and Balto-Slavonic languages, words based on the Indo-European root which gives us Irish *art* have been lost,[6] falling victim to what philologists call 'linguistic avoidance'. In these languages a variety of new descriptions has been substituted for the original word. These include *i.a. björn* 'the brown one' in Scandinavia and *lokýs* 'the (honey) thief' among the Balto-Slavs.[7]

The Irish bear names *mathghamain* (the word survives in Scottish Gaelic *mathain*) and *milchobur* also fit into the category of Noa names. The former is a compound containing the elements *math* – (in the likely meaning of 'good', 'auspicious', perhaps, 'timely' and also meaning 'bear' in its own right) and *gamain*, meaning 'calf', a word (according to Pokorny) to be connected with Indo-European *$\overset{*}{g}hi\bar{o}m$ 'winter'.[8] Mathgamain finds anthroponymic representation in the Irish surnames Mac Mathúna/Ó Mathúna while the initial element math occurs in the Gaulish Matugenos in which context we might also mention its partner Artigenos, both of which mean 'son of the bear'.[9] *Milchobur* means, of course, 'honey-lover'.[10] This completes an interesting trio of names in the Irish language for a beast which by the most generous of estimates disappeared for good from the island of Ireland more than 4000 years ago.[11]

Still in etymylogical mode, I wish to make brief reference to two other creatures which like the bear have names enjoying a common distribution within the Celtic, Germanic and Balto-Slavonic languages[12] and which in other ways show a variety of ecological, palaeo-biological and mythological connections with the bear. I refer to the bee and the wolf. The former, together with the bear, constitutes what Hamp has called a 'honey culture' peculiar to northern and western Europe where the Indo-European root *bhi-* represents 'early borrowing from some North European source(s)'.[13] The Indo-European root *$l\underset{\circ}{k}^{w}os$ or *$lúk^{w}os$[14] which gives us 'wolf', Latin *lupus* etc., is also shared between the Celtic, Germanic and Balto-Slavonic peoples. Aspects of the relationship between these three creatures, wolf, bear and bee, are revealed in a series of literary and folkloristic forms as we shall see anon.

* * *

It will be appropriate at this point to say a few words about the wolf and its part in the scheme of things, leaving the stage to Brigit and the bears thereafter. Ó Cathasaigh in his *The Heroic Biography of Cormac mac Airt* has listed a whole variety of lupine and canine connections including Art's family relationship with Olc Aiche, canine guardian of the Otherworld (Olc being, he argues, a Noa name for 'wolf'), Cormac's being suckled by a she-wolf, and/or his rescue by a character called *Conamail Conriucht* 'Wolf-like Wolf-shape'.[15] The wolf as fertility figure

Chapter 2

Fig. 20: *dea Artio* – Bronze group from Bern showing the goddess Artio offering fruit to a large bear standing beneath a tree.

Fig. 21: Pre-Christian stone sculptures of bears, St Patrick's Cathedral, Armagh.

features in the Roman tradition of the Lupercalia, the ancient Roman fertility rite held on the fifteenth of February, said to have been established by Romulus and Remus, but probably older than Rome itself. The word *lupa* came to mean 'a lewd woman'. We may also recall the fertilizing activity of the Luperci, who at the Lupercalia, ran through the city rendering women fruitful by their blows and the custom whereby the Roman bride anointed with wolf's fat the doorposts of her husband's house, from which custom she was believed to derive her name *uxor*.[16] Fat or marrow was identified with seed and Pliny tells us that there was believed to be in the wolf (as in the horse) *amatorium virus* in the tail.[17]

Turning to the Nordic world and Norwegian folk tradition, we get a useful and interesting perspective on the relationship between the bear and the wolf (as also the fox):

> The Virgin Mary came to a broad river or lake and wished to cross over but there was no-one to help her. A fox came along and she asked him for help, but the fox excused himself saying that he wasn't strong enough to carry her. 'You will always remain weak', said the Virgin Mary. From that day onwards, the fox is so miserable you could beat the back off him with a woollen sock. Shortly after that a wolf came along. She asked him for help. The wolf too excused himself saying that he didn't have the time for he was too hungry and had a lot of ground to cover. The Virgin Mary said: 'You will never get a rest, you will run and run up hill and down dale and you will never get your fill, though every time you find dog-meat, you will feel no hunger.' From that time onwards, the wolf roams restlessly never staying in one place, seldom filling its emaciated hide, always in pursuit of all dogs to satisfy its hunger. So at last a bear came along and the Virgin Mary asked him to help her over. He immediately agreed and carried her across on his back. As a reward, the Virgin Mary milked some of her breast milk onto his paws saying: 'All winter long you will lie peacefully in your den and you need do no more than suck your paws and only once will you turn over on your other side.' From that time onwards, the bear sleeps the winter long and only turns over in his den at Candlemas.[18]

In this account, as in other manifestations of Nordic folk tradition, the wolf definitely appears in an inferior light to the bear who was said to have 'twelve men's strength and ten men's knowledge' (the proportions can vary somewhat – ten/twelve; and twelve/six are also quoted) and was viewed with reverence and fear.[19] The picture of the bear in animal tales, where it is classed as stupid, contrasts sharply with the folk belief that it is both extraordinarily strong and clever – *in summa*, clearly man's superior.[20] The wolf, by contrast, is thought of as *olc* 'evil' (to use what appears to be one of its Irish Noa names), while its condemnation to a life of constant roaming in search of sustenance casts light upon its other Irish Noa name *mac tíre*, literally 'son of (the) country'.

Both bear and wolf were feared by man and both were regarded as being capable of transforming themselves into human shape just as the opposite was also considered possible.[21] A Norwegian account describing how a woman was warned by a *skogsrå* or Forest Maiden (a figure of no little interest in her own right in the context of her role as Owner of Nature/Mistress of the Animals) about the 'Big Dog' (by which she meant the bear[22] might be interpreted as indicating awareness of a *quondam* relationship of even greater intimacy between these two. This serves to remind us that, in fact, bears have evolved from a line of dogs (Fig. 21).[23] The *Waralde Biri* 'bear of the sky' seen on Sámi shaman drums was also known as 'God's sacred hound' (while the wolf was called 'Satan's dog') and the bear was also called the pasture-ground dog of the trolls[24] and, sometimes, by fairies who lived under the ground, their 'great boar'.[25]

The 'bear-line' was first identified in fossils from the tertiary Miocene Age and the modern family of Ursus did not appear before the late Pliocene.[26] We are not talking here in terms of a mere 4000 or so years ago, of course, but rather tens of millions of years and it is, no doubt, asking too much for us to believe that from whatever point human kind entered the picture, people would have had been in a position to know and understand the particulars of this process of evolution and to subsequently preserve knowledge of it in continuous memory as recorded in folk tradition and ultimately reflected in literature of the Christian era. Be that as it may, there is a substantial body of folklore concerning both these animals, elements of which, as I say, would seem, nevertheless, to signify some hierarchical preference or ancestral prioritization of the wolf over the bear.[27]

In the end, the wolf turned out to be a better survivor than the bear, outliving it in Ireland, for example by millenia, even surviving in isolated parts of the island almost into our own time.[28] The bear appears to have survived a good deal longer in

Scotland, perhaps until as recently as a millennium or so ago.[29] In these circumstances, it is no surprise, therefore to find the wolf substituting for the bear in Irish folk narrative as in, for example, the international tale type AT 425 *The Search for the Lost Husband* in which the wolf, or as some Irish versions of the tale would have it *'an madra bacach bán'* ('the lame white dog') or *'madra na n-ocht gcos'* ('the eight-legged dog') generally plays the leading part.[30] There is every appearance then that for good or for ill this would more or less render complete the record as far as bears are concerned in Ireland or in Gaelic tradition as a whole.[31] In order to test the truth or otherwise of this statement, it will be necessary to follow the bear northwards, re-entering the domain in which it continued and continues to survive long after it became extinct in Ireland or Scotland and so, we now turn to look at some further pertinent aspects of Nordic and other European bear tradition in somewhat greater detail.

* * *

The bear was popularly believed to possess superhuman qualities and to be able to see and hear everything humans do, say and even think about it: it was simultaneously both dangerous and good-natured; its human-like gait and the fact that its body, after it had been skinned, bore uncanny similarity to the human frame further added to the illusion.[32] Zoological works traditionally granted an important place to the description of the bear and ascribed sexual behaviour to it, similar to that of humans.[33] The medieval enclyclopaedist, Vincent de Beauvais (c.1190 - c.1264), for example, tells us that: 'Bears do not make love like other quadrupeds, but can embrace each other mutually, like human beings.' William of Auverge (1180-1249) believed the bear to be capable of producing semen compatible with human modes of reproduction.[34] According to the medieval mentality, relations with animals often acted as a transition towards the supernatural world; when supernatural creatures decided to fertilize a woman, they would choose to do so through the intermediary of a seed capable of generating life in a human womb and, accordingly, from this point of view the bear was believed to represent the greatest advantage.[35]

The bear, then, was seemingly both interested in women and apparently also of special interest to them. In Norwegian folk tradition it is said that the special odour which pregnant women exude could be attractive to bears.[36] Tradition also says that if the bear catches a pregnant woman, it will rip her open and remove the foetus, the worst offender of all being the type of bear which follows a woman bearing a male child.[37] The eighteenth-century Danish bishop Pontoppidan opined that the bear's taste for the foetus was merely an expression of his desire for a tasty morsel,[38] while others took the view that, quite simply, the bear had been created with this characteristic in order to deter women from roaming the woods and fields while pregnant.[39] It has even been considered especially dangerous for pregnant women to eat game especially bear meat.[40] On the other hand, it is said that women picking berries need not fear the bear if they show what sex they are, something, perhaps, which might be interpreted as indicative of an attitude of respect towards women;[41] in similar vein, a bear's paw was believed to be of assistance in the case of difficult deliveries, the belly of the parturient woman on such occasions being stroked with it,[42] a usage which might impute a benevolent and sympathetic disposition to the one-time owner of the said claw, though, of course, this action could also be interpreted as a grotesque parody of the bear's penchant for disembowelment.

The disposition of folk fantasy towards providing the bear with human properties is clearly mirrored in numerous commonly believed descriptions of the occurrence of sexual relations between male bears and women.[43] It will be helpful to view traditions of this kind against the background of Nordic bear-hunting and bear-feasting customs in general while also keeping in mind certain aspects of Nordic – particularly Swedish and Finnish wedding custom and ceremonial. The following account of the Sámi bear ceremonial revealed to an eighteenth-century Swedish clergyman (with the greatest reluctance, it is said), as it was feared that the revelation of this information would cause the hunting to fail, will serve to set the scene:

> Three brothers had an only sister who was so despised by them that she was forced to take refuge in the wilds. Exhausted, she finally happened upon a bear's den and entered it for a rest. A bear returned to the den and, on closer acquaintance, he wed her and begat a son by her. Time passed, the bear grew old and the son grew up. The bear informed his wife that, on account of his great age, he no longer wished to live but rather to trample around on the first of the autumn snows so as to enable her three brothers to find his tracks

and then 'ring him in' and kill him. She tried everything she knew to prevent him following this course of action, but he did not allow himself to be dissuaded. He asked to have a piece of brass attached to his forehead in order that he might be distinguished from other bears by this sign and also to prevent his own son who had now left him from killing him. After a deep fall of snow, the three brothers went out together to fell the bear which they had already 'ringed in'. The bear asked his wife if all three brothers had been equally spiteful to her and she answered that her two eldest brothers had been more spiteful than the younger one who had been somewhat more clement. When the brothers approach the den, the bear ran out and attacked the eldest brother, mauled him rather severely and returned uninjured to the den. When the second brother came, the bear ran at him in the same manner, causing similar injury to him and again returned uninjured to his den. At that point, the bear ordered his wife to catch hold of him around the waist and when she had done so, carrying her, he walked out of the den on his hind legs. She ordered her youngest brother to shoot him which he did. The wife then sat down some distance away, covering her face, as if she had not the heart to see the bear shot and flayed, but still she watched out of one eye. This is the origin of the old custom that no woman may see the bear or the men handling the bear, unless she has her face covered and is peering through a brass ring. When the bear had been killed and all the meat had been put in the pot to boil, the son arrived on the scene and the brothers told him that they had shot a strange animal with a piece of brass attached to his forehead. The son declared that it was his father who had been marked with just such a piece of brass and he maintained that, therefore, he should have an equal share in the bear with them. When they kept on refusing this, the son threatened to wake up his father and taking up a rod and saying – 'My father, arise! My father, arise!' – he began to beat the skin with it. Then the meat in the pot began to boil so violently that it looked like it would rise up out of the pot and so they were forced to give him an equal share. This is said to be the origin of the following custom: when the bear has been felled, the bear hunters immediately drag him out of his den and beat him with twigs or pliant rods. From this comes the proverbial saying – 'Beating a bear with rods'. The fact that the bear hunters as well as all the implements used in the capture of the bear must be adorned with brass chains has its origins in the piece of brass attached to the bear's forehead.[44]

Another seventeenth-century description of the Sámi bear hunt and festival provides some extra detail, telling us that:

> They approach the den where the bear is lying and bravely kill him with spear and gun, upon which they drag him immediately out of his den and beat him with rods or slender switches, wherefore the saying: Beating the bear with rods. Thereafter they commence to sing with joy the Bear Song which in their tongue amounts to their thanking God who has provided them with the creature and has given them the courage and power to overcome such a mighty and terrible beast.[45]

C.-M. Edsman argues that the establishment of the bear festival as something instituted by divine order is to be seen against the background of the circumpolar stories about the Bear Wife or the Bear's Son and that this is the key to understanding it.[46] This idea, he says, has been little noticed by Scandinavian scholars who regard the story only as a rationalizing of rites already existing. Edsman points to different versions of the Sámi origin myth which are found in medieval sources. Saxo Grammaticus relates this episode in his *Gesta Danorum*, which gives us the date 1200 AD or so as a *terminus ante quem*. The story, as Edsman points out, is even older, for it is met with in an early English historical source describing struggles between Danes and Anglo Saxons in the eleventh century.[47] According to Axel Olrik, the bear story has been aetiologically attached to the name of Beorn Beresun, the latter element of which derives from the female name *Bera*[48] a circumstance which leads our footsteps northwards again – this time to Iceland – and the sources in which the origins of one Bǫðvar Bjarki are described.

Bjarki means 'little bear'. It is found in the *Hrólfs Saga Kraka* and the *Bjarkarímur* (both dating to the fourteenth or fifteenth centuries) where we learn about him and what lies behind his name.[49] According to *Hrólfs Saga Kraka*, the Norwegian king Hringr's new queen Hvít, who is skilled in the magic art, attempts to seduce her stepson Björn. He spurns her and for his pains is struck with a (magic) glove made of wolf-skin and is transformed into a horrible bear *('Hún lystr nú til hans með úlfhanzka ok segir, at hann skyldi verða at einum híðbirni ólmum og grimmum...')*.[50] Björn's childhood friend, Bera, remains faithful to him and follows him to the cave where at night he resumes his human shape. He prophesies his own death and tells Bera not to forget to ask for the ring in the joint of his left fore-leg and to be careful not to eat the bear meat after the hunt. When in spite of that, she is forced to eat some of the meat, one of her sons (Elgfróði) is later born with elk's feet and another (Thórir) with dog's feet, whereas the third Böðvar, Böðvar Bjarki, becomes the most beautiful child of all.[51]

Edsman argues further that the marriage rites of the Finnish bear festival may be regarded as fresh dramatic representation of the mythical bear marriage and adds that knowledge of these rites may have given rise to some Swedish marriage customs and linguistic expressions among country people characterizing courtship and betrothal as bear-capture.[52] We may now proceed briefly to consider these in turn.

Once killed, the dead bear had to be asked for forgiveness and/or an outlandish pretence was made of blaming others, even distant nations such as the English, the French and the Germans, for its demise. It was believed that the bear, which was treated as if it were still alive, would eventually reappear as its former self in due course. It was generously entertained, celebrated and begged to be of a benevolent frame of mind towards its hosts should it return to its home in order to allow itself to be killed again the following year, so as to be able to enjoy such hospitality once again. A feature of the celebrations was the use of wedding poetry in greeting and welcoming the bear as the guest of honour. Indeed, the occasion took on the appearance of a wedding itself, for the bear, if of the male sex, might have a young female nominated as his bride or, if of the female sex, a young man of the village might act as groom. Represented by its skull and accompanied by its bride or bridegroom, the bear was allocated a place at the head of the table. When the feasting was done, the skull was borne outside and fixed with great ceremony to a pine tree; some such trees, over a period of time, became the repository of large numbers of skulls.[53]

The derivation of certain Sámi and Swedish wedding customs from the bear festival itself is clear. The custom of newly-weds donning a bear-skin was observed in the middle of the last century among the southern Sámi and corroborated in Härjedalen as late as 1914. Between the time of engagement and the wedding, the bridegroom was called 'the bear'. The salute in honour of the young couple was called 'shooting the bear'. These customs survived up to the latter part of the nineteenth century, not only in various northern Swedish counties but also as far south as Västergötland. A man dressed up in a bear-skin, or, if lacking such, any animal skin made an appearance at the wedding house or hid in the forest nearby where he was subsequently hunted and captured by the male wedding guests. He was 'killed' and carried with great ceremony to the wedding house where he was 'flayed'. Under the animal skin, the 'wedding bear' carried a bottle of spirits and from this was drunk what was called 'the bear's funeral drink of his own blood', following which the newly married couple and after them all the men and girls of marriageable age were placed couple by couple sitting on the bear skin.[54]

The Dalecarlian wedding bear does not manifest himself exclusively in a wedding context, but sometimes also makes an appearance on the 24th of February, St Matthew's Day or *Matsdagen*, which was, in certain areas, regarded as being the first day of spring. In this case the 'bear' was accompanied by a 'bridal couple'. This 'wedding bear' has been thought of as being identical, or at least closely connected with the Lenten bear we know from the Middle Ages in various parts of continental Europe.[55] The importance of focusing upon the Nordic heartland (where the bear survives, or has done so until recently) as the richest source of European bear tradition is beyond dispute, but this does not compel us to rule out as irrelevant and redundant to our understanding of this tradition, some fascinating vestiges of it which may survive in one form or another elsewhere. It is at this point, therefore, and on such a note that we begin the long trek from the farthest reaches of the inhabited regions of Arctic Europe to the fringes of its south-western Atlantic seaboard.

* * *

The content and tone of the dancing and pantomimes which sometimes constituted a part of the bear festival in Finno-Ugrian and Siberian culture has been characterized as ranging from 'dignified pious ritual to comedy and grotesque farce' in which insults 'flew to and fro' and "rude sexual gestures and imitation of the phallus and copulation were normal'.[56] At the Sámi bear feast, the proceedings commenced with the handing over of a plaited twig by the leader of the hunt. This twig was kept in a linen cloth during the three days of the celebration.

Decorated with brass ornaments, the bear's tail was fastened to the twig and finally buried with the skeleton of the bear.[57] From Fjellström's description of the bear festival among the Sámi of Västerbotten (Sweden) we learn:

> Last the bear's tail or stump, which unflayed and with some accompanying fat had been boiled: *Soiwe neit* or the bear hunter's wife, who had hidden the previously mentioned birch ring (upon which all the women present and children had fixed a ring or two or a piece of brass chain) in a linen cloth, now takes it out and when they had eaten what they could of it and sucked up all the fat that had stuck to the bear's tail, it was bound up with the above-mentioned decorated birch ring, and handed over thus to the hunters who preserve it for inclusion with the other bones... At this point all the women folk cover their faces and they are kissed by their husbands for their trouble in connection with honouring the bear.[58]

As far as I know, the Norwegian scholar, Nils Lid, was the first to advert to the remarkable similarity between this account and some Faroese (and Scottish) customs involving a *drunnur* or *(dronn)* by which was meant 'a rump with an animal's tail on it' (Fig. 22)[59] 'The Faroese custom', adds Lid, 'of passing around such a *'drunnur'* with a decorated tail during the [wedding] meal so that each one of the guests would have an opportunity to rhyme something over it... casts a useful light over an account in *Vǫlsa Þáttr* and thereby also over *Fløksandsinnskrifti* which i.a. bears witness to the use of linen in similar rituals'.[60] The tale of the *völsi* referred to by Lid and others is found in *Flateyjarbók*, a manuscript dating from the later part of the fourteenth century. The tale, however, must have existed earlier as an independent story, dating, perhaps, from about 1300 AD or even earlier, but it is set in eleventh-century Norway. The hero of the tale is Olaf Haraldsson (995–1030) – better known as St Olaf – and the story tells how he weaned a family away from their pagan worship of the *völsi*, a pickled horse's penis, and thereby converted them to Christianity.[61]

The account in *Vǫlsa Þáttr* is, as we might well expect given the nature of the subject matter, blatantly erotic in content, the Faroese rhymes that accompanied the *drunnur* no less so, both having the saving grace, however, of being humorous and witty to a degree.[62] As Lid's reference to Scotland implies, the possibility of a Celtic context for this custom was not lost on Scandinavian scholars. In fact, this had been raised originally by Jakob Jacobsen, and the whole subject subsequently examined in detail by his Faroese compatriot, Christian Matras, in an article published in 1957. More recently again, W.B. Lockwood has summarized the findings of these scholars – though, strangely, his review makes no mention of Lid's contribution and the Sámi connection.

[This] remarkable term *drunnur* 'rump'... was first treated in Jacobsen's article and reference to a (still not extinct) Faroese wedding custom when the rump of an ox or a large sheep, together with the tail, decorated with coloured paper or ribbons, is handed round the table on a platter. On receiving this platter, each guest is expected to make some witty pronouncement in verse, either about the corpus delicti or on some other topic lending itself to humorous treatment. Jacobsen wondered if this custom had once been current in the Celtic area, for this would explain why the word had been borrowed... There the matter rested until taken up by Matras... [who] traced [the custom] to Gaelic tradition [quoting] *The Metrical Dindshenchas* I:26, 177: *Dromanna dronna in cech thréibh /do drúithih, do doirseóirib* 'backs, chines (i.e. parts of meat) in every dwelling to jesters, to doorkeepers'. Reports of customs nearer to the Faroes come from Scotland starting with the H[ighland] S[ociety's] D[ictionary], 1828: *dronn*: 'a rump, the Bard's portion of a mutton, on receiving of which any one is obliged to compose a verse...' Lastly from Dwelly, the detail – 'At weddings; the man to whom the *dronn* would come was obliged to make a verse', thereby completing the connection which Jakobsen had envisaged when he first drew attention to the Gaelic antecedents of the word...[63]

To the list of names for the object passed around in this context, we may now add, thanks to MacAonghais, the curious appellation *'Dubhchapall'*, which, on the face of it, would appear to mean 'Black horse'.[64] The *dronn /drunnur /dubhchapall /völsi* and *Sámi bear's tail* complex comfortably spans the area contained within the arc of north-west Atlantic Europe from the Kola Peninsula to Corca Dhuibhne and would appear to represent a tradition once common to that whole area. This custom would repay a much more detailed examination than is possible in the context of the present exercise. I venture to say no more at this stage than that this might involve consideration of such matters as Nordic Shrove-tide customs with which linen is associated,[65] the *fénnidi* of Irish tradition[66], perambulatory mummers bands (Biddy Boys and other such groups),[67] wake games imbued with sexual overtones[68] and, most fundamentally of all, perhaps, the venerable institution of the Aśva Medha itself.[69]

The issue has yet to be fully teased out; in the meantime, however, one may be justified, perhaps, in vouchsafing the opinion that we are dealing here with some of the basic elements and reflexes of an ancient bear cult and culture which, like the bear itself, found a lifeline to survival on the European periphery. On the edge, in parts such as Lapland and Finland where bears still roam, the evidence for this is clear and explicit, though, admittedly, relatively late in terms of its documentation. At the other end of the scale, we have Ireland and Scotland, environmentally bear-less, but both boasting a culture with a long literary history, which preserves, aś we have seen, a number of intriguing names for the bear. Here, I believe we can glimpse tantalizing reflexes of this same bear culture expressed through folklore and mythology as well as etymology. The establishment of a Gaelic origin for the name *drunnur* provides a link between earlier phases of the Irish language and the Irish literary tradition and modern Gaelic folklore; it also serves to emphasize the importance which attaches to both of these and, so far as the latter is concerned, demonstrates the folly of ignoring the potential of folk tradition in helping us towards a deeper understanding of topics such as the one here under discussion. In view of these sentiments and with the stage now shifted back to Gaelic soil, as it were, it would seem appropriate to introduce at this point some further evidence of bear culture in Gaelic folk tradition.

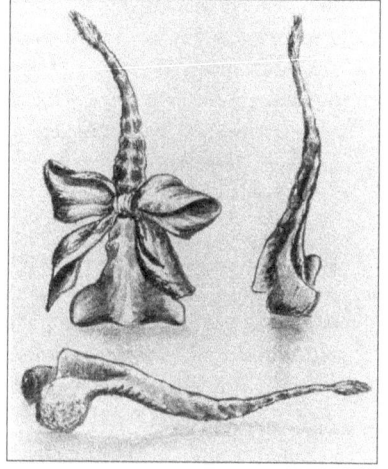

Fig. 22: *Drunnur*

* * *

Chapter 2   63

Alexander Carmichael in his wide-ranging account of Scottish (and some Irish) customs associated with the Feast of St Brigit, preserves for us a detailed description of a strange episode which caused him some puzzlement and which he dubbed 'the pounding of the serpent in effigy'. It goes as follows:

> One of the most curious customs of Bride's Day was the pounding of the serpent in effigy. The following scene was described to the writer by one who was present: 'I was one of several guests in the home of Mr John Tolmie of Uignis, Skye. One of my fellow-guests was Mrs Macleod, widow of Major Macleod of Stein, and daughter of Flora Macdonald. Mrs Macleod was known among her friends as 'Major Ann'. [Carmichael's informant goes on to describe Mrs Macleod's manners, wit, generosity, courage, dignity, grace and, last but not least, athleticism in dancing jigs, reels and strathspeys – though in her 88th year.] One morning at breakfast in Uignis, [this account continues],'some one remarked that this was the Day of Bride. 'The Day of Bride', repeated Mrs Macleod meditatively, and with a dignified bow of apology rose from the table. All watched her movements with eager curiosity. Mrs Macleod went to the fireside and took up the tongs and a bit of peat and walked out to the doorstep. She then took off her stocking and put the peat into it and pounded it with the tongs. And as she pounded the peat on the step, she intoned a 'rann' rune, only one verse of which I can remember:
>
> | | |
> |---|---|
> | *An diugh La Bride,* | This is the day of Bride, |
> | *Thig an righinn as an tom,* | The queen will come from the mound, |
> | *Cha bhean mise ris an righinn,* | I will not touch the queen, |
> | *Cha bhean an righinn rium.* | Nor will the queen touch me. |
>
> Having pounded the peat and replaced her stocking, Mrs Macleod returned to the table, apologizing for her remissness in not remembering the Day earlier in the morning. I could not make out whether Mrs Macleod was serious or acting, for she was a delightful actress and the delight of young and old. Many curious ceremonies and traditions in connection with Bride were told that morning, but I do not remember them.[70]

Remarking on his anonymous informant's description of this incident, Carmichael adds:

The pounding in the stocking of the peat representing the serpent would indicate destruction rather than worship, perhaps the bruising of the serpent's head. Probably, however, the ceremony is older, and designed to symbolise something now lost.[71]

I trust that it is obvious from the thrust of the argument hitherto that we are already headed in the general direction indicated by Carmichael's portentous comment. It may be appropriate, therefore, at this point, to see if it is possible to fit Carmichael's 'pounding of the serpent in effigy' episode within the framework of the material which has already been adduced.

One could be forgiven for dismissing this incident as something which the octogenerian Mrs Macleod (seemingly game for anything) may simply have executed for a laugh. Carmichael's informant himself indicates a degree of doubt in the matter – 'I could not make out whether Mrs Macleod was serious or acting, for she was a consummate actress and the delight of young and old'.[72] Add to that the fact that Carmichael's reputation and integrity as a collector has occasionally been called into question[73] and, on top of that again, that only once has a corresponding incident been hinted at Irish folk tradition, as far as I know,[74] and one might possibly conclude that all of this is nothing more than far-fetched Caledonian nonsense and fabrication.

Nonetheless, however bizarre it may seem at first glance, the description of the incident involving Mrs Macleod does have a ring of authenticity to it, from the folklore point of view. The action takes place on the morning of St Brigit's Day partly indoors, partly outdoors – liminal circumstances entirely appropriate to the celebration of this feast;[75] furthermore, the narrative is set in the folkloristically congenial context of reverie and reminiscence devoted to discussion of a range of practices relevant to the season in question – the 'many curious customs and traditions in connection with Bride' spoken of by Carmichael's informant.

Various Nordic accounts of beating the bear 'with slender switches', following its demise, also add a further dimension to the whole affair. Admittedly, belabouring a sod of peat with a tongs on the doorstep may not seem, on the face of it, to have much to do with whipping a bear-skin in the snow but, in the light of various ramifications of the 'beating of the bear with slender switches' syndrome,[76] I think it may be possible to substantiate the connection between the two and effectively demonstrate that they do, in fact, hang together forming a highly significant element of a wider common tradition.

We have already noted in passing that the bear was killed while in hibernation having been previously 'ringed in', as it is put, and then dragged forward and beaten as part of what has been called 'a revivification ritual'.[77] 'Beating' was believed to promote fertility.[78] During the autumn, while the bear is seeking out a winter den for itself, should a hunter succeed in tracking it and 'ringing' it, it was not the practice for him and his fellow hunter to seek out the bear in order to kill it in his winter abode but rather wait until the following March or beginning of April. The changing nature of the seasons of the year give rise to circumstances which enabled hunters to track the bear through the first flurry of winter snow, eventually – months later – to kill it and, with a minimum of effort, drag it back to camp across the deeper snows of spring.[79] However, the shifting balance of light and darkness between the seasons is a factor which plays an even more important role in terms of its crucial effect on the behaviour of the bear, being the cause of its singular habit of hibernating through the long winter night in the first place.

Hibernation is 'a complex process which requires adaptations or modifications at all levels of physiological organization...'[80] One of the most interesting of these modifications is the fluctuation of reproductive capacity on a seasonal basis. Seasonal reproductive cycles are under the influence of a number of factors, one of the most important of which is day length. If the species is to survive, it is vitally important that reproductive rhythms be timed to perfection, particularly with regard to the cycle of birth of the young which must occur in the spring or early summer, thus providing the new-born with maximum chance of survival. Many animals, including the bear, respond to the changing photoperiod (i.e. the annual change in day length) by making physiological adjustments to prepare for the forthcoming seasons;[81] the daily photoperiod thus becomes 'the major *zeitgeber*', a phenomenon which both 'clearly involves anticipation of future events and a system of measuring day length'[82] or to put it another way, it is not only necessary for bears to be aware of the season at hand but they must also be able to predict what the environmental situation will be months into the future.[83]

The process of synchronizing with the annual cycle of vegetation the crucial business of insemination, pregnancy, parturition and nurturing of their young by a wide variety of mammals is more and more thought of by experts in the field of endocrinology as being ascribable to an organ called the pineal gland.[84] Long days are believed to be inhibitory to the pineal gland and consequently have the effect of stimulating reproduction; short dark days, on the other hand repress reproductive function by triggering the secretion of certain hormones.[85] The pineal gland is situated at the geometric centre of the skull and is so called because it is generally shaped like a pine cone. It was known to the Greeks and Romans and dubbed by some authors *conarium* on account of its form,[86] but, otherwise, until recently, very little was known about its real function.[87]

Effectively, through its hibernating habits, the bear acted as a time indicator with respect to the seasons, its biocosmic rhythms subtly responding to changes in light and darkness. The hibernation of the bear acted as a stable, reliable sign of the limits of the seasons and became a dominant symbol of the entire transition from summer to winter and back again.[88] As such, it led to the bear being associated with the loss and recovery of fertility in nature.[89] This represents the basic source and impetus of what lies behind the bear feast itself, the celebration of which was imbued from beginning to end with notions of revivification, rebirth and renewal.

The bear may have been identified by humans as a kind of biocosmic clock and even its behaviour taken as some kind of indicator of the nature of the individual life-span.[90] Similarly, traces of the pattern set by its annual programme of sexual revivification may be seen in a number of the highly charged sexual images[91] associated with the celebration of the Feast of St Brigit some of which have already been adverted to above.[92] We shall not dwell further on these matters at this juncture but rather return briefly to the 'beating with slender switches' syndrome and to consider in particular its connections with the commencement of the spring season as a turning point in the year.

The belief referred to at the outset that the bear would turn over but once in its den during that long hibernation was an occurrence interpreted as marking the half-way point or midwinter. If it comes out and finds that it is cold, the bear romps around joyfully but if the weather is mild, it squeezes further back in the den than before.[93] The final emergence of the bear from hibernation, however, constituted the most dramatic proof that winter was indeed over and that spring had at last arrived. Should there be any delay in its arrival, however, folk tradition offered a number of options designed to hurry it along: the Sámi, if the winter seemed to last too long, would beat a bear skin[94] and similarly a woman born in winter was believed to be able to cause warm weather by doing the same.[95] With this, following Collinder, we may compare the Scandinavian Easter Sunday custom whereby children were lashed with a birch twig in the morning[96] and, I would also argue, the Hebridean 'pounding of the serpent in effigy'.

We are fortunate that Carmichael did not depart from his customary mixum-gatherum methods in the case of the 'rann' which was intoned by Mrs Macleod but, as was his wont, proceeded to supply further versions of this 'propitiatory hymn', as he described it, from other sources. Two of these are of particular interest to us and I quote them here in full:

La Fheill Bride brisgeanach	On the Feast of Bride,
Thig an ceann de'n chaiteanach,	The head will come off the *'caiteanach'*,
Thig nighean Iomhair as an tom,	The daughter of Ivor shall come from the knoll,
Le fonn feadalaich.	With tuneful whistling.

Thig an nathair as an toll,	The serpent will come from the hole,
La donn Bride,	On the brown day of Bride,
Ged robh tri traighean dh'an tsneachd	Though there should be three feet of snow,
Air leachd an lair.	On the flat surface of the ground.[97]

Our attention is immediately directed here, to Carmichael's having neglected to offer a translation for the adjective *brisgeanach* and equally his seeming reluctance to render *caiteanach* into English. To judge by Dwelly, at least, no particular degree of obscurity attaches to either of these words.[98] It is probably safe to conclude, therefore, that Carmichael's coyness concerning them stemmed from his inability to fully comprehend their relevance in this context. Leaving aside *brisgeanac*h (one of a number of adjectives used to qualify *La Fheill Bride* in one way or another) to concentrate on *caiteanach*, a word which would seem to mean 'hairy, shaggy' or the like, one might go as far as to suggest that the latter may well represent yet another name for the bear corresponding to the likes of the Norwegian Noa name *lodne gofar*[99] 'hairy grandfather', for example. We have already seen the importance that attaches to 'the head that comes off the hairy one', if we may so paraphrase

Carmichael, in the context of the bear feast where the head of the bear is given the place of honour at the feast to be subsequently removed with great ceremony for lodgement in a pine tree specially designated for this purpose. If this interpretation is correct, it would follow that Carmichael's *nathair* ('serpent')[100] or *nighean Iomhair* ('daughter of Ivor' – by which is meant, he believes, the serpent) which emerges from its 'hole' or 'knoll' on St Brigit's Day is to be identified with the bear awakening from hibernation and emerging from its den at the end of winter. The second of the two verses quoted above, with its reference to 'three feet of snow on the flat surface of the ground', is also reminiscent of the stress laid upon the importance of suitable early and late winter snow conditions for a successful bear hunt.[101]

Finally, I believe the enigmatic reference to the 'daughter of Ivor' emerging from the knoll 'with tuneful whistling' may also prove capable of yielding up some interesting Nordic connections in which the bear has a considerable part to play. The progress of herders leading their cattle through areas where bears might pose a problem was often a tumultuous business in the course of which as much noise and hullabaloo as possible was made in order to discourage any potential attacker.[102] This cacophony of bawling and yelling was not to the bear's liking, it seems. On the contrary, its tastes appear to have been much more refined, even extending to a capacity to discriminate between different kinds of musical sounds, as is implied by the Kalevala[103] In a verse well-known in Norwegian tradition the bear is allowed to express his preferences as follows:

> *Tutarhonn og langelur,* Trumpeting and herders' horns,
> *Det vil eg ikkje høyre:* I do not wish to hear:
> *Men fløytelåtog båne gråt,* But whistling tunes and crying bairns,
> *Det leikar i mitt øyre.* Are music to my ears.[104]

Here, the expression *'fløytelåt'* matches Carmichael's *'fonn feadalaich'* exactly, thus fashioning another intriguing link between Nordic bear-lore and the Hebridean Gaelic tradition surrounding St Brigit. Scottish tradition does not stand alone in this regard for it is possible to find evidence allowing us to widen the Gaelic base of our enquiry to include Ireland and, in the Nordic context, to extend its scope to embrace both Denmark and Iceland.

* * *

Chapter 2 69

In 1891, under the heading 'Making Weather' in Denmark, H.F. Feilberg drew attention to what he described as a 'most curious custom… still observed in some parts of Denmark'.[105] His account goes as follows:

> During the months of February and March, the farmer, housewives, thereafter their husbands and at last their servants, female and male, 'make weather'. Commonly, the parsonage being No. 1 on the list, the parson's wife 'makes weather' on the first of February. Is the weather that day good, Mrs N.N. is said to be a very benevolent lady, in good humour, and neighboresses go visiting her, congratulating on the fair weather, and are friendly received, treated to coffee and cakes. Is the weather on the contrary foul, Mrs N.N. is in bad humour, we will go to punish her or to divert her. Maybe she is pulled out into the yard and tied to the waterpump, that she may herself try her own weather. Her neighbours come wrapped up in large cloaks and shawls, whereas they come summerclad when the weather is fair. Otherwise a neighbour may creep cautiously along the house wall and tie some hards on the doorlatch. It is instantly understood, and everything ends with a cup of coffee, given by the person who 'makes' the foul weather, some jokes and everybody goes home again… Is this custom known elsewhere? Wherefrom may this 'making weather' be derived? Why in the months of February and March?

Icelandic tradition provides an answer to some of these questions as Axel Olrik pointed out a decade or so later.[106] *Thorri* is the Icelandic name for the fourth winter month beginning roughly in mid-January.[107] It was, according to the famous nineteenth-century Icelandic folklore collector Jón Árnason, an age-old custom to have a celebration in the home on the first day of *Thorri* in order to greet it with proper respect. He describes it as 'the duty of the farmer to welcome *Thorri*' or 'usher it in' by rising earlier than anyone else on the farm the first morning. The farmer should get up, and go out clad only in a shirt, barefoot and partly barelegged, for he was to wear only one leg of his underpants, while the other was to be dragged behind. Thus attired, he was to hop on one foot all around the farmhouse, still dragging his underpants by the other, and bid *Thorri* welcome to his home. Then he was to provide a banquet for other farmers in the district. In some places in northern Iceland, the first day of *Thorri* is called 'husband's day'. On that date, the lady of the house is supposed to treat her husband exceptionally well; such festivities are still called *Thorrablót*, that is 'sacrifice to *Thorri*'. The word *Thorrablót* ocurs in *Flateyjarbók* in a text which must have existed at least as early as 1230 AD; there we learn of old King Thorri who was a great one for sacrifices and made one every year in the middle of winter. He had a daughter Góa, to whom we shall return in a moment. The existence of the word *Thorrablót* indicates that some such ceremony was customary at some time, the natural purpose of which was presumably the same as any other sacrifice, namely, to win the favour of the power to whom the sacrifice was made.

In Icelandic tradition, the following month, the fifth month of winter, beginning around the 18th of February, is called *Góa* : other forms of the name include *gue, gøj, gø, go, goi, göja*, and *gyja* and the Sámi *guovva-manno*, which apparently derives from *góimánaðr*.[108] The same lore pertains to the welcoming of *Góa*, as that of *Thorri* and a couple of subsequent months as well – their hosts are supposed to hop, scantily clad, on one foot around the farmhouse, preferably dragging their underpants on one leg.[109] The institution of *Góablót* also existed in mainland Scandinavian tradition being associated with the custom of welcoming the first new moon after *Thorri/Torre*.[110] In Sweden, *Torsmånad* and *Göjemånad* were the names given to January and February respectively while a widely distributed Scandinavian weather rhyme also links these two names in various permutations – one of the Norwegian versions going as follows:

> *Torren med sit skæg,*   Torren with his beard,
> *Lokker börnene under sole væg,* Tempts the children out in the sun,
> *Gjø med sit skind,*   Gjø with her skin,
> *Jagar börnene i stuen ind.* Hunts the children in.[111]

In Iceland, Góa was approached directly and addressed as follows:

> *Velkomin sertu Góa mín,*   Welcome dearest Góa,
> *Og gakktu inn í bæinn,*   And step in, pray,
> *Vertu ekka úta í vindinum,* Don't stay out there in the draught,
> *Vorlangan daginn.*   The whole spring day.[112]

Nils Lid sought to establish a connection between the spring celebration of Góa and certain harvest customs in other European cultures, principally, White Russia, Lithuania and Gaelic Scotland.[113] In the latter case he concentrated on an examination of the traditions pertaining to the *Cailleach*, a figure with strong harvest connections but which, in Scottish tradition, also happens to be the name given to the period of time lasting from 12-18 April.[114] Quoting from Martin Martin's *A Description of the Western Islands of Scotland*,[115] Lid then proceeded to make the connection with Brigit:

> Another ancient custom observed on the second of February which the papists there (Islay) yet retain is this: the mistress and servants of each family take a sheaf of oats and dress it up in women's apparel, put it in a large basket, and lay a wooden club by it, and this they call Briid's-bed and then the mistress and servants cry three times; 'Briid is come, Briid is welcome'.

The significance of the setting and wording of the welcome extended by Irish households to the saint (believed to be making her rounds on the eve of her feast) has already been highlighted.[116] Descriptions of this dramatic encounter, embodying a situation where the husband seeks admission to his own house in the name of Brigit, can be recorded to the present day. The words of the Irish ceremony go as follows:

> *Gabhaígí ar bhur nglúine,*   Go on your knees,
> *Fosclaigí bhur súile,*   Open your eyes,
> *Agus ligigí isteach Bríd !*   And admit Brigit !

— to which the reply is:

> *Is é beatha !*   Welcome !
> *Is é beatha !*   Welcome !
> *Is é beatha na mná uaisle !*   Welcome to the holy woman ![117]

Lid, though well aware of the importance of Carmichael's material, chose, nevertheless, to bypass this source where details of the Scottish equivalent to the Irish tradition quoted above are given. Carmichael's account goes as follows:

> The older women... are also busy on the Eve of Bride, and great preparations are made to celebrate her Day, which is the first day of spring. They make an oblong basket in the shape of a cradle, which they call *'leaba Bride,'* 'the bed of Bride.' It is embellished with much care. Then they take a choice sheaf of corn, generally

oats, and fashion it into the form of a woman. They deck this ikon with gay ribbons from the loom, sparkling shells from the sea, and bright stones from the hill. All the sunny sheltered valleys around are searched for primroses, daisies, and other flowers that open their eyes in the morning of the year. This lay figure is called *'dealbh Bride,'* 'the ikon of Bride.' When it is dressed and decorated with all the tenderness and loving care the women can lavish upon it, one woman goes to the door of the house, and standing on the step with her hands on the jambs, calls softly into the darkness, *'Tha leaba Bride deiseal,'* 'Bride's bed is ready.' To this a ready woman behind replies, *'Thigeadh Bride steach, is e beatha Bride'*, 'Let Bride come in, Bride is welcome'. The woman at the door again addresses Bride, *'A Bhride! Bhride thig a steach, tha do leaba deanta. Gleidh an teach dh'an Triana'*, 'Bride, Bride, come thou in, thy bed is made. Preserve the house for the Trinity'. The women then place the ikon of Bride with great ceremony in the bed they have so carefully prepared for it. They place a small straight white wand (the bark being peeled off it) beside the figure. This wand is... called *'slatag Bride'* 'the little rod of Bride'... The wand is generally of birch, broom, bramble, white willow...[118]

The ritualistic welcoming of Góa and of Brigit as harbingers of spring and symbols of the commencement of a new season and cycle of rebirth and renewal in nature as in the animal world finds them slotting in easily as part of the picture that I have attempted to sketch here. This and a number of other interesting issues raised by this Scottish account will be dealt with anon. Etymologically, the name Góa is of uncertain derivation a meaning 'snow' or 'winter' has been suggested and Pokorny puts forward the idea that it is connected with *$\hat{g}hi\bar{o}m$, the same Indo-European root that yields, he says, *gamain*, meaning 'calf' which, as we saw at the outset, constitutes an element of one of the Irish Noa names for 'bear' – *mathgamain*.[119] Góa, however, is a much more shadowy figure than her counterpart Brigit who looms large in Gaelic folk tradition as in early Irish literature.[120] Brigit's name too appears to be much more readily understood; its basic element means 'to grow, to increase' signifying both physical growth as well as increase in size and stature.[121] Likewise, her descent is traced with surefooted observation of her ursine and lupine connections and, as was the case with Góa, her counterpart in the Nordic world, she was remembered in the Gaelic folk tradition of Ireland and Scotland down to our own time.

Chapter 2

The genealogy of the holy maiden Bride,
Radiant flame of gold, noble foster-mother of Christ.
Bride the daughter of Dugall the brown,
Son of Aodh, son of Art, son of Conn,
Son of Crearar, son of Cis, son of Carmac, son of Caruinn.

Every day and every night
That I say the genealogy of Bride,
I shall not be killed, I shall not be harried,
I shall not be put in cell, I shall not be wounded,
Neither shall Christ leave me in forgetfulness.

No fire, no sun, no moon shall burn me,
No lake, no water, nor sea shall drown me,
No arrow of fairy or dart of fay shall wound me,
And I under the protection of my Holy Mary,
And my gentle foster-mother is my beloved Bride.[122]

Fig. 23: St Brigid's Well,
Inishowen, County Donegal

Notes to Chapter 2

1 Vendryes A-91. Scharff 1915 (46-7), lists *mathgamhain, beithir, art, béar* and *ursóg*, adding: 'Although we know from the large quantity of bear remains found in Ireland that bears must have been very abundant in this country in the past they had evidently been exterminated before the 9th century AD, as St Donatus clearly states that bears did not exist in Ireland about the year.' Scharff 1907 (26-47), surveys the evidence for and speculates about the origin of a range of extinct animals in Ireland including the brown bear.

2 For the etymology of *art*, see Vendryes (A-91); Walde & Pokorny (1.322). Pokorny 1959 (1. 875); Buck (186) – following Walde & Pokorny – who suggests the interpretation 'destroyer of beehives' as being what lies behind the Indo-European root rk^ho. For a wide-ranging discussion of the name 'Art' and various manifestations of it, see Guyonvarc'h (215ff). The derivation of the word *milchobur* 'honey-desirer' is dealt with by Watkins (114-6). *Math* is described as being 'an archaic word for bear... replaced in Mid[dle] Ir[ish] by *mathgamhain*' (*DIL* M, 70; cf. also Vendryes (M-12, M-24). *Mathgamain*, according to Watkins (114), literally means 'bear-calf'. As to *bethir*, Watkins (114) believes the word to be a Celtic or 'Italo-Celtic' creation and suggests a connection with the root of the Old Irish verb *benaid* 'strikes, smites' (cf. note 100 below). The remaining items would appear to be of a much later vintage loaned from various sources. A range of Noa names for the bear is listed in the following sources: *HDA* 1. 881,893; Hallowell (43-53); Gaski (20-3); Honko *et al.* (120).

3 Ó Cathasaigh (24).

4 Personal communication.

5 Cf. Mac Cana 1970 (51, 54). *Dea Artio* is depicted in a little bronze group from Berne seated with a basket of fruit by her side before a bear standing under a tree. Green 1989 (139), in drawing attention to the paucity of bear-imagery 'apart from that of the bear–goddess Artio herself', characterizes Artio as being (together with Arduinna 'a denizen of the forests of the Ardennes' a 'inhabitant of the woods' (27) and she judges the relationships between Arduinna and the boar and Artio with the bear to be equivocal: 'their role appears to be that of protectress but at the same time they are helpers of the hunt. Indeed, it is not clear from the Muri [Bern] bronze whether Artio is communing with or warding off her ursine companion who, incidentally, is depicted very much larger than the goddess herself', (27-8) and she again emphasizes: 'the bear–goddess is dwarfed by her accompanying animal, as if it were divine' (208); cf., also in this respect Green (1992, 217-8). The bear is especially associated with Bern, the name of which means 'bear' and the town has kept bears for centuries (*EORE* 1, 504). Cf. note 89 below.

'In Greek cult bears were burnt in honour of Artemis... at Patrae ... and 'bear Artemis' was one of the names by which she was known... Moreover, at Brauron, Athens, and Munychia, Artemis Brauronia was worshipped... in ceremonies which were perhaps a survival of initiation customs. Young maidens danced in a saffron robe, and, like the priestesses, were called 'bears'; the dance was called *arkteia*, and the participants were of ages from five to ten; the celebrations were quinquennial and no girl might marry before undergoing the rite' (*EORE* 1. 504).

According to Gimbutas 1985 (20-1), the bear is also associated with Laima 'Giver-of-All, Goddess of Life and Death' and one of the main Old European goddesses of Baltic mythology – cf. in this context p.199, 230(note 103) below. Gimbutas 1985 (21-2) also notes that Laima can also be a stone 'incarnate with the Goddess' powers and that 'offerings of linen materials, usually towels, belts, and shirts, were made to the stones' – in which context, cf. Chapter 3, note 60 below.

6 Cf. Emeneau (56-63) and also Smal-Stocki (489-93).
7 For *björn*, see J. de Vries 1961a ([henceforth de Vries], 41). Watkins (114), takes *lokŷs* to mean 'the licker' and Buck (186), in deriving it from **tlakis*, tentatively suggests a meaning 'hairy, shaggy'. However, according to Hamp (personal communication), it means 'honey thief', behind which description lies the reality of the bear competing directly with humans for access to honey and the notion of its success in capturing this commodity first being regarded in effect as an act of theft from humans as much as from the bees themselves.
8 Pokorny 1959 (1. 425).
9 For a discussion of these names, cf. Vendryes (M-12, M-24) and J. de Vries 1958 (53-4): the latter also deals with dea Artio.
10 Mention might also be made of *Conchobur* 'dog (or wolf)-desiring' (cp. [O'] Con[n]or), Watkins (116).
11 Scouler (228) quotes St Donatus (obit 840) in support of his contention that the bear was not native to Ireland:
> *Ursorum rabies nulla est ibi, saeva leonum,*
> *Semina nec unquam Scotica terra tulit;*
> *Nulla venena nocent, nec serpens serpi in herba,*
> *Nec conquesta canit garrula rana lacu...*

According to van Wijngaarden-Bakker (317-8), however, *Ursus arctos* was among the members of the arctic fauna which adapted themselves to the ameliorated climatic circumstances which attended the end of the glacial period in Ireland. The brown bear, she tells us, 'can be assumed to have survived in the southern part of Ireland that was not covered by ice at any time' or was 'among the very first invaders after the glaciation when conditions were still arctic and no barriers existed between the continental mainland, Britain and Ireland... the brown bear also became extinct after the arrival of man.' I am grateful to my colleague Dr Rhoda Kavanagh for these references.

Mitchell (105) states: 'In a paper published in 1954 Ó Ríordáin described seven sites on Knockadoon, an island in Lough Gur [County Limerick]. All the sites were mainly Neolithic, but some had continued in use until the opening of the Bronze Age... Bear [bones] occurred on two sites and it is thus clear that the bear must have survived until this time in Ireland'.
12 Personal communication (E. Hamp).
13 Pokorny 1959 (1.184); Buck (192). Cf. in this general context, Polomé

1970 (55-72) and 1970 (66) for comments on the distribution of various words for 'wax'; Hamp 1971 (187) and Wagner 1960 (81-4).
14   Pokorny 1959 (1. 1178-9), Buck (185) and McCone 1985 (17).
15   Ó Cathasaigh (33-7) and (49, n.187 where he contrasts the elements *maith* 'good' and *olc* 'evil', employed in Noa names for the bear and wolf respectively). Cf. also note 2 above.
16   According to Leem 505f [quoted in *KL* 16. 410]) the Sámi people of Finnmark greased their doors with fat on the sun making its first appearance in spring.
17   Onians (471-2). Cf. Notes 56 (p.38-9), 59 (p. 39) and 106 (p. 48-9).
18   My translation from Lid (1928 (ed.), 114-5. The story was also known in Sámi tradition – cf. Qvigstad 1927 (1. 124-7 and Notes, p. 544). The bear is also brought into association with the Virgin Mary in the context of various charms used to protect cattle against the ravages of bears and other wild animals. Interestingly, in these the Virgin Mary is requested to lock up with her keys all the wild animals of the forest: *Jomfru Maria reste te skogjen/mæ ni hengde nyklar/å læste alle klodyri i skogjen,/ulvetonn, bjønn å gram,/berr' ikkje buhonden den goe'* (Bø, 97). By contrast, in assuming the role of 'Frigg and Freya and other gods' the Virgin Mary was invoked by women about to give birth to lend her keys so that they might open their loins *'Jomfru Maria! Lån mig noglerne dine, at jeg må åbne lænderne mine'* (*KL* 1. 358). For a discussion of these and other traditions associated with the Virgin Mary and her keys, cf. Backman (esp. 195-99 [and for a useful discussion of key symbolism in general,167-79]).

Key-bearing divinities are a well-known phenomenon in ancient tradition, including among their number, Cybele, who 'holds the key to Earth, shutting her up in winter and opening her again in spring'– *EOR* 8. 227 (cf. note 89 below). In Ireland, we are told: 'From St Brigid's Day [1 February] on, half the lock is taken out of the bird's throat (for singing), but the lock is completely off from St Patrick's Day [17 March]' (NFC 901:129), a notion which we also find reflected in a couplet from an early Irish poem on the 'birds of the world': 'On the festival of Rúadán, no petty saying,/their fetters are then unloosed...' (Best & Lawlor, 94 [for which reference I am indebted to Dr Miceál Ross]).

In Kalevala poetry, the Virgin Mary is referred to as *Maria, metinen neiti* ('Mary, honey virgin') and honey is, of course connected with the bee, which the Virgin Mary has as one of her many symbols (Edsman 1953, 84), as well as with the bear (cf. note 2 above). Likewise, in Finnish tradition, certain plants, designated *Neitsyt Marian sänkyheinä* (literally 'the Virgin Mary's bed-grass) – in allusion to her childbed – were placed in the bed of a woman about to give birth in order to ease the delivery (*KL* 11. 368). *Jungfru Marie sänghalm* ('The Virgin Mary's bed–straw' = *Galium verum*) is also held in similar regard in Swedish tradition (Backman, 185-6).

In Irish tradition, a piece of straw, drawn from the bed on which the woman about to give birth lay, was singed in the fire and replaced in the bed as a protective measure (*NFC* 469:124-5 and 1202:235-6, for which references I am grateful to Dr Pádraig Ó Héalaí. *Jomfru Marias særk* ('the Virgin Mary's sark',) which is preserved in Lund [Cathedral] in Sweden, is said to have been borrowed in 1468 by Christian I in connection with a birth (*KL* 11. 368) and may be compared directly with the *Brat Bríde* of Irish tradition; its use is adverted to in the Swedish prayer *Hjelp Gud! Jungfru Maria läna [låna] mig sarken tin then vijda* ('Help [me] God! Virgin Mary, lend me your broad shift'), *KL* 11. 368. Cf. also in this context, p. 6 above & pp. 124-126 below.

Lorenzen, in his chapter *'Ulv og bjørn i Dansk folkeminde'* (62-114) treats a wide range of tradition material common to the wolf and the bear, while Lid 1928 (ed.), 110-31 under the heading, *'Bjørnen, Ulven og Ræven'* deals in similar fashion with traditions pertaining to the bear, the wolf and the fox.

19 Lid 1928 (ed.), 111.
20 Bø (89).
21 *HDA* 1. 885-7, *KL* 1. 662-3 and Bø (95-6). For examples of shape-shifting involving bears in Sámi tradition, cf. Qvigstad 1927, (1. 402-13 and Notes, p. 548-9).
22 A woman in Västmanland (Sweden) was warned by the Forest Maiden about the 'Big Dog' by which she meant the bear, (Lid 1928 [ed.], 112), which was also called the 'pasture-ground dog' of the trolls (Edsman 1953, 89) and the same writer *(loc.cit.)* recounts how otherworld bears, in a further extension of this topsy turvy style, became cattle, the roles of prey and predator thus being reversed and the trolls issuing threats to a famous bear-hunter who, they complained, had killed their last 'cow' i.e. bear. Cf. also G. Granberg (105-17); Rooth (72-90). For a comprehensive survey of European folklore relating to this theme, cf. Röhrich (79-161).
23 Cf. Mysterud (101).
24 'No. 8. [referring to the figure of a bear on a particular Sámi shaman drum] *'Ist der Bär des Himmels und wird Waralde Biri, das ist der Bär des Himmels, genannt. Diesen Bären zeichnen sie ab bei den Göttern im Himmel, da sie jeden Bären auf der Erde für ein heiliges Tier halten und ihn Gottes Hund nennen; dagegen nennen sie den Wolf Satans Hund...'* – quoted by Manker in translation from the Nærö-manuscript of Johan Randulf (1723) (194).
25 Solheim (462).
26 Mysterud (101).
27 Cf. Langford (293-304). Among the six stone sculptures 'of probable Christian date' from Cathedral Hill in Armagh we find three bears and, intriguingly, on either side of the largest bear, we find 'carved in relief between the legs, and facing towards the rear... the head of a large dog or wolf', Rynne 1972 (80, 82) for which reference I am grateful to my colleague, Professor Barry Raftery.
28 'The presence of the wolf in historic times is attested by a great number of written sources, place-names, folk-tales etc.' Van Wijngaarden-Bakker (34 and sources quoted there). The 'last wolf' was shot around 1786 (Fisher, 41), or in 1790 or 1810 (McMillan, 103). The evidence is also surveyed by Moffat (74-5). Cf. also O'Dowd (287).
29 Harting (20-1, 24), for which reference I am grateful to Dr John Kennedy.
30 Swahn's comprehensive study – *The Tale of Cupid and Psyche* – lists the supernatural husband as appearing in one or other of the following guises –

bear, dog, snake, swine, wolf, 'beast' or 'monster' (26); of these variations, he states, the bear 'is most usual in the Germanic and Slavonic areas outside of which it seldom occurs' while the dog 'is, with few exceptions confined to the Germanic and Celtic areas' (228). The hero of *AT 301 The Three Stolen Princesses* is of supernatural origin and strength, in the most primitive forms of the story being the son of a bear who has stolen his mother. An Irish version of this folk-tale with English summary and notes, can be found in Ó Duilearga 1935 (189-210) reprinted in Ó Duilearga 1948 (27-53) and in full English translation in MacNeill 1981 (23-45 [Notes, p. 382]). *FW* 1, 127 provides a short survey of this tale, its distribution and various literary associations.

31 It is noteworthy that Cross contains no reference to bears, though many other animals, domestic, wild, mythical and magic are mentioned therein.
32 Cf. *EORE* 1. 502-4; Edsman 1987 (87-9) provides a comprehensive survey of different kinds of bear lore together with a useful bibliography.
33 Jacquart and Thomasset (162).
34 Jacquart and Thomasset (163). According to Pliny, bears couple lying down like human beings (A. de Vries 1974,38).
35 Jacquart and Thomasset (165).
36 Mysterud (115) and Weiser-Aall 1968 (15-8). Bø (93), mentions that a recent Norwegian radio programme in which – in the course of a debate between a local politician and a member of the medical profession centering on the question of bears which were causing a nuisance in that particular area – an argument (against protecting them) was advanced by the local representative on the basis that they might prove dangerous to pregnant women.

A recent *Reuter's* report from Oslo, quoted in the British newspaper *The Independent* on 5 December 1992 (for which reference I am grateful to Coinneach Mac Gill-Eathain), would seem to indicate that Norwegian folk belief about bears still carries a certain currency – 'A biology professor said Norwegian imagination had gone too far after suggestions that 18 cows found killed had been raped by a sex-starved bear. 'The limit for fantastic theories has been overstepped', Kaare Elgmork of the Biology Institute of Oslo University said. The 'rape' theory was launched by a university lecturer to explain the mysterious deaths of 18 cows in Norway.'

37 Lid 1928 (ed.), 120, where we are told that the bear sheds tears if the foetus turns out to be female and Bø (94), where it is also noted (p. 96) that, following a kill, the bear often takes its victim's kidneys first.
38 Bø (94).
39 Bø (94).
40 *KL* 1. 674.
41 Edsman 1987 (87); Lid 1928 (ed.), 120 and Weiser-Aall (17). In 1967, in the Sámi community of Nesseby (Varanger, Norway), I heard how the rejection of a suitor for the hand of a certain female had been intimated by the mother of the girl taking her position on the dunghill and baring her bottom to the approaching male as he drew near the house.

In her account of custom and belief associated with courtship and marriage in the Nordic countries, Frimannslund (43) describes the Swedish and Swedish-Finnish fashion of females turning their backs to unwanted suitors, concerning which individuals it was then said that they had got *kalvskinnet* 'the calf skin'; similarly a girl who had been rejected by her boyfriend was likewise said to have got *kalvskinnet* and in both cases, receipt of *kalvskinnet* was regarded as a disgrace.

The dunghill is central to a seasonal festival called *'Dyngkalaset'* – 'The Dung Party' – which took place on the completion of the chore of wheeling manure from the dunghill and spreading it on the land. Men and women joined in this task – the men wheeling and the women forking manure from the dunghill or spreading it in the fields. At the celebration which marked the successful completion of this work, festive food was served and a 'wedding' dance (complete with 'bride') was not an unknown feature (cf. Lithberg [24-42] and Klein [1-14]).

42 Bø (96) and *HDA* 1. 900. E. Granberg 1931 (47), mentions that, in the Swedish provinces of Härjedalen and Jämtland, in the event of a difficult birth, it was believed that a man who had been mauled by a bear but succeeded in escaping from it subsequently had the capacity of assuming the role of accoucheur; the woman in childbed, in imitation of the manner in which the man had been delivered from the clutches of the bear, simply held him in a firm embrace in order to be delivered of her child. As a means of avoiding pregnancy, a contraceptive consisting of a suppository containing bear gall was inserted before intercourse (*HDA* 1. 903).

43 *HDA* 1. 885-7; *KL* 1. 662.

44 Slightly paraphrased in translation by me from the account in Fjellström 1981 (14-7). Edsman 1956 (*passim* 36-56) provides another translation, together with a range of other stories concerning relations between bears and human beings.

45 My translation from Rheen (44).

46 Cf. Edsman 1956 (49).

47 *Ibid.*, 50.

48 A. Olrik 1903 (199–203). Cf. also von Sydow 1923a (1-46, [esp. in this context 36-41]); Pizarro (263-81); Barbeau (1-12).

49 *KL* 1. 672.

50 G. Jónsson (ed.) Chapter 25, p. 47.

51 Cf. Edsman 1956 (50-1) and von Sydow 1923 (37-8). In the story concerning the Virgin Mary, the fox, the wolf and the bear cited above (p. 37), the Virgin Mary ordains that the fox will become a weakling whose back can be broken by a single blow from a woollen sock and the same is also said of the wolf (Lid 1928 [ed.], 115).

52 Cf. Edsman 1956 (53).

53 Honko *et al.* (117-40 *passim*). K. Vilkuna, in his account of the Finnish bear feast (*KL* 1. 676), notes that the trees in which bear skulls were deposited usually stood by a [lake] shore and in the vicinity of a good nesting place. Emeneau (63) notes a rather similar custom in connection with the tiger in India: 'When a tiger is killed, it is set up on a chair-like frame alongside the seated hunter, and a ceremony is gone through which is said to be in general like that of a wedding, consisting of formal salutations by the household and friends and the sprinkling of rice on and the feeding of milk to the hunter'.

54 Hammarstedt 1929 (2). Cf. also Hagberg 1913 (9–-6); E. Granberg 1941 (22-35); and, for a review of this and other relevant material, cf. Danvir 1943, (6-82 and a revised version by the same author under the name Karin Johansson (1975, 35-52).
55 Hammarstedt 1929 (4-5), and *KL* 1. 676. In North Bohemian tradition the bear appeared in the company of a bride called *die Aschenbraut* (Hammarstedt 1929, 4]). It is possible that the Dalecarlian Wedding-bear /St Matthew's Day-bear customs may represent the fusion of two stages of one and the same tradition widely separate in time but ultimately claiming a common origin datable from a period when customs and legends, rites and ceremonies associated with the bear were probably as widely distributed in Europe as the bear itself. As Hammarstedt 1929 (1) points out, it is almost axiomatic that traditions such as these attaching to a certain animal are bound to disappear soon after the animal disappears. They no longer have something to which they can attach themselves and so, with a greater or lesser degree of abandonment of their form and character, they adopt a different context, degenerating, perhaps, in the fullness of time, to the point where they can no longer be recognized for what they once were.
56 Honko *et al.* (127). Among the Ob-Ugrians, especially, it developed into something close to real theatre (Edsman 1987, 86-7) with what are described in the songs that accompanied the actions as 'hand-twisting, leg-twisting plays' (Cushing [155] – for which reference I am grateful to Dr Miceál Ross). For a full account of these performances, cf. Tschernjetzow, (285-319).
57 Norlander-Unsgaard 1983 (198). She interprets this as being 'a sign of a joyful union between the sexes: the male and female principle, joined under happy circumstances', also pointing out that 'allusions and jokes accompanied this activity'.
58 My translation from Fjellström 1981 (27-8).
59 Lid 1926 (154).
60 *Loc. cit. Völsi* is defined by de Vries (673), as '*geschlectsteil des hengstes*' and derived by him from proto-nordic **walusa*, possibly being ultimately related to Latin *valor, Valerius*. According to Reichborn-Kjennerud (24), Magnus Olsen's interpretation of this fourth-century inscription from Nordhardland in western Norway indicates that it contains a formula for a defence against the evil eye incorporating a reference to linen. Flax seed was also regarded in the Nordic world as having much to do with fertility e.g. three handfuls of flax seed were scattered over the plough when it was first used in spring (*KL* 10. 580).

Linen also features in the Finnish 'Flax Festival', an important element of which was 'Shrove gliding' – "Tobogganing down long slopes was regarded as a means of securing the largest flax, but it had other flax magic associations. The length of the slope was naturally associated with the length of the flax fibres, but if the toboggan capsized in its course down the slope the omen meant that the flax should be flattened before next harvest (Enäjärvi-Haavio, 23)... The cry 'I slide Shrovetide, so long are my linens [is my flax]' – along with a colourful range of vulgar expressions – relating in particular to anatomical details of the male genitalia – which accompanied 'the coasting downhill' – played an important part in the supplementary magic associated with Shrovetide" (35). Some Shrove-tide customs were performed naked or partly so – in southern Karelia, for example, we are told that 'there is evidence that peasant women tobogganed down hill on their bare behind so that the flax would thrive' (25). In central and northern Sweden, coasting downhill in this fashion was also quite common. Further south in Sweden, the notion of encouraging 'tall flax' was associated with St Knut's Day (7 or 13 January). In south-west Sweden, this day was commemorated by groups of people – often in various kinds of animal disguise and/or with the men dressed as women and vice versa – who proceeded from farm to farm carrying a doll effigy constructed of straw wrapped around a pole, dressed in old clothes and sometimes equipped with male genitalia of monstrous dimension (Ordéus, 17-9) and pp. 197-198 below. Across Europe, the general belief was that flax or hemp seed should be planted on the days of saints who were thought to have been tall and, in Germany, long steps are taken while sowing the seed which is thrown high in the air. For these and further references, cf. Benet (42-3).

61 A full account of the custom and a discussion of its origins can be found in Joseph (245-6). For another account of the *völsi*, cf. Heusler (2. 372-87) and for a survey of the phallus cult in Nordic tradition, cf. *KL* 4. 157-8 and sources quoted there. Cf. also Matthiessen (73-6) who quotes a seventeenth-century Danish source citing the use of '*priapus equi*' as a cure for diarrhoea (76).

62 Examples are quoted in Joseph and Heusler as also in Coffey (7-16).

63 Lockwood 1978 (116-7).

64 MacAonghais (102). The fact that a horse's penis is black in colour may have some bearing on the name *dubhchapall*. I am grateful to Dr Seosamh Watson for the above reference.

65 For a review of these in Finnish and Swedish tradition, cf. Enäjärvi-Haavio (20-3).

66 Cf. J. F. Nagy 1985 (44 and Notes p. 245) compares the *fénnidi* of Ireland with various warrior and outlaw bands of other traditions, depicted in 'myth and ritual as packs of wolves or dogs'. *KL* 1. 501-3 provides a review of the Nordic berserker tradition and various Sámi connections are dealt with by Collinder (1965, 1-21). For a fuller discussion of this theme, cf. McCone 1984 (1-30) and McCone 1987 (101-54).

67 Cf. Danaher 1972 (24-31); Gailey 1969; Harrison (293-307). For various artefacts and costumes of straw play a major role in Nordic festivals of the winter season, cf. e.g. Celander 1920 (168-76); Hallström (227-31); Hagberg 1921 (33-47); Nilsson 1938 (6-8); Eskeröd 1947 (16-41 and literature cited there), Cf. also note 17 above.

68 Counterfeit matchmaking and 'marrying' were a feature of many wake games and frequently condemned by the clergy – cf. S. Ó Súilleabháin 1967 (92-8). The Synod of Armagh (1614) railed against 'unseemly behaviour at wakes' declaring that 'the pious feelings of devout people were outraged by the singing of lewd songs and the playing of obscene games' (*ibid.*,148).

69 For an account of this ceremony in the context of 'the wedding of king and country a *hieros gamos* between the sacred king and the goddess' in Irish

tradition, cf. Byrne (16-8) and particularly an assessment of the following 'notorious account given by Giraldus Cambrensis in the late twelfth century of a grotesque ceremony allegedly performed in Donegal' (*ibid.*, 16): 'There is in the northern and farther part of Ulster, namely in Kenelcunill (Tyrconnell), a certain people which is accustomed to consecrate its king with a rite altogether outlandish and abominable. When the whole of that land has been gathered together in one place, a white mare is brought forward into the middle of the assembly. He who is to be inaugurated, not as a chief, but as a beast, not as a king, but as an outlaw, embraces the animal before all, professing himself to be a beast also. The mare is then killed immediately, cut up in pieces and boiled in water. A bath is prepared for the man afterwards in the same water. He sits in the bath surrounded by all his people, and all, he and they, eat of the meat of the mare which is brought to them. He quaffs and drinks of the broth in which he is bathed, not in any cup, or using his hand, but just dipping his mouth into it round about him. When this unrighteous rite has been carried out, his kingship and dominion has been conferred (Translated in O'Meara [33-4]). Cf. also Pokorny 1927 (123-4) and Schröder (310-2). In Hindu tradition, the Aśva Medha is 'a three–day *soma* sacrifice...' in which 'the chief consort of the sacrifice has to go through a sham copulation with the immolated horse while exchanging prescribed obscene and enigmatic phrases with the other consorts' (*EOR* 15. 230).

70   *CG* 1. 169-70.
71   *CG* 1. 170.
72   *Loc. cit.*
73   Cf. Chapter 1, note 63.
74   My colleague, Mr. T. A. McGeady, tells me that this account awakened in him a vague recollection of hearing a lady from Burt, County Donegal describe a similar ceremony, some fifty years ago.
75   For a discussion of which, cf. pp. 55-56 above.
76   Cf. pp. 55-56 above.
77   Edsman 1987 (88).
78   A. de Vries 1974 (40).
79   Norlander-Unsgaard 1983 (194).
80   Reiter 1981a (1). Cf. also Mysterud (102).
81   Reiter 1981a (2). Variation in the duration of pregnancy among different species is a factor which must be taken under consideration and, more to the point, perhaps, in the present context embryonic diapause or delayed implantation of the fertilized egg in the womb – a practice indulged in by the bear – both of which elements may be 'directly or indirectly regulated by the photoperiod and the pineal gland' (Reiter 1973, 315]. I am grateful to my colleague, Mr T. A. McGeady for this reference as also for the references to Arendt, Gladstone and Wakeley and Reiter 1981b below.
82   Arendt (266).
83   Reiter 1981 (3).
84   Reiter 1973 (314).
85   Reiter 1981a (2).
86   Gladstone & Wakeley (3).

87 Reiter 1981b (289); Gladstone & Wakeley (3), who also observed that 'in 1637 René Descartes taught that the human body was an earthly machine which was presided over by the 'rational soul' which was situated in the pineal gland, 'the little gland in the middle of the substance of the brain". In Reiter 1973 (305) and Reiter 1981b (308) it is also argued that in effect 'the pineal gland keeps the organism in proper synchrony with the prevailing environmental conditions. The information i.e. the pattern of hormones that the pineal supplies is utilized differently by various species. In some it is obviously used for the purpose of impelling the annual cycle of reproduction. In other animals, the same information may be used to regulate body temperature, influence lipid metabolism or determine activity rhythms'.

Arendt (308) states that 'Winter depression', or 'seasonal affective disease', appears closely related to photoperiod length and, in regard to the effect of the hormone, melatonin, secreted by the pineal gland, she states that it 'may be partially responsible for mood changes in the course of the day and the year' and also that recent 'evidence suggests that when given rhythmically it [melatonin] may entrain the fatigue/alertness rhythm in man: it certainly has hypnotic properties... If it can bring about shifts in phase in man, it should find extensive use in the treatment of biological rhythm disorders such as are found in shift-work, jet-lag, depression and old-age'; she further states that 'from being an obscure corner of endocrinology, the study of the pineal function has led to major insights into the relationship of physiology to environment... and has provoked thought as to our own adaption to our environment, possible residual photoperiodism and the conceivable relationship of depression and neurosis to the incompatibility of our biology and our culturally imposed behaviour (309)'.

Norlander-Unsgaard 1983(198) observes that the 'bear feast was celebrated at the time when the light was changing. Many people became depressed at that time. Modern medical research has found that a disturbance in the hormone balance is involved in the trouble. By keeping the patients awake for a few nights, a simple cure is achieved. The bear festival which lasted for three nights, must for this physiological reason have given those taking part a feeling of wellbeing, not only mentally'. My colleague, Professor J. Bannigan, informs me that, in humans, there may be a connection between the secretory products of the pineal gland and the commencement of the menarche in females and the onset of puberty in both sexes.

88 Norlander-Unsgaard 1987 (84, 89).

89 Honko *et al.* (120). The motif of the cosmic hunt among the Evenks of Siberia formed one of the central points of their spring religious rites, called *'ikinipke'*, which means 'revivals'. These lasted many days and their basic content consisted of pantomimes which imitated the hunt after the cosmic elk. The cosmic animal 'killed by the hunters, miraculously came to life again, and together with it all of nature came to life: the ice broke up, the earth was freed from snow, fresh green appeared in the taiga, calving took place among the domesticated reindeer, and offspring came forth among

the beasts and birds of the evergreen forest and among the water fowl. With the rebirth of nature, the blessings of man increased – the sources of his food and everything necessary for life in the taiga…' (Anisimov, 164-5).

90 Norlander-Unsgaard 1987 (87).

91 The association between bear-hibernation, sexual atrophy and the pineal gland on the one hand, and the singling out of the bear's skull for special treatment in a context strongly suggestive of fertility connections and culminating in its consignment to a final resting place in the branches of a pine tree, on the other, also project a series of striking sexual images. In Semitic tradition, the pine-cone was the symbol of life and in the Tyrol, pine was planted as a marriage tree (*FW* 2, 870).

An interesting parallel may be struck between sexual atrophy (effectively a kind of temporary castration) in the bear and the extraordinary action of Attis, the young male partner or 'servant-lover' of Cybele, in castrating himself beneath a pine tree. According to a legend of classical tradition, Attis 'was turned into a fir tree by Cybele as he was about to commit suicide. She sat mourning under the tree until Zeus promised that the tree should be evergreen' (*FW* 1. 388). Alternatively, it is said, driven 'by Cybele, his angry mother, Attis died of self–castration and then returned to life in response to his mother's intense mourning. This death and rebirth theme was celebrated during a series of holidays at the beginning of spring; the rituals included a procession carrying a pine tree (representing the dead Attis) into the temple of the Magna Mater, violent ritual mourning, a celebration of the birth of Attis, and the bathing of Cybele's statue' (Preston, 39).

We further learn that this pine tree was subsequently swathed in woollen bands and decked with violets 'an effigy of a young man (Attis) was tied to it', and that 'the ceremonies were characterized by blood-letting, the barbaric music of flutes and cymbals, and the whirling contortions of the lesser priesthood, who in a frenzy of excitement slashed themselves to bespatter the altar and the sacred tree with their blood' (*FW* 1. 90). We may also note here the observation by Schefferus (dating from 1704) concerning the Sámi bear ceremony custom which had the women folk tie red woollen threads around the legs of the men – quoted by Norlander-Unsgaard 1983 (199).

The cult of Attis involved 'ritual performances in which in a frenzy of dances, obsessive beating of drums, and self–flagellation' during which the participants, 'reached paroxysms of exaltation' (Cosi, 111) – conduct that is highly reminiscent of the 'whirling, beating, lashing and jumping' characteristic of the Sámi bear-ceremony, and 'of a shamanistic society' in general (Norlander-Unsgaard 198 (190). The priests of Attis (called the Galli) dedicated themselves to the goddess Cybele 'after having willingly castrated themselves during ritual performances' (Cosi, 111). The transvestism of the Galli, who 'wore female clothing, heavy make-up and their hair long and loose' (*loc.cit.*) would seem to find a comfortable parallel within the world of shamanism (cf. Bleibtreu-Ehrenberg (189-227). Flint (208), informs us that '…the tenth–century Berne glosses on Lucan speak of the castration of pigs in *'nemorosa loca'*, groves and enclosures full of trees' and that 'Pliny... speaks of the dedication of particular trees to particular deities, and Saint Martin has a good deal of trouble with a revered tall pine, probably dedicated to the goddess Cybele and growing near a pagan temple. The pine tree very nearly fell upon the holy man, to the glee of his opponents. It was only persuaded to fall the other way (almost upon the gleeful opponents and giving them a scare) by the sign of the cross and a miraculously conjured up gale.' For further discussion of this cult, cf. Vermaseren and for the theme of self-castration, cf. Cosi and Marglin 1987a, 311.

Catullus, in his poem Attis, illustrates the 'almost animal rage *(furens rabies)* by which the goddess possesses her devotees', a rage which drives the Attis of his poem to self-emasculation. In the end this *furor*, leaves his Attis 'barely human screaming wildly through the woods...' (Musurillo, 105,106). This description calls to mind the image of Suibhne Geilt, the wild man of the woods of Irish tradition, renowned for his intimate connections with trees, who subsisted by drinking milk from the cavity created by a heel-mark in a dunghill.

The periodic occurrence of sexual atrophy in the bear may also be reflected in the belief that it lacks sinews, a notion which Almqvist (93-102) has shown to be connected with the idea that the bear also lacks death throes. Almqvist's argument provides us, as he says himself, with 'the key to the understanding of how the bear sinews... could be said to be one of the ingredients of Gleipnir the fetter with which the wolf Fenrir was chained according to Snorri Sturluson's Edda' (102). Sinews – or the supposed lack of them in the bear – may, perhaps, be equated with his sexual potency or the periodic lack of it – ἰνεσ μελέων – is one of the many words used for 'penis' in Attic comedy (Henderson, 20).

Given that we may be justified in positing a connection between the supposed lack of sinews and the (temporary) abeyance of sexual capacity in the bear, Almqvist's explanation of the crux concerning the inclusion of the bear's sinews as one of six fanciful ingredients (the others being 'the noise the cat makes when it walks, women's beards, the roots of mountains, the breath of fishes and bird's spit' (i.e. things that do not exist) that go to make up Fenrir's fetter, immediately acquires a new dimension.

The Finnish and Sámi words for 'pine' – *kuusi* and *guossa*, respectively (for the wider Fenno-Ugric and Ural-Altaic connections, cf. Collinder 1955 [30, 145]), bear a remarkable similarity to the Irish word for 'pine' – *giús* (*DIL* G, 86) – a word which, intriguingly, seems to have no Indo-European parallel (cf. Kelly (111-3), for which reference I am grateful to Professor P. Mac Cana). Cf. note 7 above. Cf. also in this context, L. Campbell, (149-80, esp.152-3 and 174-5).

92 Cf. pp. 28-30 above.
93 Lid 1928 (ed.),112. Similar traditions attach to the badger in Germany (cf. *HDA* 2. 130-1) and Denmark (Olrik & Ellekilde, 2. 1015) and the groundhog in North America: 'The animal is associated with Candlemas Day (February 2)... If the groundhog comes out of his hole on February 2 and sees his shadow, he will go back in and stay for six more weeks. So, if the day is sunny, winter will continue and the result will be bad crops; if it

is cloudy, the groundhog will see no shadow, and the reverse will be true' (*FW* 1. 466). In Maltese tradition, we are told that the bear comes out on Candlemas Day and that 'if he finds the ground wet, or his legs remain dry, he says; 'Winter is coming'; if he finds it dry he says 'Winter is over"; in Calabria, the bear is sometimes replaced by the wolf or the lion (Aquilina) and, for remarks on this theme in the context of Carnival, cf. Ladurie (286-287).

In Irish tradition, the badger (cf. p. 201 for Irish badger names), the hedgehog and even the snail are mentioned in this connection (NFC 902:233,261 and Chapter 5, p. 201 below). In the Isle of Man, the list is even more extensive: 'There is a curious tradition that all the following creatures pass the winter in a torpid condition. There are seven in number (though as will be seen, some of the names vary), and they are consequently called *ny shiaght cadlagyn* 'the seven sleepers'... They are Craitnag 'the Bat'; *Coag* 'the Cuckoo'; *Cloghan–ny–cleigh*, 'the Stonechat'; and *Gollan–geayee*, 'the Swallow'; which are found in all the lists; the others being *Crammag*, 'Lizard'; and *Cadlag*, 'the Sleeper,' a mythical animal' (Paton, 2).

The bear is said to turn over in its den on a variety of dates, ranging from 7 or 13 January (St Knut's Day) to 25 March, the Day of the Annunciation, but the most common date mentioned is Candlemas – cf. Hammarstedt (*Fataburen* 15, 227-35) and Wessmann 1916 (104-5) and 1917 (71-2). This event is taken to mark the half-way point of the winter season in Nordic climes, whereas the equivalent phenomenon in Ireland etc. is taken as an indication that winter has ended. Cf. Olrik & Ellekilde (2. 1010-5).

For a review of relevant Finnish calendar customs in the month of February, cf. K. Vilkuna 1969 (47-61). It is noted there (*ibid.*, 48) that 1 February was known in Finnish since medieval times as *Riitanpäivä* i.e.'[St] Brigit's Day'. A number of weather signs and sayings such as '*Kirkas Riitanpäivä tekee poutavuoden*' 'A clear Brigit's Day makes a fine year' and '*Riitanpäivän sade kestää koko viikon*' 'Brigit's Day rain lasts a whole week' have also been recorded in Finnish folk tradition (Folklore Archive Card Index, Suomalaisen Kirjallisuuden Seura, Helsinki).

94 Hammarstedt 1929 (14).
95 Norlander-Unsgaard 1983 (195).
96 Collinder 1953 (198). For a discussion of this custom and its distribution in Sweden, cf. Ejdestam 1940 (52–81) and Ejdestam 1976 in *Campbell & Nyman* (105-6).
97 *CG* 1. 169.
98 E. Dwelly, *The Illustrated Gaelic Dictionary*, 1, Fleet, Hants 1918 [HENCEFORTH Dwelly], 125, where the noun *brisgean* is quoted as meaning '1. Cartilaginous part of a bone. 2. The part of tripe called brisket or gristle. 3. Silverweed, white tansy, – (*lit.* the brittle one) – *potentilla anserina*. 4. Wild skirret – *sium sisarum*'. *Brisgean milis* is also listed there as meaning 'the sweetbread of any creature' and also 'Moor–grass' and, similarly, the adjective *brisgeanach* itself as meaning 'abounding in gristle, like gristle, gristly' and 'abounding in silver tansy'. The noun *caitean* is said to describe 'Classes of plants called amentiferae and cupuliferae' and an alternate form

caitein means 'Shag, nap on cloth' with its adjective carrying the meaning "Shaggy, hairy, rough, nappy' (154). Dr Miceál Ross has drawn my attention to the words *bruiteanach* and *paiteanach*, the latter meaning, apparently, 'chicken' or 'chickens', both of which occur in a similar context in the Irish of Rathlin Island (cf. Holmer, 222). There the rhyme goes: *'Oidhche féil' Bríde bruiteanach(=?)/ Buail* (alternately *Tuir* [149]) *an ceann de'n phaiteanach'* (145). Carmichael's observation that the oblation offered by families to propitiate Bride 'generally is a cockerel, some say a pullet' (CG 1. 168), may not be without special relevance in this regard.
99   Bø (90).
100 Curiously, Watkins (114), draws a parallel between the possible development of the word *beithir* 'bear' and the word *nathir* 'snake'.
101 Cf. p. 65 above.
102 Bø (100).
103 Rune 46 refers to the 'loud-playing' and 'singing' of Väinämöinen, 'the great primeval minstrel' as he wander with his 'shaggy friend' (=the bear) and describes the general reaction to it: 'In the house there cried the people,/ And exclaimed the handsome people:/Listen to the noise resounding,/Like the singing of the crossbill,/Or a maiden's flute in forest!', Kirby (584). Norlander-Unsgaard 1983 (191), asks: 'What is known about the cry of the bear?' to which she supplies the following answer: 'According to Zetterberg, the well-known bear-hunter and writer, the bear produces other sounds as well as the usual growl. If he is angry, he roars and bawls; when he is disturbed by people, he emits a coughing sound. It can also happen that the bear remains silent, although he is in a rage. During the late summer and early autumn, the bear lets out a sharp whistle, generally called 'blowing', which was considered by country folk and others to be a mating call. Nowadays, it has, however, been established that the mating season for bears is in May and June. Thus the blowing sound must be an ordinary call. Some people have noted that bears make contact with another by way of this call. Like other people living in that part of the country, the Saamis were very familiar with these sounds. And there is reason to suppose that when 'making music' in connection with the bear the Saamis wove the bear's calls and cries into the melodies.'

In describing 'bear veneration among the Ostyak', Halliwell (89) quotes the following account from 1706: 'Once several Ostiacks came on board the ship in which I was, to sell us Fish, and one of my Servants had a Nuremberg-Bear in clock work, which when wound up drummed, and turned his head backward and forward, continually moving his Eyes, till the Work was down. Our people set the Bear at play a little: as soon as ever the Ostiacks saw it, all of them performed to it their customary Religious Worship, and danced excessively to the honour of the Bear, nodding their Heads, and whistling at a great rate...'. A. de Vries 1974 (499) notes that 'Whistling and clacking of the tongue [and roaring] are archaic devices for attracting theriomorphic deities'. Cf. also pp. 101 & 104 below.
104 Bø (91).
105 Feilberg 1891 (133).

106 A. Olrik 1910 (57-61); Olrik & Ellekilde (2. 1119-20).
107 This account of Thorri draws heavily on the description contained in Björnsson (14-6). Olrik & Ellekilde (2. 1102-3).
108 *KL* 5. 367 and Celander 1950. The '*guovva*' of '*guovva–manno*' is sometimes associated with to the Sámi word for a special kind of straw. The Sámi custom of binding reindeer antlers with straw, the antlers in this instance being taken to represent the 'horns' of the moon is also adverted to; reindeer with antlers shaped like the 'horns' of the moon were singled out for sacrifice and their antlers greased with fat from their hooves or with bear fat – Lundmark (78-9). Cf. also in this context, Olrik & Ellekilde (1. 121) who, while acknowledging the connection with straw, nevertheless support the derivation of *guovva-mánno* from *góimánaðr*.
109 Björnsson (27-9).
110 Olrik & Ellekilde (2. 605, 1000-8, 1116-21).
111 *Ibid.*, 1002. 'Torre' and 'Gje' were frequently personified, sometimes as brother and sister, sometimes as man and wife (*ibid.*, 1001-2). The month of February was sometimes addressed: '*Góa goakvinna*' ['Góa, good woman'] when my cow calves, my sow farrows and my hen clocks' (*ibid.*, 1116). Cf. Svensson (122-40).
112 Lid 1928 (199) and Björnsson (28).
113 Lid 1928 (199-206).
114 Lid 1928 (203-6). Cf. also Black (6).
115 Martin (119).
116 Cf. pp. 10-11 above.
117 As recorded by me from Conall Eoghan Phádraig Mac an Luain, Cruach Mhín an Fheannta, Na Cruacha, County Donegal in 1972.
118 *CG* 1. 167-8.
119 *KL* 5. 367, and p. 53ff. and notes 4 and 10 above.
120 For Brigit, the Celtic goddess, cf. Ó hÓgáin 1990 (60) and for St Brigit of early Christian Ireland and modern folk tradition, *ibid.*, 60-4. For the various 'Lives' of St Brigit and other early manuscript materials pertaining to her, cf. Kenney (356-64) and McCone 1982 (30-92 and sources cited there).
121 Cf. Chapter 1, note 110 and also Heiermeier (39-41); Hamp 1956 (50) and Hamp (personal communication).
122 *CG* 1.174–5. For an Irish version of this invocation, cf. Ó Cróinín (282 and Notes, p. 434-4).

— *Chapter 3* —

An ghrian sa ló agus an tine san oíche
The sun by day and the fire at night[1]

MÁIRE MACNEILL NOTES that the 'customs which have survived in connexion with *Samhain*, St Brigid's Feast and *Bealtaine* are of a kind which can be performed in or near the dwelling-place. The social unit taking part is the household or, at most, the youth of a townland'.[2] This feature is emphasized in a variety of ways in the many accounts of the celebration of the Feast of Saint Brigit – 1st February, traditionally the first day of spring in Ireland.[3] Much effort was expended in the preparation of the dwelling-place within which an atmosphere of great expectation prevailed on the eve of the feast, as is revealed by this account from Erris, county Mayo:

> [The Feast of St Brigit] is a very noted festival of the year in the life of the country people in this part of Ireland. It is to the present day observed, but in a gradually diminishing degree, in the old time-honoured way, and the feast is commemorated among most households as of old, the same ritual and ceremonial being observed and celebrated... The house received some particular attention in the way of cleaning and tidying up and might be given even a limewashing inside. Then with the approach of night or about nightfall, a good big fire was put down, the animals were bedded (those in the dwelling house) with fresh clean straw and everything – the whole interior – had an air of cosiness and comfort to receive Brighid into the house.[4]

Much of the indoor activity associated with the celebration of the feast took place in the vicinity of the hearth or, as with the preparation of the modest ceremonial repast, was actually centred upon it.[5] A symbolic extra place might be set for the visiting saint and, similarly, sometimes a 'shakedown' bed of straw laid out for her by the fire-side.[6]

In Scotland, as Carmichael tells us 'an oblong basket in the shape of a cradle, which they call *'leaba Bride'* the bed of Bride' was made and, as he says, 'embellished with much care.' In it was placed a sheaf of corn, fashioned in the form of a woman and decked with ribbons, shells, stones and flowers and beside this figure was laid 'a small straight wand (the bark being peeled off)... of birch, broom, bramble, white willow, or other sacred wood... '.[7] Though it is not stated, perhaps we may assume that – as was the custom in Ireland - this *'leaba Bride'* was also placed somewhere near the hearth. The procedure that followed was at any rate closely associated with hearth and fireside:

> The women then level the ashes on the hearth, smoothing and dusting them over carefully. Occasionally, the ashes surrounded by a roll of cloth, are placed on a board to safeguard them against disturbance from draughts or other contingencies. In the early morning the family closely scan the ashes. If they find the marks of the wand of Bride they rejoice, but if they find *'lorg Bride,'* the footprint of Bride their joy is very great, for this is a sign that Bride was present with them during the night, and is favourable to them, and that there is increase in family, in flock, and in field during the coming year. Should there be no marks in the ashes, and no trace of Bride's presence, the family are dejected. It is to them a sign that she is offended, and will not hear their call. To propitiate her and gain her ear the family offer oblations and burn incense. The oblation generally is a cockerel, some say a pullet, buried alive near the junction of three streams, and the incense is burnt on the hearth when the family retire for the night.[8]

Carmichael's account does not advert further to fire, hearth, incense or ashes. However, his description of the levelling and smoothing of the latter in the manner described would seem to imply a distinct departure from the customary nightly habit of piling the ashes on the fire in order to cover it at bed-time. Such was normally the case on *Samhain* eve, when, instead of covering the embers with ashes, a roaring fire was built and the ashes spread around it in the expectation that the family dead as they gathered to warm themselves might leave some track of their presence in them.[9]

In Irish tradition, the process of covering the fire at night was designated *coigilt na tine* or 'raking the fire' [literally 'saving the fire']. This facilitated the survival of the glowing embers of the last fire of the day till morning. From these, 'the seed' or *an mháthair tine* 'the mother fire', as it was also known, was obtained to kindle the next day's fire.[10] In the Gaelic culture of Ireland and Scotland, the task of securing the hearth fire for the night in a manner designed to keep it alive until morning while at the same time avoiding any possible threat of nocturnal conflagration was accompanied by a special prayer, one recently collected Irish version of which goes as follows:

Coiglímse an tine seo mar a choiglíonns cách,	I rake this fire like everyone else,
Bríd ina bun agus Muire ina barr;	Brigit below it with Mary on top;
Dhá aingle déag d'aingle na ngrást,	Twelve of the angels of the graces,
Ag cumhdach mo thí-sa go lá.	Protecting my house till dawn.[11]

In Scotland, the word *smaladh* is applied to the corresponding ceremony which is elaborated upon by Carmichael in the following terms:

> Peat is the fuel of the Highlands and Islands. Where wood is not obtainable the fire is kept in during the night. The process by which this is accomplished is called, in Gaelic, *smaladh*, in Scottish, smooring; and in English, smothering, or more correctly, subduing. The ceremony of smooring the fire is artistic and symbolic, and is performed with loving care. The embers are evenly spread on the hearth – which is generally in the middle of the floor – and formed into a circle. The circle is then divided into three equal sections, a small boss being left in the midde. A peat is laid between each section, each peat touching the boss, which forms a common centre. The first peat is laid down in the name of the God of Life, the second in the name of the God of Peace, the third in the name of the God of Grace. The circle is then covered over with ashes sufficient to subdue but not extinguish the fire, in the name of the Three of Light. The heap slightly raised in the centre is called '*Tula nan Tri*', 'The Hearth of the Three'. When the smooring operation is complete the woman closes her eyes, stretches her hand, and softly intones one of the many formulae current for these occasions.[12]

We may safely assume that among these formulae were prayers of the same ilk as that quoted above, a Scottish Gaelic version of which goes as follows:

BEANNACHADH SMALAIDH	SMOORING BLESSING
Smalaidh mise an tula	I will smoor the hearth
Mar a smaladh Muire;	As Mary would smoor;
Comraig Bhride 's Mhuire,	The encompassment of Bride and Mary,
Air an tula 's air an lar,	On the fire and on the floor,
'S air an fhardaich uile.	And on the household all.

Co siud air-liana mach?	Who is on the lawn without?
Muire ghrian-gheal 's a Mac,	Fairest Mary and her Son,
Bial Dia dh'iarradh,	The mouth of God ordained,
aingheal Dia labhradh;	the angel of God spoke
Ainghle geallaidh faire an teallaidh,	Angels of promise watching the hearth,
Gu'n tig latha geal gu beallaidh.	Till white day comes to the fire.[13]

Another Scottish version would seem to relate directly to the *Tula nan Tri* 'The Hearth of the Three' mentioned by Carmichael:

An Tri numh	The sacred Three
A chumhnadh,	To save,
A chomhnadh,	To shield,
A chomraig	To surround
An tula,	The hearth,
An taighe,	The house,
An teaghlaich,	The household,
An oidhche,	This eve,
An nochd,	This night,
O! an oidhche,	Oh! this eve,
An nochd,	This night,
Agus gach oidhche,	And every night,
Gach aon oidhche.	Each single night.
Amen.	Amen.[14]

Carmichael's observations on the complicated mechanics of covering the fire and the wording of the various 'Smooring blessings' foretoken a number of important issues. A discrete adjunct of this complex is the emphasis on triplication: the tripartite division of the hearth-fire by strategically placing sods of peat around a central 'boss', to use Carmichael's word, and the invocation of 'The Three of Light' and the 'Sacred Three' of the 'smooring blessing' cited above. Another important ingredient is the concept of circumambience – 'the encompassment of Bride and Mary on the fire and on the floor and on the household all'.[15] There is also the symbolic role of sparks and smoke, not forgetting ash, all of which feature in various riddles, proverbs and pithy sayings.[16]

The function of ashes and embers in securing the fertility of crops by their being claimed as trophies from midsummer bonfires and deposited in field and furrow for that purpose is well documented. We also know that among the Celts:

> Evil spirits could be repelled by both men and women exposing their genitals to them and at the famous Celtic solstice bonfire festivals women used to stride over the fire, exposing their vulvas to the beneficial influence of the flame, and blessing it with their own power... [17]

Various circumpolar peoples practised similar rites of purification by incense, a process executed in Sámi tradition by jumping over fire.[18] In fact, in Sámi bear festival ceremony we find all three elements represented – triplication, circumambience and purification:

> 'When everything is over, the men wash themselves in a mixture of strong lye and... and go through the pässio or back door, jumping over the fire and out through the proper door, – and this three times' writes Fjellström. According to other accounts it is also stated that following the completion of the circling of the tent and the fire, the women throw ashes at the mens' legs, upon which they may 'approach their wives' ...which means that the men return to their everyday situations. The ashes are clearly a purification agent.[19]

In view of her manifold overt connections with fire as documented in early Irish literary as well as in modern folklore sources, it is hardly surprising that Brigit's name should be very much to the fore in this particular context nor that it should find it so closely coupled with that of Mary. In the Lives,[20] we read of Brigit having sent a house in which she was staying in flames up to heaven and we hear of a fiery pillar rising over her head.[21] Giraldus Cambrensis, the twelfth-century commentator, writes about her 'perpetual ashless fire watched by twenty nuns, of whom she herself was one, blown by fans or bellows only, and surrounded by a hedge within which no male could enter'.[22] Irish monks are described in another medieval source as believing Brigit to be Christ's mother[23] and nineteenth- and twentieth-century Gaelic folk tradition depicts her as a near companion of Mary or even as midwife to her and the foster mother of her Son.[24]

Máire MacNeill's treatment of *Lúnasa* has exposed a range of legend types a number of which is concerned with Brigit whose shadowy figure almost appears at times to dog this majestic study.²⁵ The most immediately relevant of these is that which she calls 'The Woman Fire-Carrier', one of two types she concedes which 'may not be peculiar to *Lughnasa*'.²⁶ MacNeill comments:

> The Tripartite Life tells that Saint Patrick visited the district and established a church at Ardagh [county Longford] close to the hill. This church was important enough to give its name to the diocese. He installed Saint Mel in pseudo-tradition, his nephew, as bishop and patron. Mel's sister, Eiche lived in the same house with him, and scandalized gossip about it reached Saint Patrick who came to rebuke them. Their innocence was proved by two miracles: Mel caught a salmon in a rain-filled furrow and Eiche carried burning coals in her dress unscathed... Saint Brigid, too, was traditionally connected with Ardagh. Indeed she now overshadows the saints of the early Patrician foundation. It is her feast, February 1ˢᵗ, not Saint Mel's on February 6ᵗʰ, which is the patron day of the parish, and there is a holy well dedicated to her at the north-eastern foot of the hill and a half-mile from the village of Ardagh. Saint Mel's sister and the story of the carrying of the burning coals is now told of Brigid. The distance she walked is pointed out, and the well is said to have sprung up where the coals fell from her dress.²⁷

This legend is also associated with St Latiaran of Cullen (Duhallow, County Cork) with whom another type, dubbed by MacNeill 'The Three Sisters at the Site',²⁸ is also connected. The latter type relates to five *Lúnasa* sites in all. The eponymous three sisters of this legend title are ill-defined figures with the exception of those associated with Cullen Well, a fact which MacNeill interprets as signifying the existence of 'an older cult there... almost submerged in other parts of the island by an in-coming male-dominated religion'.²⁹ Concerning Latiaran, MacNeill tells us:

> We know only of her from popular local tradition. She was one of three sisters whose names... are constantly given as Lasair (Flame), Inghean Bhuidhe (the Yellow-haired Girl) and Latiaran... Her name seems to be unique and its meaning unknown.

And she concludes:

> In the legends of these saints we have a conflation of Christian and pagan elements... as we must assume that there was some solid

foundation for the tradition of the holy women at Cullen, it seems likely enough that in early Christian times there was a nunnery there, and that the foundress in course of time attracted to herself the stories told of pre-Christian goddesses... It would be unrealistic, of course, to assume that the Duhallow saints are just goddesses redressed in Christian garb. The enduring tradition connecting them with parish centres and early Christianity suggests that there were settlements or hermitages of devout Christian women there, and that in the course of time the foundresses attracted to themselves the legends and attributes floating in folk consciousness from old times as the properties of the beneficient female powers...'[30]

'Oblivion', MacNeill remarks, 'has almost quenched memory of Lasair'[31] and Inghean Bhuidhe 'The Yellow-haired Girl' appears to have fared but little better. Latiaran, though the youngest of the three was 'the chief figure of the three and of the legendary traditions which have gathered around them'.[32] Since Latiaran Sunday, the Sunday falling on or before July 25th, was regarded as signalling the start of harvest and Inghean Bhuidhe's day marked the beginning of summer, MacNeill postulates that Lasair, the eldest, also presided over the beginning of a season and that her feast-day would have been at the beginning of spring.'[33] This assignment of the eldest of the three saints, to be patron of the youngest of the seasons appears somewhat arbitrary and it may well be that MacNeill has overreached herself somewhat in arriving at such a conclusion.

As it happens, tradition leaves room for possible realignment of these affiliations in so far as it permits a number of other names to enter the lists – e.g. Crobh Dhearg, literally 'Red Claw' and Gobnait turn up to join Latiaran (supplanting both Lasair and Inghean Bhuidhe in the process).[34] Crobh Dhearg boasts an association with May Eve[35] and, therefore, the beginning of summer, while St Gobnait's feast-day fixed at 11th February, translated from Old Style to New Style becomes 1st February, the first day of spring and identical, therefore, with the Feast of St Brigit.[36] Indeed, it would appear that Gobnait and Brigit – both equally celebrated, honoured and remembered in the folk tradition of County Cork – are really one and the same person. The numerous parallels between these figures as recorded in folk tradition is a subject which need not detain us further here. By the same token, the seeming difficulty of reconciling the rankings of the fire-carrying holy women – Latiaran and Brigit – fades into insignificance when considered in the light of the description of Brigit given by the tenth-century glossator, Cormac mac Cuillenáin:

> Brigit i.e. a learned woman, daughter of the Dagda. That is Brigit woman of learning i.e. a goddess whom *filid* worshipped. For her protecting care was very great and very wonderful. So they called her goddess of poets. Her sisters were Brigit woman of healing and Brigit woman of smith-work, daughters of the Dagda from whose names among all the Irish a goddess used to be called Brigit.[37]

The story of the Saint and the Ember, which is the main story about Latiaran, contains a smith motif which points directly towards the possibility of establishing a connection between her and one of the three Brigits. It is summarized by MacNeill as follows:

> Every morning Latiaran went from her cell to a nearby forge for the 'seed' of the fire and carried it back in her apron, but on one memorable morning the smith spoke to her of the beauty of her feet and in a moment of vanity she looked at them and in that instant her apron took fire. In her chagrin and unsaintly anger she cursed the smith and prophesied that the sound of a smith's anvil should never more be heard in Cullen. And so it has befallen, according to accepted belief: several attempts to establish smithies in Cullen failed, and no irons will redden in the townland... As to Latiaran, tradition gives varying sequels to her story. One says that when her clothes blazed up about her, she remained unharmed; another that the ember burned through her apron and dropped to the ground... After uttering the curse she sank into the ground... and came up again in her cell. She never afterwards went out in daylight so that she might avoid being a cause of sin to anyone, and her subterranean journey from forge to cell is interpreted as a penance performed for her sin.[38]

The three sisters of Cormac's account – Brigit, Brigit and Brigit – differentiated by their special interests in poetry, healing and smith-work, are matched by Cullen's holy trio: Latiaran/(Brigit), Inghean Bhuidhe/Crobh Dhearg/(Brigit) and Lasair/Gobnait/(Brigit) each with her own particular profile. It is to a distinguishing feature of the latter trio I now wish to direct particular attention, namely the association of Brigit in her Gobnait persona with bees, a circumstance remembered as follows by a famous storyteller of this same locality:

> The Beehive – an object shaped like a beehive, but not quite as big. Once soldiers made a raid on Ballyvourney and they had penetrated as far as a place they call *Goirtín na Plá* ('The Little Field of the Pestilence')... when Saint Gobnait loosed the bees from the beehive. They alighted on the soldiers and began to sting them and they were fortunate indeed to be able to make their escape leaving behind them the plunder, that is the cattle. The place has been called *Goirtín na Plá* ever since and if you were to ask anyone what that pestilence was they would reply 'a pestilence of bees'. No one really knows what became of that beehive.[39]

This tradition provides crucial evidence for a central element of the pagan goddess paraphernalia that Brigit brought in her train into the Christian era, as we shall shortly see.

*   *   *

Bees are thought to have evolved from a wasp ancestor having at some stage abandoned predation in favour of provisioning nests with nectar and pollen.[40] The honey-bee has been described as exhibiting 'a combination of individuals traits and social cooperation which is unparalleled in the animal kingdom'.[41] It has been eulogized by poets, philosophers, historians and naturalists 'as unique among insects, endowed by nature with wondrous gifts beneficial to mankind in a greater degree than any other creature of the insect world'.[42]

From cave paintings dating back many thousands of years we can glean details of honey-bee nests, but primitive peoples, while clearly interested in honey, were honey hunters rather than bee-keepers.[43] Bees are also depicted in Egyptian tombs dating back to 3000 BC[44] and there are references to them in the Hittite laws of about 1300 BC and also later frequent mention of them in early Greek and Roman sources.[45]

In his writings, Aristotle recognized the different races of bees but for all his close observation of them he confessed the 'generation of bees to be a great puzzle'.[46] In the judgement of

Irish folk tradition, *Obair na mbeach* ('The work of the bees') – together with *Intinn na mban* ('The mind of women') and *Imeacht agus teacht na taoide* ('The coming and going of the tide') – were among the few things which seem to have surpassed even Aristotle's understanding.[47]

Bees are found in a number of varieties all over the world. In Europe, the natural habitat of the honey-bee *(Apis mellifera)* reaches the northerly limits of its range in southern Scandinavia.[48] As regards Ireland, there seems to have been some division of opinion: Solinus, for example, in his famous description of Ireland and its inhabitants, tells us:

> No bees have ever been there; and if sand or pebbles brought from thence be sprinkled among beehives, the swarms will abandon the combs.[49]

On the other hand, the seventh-century Irish text – *Bechbretha* 'Bee-Judgements' – details a variety of legal points concerning bees and bee-keeping contained in 'glosses and commentary ranging in date from about the ninth to the sixteenth century'[50] and elsewhere, early Irish tradition also records that the honey-bee was, indeed, introduced by man:

> According to the 8th century *Félire Oengusso* (Feb 13) a swarm of honeybees was brought from Britain by the saint Mo Domnóc, who flourished in the early 7th century AD. This tradition was known to Giraldus Cambrensis (*Topographia Hiberniae* i c. vi) in the 12th century.[51]

As this same source points out the truth may be that:

> ...monasteries practised bee-keeping on a larger scale than was known in pre-Christian Ireland, and so acquired the reputation for having introduced it... the linguistic evidence – though uncertain – indicates that the honeybee was present in Ireland before (probably long before) the arrival of Christianity.[52]

Among the ancient beliefs about bees was the notion that they were begotten of bulls. One of the earliest writers to mention the bull-born bee is Antigonos of Karystos, about 250 BC, who informs us that:

Chapter 3

99

In Egypt if you bury the ox in certain places, so that only his horns project above the ground and then saw them off, they say that bees fly out for the ox putrefies and is resolved into bees.[53]

The same source further informs us that the most appropriate time for this method of reproducing bees was when the sun entered the sign of the bull (Taurus).[54] A different origin for bees is suggested by one Irish tradition that describes them as having been created from the tears shed by Jesus on the cross[55] while another relates that they emerged from the sores of the dying Job as his soul left his body.[56] Accordingly, traditions about bees touch upon matters concerned with either end of the life cycle.

As elsewhere in Europe, there is a strong tradition in Ireland of telling bees of a death in the family.[57] The bee as a symbol of chastity and of the Virgin Birth as well as Mary's special powers over bees are points strongly emphasized in German tradition which also boasts a range of other interesting connections:[58] the branch of a tree on which a swarm has alighted on Good Friday broken off and used to drive cattle to market would guarantee plenty of offers to buy; it was believed; when a young cow had her first calf, the afterbirth was dragged three times around the beehive so as to prevent the bees swarming and this could also be prevented by hanging up the bark of an oak hit by lightning; a female beekeeper may be unable to become pregnant while, on the other hand, by eating a bee, a barren woman can ensure that she does so; at Candlemas, the beehive was surrounded by lighted candles.

Virgil states (fourth *Georgics*) that bees 'do not give themselves to love, do not seek pleasure which weakens, do not know the union of the sexes, neither the pangs of maternity'.[59] According to Plutarch, they are capable of detecting lack of chastity in men or women.[60] Artemis at Ephesus, had the bee as her cult animal and according to Gimbutas:

> ...the whole organization of the sanctuary in classical times seems to have rested on the symbolic analogy of a beehive, with swarms of priestesses called bees – *melissai*, and numerous eunuch priests called 'drones' – *essênes*.[61]

In Mithraism, a bull's head and three hundred golden bees was featured on the altar, while for Christians, the bee became the symbol of Mary and of Christ (in the latter case, Mary being thought of as the beehive).[62]

Gimbutas, in answer to her own question – 'Why was the bee chosen for the symbol of regeneration?' recommends that this issue should be viewed in the context of the Egyptian beetle or scarab 'which symbolizes the moon and eternal renewal' both of which have 'antennae like bull horns and wings in the form of a lunar crescent.' And she adds – 'The periodic swarming and buzzing of bees, when a new generation is born, and the creative activity associated with the production of honey must have greatly impressed our forefathers who regarded it as the food of the gods.'[63]

Ancient scientists, like Aristotle, who passed years of their lives studying the wonders of bee-life, and often left accurate records of their observations, were intrigued by the intangible quality of honey-bee society. Before that again, man had begun to register and interpret the almost mystical dimension that pervaded their nests by incorporating it in his symbolism of seven or eight thousand years ago. In striving to reach a deeper understanding of the thinking behind this symbolism and the commentaries that classical authors and other sources have left us as well as the complex of beliefs that found a lifeline to survival in folklore, it will be necessary to review the structures of honey bee society, examining briefly its three castes – queens, drones, and workers – each with its own specialization and place.[64]

First, there is the queen who reigns over the nest, surrounded by attendants; she is fed the rich food she requires to perform her crucial task in the colony which is to function as an extraordinary egg-laying machine, capable of laying thousands of eggs a day. Queens are the most long-lived of the honey-bee castes, generally surviving for one to three years. However, it is not her amazing rate of egg production which determines the queen's natural life span, but rather the amount of sperm she can hold and her efficiency in releasing it in miniscule amounts over a period of time – a process called 'partial parthenogenesis'.[65] Put simply, when the queen runs out of sperm, she runs out of time and is superseded and killed by the colony.[66]

The drones – the other sexual members of this society – are tended and fed by the workers. They perform one function only, a task for which they are magnificently constructed and after the fulfillment of which they die, the all-important service of mating the queen. The few drones who succeed in mating queens do so only once, since they die immediately after mating, when their abdomen and genital apparatus rupture.[67]

The life of the drone generally extends to up to three months during the spring to mid-summer period; hundreds or thousands of drones fly out to congregation areas where they compete for the favours of the small number of queens which make their way to the mating sites. Although drones exist only to mate and perform no other useful functions in the nest, actually most of them die before they get a chance to do so, either because they grow old or are thrown out of the nest by the workers. The peak of drone rearing precedes the emergence of virgin queens in the spring; they are produced and maintained only when colonies can support them and when queens are potentially available for mating and the timing and extent of production is controlled by many of the same factors that are involved in the spectacular event of reproduction by swarming.

Preparations for swarming by honey-bee colonies in cold temperate climates actually begin in the dead of winter[68] and most swarming takes place in mid-spring, usually sometime in May or early June.[69] Emerging queens produce a series of audible high-pitched sounds called 'piping'. The frequency of piping is greatest between the time the first virgin queen emerges and the end of the after-swarming when the remaining queens fight. The direct effect of piping is to cause workers to freeze in place on the comb until piping is completed, but otherwise, there appears to be no clear explanation as to its function or value.[70]

Like the bear, which also produces a whistling sound,[71] the bee was believed to show a predilection for certain kinds of musical sounds. According to Ovid (*Fasti* 3, 736 ff.), for example, the tempting of the swarm must be accompanied by tinkling sounds and the clashing of Cybele's cymbals, for the bees love rough music.[72] Likewise, Vergil (fourth *Georgic*, 63), describing the noise made to attract swarming bees, tells us that 'they clash the cymbals of the Great Mother'.[73] The motif of castration figures prominently in the cult of Cybele and a reflex of this may be detected in various manifestations of the European and north-Eurasian bear cult, as I have already pointed out.[74] This would seem to represent, therefore, a further notable parallel between the bear and the bee which, of course, already share a number of well-known links in any case. Honey-bee nests as sources of food have long provided a rich and concentrated source of food – brood, wax, honey, pollen as well as the adult bees themselves – for a variety of would-be predators.

Humans are among the most serious bee predators and high on the list of other vertebrates which attack bee nests are badgers[75] and bears: with their powerful legs and claws, bears can easily tear open most wild nests, their thick fur making them almost oblivious to sting. The bear was an efficient honey hunter and was regarded by humans as competing with them for this important source of nourishment, thus earning for itself the name 'honey-thief'.[76]

Inherent in the hapless circumstance of the drone, cast centre-stage in the role of a transiently powerful sexual figure, then – like Attis[77] – cast aside, castrated and killed – there is a paradox which may also find a reflection in bee nomenclature and etymology. Old Irish *bech* and *beth* are among a number of bee-words which constitute a partial Indo-European agreement[78] on the name for this insect within which is included a North European or Baltic-Celtic isogloss, as Hamp[79] and Heiermeier[80] have both noted.

Old Irish *foich*, 'a wasp', a Brythonic loanword,[81] – is glossed thus by O'Rahilly:[82]

> Just as *speach*, 'a darting blow,' is derived from *beach*, 'bee'... so *spoch*, 'attack angrily', is derived from *foich*, 'wasp,' and means literally 'attack (one) like a wasp.' The broadening of the *ch* in *spoch* may have been due to the influence of *speach*.

And O'Rahilly adds:

> Quite distinct from *spoch*, 'attack' is Irish *spoch*, Sc. *spoth*, Manx *spoiy* in the sense of 'geld'. These seem to be ultimately derived from Lat. *spado*... though their form presents certain difficulties.[83]

Despite O'Rahilly's strictures, the possibility of seeing (etymologically or otherwise) a direct connection between *speach* 'bee' and *spoch* 'geld' is still worthy of consideration, especially since the existence of a relationship between them would also see the concept of stinging or sticking i.e. penetrating as in sexual intercourse, accommodated alongside the drastic deprivation of the ability to execute such a function – the fate of the drone.

An examination of certain expressions for 'maleness' in the Finno-Ugrian group of languages may also help to cast some light on the matter. The Hungarian word *here* 'drone, male bee; testicle' is related by Collinder[84] to the Kola Sámi word *gujj* 'husband', which has a similar meaning in a range of related languages, for example, Vogul *huj, hoj*, 'the male of animals'. Here too we find the derivation of the Finnish word *koira* 'dog' (and also 'the male [of animals]', reminiscent of Old Irish *gagar* 'a hunting dog, a beagle',[85] a word which, as Marstrander,[86] observed, stands alone in Irish and which he believes to have been borrowed from Old Norse *gagarr*, a poetic word for 'dog'.

The evidence of the Finno-Ugrian complex (in so far as it may be accepted as having a bearing on the issue) would seem to imply that Old Norse *gagarr* also carries a core meaning of maleness. Modern Irish *gadhar* (Old Irish *gagar*) is generally felt to mean 'dog' rather than 'bitch' while *madra* (Old Irish *madrad*) may possibly be taken as referring to a dog of either sex.[87] According to Vendryes[88] *madrad* contains the root *mad-/mat-* also preserved in *math* [89] meaning 'good' – one of a number of Noa names for the bear in Old Irish.[90] This raises the possibility of seeing *madradh* and *gagar* as comparants to *math* 'bear' = 'good' and *olc* [91] (a Noa name for 'wolf') = 'evil'. The effect of this would be to invest Old Irish *gagar*, Old Norse *gagarr* with a rather negative connotation of maleness, of course, which concept, as we have seen, would be eminently applicable in the context of the disastrous consequences arising from the dilemma of the drone in the bee-world. In this bear/dog (wolf) and bear/bee equation the bear acts as common denominator. With Brigit's ursine connections as previously discussed, as well as her apian associations as revealed above both in mind, we venture once more into the realms of the bear cult as evidenced in the Celtic and Nordic (including Finno-Ugrian) worlds. Impetus will be added to the further exposition of this theme by reverting to the queen bee at this point and focusing in particular on the circumstances which surround her dramatic emergence from the nest in order to mate.

Carmichael, in his review of Scottish customs attaching to the Feast of St Brigit, speaks of what he calls 'a propitiatory hymn' sung to 'a serpent' which 'is supposed to emerge from its hollow among the hills on St Bride's Day'.[92] The various versions of the verse which he quotes contain references such as *Thig an nimhir as an toll* alternatively *Thig an nathair as an toll* ('The serpent shall come from the hole'), *Thig nighean Imhir as a chnoc* ('The daughter of Ivor shall come from the knoll')[93] upon which he comments:

The 'daughter of Ivor' is the serpent and it is said that the serpent will not sting a descendant of Ivor, he having made *'tabhair agus tuis'*, offering and incense, to it, thereby securing immunity from its sting himself and his seed for ever.[94]

In some of the versions of the 'hymn' quoted by Carmichael, the wording specifies the agreement on immunity as having been concluded between *an nimhir* – which he translates 'the serpent' or *nighean Imhir* which he renders as 'the daughter of Ivor'. However, other variants cited by him describe what emerges from a *tom*, 'the knoll' as *rigen ran*, 'a noble queen'. On the basis of my argument hitherto, I take this to be a clear reference not to any serpent, but rather to the queen bee and, therefore by implication, to Brigit herself:

> *La Bride nam brig ban;*   On the day of Bride of the white hills;
> *Thig an rigen ran a tom,*   The noble queen will come from the knoll,
> *Cha bhoin mise ris an rigen ran,*   I will not molest the noble queen,
> *'S cha bhoin an rigen ran rium.*   Nor will the noble queen molest me.[95]

By way of garnering further support for this reading, an emendation of Carmichael's interpretation of a *tom* as 'the knoll' can easily be made, substituting for 'knoll', 'round heap', 'conical knoll', 'ant-hill' – dictionary definitions of *tom*,[96] – one or all of which readily could be taken as referring to a bee-nest or bee-hive. Likewise, Carmichael's reading of *rigen ran* as 'noble queen' may also be open to an interpretation other than that offered by him here: the qualifying element *ran*, taken by Carmichael to be the adjective *ran* 'noble', constitutes a suitable soubriquet for a royal personage, to be sure, but it is also a word which might easily be confused with *ràn* meaning, among other things, 'melancholy cry', 'drawling, dissonant roar or cry.'[97] Needless to say, the idea of a 'noisy' rather than a 'noble' queen chimes well with the tumult which accompanied swarming according to early writers as with the phenomenon of 'piping' queens mentioned above.

From Carmichael's account of the Feast of St Brigit we have now succeeded in extracting evidence pointing directly towards the association of Brigit and the feast in her honour with two powerful fertility symbols – the bear – 'a ubiquitous cult figure... often associated with motherhood and nurturing'[98] – on the one hand, and the bee, 'the mythical image of the Great Goddess... [and] the

Goddess of Regeneration',[99] on the other. However, we have not yet succeeded in exhausting the potential of Scottish and Irish folklore and kindred sources to reveal more about Brigit as the examination of some other aspects of the celebration of her feast will show.

* * *

The oyster-catcher is one of the most conspicuous birds of European coasts. It ranges from Iceland to the Red Sea and '...lives chiefly on marine worms, crustacea and such molluscs as it is able to obtain. It is commonly supposed to be capable of prizing limpets from their rock... [laying] its head sideways on the ground, and then, grasping the limpet's shell close to the rock between the mandibles... [using] them as scissor-blades to cut off the mollusc from its sticking-place.'[100] In Ireland, this bird is remembered for its foolish generosity in lending its swimming-gear to the seagull who never returned it, thus giving rise to the wry comment *'iasacht an roilligh don bhfaológ'* – 'The loan given by the oyster-catcher to the sea-gull', that is to say a loan that will never be returned.[101] The distinctive call of the oyster-catcher, interpreted in Scotland as *'Bi glic, Bi glic'* – 'Be wise! Be wise!', is supposed to be a warning to approaching strangers;[102] in the Faroe Islands it was rendered onomatopoeically as *'klipp! klipp!'*[103] Scottish tradition ranks the oyster-catcher with those birds which help to conceal the presence of certain individuals from pursuers in its case by hiding Our Lord under seaweed.[104]

Common to the Gaelic tradition of Ireland and Scotland is the ascription to the oyster-catcher of the Noa name *Giolla Bríde* 'servant of Brigit'[105] which Carmichael elaborates upon as follows:

In Lismore the oyster-catcher is called *'gille Bride'*, page of Bride:

Gille Bride bochd,   Poor page of Bride,
Gu de bhigil a th'ort?   What cheeping ails thee?

In Uist the oyster-catcher is called 'Bridein', bird of Bride.[106]

In the Faroe Islands, the oyster-catcher goes by the name of *tjaldur*, a word with a wide Nordic distribution which may be descriptive of the bird's wobbling gait.[107] Lockwood, describing the oyster-catcher as 'the best-loved bird in the Faroes', adds:

Doubtless its popularity originally derived from its usefulness in the *hagi* ['haggard'], where it was considered to keep at bay such undesirables as ravens and crows... The bird is a migrant to the Faroes and its return in the second week of March – on *Graekarismessa* ([St Gregory's Day] March 12th) they say – was counted as the beginning of spring.[108]

In *sjómál* 'sea-language' (the argot of Faroese fishermen) the oyster-catcher was called *rúðurbori* 'shellfish-borer', *hitt nevreyða* 'the red beak' and, most interestingly of all from our point of view, *gestur*, meaning 'a guest'.[109] According to Lockwood, the latter designation is really an aphetic form of *nornagestur*, which evokes the name of '...the famous hero of the Old Norse *Norna-Gests tháttr*... equally well known in Faroese balladry.'[110] The reasons for this particular association are unclear. However, in view of the oyster-catcher's unequivocal link with Brigit and on account of her connections with the Norns, it seems reasonable to suppose that *nornagestur* – one of the Faroese Noa names for the oyster-catcher – must also relate in some way or other to the famous fate-spinners of Nordic tradition.[111]

The folklore of the wren, the (grey) crow, the raven and particularly the crane (or heron) is not without its own measure of interest in the context of the present discussion.[112] It is to the last of these, the crane, that we now turn on the next stage of our investigation. Throughout the early iconographic and literary material this bird is characterized as being of a singular and consistent character.[113] Ross describes it as being:

> almost exclusively associated with transformed women, sometimes owned by a god... [something which] seems to have given rise to a superstitious dislike for it when its cult significance ceased to be operative. Although clearly venerated in the earlier period, the bird seems to have developed a quality of mystery in the popular mind, and to have inspired a certain amount of fear and dislike in the emotions of the Celtic peoples. Its flesh was tabu in Ireland and it was believed in more recent traditions to have the power of bringing death upon anyone who ate it. Its impact upon the Celtic imagination was clearly considerable and the consistency of its appearance throughout a long and heterogeneous tradition is remarkable.[114]

The eighth-century BC writings of the Greek farmer Hesiod

ascribe a weather-forecasting role to such birds and imply that they had a strong link with agricultural activity:

> Take heed what time thou hearest the voice of the crane, who year by year, from out the clouds on high clangs shrilly. For her voice bringeth out the sign for ploughing and the time of winter's rain, and bites the heart of him that hath no ox.[115]

This theme may be echoed in the crane symbolism which occurs in two Celtic monuments from the early first century AD, one from Paris (Figs. 24, 25 *overleaf*), the other from Trier. The imagery of these two stones features an association of a bull with three egrets and is described by Green as follows:

> ...on one a large bull stands in front of a willow-tree, two birds on his back and a third perched on his head on an adjacent panel, a woodcutter hacks at the branch of a willow. The inscription above the bull reads *'Tarvostrigaranus'* ('the Bull with Three Cranes'); that above the man reads *'Esus'* ('Lord')... [on the other] a woodcutter chops at a willow tree in which are a bull's head and three cranes or egrets.[116]

The Celtic languages have two different words for the crane, one of these *(corr-)* being categorized as a North European *Wanderwort* which may belong to a pre-Celtic, pre-Germanic substratum with a possible chain of relationship extending into northern Eurasia.[117] With the word *corr-* and its compounds[118] standing alongside a range of Noa names such as *Máire Fhada* ('Long Mary'), we thus find ourselves in a position to complement the naming profile of the oyster-catcher and the bear with that of the crane within the Gaelic languages.[119]

Green's conclusion that 'the whole symbolism of woodcutter, tree, birds and bull reflects a complex mythology', possibly involving the Tree of Life, the 'destruction' of winter and the departure of the tree's spirit in the form of birds as well as the resurgence of the forces of regeneration in nature as represented by the bull is perhaps not entirely happy, but still not far off the mark in perpetuating the identification of the crane with the coming of spring in the Celtic world as also in the Classical.[120] As far as Ireland and Scotland are concerned, however, the indications are that other birds may have arrogated that particular role to themselves and that, as in the Faroes, the oyster-catcher, through

Fig. 24:
Celtic monument, Paris –
Tarvos trigaranus
('the bull with three cranes').

Fig. 25:
Celtic monument, Paris –
Esus side
(with woodcutter).

its association with Brigit, holds some special sway in this respect. In mainland Scandinavia, however, it is the crane rather than the oyster-catcher which functions as harbinger of spring as we shall shortly see.

The Icelandic ceremonies to welcome Góa (the fifth month of winter beginning around the eighteenth of February), as with *Thorrablót* which preceded it, involved the man of the house rising early, going out clad only in a shirt, barefoot and partly barelegged and hopping all around the farmhouse and it has been suggested by Olrik that it is here the Danish spring custom of 'Making Weather' finds its explanation.[121] Similarly, Celander has argued strongly for a connection between this Icelandic custom and the (mainly) west Swedish tradition of *barfotaspringning* ('running barefoot'), a custom frequently associated with either St Gregory's Day (12th March) or Lady Day (25th March).[122]

The habit of running barefoot around the dwelling house or over a wider area of ground at this time of year also went by another name viz. *att springa trana* literally 'running (the) crane'.[123] *Trankvällen* ('Crane-evening') and *trandagen* ('Crane-day' were names commonly applied in parts of Sweden to the eve of Lady Day and to Lady Day itself and, somewhat incongruously it might seem, these names were also sporadically associated with Candlemas.[124] The saying *Tranan bär ljus i säng* ('The crane comes with the light' [lit. 'takes the candle to bed']) was cited by way of encouraging people to abandon the use of artificial light for a period from that night onwards and was accompanied by the injunction that thenceforth one should go to bed in daylight. The onset of such modes of behaviour in Scandinavia was signalled by the arrival of flocks of migrating cranes from the south.[125]

The same principle, minus articulation of any connection with cranes or other such birds, is witnessed in Ireland and Scotland by sayings such as *'Suipeir is soilse Oidhch Fheill Bride // Cadal is soilse Oidhch Fheill Paraig'* ('Supper and light the night of St Bride //Sleep and light the Night of St Patrick' [17th March]).[126]

Mention of the crane is not lacking altogether, however, in the context of British weather rhymes for on the Isle of Man, we are told that March borrowed three days from February in order to catch the crane (heron) on the nest but he only caught her tail, and so the crane has no tail since that time.[127] In the Lowlands of Scotland, we also find something corresponding roughly to the Manx crane tradition:

> March borrowed from April,
> Three days and they were ill
> The first it was snaw and sleet,
> The second it was caul and weet,
> The third it was sic a freeze,
> The birds' nibs stack t' the trees.[128]

Considerations of time, space and future prospects are among the important themes that are highlighted in one way or another by the traditions attaching to the crane and the oyster-catcher as well as the other birds mentioned above. These are issues which are given a special coherence in the personality, so to speak, of the bird called in Irish *gobadán*, a wading bird with a distinct migrating profile.

The word *gobadán* is described by Dinneen as meaning 'a little bird that frequents sea-strands',[129] and given more specifically by Ó Dónaill as 'sandpiper'.[130] Dinneen also quotes the well-known saying *'Ní thig leis an ngobadán an dá thrághadh a fhreastal'* – 'the *gobadán* cannot attend the two ebb-tides' – cannot work night and day (al. rendered the *gobadán* cannot attend to the two strands, reading *tráigh*, for *trághadh*...),[131] which Ó Dónaill in turn glosses 'one cannot be everywhere, attend to everything, at once', the implication obviously being that this is the very impression given by the scurrying *gobadán* as it makes its 'short, tripping runs along the water's edge',[132] bobbing and rising in short flights – 'piping' as it goes about its business.

The word *gob* 'a pointed or beak-like mouth'[133] (on which the name *gobadán* is formed) while quite apt in describing the sandpiper would be even more applicable to the oyster-catcher whose long, sharp beak is much more pronounced and who also feeds at low water, poking and prodding as it moves along. In short, *gobadán* is a name as suited to the oyster-catcher as it is to the sandpiper and, perhaps, it may be classed along with *giolla Bríde* as a Noa name for it. The sayings which credit the *gobadán* with aspirations to achieve bilocation or alternatively to successfully address different tasks simultaneously may be a reflection of much more than straightforward nature observation. They imply a degree of empathy on the part of the observer embodying, perhaps, recognition of a shared dilemma. Whether as sandpiper or oyster-catcher, the *gobadán* vividly conveys by its behaviour, feeding and migration habits, a sense of being between two worlds and as such powerfully expresses the notion of liminality (Figs. 26 & 27).[134]

Chapter 3

Fig. 26:
Papil Stone slab, Isle of West Burra, Shetland.

Fig. 27:
Panel detail of the original Papil Stone slab (in the National Museum of Scotland, Edinburgh).

* * *

As we have seen above in regard to the preparation of *leaba Bride*, the make-believe image of the saint was decked with 'gay ribbons from the loom, sparkling shells from the sea, and bright stones from the hill.'[135] Likewise, 'primroses, daisies, and other flowers that open their eyes in the morning of the year' were laid about *dealbh Bride*, 'the ikon of Bride'.[136] Carmichael's account of the *banal Bride* – directly comparable in many respects to the Irish institution of *Brideoga*, (Biddies or Biddy Boys) – contains the following description of the doll image of the saint and the ceremony attending it:

> On Bride's Eve the girls of the townland fashion a sheaf of corn into the likeness of a woman. They dress and deck the figure with shining shells, sparkling crystals, primroses, snowdrops, and any greenery they may obtain… A special bright shell or crystal is placed over the heart of the figure. This is called *'real-iuil Bride'*, the guiding star of Bride, and typifies the star over the stable door of Bethlehem, which led Bride to the infant Christ. The girls call the figure 'Bride'. 'Brideag,' Bride, Little Bride, and carry it on procession, singing the song of *'Bride bhoidheach oigh nam mile beus'*, 'Beauteous Bride, virgin of a thousand charms'. The *'banal Bride,'* Bride maiden band, are clad in white, and have their hair down, symbolising purity and youth. They visit every house, and every person is expected to give a gift to Bride and to make obeisance to her. The gift may be a shell, a spar, a crystal, a flower, or a bit of greenery to decorate the person of Bride. Mothers, however, give *'bonnach Bride'*, a Bride bannock, *'cabag Bride'*, a Bride cheese or *'rolag Bride'*, a Bride roll of butter.[137]

Carmichael observes:

> Customs assume the complexion of their surroundings, as fishes, birds, and beasts assimilate the colours of their habitats. The seas of the *'Garbh Chriocha'*, 'Rough Bounds' [= Highlands and Islands]', in which the cult of Bride has longest lived, abound in iridescent shells, and the mountains in bright sparkling stones and these are used to adorn the ikon of Bride. In other districts where the figure of Bride is made, there are no shining shells, no brilliant crystals, and the girls decorate the image with artistically interlaced straw.[138]

This commentary articulates a basic principle as apt for the proper assessment and comprehension of Scottish folklore as for that of any other country while, at the same time, holding forth a fascinating and, as far as I know, hitherto unnoticed prospective concordance with Irish folk tradition on an issue of central relevance to the theme here under discussion.

In the course of his comprehensive and penetrating review of the celebration of the Feast of Brigit in Ireland, Danaher adverts to a custom which does not appear to have existed without the bounds of County Leitrim. There, he says:

> children... got a small piece of a flat wooden board about 30 cms by 15 cms and with the viscous exudation of a partly boiled or roasted potato fixed peeled rushes upon it in figures representing 'the sun, the moon and the stars' this was then hung up with the cross.[139]

A full description of the local setting is provided by a Leitrim collector:

> The feast of St Brigid was observed in this locality by the visit of a young girl, specially chosen, to a certain house which was selected by all the neighbours in the townland. The neighbours gathered in the appointed house at a given time and awaited the arrival of the Saint's representative who came and knocked for admission at the back door. The knock was questioned in the Irish language from inside 'Who is there?' The answer from outside was in Irish *'Bríd bheannaithe'* ['Blessed *Bríd*']. The door was immediately opened and the 'Saint' was admitted and given the best seat in the house. The feast then commenced and any food left by the Saint's representative was carefully left over and divided among the guests who took their portion home with them and afterwards busied themselves making St Brigid's crosses. These were made of green rushes and chips of timber and in the making of the cross a piece of the food left by the Saint's representative was inserted. A board about eighteen inches long was then procured and on this board was made a representation of the moon and stars constructed from peeled green rushes [and] in the moon and in each star there was also placed a particle of the food. The cross and board were then placed over the door which the Saint entered and the Rosary was recited in honour of St Brigid and her assistance was invoked for the protection of the family from

sickness, sin and scandal for twelve months, at the end of which the same ceremony, as described above, took place.[140]

It requires but little effort to detect a reflection here in the 'sun, moon and star of Leitrim – of Carmichael's 'iridescent shells', 'sparkling stones' and 'brilliant crystals', likewise his 'artistically interlaced straw decorations', while his *real-iuil Bride*, the special bright shell or crystal, looked upon as the guiding star of Bethlehem and placed over the heart of the figure representing Brigit, is clearly also paralleled over wider areas of Ireland by the cross, with all its multivalent symbolism,[141] that was commonly pinned to the *brídeog*, the Irish doll image of Brigit. Peeled green rushes and the juice of half-boiled potatoes may appear at first sight to be a poor match for glittering crystals, stones and shells but from these humble raw materials, shining images were created and, in much the same spirit as in Scotland, subsequently allocated a special place of honour in the family home.

Elsewhere in Ireland, we also find shells together with their live contents coming into play, though not by way of decoration, it would seem:

> In a few places around Galway Bay, a live shellfish, such as a limpet or periwinkle, was placed at each end of the four corners of the house, to bring fishing luck and ensure plentiful shore gathering.[142]

I believe Evans is quite correct in regarding this custom (which is still remembered, perhaps also practised in this part of Ireland) as hinting 'at a remote pre-agricultural origin for the festival…' [143] In Old Europe, the shell was, regarded as an emblem symbolizing, as Gimbutas says, 'rising life power at the moment of death'.[144] It carries manifold fertility connotations: as a symbol of the vulva, it represents the Female Principle;[145] the so-called plaques (= shells) of Ashtart (Astarte), the [Semitic] goddess of fecundity,[146] and a special favourite of maritime communities,[147] feature a goddess with emphasized genitals holding up her breasts;[148] murex shells, long connected with divinity and royalty, were regarded as being sacred to Aphrodite because a murex once stopped a ship and thus prevented boys being castrated;[149] shells were reputed to possess prophylactic virtues[150] – the image of a shell was imprinted on amulets which were used against the Evil Eye[151] and as a luck token given to married daughters;[152] shells were also employed in weather prognosis.[153]

Barnacles – one of the shellfish mentioned in the context of the County Galway custom referred to above, are themselves the subject of 'one of the most extraordinary and persistent myths of medieval natural history, dating back to the twelfth century at least,'[154] namely that the rotting timber of ships turns into barnacles and that these then turn into barnacle geese or alternatively that barnacle geese are hatched from the fruit of a tree or from the shells growing on it.[155] The fact that the barnacle goose was a winter visitor to Ireland and that its nesting-place was unknown, undoubtedly lent credence to these beliefs. Barnacles, together with acorn shells (multivalve cirripeds), belong to the division *Cirripedia* or *Thyrostraca* and as such are hermaphrodite by nature.[156] Parthenogenesis is of frequent occurrence in many of the lower crustaceans such as the brine-shrimp Artemia.[157] The latter phenomenon is not confined to the animal world: the term is applied in many cultures in the context of myth and religion to any miraculous conception and birth and features. It would seem that the physiological quirk in certain kinds of shellfish and other hermaphroditic species which permits parthenogenesis was observed by man and understood by him as a metaphor for the notion of divinity entering the human experience.[158] It is a process basic to the idea of the primordial, an essential component for the appearance of all the species of animals and plants born from the body of a primordial being.[159]

Faechóg, the Irish name for the humble periwinkle, should not be forgotten here for it is possible that it may conceal a crucial connecting link between the mollusc and apian worlds wherein reside prime symbols of parthenogenesis and fertility. Like *foich* 'a wasp' (gl. *eruca*, 'cankerworm'), *faechóg* has a number of p-Celtic counterparts: while *foich*, is quoted as glossing Latin *eruca* 'cankerworm', Brythonic *guohi* (<*uuochi*) which has given rise to *foich* in Irish),[160] glosses *fucos* 'rock-lichen, the reddish juice with which bees stop up the entrance to their hives; bee-glue; a drone'. *Guohi* in turn, goes back to *uobh(e)sa* 'wasp' and ultimately to *uebh-* 'to weave'.[161] This complex of derivations and glosses embracing the wasp, the drone, rock-lichen (seaweed), and bee-juice all seem to be related in one way or another to a basic root meaning 'to weave'.[162]

Faechóg, which is related to Welsh *gwichiad*, Cornish *gwihan* also meaning 'periwinkle', is listed by Pedersen cheek by jowl with *foich*, but merits no comment from him as to its origins or to the possibility of its having been borrowed in the same direction as *foich*. In fact, this is precisely what appears to have been the case. The derivation of the Welsh and Cornish words from **ueik-*, **ueig-* 'to bend, twist, spin',[163] offers the possibility of substantiating a connection between *foich* and *faechóg* in broad thematic terms; for the ultimate derivation of *faoch* from this root would seem to have a direct bearing on the spiralled appearance of the winkle shell and the crooked nature of its contents. The weaving of the bee in designing and constructing the honey-comb (one of the marvels of animal architecture) set alongside the twisted winkle reproduces a combination which mirrors central elements of the imagery and symbolism permeating the folk tradition that surrounds the Feast of Brigit. I refer, of course, to two outstanding features of that feast, to wit the express ban on spinning (or the turning of wheels) which is counterbalanced by an explicit injunction on the participants to engage in the weaving of crosses for her day.[164]

Apart from the medieval legend which it inspired, the word 'barnacle' also presents its own fascinating problems. The history of 'barnacle', the vernacular description applied to some cirripeds, is obscure: the name may have been originally applied to the bird – a species of wild goose, allied to the Brent goose – and subsequently to the shell.[165] Vendryes, however, believes English *barnacle* and French *bernache*, *bernacle* to be of Celtic origin, relating the Irish word *bairneach* to *bairenn*, *boirenn* 'a rock, a rocky place.'[166] This would seem to imply the opposite development, thus bringing it into line with the belief crediting the shellfish with the role of progenitor.

The ultimate derivation of 'barnacle' (whether shellfish or goose) from a word for 'rock' raises the question as to what part rocks might be conceived as playing in the matter, apart from providing a convenient surface for encrustment by the myriads of barnacles which cling to them between the coastal tide marks. The obvious place to turn for an answer to this question is to the stone itself in the first instance. We could make no better start than to approach rocks or stones in the same fashion as many cultures, both ancient and modern, namely as manifestations of the deity whose nature we are now seeking to better understand.

* * *

Chapter 3

The imagery of rocks and stones is strongly redolent of fertility and regenerative powers and is perhaps most comprehensively delineated in the concept of the 'cosmic phallus represented by the standing stone, pillar or tower', which as often as not has transposed and absorbed 'the originally female power of its material substance, the 'mother rock'.[167] For the Celts, the 'most highly significant sexual symbol of all was the human head, especially in conjunction with a pillar-stone or a sacred spring'.[168] The Celts were wont to take phalloid stones representing the deity and surmount them with a human head or draw a human face on the glans.[169] For them, the head (especially the severed head) rather than the phallus seems to have figured as the predominant symbol of fertility:

> They believed it to be the seat of the soul, the very centre of being; this must include in it the powers not only of prophecy, all wisdom and entertainment, but of generation itself.[170]

There would seem to be a *prima facie* case at least for linking the (severed) head, whether in conjunction with stones or springs, with the notion of generation on the basis of the apposition between it and the suggestively phalloid stones on which it was so often depicted. Like all great religious symbols, 'the phallus points to a mysterious divine reality that cannot otherwise be apprehended.'[171] Apprehension of the divine is a goal far beyond the ambitions of the present exercise, but by delving in search of further ramifications of this intriguing synergy between head and stone arising from the habit of singling out and highlighting the 'glans' of phalloid stones, perhaps it may prove possible to make some modest progress in achieving at least a fuller appreciation of how our forbears viewed this issue and attempted to grapple with it.

The Latin word *glans*, 'acorn', is also used to signify the conical part which forms the end of the penis or the clitoris.[172] The acorn, 'a one-seeded nut fixed in a little woody cup',[173] originally meant 'fruit of the open country' only later being applied exclusively to the oak.[174] The conical form of both glans and acorn clearly invites comparison; it is no surprise, therefore, that the acorn should be thought of as symbolizing, life, strength and virility[175] and, like the phallus, looked upon as being 'a great giver of life of one kind or another'.[176]

This pattern is confirmed in Irish where Old Irish *derucc* (later *dircu, dercu*), cited as meaning 'acorn' and glossing 'glans', stands alongside *derc* 'hole, pit, cavity, hollow, empty eye-socket, armpit', *derc* 'eye' and *derc* 'berry',[177] words which would appear to be related to one another.[178] In the Nordic world, Swedish *ollon* also carries the dual meaning 'acorn' and 'glans'. Old Swedish *alda*, from which *ollon* is derived, preserves the original sense of 'fruit-bearing tree' (as well as the more specific 'fruit-bearing oak').[179] Tree-names are notorious for their interchangeability[180] and the possibility should not be excluded that *alda*, which is perhaps the last remaining element of a very old tree name,[181] may have been applied at one stage to the alder, a tree of the genus *Alnus*. It is sufficient for our purposes, however, simply to note that the oak and the alder are both trees which produce a similarly-shaped conical fruit. That they share this common shape with phalloid decorated stones is obvious; less conspicuous – though no less significant – is the role played by the pineal gland (so-called because of its conical shape) in establishing a connection between the tradition of fertility-imbued severed heads among the Celts and some critically important elements of the bear cult of northern Europe and Eurasia.[182] This photosensitive organ is situated at the geometric centre of the skull where it functions as a third eye. As we have seen in the case of the bear, it fulfils a crucial regulatory function in the context of its reproductive cycle.[183]

In classical tradition, a direct association between phallus and eye may be seen in adversions to Pan's 'sharp eye' and an eye is actually depicted on the glans of the phallus featuring in a scene from the Haloa festival associated with Demeter.[184] Like Pan, Priapus was sometimes regarded as a son of Hermes. Among the Romans he is a god of gardens and he is shown 'as an old man holding up his robe to carry the fruits and vegetables for which he is responsible and thereby exposing to view the source of all this fruitfulness – itself almost a fruit – an unnaturally large, erect phallus.'[185] It is tempting to see a direct parallel in this image to that of the fire-carrying Brigit of Irish tradition, her gown raised to accommodate the burning coals, an exercise we may be justified in assuming which resulted in the exposure of more than her feet, the body parts usually referred to by Irish tradition in this context.[186]

The importance of various conically shaped objects – human, animal and vegetable – in the field of sexual symbolism is clear.

For an insight into the particular relevance of one of the cone-bearing trees that have entered the picture we revert to the Far North and the scrutiny of *Leib-Olmai*, 'the alder-man', ruler over all wild animals and tutelary spirit of the bear among the Sámi people. Of *Leib-Olmai*, Holmberg tells us:

> This being was only known in a very restricted region, and he appears occasionally depicted on the Lapp drum in the shape of a bear – from which one may conclude that his origin may be assigned to the bear-worship itself. The name also points to this conclusion; for the juice of the alder-bark played an important part in the bear-hunting ceremonies.[187]

The blood-red concoction of alder-juice used for painting the Sámi shaman drums, Bäckman tells us, was occasionally replaced with bear's blood. Commenting upon Pehr Fjellström's mid-eighteenth-century account of Sámi bear-hunting and bear-feast ceremonial, Bäckman describes the further use of alder-bark juice in the following terms:

> When the hunters have returned from the kill bringing news of its successful outcome, the women squirt chewed alder bark in the eyes of all the bear-men i.e. hunters and also on their dogs. Formerly they would sprinkle themselves and make the sign of the cross on their own eyes with it and this is a rite which must be seen as a defensive action in order to prevent their becoming the object of revenge on the part of the bear...[188]

The striking emphasis upon eyes is paralleled in a similar context in other Eurasian cultures. For example, among the various Turkish tribes of Siberia we learn that:

> The Yakut after having killed the bear, tear out the warm heart from the body and swallow it raw in small pieces, and they croak like ravens: 'khakh, khakh'. When approaching the cooked meat the young hunters must croak like ravens. They perform over the bear's carcase some movements resembling those of sexual intercourse. The eyes of the dead bear are also removed. The Shortsi believe that the hunter who has swallowed the eyes, will not fear the bear anymore on the contrary, the bear will fear him, since the hunter will appear to him as a bear... Among the Sagai the eyes are taken out in order

that the bear may not see the people any more. The hunters swallow the eyes to gain courage. If a bear should meet such a man he would see the eyes in him (for a bear sees everything), and he would fear him and would not touch him.[189]

Chichlo tells us that *Seven* is a word used among the Tunguz peoples, to mean both 'shaman's spirit helper' and the ritual dish of rendered bear fat mixed with finely chopped bear meat which is eaten at the bear festival. The hunter scoops it with a spoon and, as with the bear's eyes, must swallow it without it touching his teeth.[190] Chichlo proceeds to explain the meaning of these rules in the light of certain strong prohibitions associated with the domestic hearth:

> The firewood and coals must not be stirred with a sharp object, nor may broken needles be thrown into the fire. Even to place a knife with its point toward the fire may put out the eyes of the spirit of the fire. This spirit, according to an Orochi myth, is a pair of bear cubs born from the mating of a bear and a woman. According to the Evenki, the bear is a culture hero who gave people fire. Reconstructing the Tunguz spirit of the domestic fire discloses his bisexual nature, corresponding to an androgynous deity like the bear. It is therefore understandable why hunters do not risk swallowing *osikta* ('bear's eyes'), preferring to return them to the taiga. The luster of these stars on top of the World tree assured hunting success, and the projections of the luster are the light and warmth of domestic hearths.[191]

This image of the bear with its all-seeing eye (within or without its skull), its fertility associations and its divine status among the bear hunting peoples of the Far North sits comfortably alongside that of the severed Celtic head as already pictured for us by Ross. As the head was for the Celts, for these peoples, the bear was clearly 'the seat of the soul, the very centre of being', being likewise invested with 'not only powers of prophecy, all wisdom and entertainment, but of generation itself.'[192]

A recurring feature that the treatment of our subject hitherto has revealed is the intriguing match between etymological and thematic ambivalence. Nagy sums up the essence of the linguistic application of the Indo-European root *$perk^w u$- to oaks in some languages (for example, Latin *quercus*) and to rocks in others (for example, Hittite *peru*) alongside the extremely common theme that man originated from trees or rocks in terms of a similar match. The root *per-* meaning 'to strike' he argues 'is associated with rocks and trees in Indo-European languages because the action of the thunderbolt on these materials was believed to be not only sacral but creative.'[193] This observation brings us a step closer to understanding the central importance of fire in the context of the present study, for the conflict inherent in its 'destructive/creative ambivalence' is ultimately what lies at the heart of the matter. This conflict Nagy sees as having been resolved in favour of creative rather than destructive force as witnessed in the characteristics of a number of thundergods such as Lithuanian Perkunas and Byelorussian Piarun, whose names, like Old Norse Fjörgyn – according to Völuspá 'mother' of Thórr[194] (whose name means 'thunderer') – or Celtic Hercynia, are derived from *$perk^w$ u-* 'oak'. Both oaks and rocks are 'singled out for sacral affinity with the thunderbolt to such an extent that their designations are interchangeable in various Indo-European languages.'[195] The explanation as to why this should be so Nagy believes lies in there being something intrinsic in (oak) trees and rocks 'which is like the thunderbolt and which therefore attracts them.'[196] This quality he suggests is 'potential fire'.[197] Man kindles fire by rubbing it out of wood and rock thus running the risk of attracting a thunderbolt while simultaneously standing in prospect of achieving an understanding of how the fire of the thunderbolt itself is created. Nagy continues:

> Conversely, the fact that we can rub fire out of wood and rock suggests that these materials were once infused, perhaps even impregnated with the stroke of some thunderbolt. In the folklore of many non-Indo-European peoples, it is in fact a common mythical theme that thunderbolts deposit fire in trees or rocks, which then has to be extracted from these materials by way of friction. Oftentimes the god of the thunderbolt is pictured as being actually incarnated within the material. Also there is a primitive logic which makes the friction of making fire parallel to the friction of making love... Accordingly, the stroke of the thunderbolt may be viewed as not only destructive but also procreative.[198]

Thórr was thought of as being a source of tremendous heat and was generally pictured as having a halo of fire around his head.[199] He is a powerful worker for the good of the gods and of man, however, constantly battling against the powers of evil and portrayed as such in nearly all the myths about him.[200] In Denmark, Norway, Sweden and Iceland his name occurs in many placenames some of which may provide evidence for his having associations with fertility, a feature otherwise rather poorly represented in his case. His overwhelming popularity among the Nordic peoples is indicated by the fact that his name appears as an element in personal name compounds more frequently than the name of any other god.[201] Nevertheless, the evidence of Thórr's mark upon the folk tradition of the Nordic countries would appear to be somewhat equivocal. It is to some relevant aspects of this subject that we now direct our attention.

* * *

One Nordic custom with strong fire associations which may be linked with Thórr is 'a remarkable and little known Norwegian folk memory pertaining to the end of the Christmas period' – as Celander has it – a custom, he maintains, which is 'of such a character as to constitute a ritual memory *in situ* of the old Nordic Yuletide fire.'[202] The twelfth of January, Celander tells us, 'is called in some south-eastern dialects of Norwegian, *midvet* 'mid-winter [day], by which time of year, according to a widespread European tradition, the length of the day (i.e. daylight) will have increased by an amount that can then be equated with 'a cock's step'.[203] Mid-winter day in this part of Norway was also called *Toredagen* ('*Tore*-day') and on his day it was the custom for the following ceremony to be performed:

> This was when one made the *torelut* ['*tore*-lye'], a bucketful of ashes which had accumulated in the course of the previous three days. Just after sunset, the ash was emptied over the heart of a snake and the heart of a bear, following which it was left to stand for three days in an unused wall (chimney or fireplace). Then the ash was separated from the rest and put away. This ash was used specially for mixing with bathwater intended for bathing a new-born male child. You said:
>
> Jeg lauger dig i torelut,   I bathe you in *tore*-lye,
> For du skal holde verden ut.   That you may live for many a day.
>
> The bathwater was called *torevatn* ['*tore*-water'] or *torelaug* ['*tore*-bath']. From the heart of the snake, the boy would get vindictiveness and from the heart of the bear he got courage and strength.[204]

Celander characterizes this account as being almost terrifyingly primitive in tone by comparison (especially in its reference to an era of blood-feuding) to which all else that Nordic folk tradition has to say about the magic powers of Yule ash is but a pale shadow. We may be justified, he concludes, in identifying the *Tore-* element of *Toredagen, Torelut* etc. with *Thorrablót*, the ceremony with which the month of *Thorre* 14th January – 14th February – was inaugurated and in seeing in the tradition of *Toredagen* /*Torelut*, a memory of the fire festival dimension of *Thorrablót*.[205]

The commencement of the month of *Thorre* was also the occasion for the enactment of an old Scandinavian hearth-fire ceremony known as *Eldborgs skål* or the like,[206] a custom best known in Norway, but also at home in adjacent areas of Sweden and which can be further traced to the Faroe Islands and to Iceland. This custom is variously associated with the Epiphany (5th-6th January), the twentieth day of Christmas (12th or 13th January), Candlemas, or the first Tuesday or Wednesday in Lent.[207] Ordéus has identified the oracular part of the ceremony associated with this event with a similar ceremony in Welsh tradition and, as a result of her brief survey of the Nordic and Celtic evidence (the latter represented only by the Welsh material) is convinced that we are apparently dealing with what she terms 'an east atlantic phenomenon'.[208]

However that may be, perhaps the most interesting aspect of the *Eldborgs skål* tradition in the context of the present discussion is the fire-offering element and the words which accompany it among which are counted such sayings as *'Gud beware wårt hus ifrån Eld och Brand och Thiufwe hand'* ('God protect our house from fire and conflagration and thieving hands').[209] The essential elements of this ceremony are contained in the following account of it from Telemark in Norway:

> The day after [the Thirteenth Day] called *Elbiør-Dagen* ('*Elbiør-*Day') was when you drank *Elbiør-Minde (Ildborgs Skaal)* [*Elbiør-*Commemoration ('*Ildborg's* Toast')]. The woman of the house came in with a bowl of ale, stood by the hearth and drank the health of the fire, whereupon she sprinkled a little in the fire with these words: '*Saa høit min El, og inkje høgare og heitare hel*' ('Thus high my fire and neither higher or hotter'). Afterwards you drank like this: You sat on the floor with this bowl of ale between your legs and your hands behind your back; you lifted the bowl with your mouth, drank up the ale and with a flick of your head cast it behind you; if the bowl landed upside down,

you would die within the year; if not, then you would be lucky enough to drink *Elbiør's*-Commemoration once again.[210]

Another account from Valdres in Norway, where the custom was celebrated on St Knut's Day [13th (originally 7th) January],[211] the eve of which day was called *Ildbjørsminne* ('*Ildbjør's* commemoration'), provides further interesting detail:

> A big bowl full of Yule ale specially set aside for this purpose was passed from hand to hand. As you caught hold of the bowl, you stood up, bowed low to the fire and said: '*E drikke St. Ildbjørsminne te!*' ('I drink to the memory of St Ildbjør!'). Then you took a little of the ale in a spoon and sprinkled it over on the pile of embers and prayed that the 'red rooster' would not crow over your house and property. When everyone had taken a drink, the old woman of the house or some other person took a spoonful of ale or maybe spirits and put it on the fire and let it burn up. At bedtime, you raked the ashes nicely together and recited in a low voice:
>
> | | |
> |---|---|
> | *Ikvæld vil e Elden raka,* | Tonight I shall rake the fire, |
> | *imorgo vil e han levande taka;* | Tomorrow I will receive it alive; |
> | *hjælpe me Gu aa Santa-Knut,* | Help me God and St Knut, |
> | *at alder min Verma slokna ut.* | That my heat [= *fire*] never dies.[212] |

This formula seems to have been adopted from everyday hearth and fire-care protocol and adapted to the seasonal celebration in question.[213] The twin concerns of simultaneously containing and maintaining the fire are embodied in this quatrain. The challenge of 'saving the fire' *(coigilt)* is similarly addressed in the Gaelic hearth-prayers of Ireland and Scotland where Brigit and Mary are said to have encircled it *('Bríd ina bun agus Muire ina barr')* and together with the 'twelve angels of of the graces' protected the house and all within from conflagration.[214]

The encompassment of the fire in the embrace of two powerful female figures seems to be absent in Scandinavia where hearth prayers mention only one such – the Virgin Mary.[215] The 'Santa Knut' adverted to here was, in fact a Danish nobleman (Knut Lavard), who was treacherously murdered on 7th January 1121 AD and canonized in the year 1169. The original 'St Knut's Day' (on 7th January) coincided with an end date for the Christmas season.

Fire maintenance and containment in Scandinavian hearth prayers only mention supplication to God, the Virgin Mary, St

Knut and the obscure figure of Eldborg, the 'fire-protectress'. Scholarly opinion as to the origin of the name Eldborg is fairly unanimous in seeing it as an element of the designation for the (commemorative) drink *(= skål)* which was drunk when the (hearth) fire *(eld)* was 'saved' or 'preserved' *(= bärga)*.[216] While St Knut was an historical personage, St Eldborg was no saint, but a fictional figure 'canonized' by the folk in the late middle ages. The name Eldborg, however, stems from earlier times surviving into the Christian era (which came late to Scandinavia) and then dressed up as a saint. The break-down of the elements of her name – *eld* and *borg (= bärga)* reveal her true identity as a 'protectress of fire'. In Norway, Eldborg was also popular as an ordinary woman's name which would seem to indicate the Eldborg of *Eldborgs skål* was thought of as being female.[217]

This comparison of Gaelic/Norse prayers and ceremonial has revealed some interesting parallels and it has also exposed apparent divergences. The most glaring of these relates to the encompassment of the fire explicitly by *two* powerful female figures in Gaelic tradition.

It may be speculated, perhaps, that the various names featured in the Norse cohort in question may have once occurred in other combinations such as, for example, Eldborg and the Virgin Mary working hand in hand to save the fire, in which case the former might be thought of as exercising a similar role to that of Brigit. The obeisance paid to Eldborg by Scandinavian households is also reflected in the dignified manner of the welcome accorded, on this side of the North Sea, to Brigit – 'the noble woman'.

Fire-offerings from outside the Nordic world (Bohemia and Austria in particular) are also discussed by Celander but most revealing of all is his adversion to the Sámi version of *Eldborgs skål*, borrowed by them, he maintains, from their Germanic neighbours in Scandinavia. Norwegian and Swedish missionaries among the Sámi people have left us several accounts dating to the beginning of the eighteenth century, the following being from the Nærö manuscript where it is cited as an example of the 'Satanic customs of the Sámi':

> ...every Sámi on Christmas Eve when he is sated with beer or spirits consecrates his cabin or *Kuttu* in the following manner... When Christmas Eve comes, he drinks a toast of beer or spirits with his wife and children one by one and pours the half of it in the *Paasio*

[by the main entrance to the dwelling] and with the remaining half he drinks the health of *Jemmel* or God, likewise he and his family take up position by the other door *Ux* and drink the health of *Mubenaimo* Satan], likewise also by the hearth on which the half portion is similarly poured and the health of *Sarachae* also drunk.[218]

The worship of the Sámi goddess, Sarakka, one member of a group of female divinities comparable in many respects to the Norns and other such groupings is elsewhere declared to have had 'the hearth consecrated in her honour'. Libations are stated to have been offered to her on the hearth before proceeding to church and communion, reference also being made to Thórr and the spirits of the dead.[219]

The hearth-fire associations of Sarakka and her fellow divinities and their strong fertility and childbirth associations invite comparison not only with the Norns but with Brigit too, a subject to which we shall return in greater detail in the next chapter.

Fig. 28: Sámi Turf Dwelling, Finnmark, Norway, 1925

Notes to Chapter 3

1 Ó Máille (2. 324 [No. 4708]).
2 MacNeill 1962 (12).
3 Cf. p. 4ff. above.
4 NFC 903:44-5, 50.
5 Cf. p. 22ff. above.
6 Cf. Chapter 1, Note 93.
7 *CG* 1, 168.
8 *Loc.cit.*
9 Ó Catháin 1980 (120-2).
10 *Máthair tine* is an expression commonly used in Erris, County Mayo. The 'seed' of the fire is frequently referred to in the folklore manuscripts (NFC) e.g. NFC 36:245; 266:76 and 462:24-6.
11 Noted by me (24 October 1993) from Molly Henry of Kilgalligan, County Mayo. She and other local women quoted *'Ag cumhdach an tí seo go lá'* ['Protecting my house till dawn'] or *'Ag cumhdach an tí seo agus a bhfuil ann go lá'* ['Protecting this house and its occupants till dawn')] as alternate last lines to this verse. Molly Henry reports the verse as having been commonly used by the older generation of women. Molly quoted it to me in the context of a number of traditional night prayers such as *'Ceithre choirnéal ar mo leaba'* (Cf. Ó Laoghaire (95 [No. 275]).

The 'twelve angels of the angels of the graces' – which finds a parallel in the *'ainghle geallaidh'* ['the angels of promise'] of the Scottish Gaelic prayer given below – would seem to embody a reference to fire since the word *aingeal* means both 'angel' and 'fire' (Wagner 1953a, 133-4). Lockwood 1966 (30) observing that 'the original word for fire in [Manx] Gaelic, has been replaced by the euphemism *aile [aingeal]* declares that 'this can only be explained in terms of a wholesale taboo on the original word in its concrete uses'. Dinneen, *Foclóir Gaedhilge agus Béarla*, Dublin 1927 [HENCEFORTH Dinneen], defines the word as meaning 'a burnt-out cinder taken from the fire, sometimes given in their hands as a protection to children going out at night, as it is supposed to represent an angel' (19). It was also the custom to place a burnt-out cinder – called *aingeal* – underneath the churn while making a churning of butter in order to ensure the success of the operation. Other customs observed during churning included the placing of the share of the plough in the fire (NFC 84:309) and the exercise of a total ban on embers from the fire being removed from the house (NFC 41:196).
12 *CG* 1. 234-5. A similar concern with the appearance of the fire – whether symmetrical or asymmetrical – is expressed in the belief that an odd number of peat sods should not be used when raking the fire NFC 65:205) and in the notion that for each ember removed from the fire (for example, to place on an oven lid when baking), a turf sod should be put in its place (NFC card index). The latter tradition is still remembered in Erris (County Mayo). *'Corr-choigilt'* is glossed by Dinneen as 'green and blue figures, resembling glow-worms observed on the hearth when raking the fire at night, said to forebode frost or rain' (251): *coigilt* – the word applied

to the action of raking the fire – is here combined with the word *corr-* which in compounds carries the meaning 'odd, occasional, pointed, round, -snouted' (Dinneen, 249): in the meaning 'bird of the crane or heron kind; a stork, bittern etc.' (Dinneen, 250) it occurs in words such as *corr-mhóna* ['heron']. The word *corr* also means 'a worm, a reptile; young of gannet; fly or insect; a sand-eel' *(loc.cit.)*. For *corrguine* (meaning 'magic, sorcery') – the first element of which may be connected with *corr* meaning 'heron' – cf. Vendryes (C-213). The expression *'éan an churaigh'* – used to describe the prow of the curragh – may be compared with *in chorr thuiseach 'la proue [d'un coracle]'* (Vendryes, C-211), the elements *éan* and *corr* meaning 'bird' and 'heron' respectively. *An Chorr Ghobach* is the name of a wake-game in which a hooded figure lunges at the other players armed with a pointed object [cp. S. Ó Súilleabháin 1967, 'The Speckled Stallion' (91) and also the wake game called 'Feeding the Crane' *(loc.cit.)*]. In the context of lending fire, it is also reported that only one side of the fire should be given *(An Stoc* 6. 12. *Iúl-Lughnasa* 1929, 7) and ashes should not be removed from the house while churning was in progress (NFC 236:161). St Colm Cille, who was said to understand the speech of birds and be especially adept at communicating with the heron *(corr)*, earned the soubriquet *corrchléirech*, 'crooked' or 'heron cleric' (cf. J.F. Nagy 1990, 374).

13 *CG* 1. 240-1.
14 *CG* 1. 236-7.
15 Della Volpe treats of the importance of the domestic hearth as a focal point for the expression of Indo-European religious ideals and practices emphasizing its role in 'forging a link between the world of the living and the world of the dead' (175). This article also contains a number of interesting remarks concerning the geometric form of the hearth (see Note 12 above).
16 For relevant riddles in Irish tradition, cf. Hull & Taylor (Nos. 160, 179, 208, 273, 319, 473 and 479).
16 For relevant proverbs in Irish tradition, cf. Ó Máille (1. Nos. 315, 1400, 1569); *Ibid.*, (2. Nos. 2852, 3696, 3827, 3828, 4708, 4997 and 4998).
17 Rawson (76).
18 Fjellström 1981 (50).
19 *Ibid.* (51). *FW* (2.912) concurs with this opinion adding that incense of one kind or other including angelica, sage and fir among other plants 'was used both to purify human beings and ritual apparatus such as drums, rattles, and other musical instruments, masks etc. Often these purificatory substances were burned in an open fire and the articles were cleansed by being held in the smoke from the fire'. For a discussion of the significance of angelica and fir (pine), cf. p. 18 and Chapter 2, Note 91 respectively.
20 For the various 'Lives' of Brigit – and other early manuscript materials pertaining to her, cf. Chapter 1, Note 119.
21 O'Brien (122, 126).
22 Cf. Kenney (357).
23 Cf. p. 27 above.
24 *CG* 1. 165-6.
25 This is particularly striking with regard to the number of *Lúnasa* sites noted

by her which have associations with St Brigit, among them the famous *Daigh Bhríde*, a holy well at Liscannor, County Clare dedicated to St Brigit (cf. MacNeill 1962, 275-86).
26 MacNeill 1962 (407).
27 *Ibid.* (240).
28 *Ibid.* (406).
29 *Loc.cit.*
30 MacNeill 1962 (271, 274).
31 *Ibid.* (72).
32 *Loc.cit.*
33 MacNeill 1962 (271).
34 *Ibid.* (27).
35 *Loc.cit.*
36 For a discussion of the impact of this calendar change upon festival dates, cf. MacNeill (1962, 20-50).
37 Kenney (357-8).
38 MacNeill 1962 (273).
39 Ó Cróinín (396).
40 Winston (4).
41 *Loc.cit.*
42 *EB* 3, 628-9.
43 Gojmerac (9).
44 Gojmerac (10). According to Winston (4 and 7) the 'earliest known fossil bees are from the Eocene period 40 million years ago… but since these specimens were highly specialized it is clear that bees arose much earlier. At any rate, the evolution and divergence of bees has been closely linked to that of the angiosperm plants… On the basis of morphological evidence, however, there has been relatively little change in honey bees during the last 30 million years… and the physical resemblance of fossil forms to modern worker bees suggests that complex social behaviour had already developed by the Miocene, 27 million years ago…'
45 Charles-Edwards & Kelly (39).
46 Peck (III. X. 759a, 333). A review of previous theories as well Aristotle's conclusions about this matter can be found on pages 333-46 of the above-mentioned publication. Gojmerac (10) observes that 'Virgil described how to make a hive of cork and suggested it be located in the shade and protected from animals. Through the centuries many others, wrote on the subject, often combining imagination with observations… By not understanding the biology and behaviour of bees, many different kinds of folklore stories developed – some very interesting, others amusing, and a few not far off, based on our understanding today.'
47 NFC 407:370.
48 Winston (8).
49 Kenney (134). I am grateful to my colleague Charles Doherty for this reference. A similar tradition is still current concerning the power of sand drawn from Inishglora (St Brendan's holy island off the Erris coast, County Mayo) to banish rats. Cf. Chapter 5, Note 36.
50 Charles-Edwards & Kelly (4). For a review of beekeeping in 'legend and

story' from the third to the sixteenth century in Ireland, cf. J. K. Watson (1-5).
51 Ibid. (40). For a review of the contents of *Bechbretha*, cf. Watson (6-11).
52 Ibid. (40-2).
53 Quoted in Gimbutas 1982 (181). The European Great Goddess, Gimbutas adds (196-7): 'In her incarnation as a pregnant doe, a chrysalis, caterpillar, butterfly, bee, toad, turtle, or hedgehog… was a symbol of embryonic life and regeneration. In this fundamental notion lies her association with the moon and horns. As a bee or butterfly she emerges from the body or horns of the bull; as a bear she takes care of all young life… In Minoan (non-Indo-European) Crete the Great Goddess is seen in association with bulls, or bull-horns, 'double-axes' (butterflies), he-goats or lions… On a gold ring from Isopata near Knossos the butterfly – or bee-headed goddess is… surrounded by worshippers in festive garments wearing insect masks.' An association between bee and butterfly is observed in the following rhyme -

'A hive o' bees in May,
   Is worth a load o' hay;
A hive o' bees in June,
   Is worth a golden spoon;
A hive o' bees in July,
   Isn't worth a butterfly.'

(NFC 978:71).
54 Gimbutas 1982 (181).
55 NFC 1231:469. I am grateful to Dr Pádraig Ó Healaí for this reference, as also the source of the rhyme in Note 53 above, as well as the reference in Note 56 below.
56 NFC 978: 70-2. According to the A. & B. Rees (136), 'In Celtic tradition, bees have a secret wisdom and hail from Paradise'.
57 Evans (289). An account from Shropshire, records how 'in 1961, a swarm of bees, having been informed in the traditional manner of his death [in the month of January, it would appear], swarmed on the grave of their late keeper a few days later and then returned to their hives that same evening' (*Folklore* 72 [1961], 408 [for which reference I am grateful to Dr Miceal Ross]).
58 *HDA* 1. 1230ff.
59 A. de Vries 1974 (42).
60 *Loc.cit.*
61 Gimbutas 1982 (183).
62 A. de Vries 1974 (42).
63 Gimbutas 1982 (183) who adds that the 'image of the Great Goddess of Life, Death and Regeneration in anthropomorphic form with a projection of her powers through insects and animals – bee, butterfly, deer, bear, hare, toad, turtle, hedgehog and dog – was the outward symbol of a community concerned with the problems of the life and death cycle (195)'.
64 The following section is largely based on Winston (Chapter 12, 199-213) and Gojmerac (Chapter 4, 27-31).
65 *EORE* 9. 650.
66 Cf. Winston (43-4) who describes the process in the following terms: 'The spermatheca holds sperm from the drones which have mated with the queen

early in her life, and nutrients supplied by the spermathecal gland ensure that the sperm will survive for many years... A small... pump and valve leading from the spermatheca to this duct [opening to the spermatheca] allows the queen to draw a minute amount of sperm and seminal fluid into the duct, thus releasing only a few sperm at a time. This is important to the queen, since she will be superseded and killed by the colony when she runs out of sperm. The spermatheca can hold up to seven million sperm... and it generally takes 2 - 4 yr after mating before all of the sperm are used.'
67 Winston (199).
68 *Ibid.* (181).
69 Winston (182).
70 *Ibid.* (187-8) and Gojmerac (28).
71 Cf. Chapter 2, Note 103.
72 A. de Vries 197 (41).
73 Gimbutas 1982 (183).
74 Cf. Chapter 2, Notes 87 and 89.
75 Cf. Chapter 2, Note 93.
76 Cf. Chapter 2, Note 97. Cf. Markey (5-6) who states that Beowulf 'has been seen as an onomastic kenning for 'bear' and thereby connected with *(Boðvarr) Bjarki* a hypochoristic form of *Björn* = 'bear', but is perhaps better seen as 'hero of the honey' = 'bear', that is, 'the rescuer of the honey'. *Bienewulf* (literally 'bee-wolf' meaning 'bee-eater'.'
77 Cf. Chapter 2, Note 91. Marglin (1987b (311-2) states that the 'sacrifice of one's reproductive capacity is symbolically akin to death; the link is particularly clear in the myths of the self-castration of Tammuz, Adonis and Attis, which is soon followed by death. The paradox of general fertility brought about by the sexual fertility of persons who have sacrificed their own fecundity may have to be understood as one symbolic expression of the widespread sacrificial theme of renewed life through death.' Similarly, Cosi (110) notes that 'Recurrences of the castration of Ouranos of early Greek tradition are found in the cosmogonies of other peoples, e.g. the Phoenicians and, perhaps – derived from Christian influences – also in ancient Germanic cosmogony where we find mention in the *Prose Edda* of the "father of everything", a personal entity with creative power who is also called "the castrated" with no further explanation.' Cf. p. 158ff.
78 Buck (192).
79 Hamp 1971 (187).
80 Heiermeier (1. 94).
81 Pedersen (1. 24, 75); cf. also *DIL fochratae-futhu* 241.
82 O'Rahilly 1931 (63).
83 *Ibid.* (64 [footnote]).
84 Collinder 1955 (13).
85 *DIL* G, 9-10. Also worthy of note in this context is the word *kai'ri*, a Sámi name for a dog with a white streak from nose to forehead (H. Grundström, 147).
86 Marstrander 1915 (158).
87 According to Dinneen (506) *gadhar* = 'a hound, hunting-dog, beagle, dog, mastiff'. However, *madadh (madradh)* is also given there with similar range

of meanings. Old Irish *suth*, 'fruit produce; offspring, issue, progeny; milk' (*DIL*, S, 432-3) can also mean 'bitch' (E. P. Hamp, personal communication). In the meaning 'milk', this word is related by Vendryes (S-206) to Sanskrit *sómah*, Avestic *hauma*- thus constituting a possible correspondence '*entre les vocabulaires religieux de l'indo-iranien et du celtique*'.

88 Vendryes (M-6).
89 *Ibid.* (M-24).
90 Cf. pp. 49-50 above.
91 Cf. pp. 27-28 above.
92 *CG* 1, 169. Cf. p. 28 above.
93 *Loc.cit.*
94 *Loc.cit.*
95 *Loc.cit.*
96 Dwelly (3, 962).
97 *Ibid.* (3, 748). I am grateful to my colleague, Dr Seosamh Watson, for this suggestion.
98 Gimbutas 1989 (117).
99 Gimbutas 1982 (185).
100 *EB* 20. 428.
101 Cf. Ó Máille (2. 15, No. 2599). This is still a common saying in Erris, County Mayo. The loan is also recorded as having consisted of *figheachán* – 'weaving' (NFC 191:281) – and as having been tendered by the *gobadán* 'sand-piper' and also the *corr-éisc* 'heron' (rendered by Ó Concheanainn (17-8) as incorporating *riasc* 'marsh' rather than *iasc* 'fish'). Cf. Ó Súilleabháin and Christiansen (AT 234 *The Nightingale and the Blindworm* (54-5) and AT 235 *The Jay Borrows the Cuckoo's Skin* [55)]), the latter generally featuring the wren and the crane as opponents. Cf. Note 12 above.
102 J. F. Campbell 1860 (1. 275). Carmichael tells the story of an oyster-catcher in Uist which 'was so elated with his own growing riches that he thought he would like to go and see something of the great world around him. He went away, leaving his three beautiful, olive-brown, blotched black-grey eggs in the rough shingle among the stones of the seashore. Shortly after he left the grey crow came hopping round to see what was doing in the place. In her peering she saw the three eggs of the oyster-catcher in the hollow among the rocks, and she thought she would like to try the taste of one of them, as a variant upon the refuse of land and shore. So she drove her strong bill through the broad end of an egg, and seizing it by the shell carried it up to the mossy holm adjoining. The quality of the egg was so pleasing to the grey crow that she went back for the second, and then for the third egg. The grey crow was taking the last suck of the third egg when the oyster-catcher was heard returning with his usual fuss and flurry and hurry-scurry. He looked at his nest but there were no eggs there – no, not one, and the oyster-catcher knew not what to do or say. He flew about to and fro, hither and thither in great distress, crying out in the bitterness of his heart, '*Co dh'ol na h-uibhean? Co dh'ol na h-uibhean? Cha chuala mi riamh a leithid! Cha chuala mi riamh a leithid!*' 'Who drank the eggs? Who drank the eggs? I never heard the like! I never heard the like!' The grey crow listened now on this side and now on that, and gave

two more precautionary wipes to her already well-wiped bill in the fringy, friendly moss, then looked up with much affected innocence and called out in deeply sympathetic tones, *'Cha chuala na sinne sinn fhein sin, ged is sinn is sine 's an aite.'* 'No, nor heard we ourselves that, though we are older in the place.' (*CG* 1, 171-2). W. Thompson, observes: 'When a flock of oyster-catchers have been on the wing for a short time, they utter a peculiar brief note, so frequently repeated, that it gives the idea of a general conversation, interrupted occasionally by a whistle of longer duration' (126). For examples of sea-birds' talk in Ireland, cf. S. Ó Súilleabháin 1942 (652-653).
103 Lockwood 1961 (62).
104 Armstrong (28).
105 Cf. Dinneen, 536, Dwelly, 2. 492. *Na Roilligh* 'The Oyster-Catchers' is a name applied to an Erris (County Mayo) family of my acquaintance in an area where other families are nicknamed *Na Cait* 'The Cats', *Na Feadógaí* 'The Plovers', *Na Bulláin* 'The Bullocks', and *Na Rónta* 'The Seals'. The family known as *Na Roilligh* are so called because they live by the edge of the shore.
106 *CG* 1. 171.
107 Lockwood 1961 (62) and de Vries, 591.
108 Lockwood 1961 (62).
109 *Loc.cit.*
110 *Loc.cit.*
111 Cf. 157ff.
112 For a comprehensive review of the range of tradition pertaining to these and many other birds, cf. Armstrong. In Shetland (MacLeod Banks 1946, 47), for example, it was said of crows that at Candlemas 'the lasses' chased them and that in 'the grey dawn of the morning a maid would steal forth and with fluttering heart give chase to the first 'craw' she chanced to see and watch with anxiety the direction to which it flew, for there dwelt her husband to come, and there lay her future home. But should the crow go the way of the churchyard, it was a sad omen, for it betokened that the lass would die an old maid.'

Among the Sámi people, the crow is accorded similar powers: I was told by Ellen Bertha Lindseth of Nesseby, Varanger, in north-east Norway (14 October 1988) that she once lost a sheep for which she searched in vain high and low. She sought advice from a local man renowned for his ability to cure people and he told her to go back home and if she happened to see a crow on the way to follow it. She duly spied a crow, followed it and a short time later came upon her lost sheep. Ellen Bertha's husband, Thomas, also told me that he and other fishermen of the locality firmly believed in following whatever course a crow might happen to set for them when they went fishing on the waters of Varangerfjord. Invariably the crow they followed would lead them to the best place for catching fish. Younger fishermen would laugh at them, but Thomas had seen this course of action proved right again and again.

According to Vendryes (P-14), *préchán*, the Irish word for 'crow' is related to Latin *praesagus*, medieval Latin *praesaga* 'a bird of ill omen'.

Dinneen (860) quotes *préachán* as meaning not only 'crow' but also 'periwinkle' giving as his opinion that this may be a corruption of *faochán*. (cf. in this connection Note 163 below).
113 Ross 1967 (296).
114 *Loc.cit.*
115 Quoted in Green 1992 (160). Barns (453) in discussing various tree-offerings and tree-rites, notes that at the close of the bear-festival, 'the head of the bear is set up on a pole, called 'the pole for sending away' and the skulls of the other animals which are hung up with it are called 'divine preservers' and are at time worshipped' and he adds – 'This is a link with the *bucrania* which form so integral a part in the sacrificial tokens of Aryan worship. Plutarch states that Theseus on his return from Crete put in at Delos, and instituted a dance in imitation of the mazes of the labyrinth: 'He danced it round the altar Keraton which was built entirely of the left-side horns of beasts'. This was known as the 'crane dance' and is certainly in some way associated with the cult of the Celtic tree-god Sucellos or Esus with his three cranes and with the Tarvos trigaranus of the Paris monument.'
116 Green 1992 (214).
117 Cf. Wagner 1964 (301-4) and for remarks on *corr* and its compounds Note 12 above. According to Pokorny 1959 (1. 283-4), Brythonic *garan* 'heron' and Icelandic *trani* 'heron' and *krákr* 'crow' all derive from the root *ger-* meaning 'to cry hoarsely'. Cf. also in this respect Pedersen (1.38); de Vries, 328 and 596 and Hellqvist, *Svensk Etymologisk Ordbok*, Lund 1939 [HENCEFORTH Hellqvist] 1. 517 and 2. 1214. Cf. also Tillhagen 1978 (295).
118 Cf. Note 12 above.
119 Other such names include *Juny an scrogaill* 'Juny of the long thin neck', *Síle raga* 'Dissolute Sheila', and *Nóra na bportaithe* 'Norry the bogs' – Cf. S. Ó Súilleabháin 1942 (290). Interestingly, the first of these names finds an echo in *Jonee Ghorrym* 'Blue Jane', one of the Manx names for the mermaid (cf. Lockwood 1966, 32).
120 Green 1992 (214). For a full analysis of this theme, cf. Ross 1960 (405-38).
121 Cf. pp. 72-73 & 109 above, where I have sought to draw a parallel between Góa of Nordic tradition and aspects of Celtic Brigit. Góa was celebrated in *Góablót* – the sacrificial ceremonies held in her honour but, in spite of the relative frequency with which her name occurs across the Nordic world, she remains a shadowy figure, who in the opinion of Anne Holtsmark is more a personification of the month that bears her name than what she calls the 'fertility sprite' who may have been responsible for having given the month its name in the first place (*KL* 5. 366-8). For all her equivocal status, Góa presents an easily discernible profile in various sayings and traditional rhymes (cf. p. 64 above) where she and her partner, Tor, usually (though not invariably) stand for the months of January and February respectively (Svensson). Góa is also mentioned in sayings such as *Göa goakvinna* ('Göa, good woman') to which is added 'for that is when my sow farrows, my cow calves and we all live so well' (Celander 1950, 17).
122 Celander 1944.
123 Tillhagen 1978 (292-3).

124 Celander 1944 (72).
125 Tillhagen 1978 (287).
126 *CG* 1. 171. Carmichael also records that 'Bride is said to preside over the different seasons of the year and to bestow their functions upon them according to their respective needs. Some call January *'am mios marbh'* the dead month, some December, while some apply the terms *'na tri miosa marbh'* the three dead months, *'an raithe marbh'* the dead quarter, and *'raithe marbh na bliadhna'* the dead quarter of the year, to the winter months when winter is asleep. Bride with her white wand is said to breathe life into the mouth of the dead Winter and to bring him to open his eyes to the tears and the smiles, the sighs and the laughter of Spring. The venom of the cold is said to tremble for its safety on Bride's day and to flee for its life on Patrick's Day. There is a saying:

Chuir Bride miar's an abhuinn	Bride put her finger in the river
La na Feill Bride	On the Feast Day of Bride
Is dh'fhalbh mathair ghuir an fhuachd	And away went the hatching mother of the cold
Is nigh i basan anns an abhuinn	And she bathed her palms in the river
La na Feill Padruig	On the feast day of Patrick
Is dh'fhalbh mathair ghin an fhuachd	And away went the conception mother of the cold.

Another version says:

Chuir Brighid a bas ann,	Bride put her palm in it,
Chuir Moire a cas ann,	Mary put her foot in it,
Chuir Padruig a chlach fhuar ann.' (?)	Patrick put the cold stone in it.

– alluding to the decrease in cold as the year advances. [Carmichael's puzzlement as to the correctness of the Gaelic text in referring to Padruig as having put the cold stone in rather than taking it out, is, of course, entirely understandable.] Similar traditions exist in Ireland as also in Swedish and Finnish tradition (for the latter two, cf. Wikman 1943 (15-16).
127 Paton (3-4).
128 MacLeod Banks 1939 (193). Both in Britain and in Ireland, these three days are most commonly designated the 'Borrowing Days'. In Ireland, however, they are not associated with cranes or other birds, but – as in parts of Scotland – with a cow which foolishly declared that now that she had survived the winter she would surely last another year, whereupon April promptly despatched her with some days of bitterly cold weather borrowed from March. This cluster of days may also be compared, perhaps, with the time of year known in Sweden as *kråknedandet* ('the waning crow-moon'). This was a widespread old description applied to the three days before and after the first of May at which time temperatures were sometimes perceived to register a frosty downswing, without loss of animal life as far as I know. The crow is a migrant bird whose return to the colder parts of Sweden generally takes place in March (when, incidentally, it was believed to be edible) rather than May – that is to say, in or around the same time as the returning crane is scheduled to make its appearance (cf. Nilsson 1921, 48-51).
129 Dinneen, 557.

130 N. Ó Dónaill (ed.), *Foclóir Gaeilge-Béarla*, Baile Átha Cliath 1977 [HENCEFORTH Ó Dónaill], 656. 'The Common Sandpiper is found over the greater part of the Old World. In summer it is the most abundant bird of its kind in the extreme N. of Europe, and it extends across Asia to Japan. In winter it makes its way to India, Australia and the Cape of Good Hope' (*EB* 24. 141). The sandpiper first arrives in Ireland about mid-April and 'is the only common Irish wader which is a summer visitor' (Ruttledge, 98).
131 Dinneen, 557.
132 Hickin (53).
133 Dinneen, 557.
134 *Gobachán* is equated with *gobadán* by Dinneen; *gobadán* is also defined by him as 'the little bird (titling or pipit)' and, in turn, by Ó Dónaill as 'the bird that follows the cuckoo, pipit' where the proverbial saying '*Titfidh an spéir nuair a rachaidh an gobadán i mbéal na cuaiche*' is quoted as meaning 'There will be chaos (literally 'the sky will fall' when the pipit leads the cuckoo' (557).
135 *CG* 1. 168.
136 *Loc. cit.*
137 *CG* 1. 166-7.
138 *CG* 1. 167.
139 Cf. Danaher 1972 (23).
140 NFC 902: 225-6, a questionnaire reply sent in by Peadar S. Mac Fhlannchadha of Ballinagleragh, County Leitrim in July 1942.
141 Cf. p. 19ff.
142 Danaher 1972 (14).
143 Evans (270). Cf. Paton (39 and 137-8) where reference is made to a 'Periwinkle Fair' held on 6 February or Shrove Tuesday.
144 Gimbutas 1989 (263).
145 A. de Vries 1974 (419); HDA 7. 1269. Rawson (14) states that in 'the [shell a] major but rare type of Palaeolithic female emblem the symbolism becomes at once more complex and more abstract, and introduces a common theme in human symbolism which has lasted down to the present day. It is the representation of the shell as emblem of the vulva... shells of all kinds are recognised as vulva-symbols virtually the world over, especially those univalves with deeply involuted pinkish mouths, such as certain varieties of *murex*... Eye-shapes, when schematically rendered, may also be used to symbolize the vulva. In many high societies, the shell is the emblem of goddesses of love and fertility, and even bivalves have taken on this symbolism, e.g. Aphrodite's scallop... the *actual* vulva [is] not meant but the *notional* vulva, i.e. not a human but a spiritual reference. At least some of the Stone-Age peoples, particularly those who knew the sea, must also have recognized that shells came from the sea. And this recognition must have added to the compound image some such further dimension as 'maternal waters...'
146 *EORE* 3. 440.
147 *EOR* 1. 471.
148 *Ibid.*
149 A. de Vries 1974 (419).

150 *EORE* 3. 440.
151 *HDA* 7. 1269.
152 A. de Vries 1974 (419).
153 *HDA* 7. 1270-1.
154 *EB* 3. 409.
155 A. de Vries 1974 (5). Cf. also Brewer (97-8). An account of the Barony of Forth, County Wexford, written about 1680 (*Journal of the Royal Society of Antiquaries of Ireland* 7 [1862-3], 60-1) tells us that the 'Haven's mouth and Barre of Wexford… is innumerablie supplied with divers kinds of wilde fowle… with Barnacles becoming in the month of May so ponderously fatt, that not having activity nor strength to flie, are by the adjacent inhabitants in small boats pursued and taken. They are not produced nor breed in theis parts, are never hardly thence three months absent, yet returning are found to be of the ordinary proportion of equal corpulency. It is the received opinion (as in the Irish History and Scottish description of blacke Geese) that they have their originall and naturall production from pieces of Timber longe remaining in the ocean, and cannot but improperlie be esteemed flesh.' Giraldus Cambrensis in his *Topographia Hiberniae*, protesting against the eating of barnacle geese during Lent, wrote that in Ireland there were 'many birds which are called *Bernacae* which Nature produces in a manner contrary to nature and very wonderful… They are produced from fir-timber tossed about at sea, and are at first like geese upon it. Afterwards they hang down by their beaks as if from a sea-weed attached to the wood and are enclosed in shells that they may grow the more freely. Having thus in course of time been clothed with a strong covering of feathers, they either fall into the water or seek their liberty in the air by flight. The embryo geese derive their growth and nutriment from the moisture of the woods or of the sea, in a secret and most marvellous manner. I have seen with my own eyes more than a thousand minute bodies hanging from one piece of timber on the shore, enclosed in shells and already formed… in no corner of the world have they been known to build a nest. Hence the bishops and clergy in some parts of Ireland are in the habit of partaking of these birds on fast days without scruple' (quoted in Rohde, 259). The existence of a tree whose fruit when it fell into the water beneath it became endowed with new life and converted into a living bird – the 'tree goose' – was a phenomenon commented upon by Saxo Grammaticus and Gervasius of Tilbury, *inter alios*; Pope Innocent III at the Lateran Council in 1215 was persuaded to ban the eating of barnacle geese during Lent (cf. Rohde. 260).
156 *EB* 3. 409; *EB* 26. 905.
157 *EORE* 9. 650.
158 Leeming (273). Ross 1973 in *Rawson* [ed.], 80, reports that one 'of the most fascinating and early fertility figures from the British Isles is the figure, fashioned from ash-wood… [a] fetish christened by the excavators the 'God-dolly'… [which is] hermaphroditic in form… Six inches in height, it has a head, flattish but clearly demarcated breasts and an emphatic phallus projecting from below the left breast.'
159 Eliade & Sullivan in *EOR* 4. 535.
160 Cf. Walde & Pokorny (1. 258) and also Pedersen (1. 24, 75).

161 Walde & Pokorny (1. 258). So also might *uokso-* 'wax', Walde & Pokorny (1. 315). Polomé (1986, 661-2) believes Germanic **wahsa-* 'wax' to be of non-Indo-European origin, a 'technical term associated with apiculture, which may or may not derive from an Indo-European root **weg-* 'weave'. With regard to *fucus*, Walde & Pokorny (2. 184) follows Kluge in comparing it with Anglo-Saxon *béaw* 'cow-fly' both traceable to *bhouq^w ós*.
162 Austeja, the name of the Baltic bee-goddess – a protectress of married women who promoted growth and 'cared for the multiplication of the beehive and the human family' – is 'connected with the verb *austi, austyñ*, 'to weave, to turn about', Gimbutas 1985 (24).
163 *GPC* 25, 1657. Cf. also Marstrander 1910 (395-6). The root *ueg-* also meaning 'to weave', gives us Old Irish *fige* 'weaving, intertwining, plaiting' with similar meaning in Welsh *gweu* and Cornish *gwia*. Middle Irish *fí*, in the meaning 'venom, poison, evil (poetic)' according to Walde & Pokorny (1. 243-4) goes back to **ueis-* which carries various meanings including 'animal sperm, impure juices, poison' is cognate with Welsh *gwyar* meaning 'blood, gore' (Pedersen 1. 73). Hamp 1978 (152-3) in his discussion of the personages Gwion and Fer Fí sees in these names 'an archaic fragment of Common Celtic mythic onomastics'. I am grateful for this reference to my colleague Dr Nicholas Williams.
164 For a description of these ceremonies, cf. Danaher 1972 (19-23).
165 Onions (148). Cf. also Skeat (48).
166 Vendryes (B-9). Walde & Pokorny (2. 159) derives *bairnech* from *bher-*, an Indo-European root meaning 'to cut, bore, scrape, grate etc using a sharp tool' adding the comment that this range of meaning reflects the modest refinement of early Stone Age tools.
167 Rawson (72). Ross 1973 in Rawson (ed.),106, sums up Celtic art as having two forms: 'that of the La Tène phase, aristocratic, cryptic and elusive, and that which it shares with the rest of barbaric Europe, naturalistic, crude, direct. The first may contain allusions to sex and fertility in its flowing curves and sharp, keen angles, but we have no documentation to assist in an interpretation of these forms. The second is concerned with matters fundamental to life and its continuity, with sexual symbolism and fertility emblems – phalli, ithyphallic and sometimes horned men, pregnant women and breast symbols. But the repertoire is limited. We must never interpret as mere erotica images which in these barbarian societies were related directly to their preoccupation with the struggle for survival and hence with their own fertility and that of their beasts and crops.' Among the few examples of 'overt sexual or erotic expression in Celtic art of La Tène phase is the 'phallic stone... of early Celtic date [which] comes from Irlich... in the district of Koblenz – a region where there are many Celtic graves. The stone stood in the vestry of the old church, and was brought into the new church when its predecessor was destroyed. According to local tradition it promoted childbearing' (Ross 1973 in *Rawson* [ed.], 78-9).
168 Ross 1973 in *Rawson* (ed.), 5 to which she adds: 'The fertility powers of water are well-known; the severed head too was believed to be capable of conveying fertility. The combination of these objects was a very potent one. The Celts, like many barbarian peoples, were head-hunters: but the severed

head was no mere trophy of military success. They preserved the heads they took in battle in oils and herbs, and either kept them in wooden chests in their houses, displayed them on stakes around their houses and hill-forts, or set them on pillars in their sacred groves and temples. They also made heads from stone, wood or metals; they must have carried these about as amulets, or as icons portraying some particular deity or power. The archaeology of the Celtic world supported by classical writers testifies fully to this belief in the powers of the head (85-6).'

169 Ross 1973, in *Rawson*, (ed.), 86.
170 *Loc.cit.*
171 Elder (263).
172 '*glans*... an acorn and, in gen. any acorn-shaped fruit, beechnut, chestnut etc... *The glans* penis...' (Lewis & Short, 816).
173 *FW*, 1. 7. It is 'androgyne: I (Holy One) + O (generative crater or cup)' according to A. de Vries 1974 (3).
174 A. de Vries 1974 (3).
175 *Loc. cit.*
176 Elder (263). The acorn was sacred to Thórr, god of fire and fertility (A. de Vries, 1974, 3). *Mesrad Machae* 'Macha's mast' is the suggestive description given to the heads of men taken in battle when offered to 'the highly sexual and awesome raven-goddess, or rather trio of goddesses [Bodb, Macha and the Mórrígan]' (Ross 1973 in *Rawson*, [ed.], 86]).
177 *DIL*, *degra – dodelbtha*, 33-5.
178 Pokorny 1958 (25). I am grateful to my colleague Dr Nicholas Williams for this reference.
179 Hellqvist 1. 5. *Alda* is derived from the Indo-European root **al-* 'grow, make growth, nourish' (Walde & Pokorny, 1. 86-7), a root common to Celtic, Italic and Germanic (Vendryes [A-57]).
180 Friedrich *passim*.
181 Hellqvist, 2. 729.
182 Rawson's reference (20) to the portrayal on a Palaeolithic staff from La Madaleine (Dordogne) of 'a long undulent penis [which is] emerging from a realistic vulva being licked by a bear's head', is not without relevance in this context.
183 Cf. p. 49ff. We may also note here the third eye of the god Śiva – 'The frontal eye that gives him a unifying vision' (Meslin, 239). Meslin notes that Śiva's 'look of fire expressed the pureness of the present with out any other temporal dimension, as well as the simultaneity of beings and events which he reduces to ashes in revelation of the all.'
184 Elder (263) The herm – the phallic image of Hermes the father of Pan – was originally a stone heap, perhaps topped by a large upright stone. In the Homeric Hymns, Hermes is given care over 'all the animals', domestic and wild and is also a god of boundaries (cf. Elder (264-5).

Haloa was a festival of Demeter and Kore which was celebrated in Eleusis in mid-winter on dates ranging from 18 December to 14 January, in the month Poseidon (December/January) at the pruning of the vine and the tasting of the stored-up wine. It was performed by the women at Eleusis and the heart of the ritual which it involved is described as follows by Arethas of

Caesarea (quoted in Chandor, 108-9): 'In these rites images of male organs are displayed, concerning which they say that they are performed as a symbol of the procreation of men, since Dionysos, who gave the wine, made it a potion which stimulates one to intercourse. He gave it to Ikarios, whom the shepherds killed, in ignorance that drinking wine had such consequences [i.e., they thought they had been poisoned]. Then they were driven mad because of their outrageous actions against Dionysos, and they committed mad acts on this shameless image. The oracle to stop their madness, ordered them to make and dedicate clay sexual organs. When the evil had passed, they established this festival as a memorial of the incident. In this festival an initiation is given in Eleusis by women, and many games and jokes are told. Since only women are present, they have freedom to say what they want. And they say the most shameful things to each other then; the priestesses stealthily draw near to the women and discuss illicit love, whispering, as it is something unspeakable. All the women shout shameful and irreverent things to each other, holding up indecent representations of male and female bodies. Here much wine is set out, and tables full of all the foods of mystery, except the things forbidden in the mystery, namely: pomegranates, apples, domestic fowl, eggs, sea-mullet, erythynos [a fish], blackfish, crayfish, dogfish. The archons furnish the tables and leaving the inside to the women, they go outside and continue to demonstrate to all the inhabitants that cultivated foods were discovered among them [the Athenians] and made common to all men by them. Sexual organs of both sexes, made from pastry, are set out on the tables. The Haloa are named on account of the fruit of Dionysos. The aloai are the vine-shoots.' Cf. further, Chandor (124, 131).

185 Elder (264-5).
186 The Irish word *cos* means both 'foot' and 'leg', thus leaving accounts of the various fire-carrying incidents open to a more delicate interpretation. A Kerry account of a fire-carrying female – sister to St Gobnait (and alter ego of Brigit) – is a little more forthright in declaring *'gur dheas an dá cholpa coise a bhí aici'* i.e. 'that she had a fine pair of calves' (NFC 947:51).
187 Holmberg 1914 (798). Bäckman (1987b, 498) adds in reference to the bear-hunt: 'The man who found the bear in the hibernating den led the group: 'the drummer' went immediately after him, followed in a predetermined order by those whose duty it was to kill the bear. When the animal had been downed, the hunters sang songs of thanks both to the quarry and to Leibolmai ('alder-tree man'), who is variously described as the god of the hunt or the lord of the animals, but was, most importantly, the lord of the bears.'
188 Bäckman in Fjellström 1981 (49-51). The blood-red alder-juice may be compared, perhaps, with the reddish 'bee-juice' (cf. *fucos*, p. 115 above) with which bees stop up the entrance to their hives. It is interesting to note that, in preparation for hibernation, the bear evacuates its bowels completely, retaining the last pieces of excrement, however, which harden and block the rectum. On emerging from hibernation, the bear seeks out and eats Arum, a plant containing an acrid poisonous juice – consumption of which brings on a bowel movement (Dokken 37). Williams (1993, 37) lists a range of names in Irish and other languages for *Arum maculata* adverting to the

penis and sexual intercourse. He also notes that Giraldus Cambrensis (drawing on Aristotle) refers to its efficacy in relation to restoring bears to normal function following hibernation (37):

'Beares after they have lien in their dens forty dayes without any manner of sustenance, but what they get with licking and sucking their own feet, do as soone as they come forth eate the herbe Cuckowpint, through the windy nature thereof the hungry gut is opened and made fit againe to receive sustenance: for by abstaining from food for so long a time, the gut is shrunke or drawne so close together, that in a manner it is quite shut up.'

189 Dyrenkova (418-9). Dyrenkova also tells us that: 'For security of the house, the Yakut hang the bear's skull on a tree near it... The Chelei clan (Shortsi) fasten the bear's head on a pole among the beehives, turning its snout towards the hives that the bees may steal the honey from the neighbor's beehives. For the same purpose, some use bear's claws, suspending them under the hives (431).' Similarly, Chichlo (84) informs us that the 'most important detail of the Tunguz bear ceremony, which has an explanation in their religio-mythological perception of the world, is the way in which they handle the bear's eyes. Hunters, having cut off the head of the slain beast, take out its eyes with great care, seeking to touch them neither with a knife nor with their fingernails. then they wrap the eyes in grass or birch bark and carry them away into the forest, where they place them high in a tree. The Udege did this in the hope that the bear's eyes might be illuminated by the first rays of the rising sun. In the tabooed language of Tunguz hunters the bear's eyes are called ōsikta ('stars')'.

190 Chichlo (84).
191 Loc.cit., to which he adds: 'The connection of the bear with heavenly luminaries is well illustrated in a Tunguz myth in which the bear, named Mangi, follows the reindeer or moose who had stolen the sun. Having caught up with his prey, the bear returns the sun to its place. Both protagonists in this myth form the constellation of Ursa Major, the Big Dipper in Tunguz cosmology...'
192 Ross 1973 in *Rawson* (ed.),86.
193 G. Nagy (126). Perhaps the arguments put forward in this article may justify a reassessment of Polomé's dismissal (1989, 139) of Nagy's hypothesis as being 'based exclusively on etymological material without mythological support'.
194 *KL* 4. 398.
195 G. Nagy (122).
196 G. Nagy (123).
197 *Loc.cit.* Tintinnabulation, or the ringing of church bells to turn away advancing thunderstorms, was once a common practice all over Europe and 'Norse bells were also often marked with the bent cross, the hammer of Thor, the Thunderer' (*FW* 1. 133-4).
198 *Loc.cit.* Rawson (11) suggests that 'if... Palaeolithic peoples did not isolate in their idea of generation the semen as alone responsible for fertility – which seems most probable – they may have identified the male contribution to the propagation of offspring as having to do with the active friction of the male organ inside the female. There is a good deal of evidence to suggest

that this was so, both in anthropological reports and, for example, in an ancient Sanscrit text which analogizes conception with the fire produced by a hardwood rubbing-stick in the slot of a softwood stick...'

199 *FW* 2. 1100.
200 *KL* 20. 395.
201 *Loc.cit.* Cf. Markey (8) who states that: 'in late pre-historic times, Thor was demoted to the status of an intermediate deity, partially representative of the warrior class and partially of the peasantry (fertility function). He was then popularly associated with the belated harvest festival *Thorrablót*, celebrated at the beginning of Thorri = mid-January to mid-February... Then, too, he was the one deity who continued to be celebrated in the *folkeviser (Torekall, Toreliti og Skakjelokk)*. He is also the only deity whose name is collocated with *-úlfr/-ólfr*, i.e. *Thór-úlfr/-ólfr*, a name that is even widely attested runically: Torpe and Aals, Hallingdal; Fyrisdal; Isle of Man.' *Thór-* is also combined with *björn* ('bear') in the name Thórbjörn and the latter element also occurs in the compound name Arin-björn , literally 'hearth-bear' (cf. Nordseth (1-2).
202 Celander 1931 (73).
203 *Loc.cit.*
204 *Loc.cit.* According to Alekseenko (in *Diószegi* [ed.],182), the Kureika Ket had a custom 'of taking the youngsters on the bear hunt. While skinning the bear, the hunter cut out a bit of the heart, dipped it in blood, and the boy to whom it was given ate it and said: 'You are strong, my father who brought you down is stronger than you; I shall be still stronger, my heart will be stronger than his'.'

The use of a lye made from vegetable ash (sometimes supplemented by urine) as a common detergent is documented in Ireland from earliest times. It was used in washing hair and possibly also in bathing and as a cleaning agent for finishing woollen cloth. An early Irish law tract, cites as being free from fine: 'the ashes of every hearth except sea ashes' i.e. *múrluath* – the ashes of burnt seaweed – which functioned as unrectified salt in curing meat, mackerel, seal meat, sea fowl and cheese (Cf. Lucas 1965, 94 ff.).
205 Celander 1931 (75).
206 For a review of the various names by which this ceremony was known and notice of its earliest occurrence, cf. Wikman 1929 (206-7). The expression *torebrende* ('*tore*-burnt') used of cows which shed or lose their hair is also noteworthy in this context (Solheim, 345).
207 Ordéus 1975 (152).
208 Ordéus 1975 (155).
209 Celander 1931 (62).
210 Celander 1931 (65).The essential elements of the ceremony are summarized by Celander under four headings – 1) The ritual drink (supplied by the woman of the house) and the participation of all the members of the household in making an offering to the fire by drinking its health. 2) The throwing of ale and/or food and ale in the fire. 3) The utterance of a formula (whose purpose is to ensure that the fire remains within the confines of the hearth and thereby poses no threat to the house). 4) Divination by tossing the bowl (and by a variety of other means).

211 Nilsson 1936 (274).
212 Wikman 1929 (200).
213 Wikman 1929 (213).
214 The Norwegian 'red rooster' (= fire) may be equated with Carmichael's cockerel mentioned above (Chapter 2, Note 98) and its 'oblation' seen as a token that fire would not pose a threat to house and home.
215 Significantly, everyday invocations of this kind regularly invoked the Virgin Mary, for example, *Jag fäster denna ild i glö, såvist som Jungfru Maria var mö* 'I fix this fire aglow, as sure as the Virgin Mary was a maid'. [–Feilberg 1899 (70 *footnote*)].

Mary's name also features prominently in a wide range of prayers and charms recited to protect cattle against the depredations of marauding animals by causing their jaws to lock fast so that they might never close upon a likely victim. [– Cf. Chapter 2, Note 18.] Likewise, she might also be invited to use her power not to lock but to open in such sayings as *Jomfru Maria! Lån mig noglerna dine, at jeg må åbne lænderne mine!* 'Oh, Virgin Mary! Lend me your keys, that I may open my loins', a prayer said by Scandinavian women in childbed. [– *KL* 11. 368.]
216 Cf. Wikman 1929 (206) and cf. also de Vries, 39 and Hellqvist, 1. 122. Fire has been thought of in many cultures as a living entity, especially a female being (Wikman, *loc.cit.*). Cp. also the Irish term *máthair tine* 'mother fire' (Note 10 above).
217 Bø 1974 (179).
218 Quoted in Celander 1931 (72).
219 Celander 1931 (70).

—Chapter 4—

Atá Bó agam ar Shliabh...
Booley and Baile

Atá bó agam ar shliabh,	Upon the mountain brow,
Is fada mé 'nna diaigh,	I herd a lowing cow,
A's do chaill mé mo chiall	(And my sense is gone now
le nódhchar.	through a maiden).
D'á seoladh soir (a's) siar,	I drive her east and west,
A's gach áit a ngabhann an ghrian,	And where'er the sun shines best,
No go bhfilleann sí aniar (san)	To return with her white milk
tráthnóna.	laden.[1]

THE LEGEND OF A GIRL about to be kidnapped from a mountain *buaile*, henceforth referred to as 'booley' (its Hiberno-English equivalent) or transhumance site who frustrates her would-be captors by transmitting in verse (or by means of a tune) a signal concerning her plight which results in her rescue has been assigned Type Number ML 8025 by R.Th. Christiansen in his *The Migratory Legends*. It is of rare occurrence in Ireland[2] and together with some other legend types (e.g. ML 6000 Tricking the Fairy Suitor and ML 6045 The Drinking Cup Stolen from the Fairies) also shares the distinction of being largely confined to a fairly restricted area in the north western corner of County Mayo.[3]

This legend type is also listed by Stith Thompson as a Romantic Tale, AT 958 *The Shepherd Youth in the Robbers' Power*,[4] and in that guise was analysed by Robert Wildhaber in a study published in 1975.[5] His diligent enquiries unearthed versions from all over Europe, but failed to draw a positive response from Ireland. Wildhaber found this story to be especially common in three widely separated areas – the Nordic countries (particularly Norway, Sweden and Finland), Switzerland and south-east Europe (Rumania in particular).[6] He concluded that though the story showed a range of special characteristics within these areas and that while no continuous pattern of distribution was manifest, nevertheless the evidence pointed towards the existence of a common European tradition with origins lying in northern

Europe.⁷ In fact, by the time his study appeared, a cluster of Irish versions of this type had been already collected, while a few more examples were destined to be yielded up by the living tradition of Ireland in the years that followed. None of this Irish material, however, came under scrutiny by Wildhaber nor have the scholars who followed him taken account of it.⁸

A Mayo storyteller, Peadar Bairéad (1900-79) of Stonefield in the Barony of Erris, has been the source of no less than three of the eleven Irish versions of this legend which are now available to us.⁹ The first of these was taken down from Peadar in 1952 by a next-door neighbour of his, Micheál Ó Sírín, who was also a full-time collector with the Irish Folklore Commission (NFC 1230:251-4); in or around a quarter of a century or so later, it was my privilege to collect it from him again in 1975 (NFC Tape SÓC 37/1) and also in 1979 (NFC Tape SÓC 100/1), just a few months before he died. Peadar's rendition of ML 8025 on the latter occasion may well prove to have been its Last Hurrah in Ireland. The three versions taken down from him are fairly close to one another and they, in turn, resemble in all essential details the other seven versions which have been collected in the province of Connacht (six of them from County Mayo). The remaining Irish version dates from the mid-nineteenth century and stems from the booley country around Slievenaman on the borders of counties Kilkenny and Tipperary. It takes the following form:

> *Aodh beag, Aodh beag na buaile seo,* ¹⁰
> [Little Hugh, little Hugh of this boley,]
> *Téirse abhaile is fuagair, fuagair,*
> [Go home and announce, announce,]
> *Go dtáinig aoinne déag ar a gcuaird chugham,*
> [That eleven have come to visit me,]
> *Le haghaidh luach ma mbó seo,*
> [In order the price of these cows,]
> *A dh'fuadach uamsa !*
> [To steal from me !]

The Kilcash Farmer and the Band of Robbers – the foregoing words were played on a Jews-harp by the farmer calmly and seemingly unconcerned, on seeing eleven men enter his house at a late hour and shortly after his return from a fair where he had sold a lot of cows. He and his wife assumed, as it were that the suspicious visitors were wayfarers, and invited them to partake of refreshments. The mountain dew was liked by each, and was the means of delaying them until sixty armed men from the Castle and surrounding homesteads surrounded the house and made prisoners of the villains. Little Hugh ran first to his parent's house, and soon the alarm was spread. The farmer's name was Mr Richard Lawless, and the maiden name of his wife was Jane Moore...

This telling is not without its shortcomings and – as my colleague, Dr Dáithí Ó hÓgáin (who first drew my attention to it) has pointed out to me – would seem to have been confused with the circumstances of a local robbery. While its survival retaining the crucial Irish language verse message in this latterly largely English-speaking area is noteworthy, it does not bear comparison with, say, the following Mayo version (given here in English translation). This was taken down by another full-time collector formerly active in north and west Mayo – Tomás a Búrca of Portacloy. His informant in 1940, Áine Ní Chabhail (56), was a near-neighbour of his.[11] This is how she told it:

> Long ago, though, indeed, not so very long ago, they used to kidnap women. Well, perhaps there wasn't all that much of it going on in my time but it was quite common only a little before that. Sure, I often heard the old people talking about it but as with many another thing I believe we didn't pay much heed to what they were saying. Many a story we heard if we could only remember them. But I remember this one after a fashion at least. I often heard the old people telling it.
>
> Do you see, in those times, if a man came to seek a wife and the woman wasn't satisfied to go with him, well, he would just come and take her – make off with her some other night. Many a time they didn't even bother to ask for her hand at all, especially if they were of the opinion that they were unlikely to get her in the first place.
>
> You might think that a woman who would be carried off like that by a man would not stay with him, but she would. There was no point in her coming home. No other man would ever ask to marry her and at that time no woman wanted to be left on the shelf. I think they don't care much nowadays or maybe they're just pretending. But in those days when a woman had been kidnapped it was just as well for her to stay put. Indeed, it was.
>
> Well, there was a house a short distance from Cornboy they called the booley and there was a young girl living in it. There was a child in the cradle and a young boy as well – his name was Aodh, as you'll see.

This night, the people of the house were away visiting in Cornboy and only the girl, the child in the cradle and Aodh were left at home. Shortly after nightfall, a man came to get her and he had four other men with him. She bid them welcome and never let on that she knew fine well what had brought them there. But she didn't miss a bat. She made ready some food for the men and she seated herself by the cradle soothing the child. She began to sing to the child and this is what she sang:

> 'Rise up Aodh and leave the booley,
> [Go to the homestead and raise a host;][12]
> Say that a kidnapping is under way,
> Four, five, a hound and a boy.'

She was putting a tune to that, as you might say, soothing the child. She put the business about the hound and the boy in it so that the people who were eating at the table would not understand it. They were totally unconcerned about it.

But Aodh was equal to the occasion for he picked up on it pretty quickly. He just grabbed a can and out he went. They thought he was going for water and took no further notice of him. But as soon as he got out he fairly took to his heels and made all haste to Cornboy where all was revealed. As soon as they heard the news they made for the booley as fast as they could, together with a band of men from Cornboy. They routed the kidnappers who were forced to depart empty-handed.

But wasn't the young girl clever to think of it! Many a person wouldn't, but more than likely would find their heart going to their boots if such a thing were to happen to them. And don't tell me that the lad that was able to make sense of what she was about wasn't every bit as clever as she was!

In stark contrast with the Irish situation, this legend is both well-known and widely distributed in the Nordic countries; Reidar Christiansen, for example, had no less than 116 Norwegian versions[13] at his disposal on which to base the following synopsis:

> In a certain place (A1), a girl (A2) was staying alone when a band of robbers (B1) arrived, took her captive (B2), and/or killed the animals (B3). She defended herself by throwing boiling milk at them (C1). Blinded, they tried to stop her, grabbing at her skirt, but she managed to slip away (C1a). She finally had to give in (C2), but was allowed to sound her cow-horn once more (C3). Being an expert player (D1), she was able, in this way, to send a message to her people (D2) which they could understand (D3)... In the meantime, she climbed up in a

tree which the robbers were sawing through (D4). The people down in the valley heard the sound and understood the message (E1) so that assistance arrived (E2) and the robbers were caught or killed (E3).

The rescue message cited by Christiansen goes as follows in translation:

> *Till, till Tove* [14]
> Twelve men in the forest
> Twelve men they were
> Twelve swords had they
> They thrashed the herd boy
> They stabbed the great ox
> They bound the belled cow
> They hanged the watch dog
> They threw the bell up in a tree
> They stole the farmer's cattle,
> *Till, till* little lad
> Hurry to the forest, help me home
> They want to take away the cattle
> They want to take me too
> High up on Dovre mountain
> Now the spruce is half cut.[15]

This story was no less well-known in Sweden – in fact it has been characterized by Bengt af Klintberg as being the most popular robber story in Norway and Sweden[16] and Christiansen tells us that there 'is ample evidence of the wide circulation of this story from every part of the country [Norway], and the tale is generally told in explanation of the verse which is still more widely known… No song is heard as often as this in the woods and hills of the North.'[17] To give something of the flavour of the Scandinavian versions of it, here in translation is a short Swedish example quoted by af Klintberg, including a form of the message which was broadcast by the female under threat, a verse which af Klintberg implies also led a more or less independent existence as a herding song and as a lullaby:[18]

TWELVE MEN IN THE FOREST
There was once a girl who was herding cattle when twelve scoundrels bent on raping her emerged from the forest. So she climbed a tree

breaking off the branches as she went so that they could not follow her. Then she blew on her horn:

    Tilili logen,   *Tilili logen,*
    tolv man i skogen,   Twelve men in the forest,
    vallhunden hängde de, They hanged the watch dog,
    skällkoa sprängde de,   They killed the belled cow,
    löskoa drevo de,   They drove off the stray cow,
    å mej ville de våldtaga. And they want to rape me.

At the place where this happened, just west of here, they cleared a meadow which is still called 'Twelve-man Meadow'.[19]

In Ireland, Norway and Sweden, most frequently it is the girl in the booley who is the object of desire.[20] However, in the Finnish versions of which there are more than one hundred, according to Wildhaber[21] (most of them stemming from an area straddling the Finnish/Russian border) it tends to be a shepherd boy who fills this role, a change of gender which along with the emphasis on a background of border quarrels and ethnic disputes may be taken to be the main distinguishing feature of a second Nordic redaction.[22] The following is an example of the rescue message as it occurs in Finnish versions:

    Turun lurun come here
    There's a bear on his back
    The big bull was killed *(/ the black bull was murdered)*
    The bell cow was cut
    The cattle dog was hung
    The cow bells were cut
    The cattle are taken
    (The shepherd) is taken on his last journey *(/is strung up in a noose)*
    Hurry, hurry up now.[23]

In many of the versions of AT 958 quoted by Wildhaber, heavy stress is laid upon the role of altercations between warring neighbours, intercommunity strife and sectarian frictions and also on the predominantly brigandish nature of the encounter between the parties, all scenarios which are conducive to a blurring of the significance of the gender element insofar as it is it would seem to matter little in such circumstances whether it is a male or female herd that is threatened and robbed and that subsequently transmits the message which eventually frustrates the attackers.

We may conclude that Scandinavian versions of our legend exhibit a closer affinity with the Irish versions than either the continental European or, within the wider Nordic context, Finnish versions of ML 8025.

The summer pasture setting is a feature which this legend type shares with the versions of AT 958 treated by Wildhaber for various parts of central and southern Europe as also with the Nordic versions of ML 8025 discussed by Christiansen, af Klintberg and Leisiö. A striking feature of many Irish versions of this legend type is their richness of detail concerning the setting; in the case of the telling by Áine Ní Chabhail quoted above, for example, strong emphasis is placed on explaining the nature of courtship by capture, once a common enough custom in Ireland.[24] In other Irish versions quite detailed descriptions of the mountain 'booley' or summer pasture, the actual physical setting for our story and the work carried out there, figure prominently.[25] It is appropriate that it was in the context of his treatment of the custom of booleying that Caoimhín Ó Danachair should have drawn attention for the very first time to the existence of stories belonging to this legend type in Irish tradition.[26]

In addition, we may observe that this legend generally tends to occur in the context of stories concerning abduction of humans by fairies. Indeed, on the occasion when Peadar Bairéad's last telling of it was recorded from him, this followed hard on the heels of a story which he told about a girl stolen away by the fairies whose boyfriend failed to carry through a plan for her rescue from fairyland: there the girl imprisoned in the fairy mound managed – like her female counterpart in ML 8025 – to provide her would-be deliverer with the information which would enable him to effect a rescue operation and secure her release, though all to no avail on that occasion.

Transhumance and abduction (whether by fairies or others) constitute two of the important background elements for Irish versions of ML 8025. These belong together, of course, for summer pastures by their very nature tended to be located in isolated out-of-the way places, in some cases, even being disposed in or near areas reputed to have strong otherworld associations.[27] In such mountainous and – apart from their intermittent use as booley sites, generally deserted places – various forms of wild life thrived and the potential hazards posed by certain animals constituted an element which also had to be taken into account.[28]

The practice of booleying survived into the 1930s and 1940s on Achill Island, County Mayo, as we know from Pádhraig Ó Moghráin's valuable treatment of this subject.[29] Ó Moghráin stressed the need that was felt for protection against marauding wild animals, noting *inter alia* the desirability of the booley having its own dog to guard against attack from man or beast:

> He [the farmer] had to have the cattle guarded from thieves and wolves and what was just as important, he had to have them kept from going back at night to the tillage, where they might endanger his chance and their own of surviving the coming winter. This would mean the presence of boys and dogs on the pasture ground.[30]

Interestingly, Ó Danachair, in noting that wolves 'survived in some remote areas well into the eighteenth century', observes in more or less the same vein that 'the tale is told in several places of the killing of 'the last wolf in Ireland' in a summer pasture.[31] The extensive cliffs bounding the north Mayo coastline contain a tradition-rich, wild and beautiful countryside (in which the bulk of Irish versions of ML 8025 happen to have survived) where, not surprisingly, traditions of the *madar alla* ('wild dog' or 'wolf') have also been preserved. Here we stumble across a werewolf legend which, to the best of my knowledge, is the only one of its kind known in Irish folk tradition. The following, in English translation, is a version of this legend which I recorded from Peadar Bairéad in March 1975:[32]

> Have you ever heard tell of this story '*Tá mé gan Murchadh gan Mánas*'?[33] [*lit.* 'I am left with neither Murchadh nor Mánas'.] Well, this is what is behind that.
>
> Murchadh was a man, he was a tailor who lived over in Belderg along the coast out beyond a place they call Glinsk. He was a tailor [weaver][34] and lots of people used to go to him with flannel, with yarn to have tweed made. It was all looms at that time.
>
> Well, anyway this evening as it grew dark who should come to his house but a soldier and he asked for a drink of water. He gave him a drink. 'Aren't you going to stay till morning?,' said the woman of the house. 'No,' said he – he had a hound and a gun with him – 'I'm heading west to Erris (That's our place here, where we are now). 'Well,' said the man of the house, 'if I were you I wouldn't go back that way, they say there's a wild dog there,' said he, 'which comes down from the

hill and kills a lot of people.' 'Oh, what harm would the wild dog do to me? – (The 'wild dog', that's a wolf) – 'haven't I got a hound!' 'And if your hound was to let you down,' says he, 'what would you do?' 'Well, I have a gun,' says he, 'I'd shoot him.' 'Suppose,' says he, 'your gun were to fail you,' says he, 'what would you do?', said he. 'Well', says he – he thought a bit – 'well, I'd call on my grandmother', says he, 'who is living back at the far end of Erris. It is often she helped me when I was in the [battle-] field in the West Indies.'

The man didn't know at that point who the grandmother was.

The soldier left and the man of the house watched him as he went out the door. He hadn't travelled far – back by Tanaí Mhór he went – till he saw a dog making for him down the slope of the hill, a huge big white dog. He set his hound at him right away. The hound wouldn't budge. He had cast a charm on the hound. He tried the gun but the gun jammed and he wasn't able to fire it. And just when the dog was about to leap at him, he pulled a dagger from his belt and stabbed him clean through the belly. And when he stabbed him, the dog tumbled over on his back and turned into a man.

He just abandoned him there and went back to the house he left and when he got back there, the woman of the house was sitting within by the fire and she was astonished to see him step in. 'Oh,' said she, 'didn't I think,' says she, 'that you headed back,' says she, 'to Erris!' 'Well', I did,' says he, 'but I wanted to come back with the news that I have killed the wild dog of Tanaí Mhór.' 'Oh, God help us,' says she, 'I am left with neither Murchadh nor Mánas.' He was called Mánas Ó Murchadh. 'And was that your husband?', said he. 'Well, it is,' said she, 'and you've killed him,' said she. 'Well', says he, 'it would take very little for me to make me kill you too,' says he, 'for many a person he killed.'

They used to go to him with yarn, to have flannel made and when he got, when they paid him and were on their way home, he would appear before them having turned himself into a dog and he would kill them on the mountain. And many a man lies dead and buried on that mountain that that wild dog did for.

And that's the meaning of the story – you've often heard *'Tá mé gan Murchadh gan Mánas'* – 'I have neither Mánas nor Murchadh'. That's Mánas Ó Murchadh that used to kill the people. He was a weaver. But the soldier finished him off, he did away with him. And the number of people that that wild dog killed has left many a death cairn on that hillside. And that's the story and all there is to it is that I am explaining to you the meaning of the words 'Mánas Ó Murchadh' – the wild dog of Tanaí Mhór long ago.

Versions of this legend can still be heard in this part of Mayo. In his tellings of it, my friend John Henry of Kilgalligan puts the crucial response which the marauding weaver/wild dog failed to grasp as follows: *'Ghlaofainn ar mo mháthair mhór thiar in Iorras'* ('I would call upon my grandmother back in Erris').[35] Similarly, Scottish versions of this legend have the soldier protagonist declare – 'I will try my mother's sister [i.e. his dirk] on her', or the like.[36] We may also note here in passing the Irish riddle – *'Sin í suas mo mháthair mhór agus srón iarainn uirthi'* ('There's my grandmother with her iron nose') – for which the standard answer *'gunna'* ('a gun') is recorded,[37] thus equating with a weapon the maternal ancestor or relative to whom reference is made.

This werewolf story turns on the bafflement of the ill-intentioned Mánas Ó Murchadh by the soldier's final enigmatic response under close interrogation. The purpose of the information tendered in this instance is total obfuscation: the clear intention is that there should be little or no possibility for any successful decoding of it. Failure to perceive the real meaning of this reply ultimately causes the wild dog to be killed, when the treacherous assault is finally launched and Murchadh's human identity is revealed. Similarly, failure to comprehend a coded message in ML 8025 – also the issue upon which that particular story turns – results in the thwarting of a kidnapping attempt and the routing of the evil-doers. Interestingly, both these stories feature a largely redundant hound *(cú)* cast in what appears to be an entirely passive role.

In the werewolf legend, we are dealing with a relatively straightforward process concerning the delivery of an item of intelligence deliberately couched in such terms as to positively discourage correct interpretation. Also relevant to an understanding of the core element of ML 8025, namely the successful transmission and instantaneous unilateral comprehension of the rescue message, is the situation where the quick-witted delivery and the equally swift deciphering of ambiguous statements containing a play on words combine to save the skin of certain Irish rapparees who found themselves in imminent danger of capture. The successful interpretation by these daring individuals without the law of the real meaning of veiled messages, usually delivered by sympathetic servants or the like in the presence of would-be captors, invariably enables them to make good their escape. A typical example of a statement of this kind would be *'caith fuar agus te'* (lit. 'eat cold and hot') which sounds identical to '*caith fuar agus teich*' (lit. 'shoot cold and flee'), the latter rather than the former being, of course, the appropriate line of action best suited to the circumstances in question.[38]

As with the rapparees, the central exchange in ML 8025 is quite an elaborate affair, involving not one but two potential receiving parties with the added complication that, quite unambiguously in the Irish versions of the legend at least, the true import of the information transmitted *must* be understood by one of these while simultaneously being misunderstood or altogether ignored by the other. The following story set in the heart of the wild boglands of north Mayo employs more or less the same device, the robbers on this occasion, however, being cast in the role of dolts and dullards:

> [John Tiernan] told me that when his ancestors had to fly from the North [of Ireland] with his family and live-stock he settled first in Tawney Con, building himself a house there. This Tiernan had two or three sons and a daughter, who was a beautiful girl. One day when the old Tiernan and his sons were away back in Devlin or Cross, a party of men came to the house. Tiernan's wife suspected that their purpose was the abduction of her daughter, but disguising her feelings, she made the visitors welcome, and proceeded to put down a portion of a sheep to cook to feed the visitors and then going outside she blew a bugle or 'war horn', as Mr. Tiernan called it, telling her visitors that her men were away and although she did not expect them home she blew the horn to inform them that the dinner was ready if they were anyway near. When the Tiernans heard the war horn they were back at the shore at Roonith or Cross; they cut across the mountain as quickly as possible, and arrived at the house where Mrs. Tiernan was putting the meat on the table for the meal. When her men entered, taking a *scian fada* [a long knife] for each of them, she armed her husband and sons and told them to 'cut' and they, taking the hint, attacked the visitors and routed them…[39]

The dimwitted villains of this piece rather than expediting their mission with all speed, condone the creation of a thoroughly unnecessary and dangerous delay, during which space of time an emergency signal is broadcast, on top of which, with disastrous consequences for themselves, they fail to appreciate the significance of the ambiguous and somewhat heavy-handed delivery of the hint to 'cut' subsequently uttered within their hearing.

Svale Solheim in *Norsk Sætertradisjon*, his classic description of traditions associated with transhumance in Norway, records similar accounts which he argues form part of the real-life background out of which legend types such as ML 8025 grew.[40] In these Irish and Norwegian accounts, pretty well all the ingredients that go to make up ML 8025 seem to present themselves – the arrival of 'robbers' on the scene, the presence of a vulnerable desirable female, the creation of a distraction and a contrived delay, the delivery of the signal and later the message and, finally, the rescue. The setting in the example quoted above is not that of the booley site, of course (though it is no less isolated) and the signal and the message are separate communications. The main factor distinguishing accounts such as this from versions of ML 8025, however, is the fact that it is the female under threat of kidnapping who effectively engineers her own rescue and not some third party; this and the precise manner in which this feat is accomplished and, most important of all, the special form and wording of the rescue message is what lies at the heart of the matter and it is to these issues we must next direct our attention.

* * *

Áine Ní Chabhail in the course of her telling of ML 8025 was at pains to highlight the extraordinary presence of mind, ingenuity, nimble-wittedness and bravery of both the girl and her brother Aodh. Her version also introduces the motif of an infant child lulled to sleep by the crooning of the secret message, thus constituting a distinguishing feature of one of the two Irish redactions of this type.[41] In line with the Nordic versions, the second Irish redaction substitutes virtuoso musicianship for the infant child and lullaby motif; the girl's capacity so to entertain and beguile her kidnappers as to facilitate through the medium of her music clandestine communication with her brother Aodh is strongly emphasized in most of the Irish versions.

Either way, the object is, of course, for the message to be conveyed without raising any suspicions about its contents. However, buying time, so to speak, by seeking refuge in a tree and broadcasting the message quite blatantly from a (temporarily) safe position on high would also appear to be a factor which plays an important role in the Nordic versions.[42] In order for a surreptitious delivery of the message to have any chance of success, it would require the communication to be simultaneously capable of attracting attention and sufficiently transparent for it to be understood by the person at whom it was being directed. At the same time, taking into account the likelihood that it would run the risk of being overheard, the message must needs remain unremarkable enough not to excite the interest of the kidnappers and, in the event that it did so, sufficiently obscure to defy any effort made to interpret it. Even if it was unlikely to be capable of instant interpretation and immediate application in the context of this overall tense situation, the unusual wording and composition of the *ex tempore* lullaby, which, we may take it, was likely to have been repeated over and over again, would have been sufficient, one would have thought, to have succeeded in raising at least an eyebrow or two among an audience of jittery kidnappers. Such does not appear to have been the case, however.

A different set of problems arises where the message is said to have been conveyed using a musical instrument – i.e. by playing a tune to which an appropriate set of words was subsequently fitted by the recipient. Here the difficulty of explaining the serendipitous existence of a suitable tune to which an apt and applicable form of words were suddenly fitted all of which was so constructed as to be capable of unilateral recognition and interpretation on the part of the individual at whom it was aimed, yet by none other, has to be faced. The tune might also have come complete with words already, of course, either a set of words known and used only within the intimacy of the immediate family circle and, on that basis, judged unlikely to lend itself to ready comprehension by outsiders, or a set of words possessing some currency in the wider community, but which, for some reason or other, remained unfamiliar to the kidnappers. Communication, even 'conversations' between individuals or groups by means of musical sounds broadcast over considerable distances was common in the context of transhumance, not least in the Nordic world. There is evidence even for the existence of sophisticated codes of communication which may have extended to accommodating a degree of *ex tempore* composition.[43] The occurrence of such a medium or the possible uses to which it might be put would have been unlikely to have been entirely beyond the ken of the kidnappers. Perhaps, it might not be out of place to speculate here that the Nordic storytelling tradition has sought to resolve this difficulty by introducing the 'safe refuge in a tree' motif. One way or another, the successful operation of this artifice in the context of ML 8025 would seem to stipulate an unacceptable level of compliance on the part of the band of robbers.[44]

The dubious workings of these devices constitutes a problem the reality of which has not escaped some of the collectors and storytellers insofar as they exhibit a tendency to equivocate about the circumstances surrounding the apparent inability of the kidnappers, a bunch of grown men, to interpret the verse or tune sung or played by a slip of a girl, a process which miraculously seemed to pose no problems whatsoever for her young brother. As one source puts it:

> It may be asked why did the raiders act their part when they heard the words of the lullaby and seize and carry off the girl, instead of allowing themselves to delay and be captured. Surely in those days of over a century ago, there was scarcely any one in Mayo who did not understand Irish. It would be a different matter if the girl sang in English, as in that case it would be naturally assumed that the raiders did not understand English and hence their frustration. The explanation is that the wording of the song was so paraphrased and disguised that the raiders did not understand its implications or meaning, until they were late, but the boy Hugh must have been a bright and intelligent lad to grasp so quickly the hidden trend and significance of the lullaby. Folktales of the locality to this day give the words of that short famous lullaby as uttered by the moorland peasant girl of over one hundred years ago.[45]

However, despite the astute efforts of this Mayo commentator to rationalize the deficiencies of the case, the argument remains less than fully satisfying. In turning elsewhere in search of a more convincing solution to this dilemma, we could do worse than ponder more closely the wording of the rescue message as it has come down to us and to concentrate on some of the issues surrounding its deeper meaning and origin.

* * *

Elsewhere, I have described ML 8025 as belonging to a complex of fairy legends involving *fuadach* ['kidnapping'] and tentatively suggested that, along with types such as ML 6000 and ML 6045, it might ultimately find its place of origin in Scandinavia. Irish versions of these latter types, it was argued, exhibit what would appear to be the classic characteristics of peripheral versions, principal among these being the loss of the rhyme or verse central to the plot, as was shown to be the case with ML 6000.[46]

All the Irish versions of ML 8025, however, come fully equipped with a verse, which circumstance immediately signals the absence of one of the principal hallmarks of peripheral status. Not only that but the verse in question rather than taking a degenerate form based, perhaps, on some distant original model is clearly of independent composition and, as is the case with regard to the various Nordic versions, there is also evidence pointing towards its having a stable and, at least in part, a long-established form.

Despite their differing formulae, however, the purpose and the end result of the messages contained in the Nordic and Irish rhymes remain identical. Perhaps, it may be possible to go further and argue that, different as they may appear at first glance, these verses also ultimately share a common source of inspiration which is older than the particular set of circumstances with which they have become associated in the latter-day context of this legend type.

Let us then consider briefly one or two aspects of the wording of the rescue message. The first thing to note is that the formulation of the phrase *'fág an bhuaile agus téirigh chun an tseanbhaile'* finds a number of interesting echoes in older Irish literary texts as well as in the Brehon Laws: seventeenth-century Irish historian, Geoffrey Keating, uses this same terminology metaphorically on no less than three occasions, opposing 'the *buaile* to the *seanbhaile*' in a manner which leaves no doubt, as Lucas has it, 'that the latter refers to the permanent dwelling and the former to the temporary summer settlement on the hills'[47] the expression *ón mbuailidh gusan senbhaili* occurs in *Cath Finntrágha*, of which we have a text dating to the latter half of the fifteenth century but which was already in existence in some form in the twelfth; further back in time again, we find reference in the Brehon Laws to 'throwing open the enclosed grass of the permanent dwelling *(senbaili)* at *Samhain* (November 1st)', the implication being that the land was kept fenced until that date.[48] This would seem to leave room to find ample precedent for the form of exhortation used in the rescue message urging an exit from the *buaile* in the direction of the *seanbhaile*.

Chapter 4

One of the most significant of the older sources from our point of view is *Broccán's Hymn*, an Old Irish text dated to the eighth or early ninth century, which contains the following puzzling verse:

> When the first dairying was sent with the first butter in a hamper. It kept her not from her bounty to her guests; their attachment was not diminished.[49]

'A good commentary' on this verse, as Pádraig Ó Moghráin points out, 'which not only makes clear much of what is dim in *Broccán's Hymn's* puzzling allusions, [but which] is further valuable as a description of the work carried out on an *airge* [i.e. summer pasture][50] at that remote period' is the well-known story of the multiplication of the butter told in the prose lives of St Brigit:

> Brigit's mother was a slave to a druid. Brigit went once to visit her on a mountain-side pasture and found her suffering from a sore eye. She took her mother's place at the dairying leaving the herd to the druid's charioteer. Although warned by the charioteer she should store the butter, as every dairy-maid did, Brigit insisted in distributing the butter to the poor, saying: 'It is hard for me to take Christ's food from Christ.' The result was that, when the druid and his wife came with a hamper for the butter, Brigit had only the produce of a churning and a half. Still the hamper was filled, and the druid and his wife, who seem to have had some knowledge of how Brigit had been distributing their property, were so struck by the miracle that they freed Brigit's mother without asking a price, and became Christians.[51]

Brigit's association with cattle, milk and milk products is strongly marked in Irish folk tradition and is also the subject of much comment in her various *vitae*.[52] In addition to these affiliations, we see established in this instance an explicit early connection between Brigit and the practice of booleying. The phrase 'a series of miracles of folkloric interest',[53] used by one commentator in the course of his treatment of the seventh-century *Life of St Brigit* by Cogitosus, is no understatement for her *vitae* as a whole are choc-a-bloc with such material. It is not possible to touch upon this subject in any detail here other than to say that wild animals (including wolves), robbers, fire and love potions are among the many fascinating topics earmarked for attention; as one would expect in such a context, ever present also, of course, is 'the evangelical counsel of virginity...'[54]

We have already seen how the combination *'fág an bhuaile agus téirigh chun an tseanbhaile'* finds interesting echoes in the older strata of Irish literature. The girl in the booley in enjoining her brother to 'rise up' *('Éirigh a Aoidh...')* also identifies him by name *(Aodh)* and in doing so spotlights a salient name in the annals of *fianaigeacht*, and one whose meaning 'fire' also calls to mind a prominent figure of classical mythology, namely, Hestia (Vesta).[55] She, as one of the twelve great gods and goddesses and the oldest of the Olympians, was worshipped as goddess of the domestic hearth which 'represented personal security, happiness and the sacred duty of hospitality'.[56]

Hestia is etymologically and otherwise the same as Vesta; she is 'the Goddess of the Hearth and in every private house and city hall protects suppliants who flee to her for protection.'[57] Like Brigit, she resisted every amorous invitation offered her and chose to remain a virgin, 'bright and pure like the flame which is her symbol',[58] and like Brigit too she came to be regarded at the same time as standing for 'idealised maternity'.[59] A series of remarkable connections with hearth and fire which pervades the body of tradition surrounding Brigit has already been discussed above.[60]

Fionn mac Cumhaill in the oldest literature, as Gerard Murphy points out, 'is constantly being given for his main enemy... *an Aed* (modern spelling *Aodh*)...'[61] In this Murphy considers that we may well be seeing nothing new for 'looks very like the old superhuman fire-opponent of the most ancient stratum of the literature, and of the folklore, in a different form.'[62] A number of interesting parallels with our ML 8025 is also revealed in what Murphy calls 'The Story of Aed mac Fidaig (Fidga)' the main structure of which is outlined by him as follows:

> A maiden lives in a fairy-hill... Someone is interested in her (lover, father)... She has many wooers... The wooers are slain, or ill-treated in some way, by the person interested in the maiden... A wooer, connected in some way with Finn (friend, father), is killed by the person interested in the maiden... on *Samhain* night... in connection with feasting... Finn kills, or robs of his fairy hill, the man interested in the maiden, who was responsible for the death of Finn's friend, or father... Finn uses the spear of Fiacail mac Conchinn... The killing is followed by lamenting and utterance of poetry by a woman...[63]

The identity of Finn's otherworld enemy – Aed – is revealed in the lament from the fairy mound which is penetrated by the spear of one bearing the name *mac Conchinn* – 'son of dog-head', circumstances which remind us of the utterance of the girl in the booley in ML 8025, on the one hand and the story of the soldier with his dog and knife against the werewolf, on the other.

The picture still remains somewhat hazy, but, perhaps, we know enough at this stage to say with some degree of assurance that twentieth-century Irish manifestations of the legend type here under investigation must surely seek their derivation through descent at least as much from an early native wellspring, both oral and literary in character, as from any putative Scandinavian source. Neither may it be going too far to suggest that impulses relevant to the theme in hand might just as easily have radiated in the opposite direction with Gaelic tradition exercising an influence in the formation of Scandinavian, particularly Norwegian, versions of this legend. At worst, it may be claimed that analysis of the small corpus of Irish versions of ML 8025 now available to us provides a new perspective on the Nordic material extending even to possible clarification of some elements of it which have hitherto defied successful interpretation. I refer here in particular to the so-called 'nonsense words' – *'Tilili logen'* and the like – by which the rescue message in the Nordic versions is sometimes introduced.[64]

It may not be amiss in this context to seek a parallel between the opening syllables of the Nordic rescue message and the initial words of the Irish rescue message – *Éirigh a Aoidh* – and, with 'fire' in mind, to extrapolate therefrom the possibility of a not inappropriate reference to Loki.[65] The arguments advanced by Moberg and others in favour of seeing a reference to Thórr,[66] another figure of Nordic mythology and folklore with a number of interesting fire associations[67] in the closing words of some of the Scandinavian rescue messages (*'Till Tor i fjäll'* – 'To Thórr in the mountains' – and their inclination to interpret this as a kenning for the kingdom of the dead (which have been reviewed and resoundingly rejected by af Klintberg)[68] may also take new sustenance from the Irish evidence.

* * *

The transfer *'ón tseanbhaile chun na buaile'* – a movement from the homestead or permanent dwelling to the temporary abode in the summer pastures – generally took place in May with the return trip being made some time in the autumn. These movements to and from the mountain booley more or less coincided with and, indeed, may even have been signalled by the risings of the constellation Orion and the Pleiades (early in summer and late in winter).[69] In other words, the regulation and timing of the all-important aspects of farming husbandry relating to tillage of the home acres on the one hand and grazing of the mountain pastures on the other was associated with the appearance of certain stars and their position in the heavens. This connection stretches beyond annual patterns of behaviour based upon routine celestial observation in relation to the seasons to embrace a highly significant system of nomenclature which *inter alia* leads into the oldest layers of classical tradition. This is a circumstance which has profound implications for our understanding of the real meaning of the rescue message of ML 8025 as we know it in Ireland and elsewhere.

As it turns out, some of the heavenly bodies mentioned above are called by names which bear witness to their association with pastoral, dairy and other practices. The Pleiades (a small cluster of stars in the constellation of Taurus), for example, are known in Mayo Irish as *An Bhuaile Bhodach*;[70] elsewhere they are called *An Tréidín*,[71] the latter meaning 'The Little Herd' and the former possibly to be translated as 'The Penis-y Booley'.[72] In similar vein, Orion's Belt is called *Fjósakonur* 'The Byre-Women' in Icelandic[73] (and The Little Bear, *'Fiosakonur á lopti'*, 'The Milkmaids of the Sky'[74]). Mainland Scandinavian tradition, however, choses to emphasize another aspect of traditional craft and industry typical of booley culture by dubbing Orion's Belt *Friggetenen* or *Friggerocken* (Sweden), *Rok-Stjernen* (Norway) or *Mariarok* (Denmark),[75] names which refer to the spinning-wheel and which also variously advert to the Nordic goddess Frigg and the Virgin Mary. We may be justified in concluding that the association of female figures of such moment as Frigg and Mary (a later medieval substitute for Frigg in the Nordic context)[76] with this constellation is not without its own special significance. When we add Brigit replete with her special spinning and weaving affinities to the list,[77] the potential complement of *dramatis personae* in our legend type assumes rather more august dimensions than might be supplied by the humble presence of a mere 'moorland peasant girl' and her little brother Aodh.

The Pleiades make an early showing in astronomical literature, appearing in Chinese annals of 2357 BC; pictured as a flame they are also connected with Agni, the Indian god of fire.[78] Hesiod called them the Seven Virgins and they have long been familiar to many peoples under the name the Seven Sisters, 'a numerical title also frequently... applied to the brightest stars of the Great Bear'.[79] Their Sanskrit designation, Riksha, according to Allen, 'signifies, in two different genders, 'a bear,' and 'a Star,' 'bright,' or 'to shine,' – hence a title, the Seven Shiners, – so that it would appear to have come, by some confusion of sound, of the two words among a people not familiar with the animal.[80]

Two names for them found among the Sámi people, *nieiddagærreg* or the like (signifying 'a gathering of girls') and *miesse tsjora* meaning 'a group of reindeer calves'[81] rank comfortably alongside the Icelandic 'Byrewomen' and the Irish 'Booley' and 'Herd' names mentioned above. In Finnish tradition, the Pleiades were accounted 'young and beautiful maidens highly skilled in spinning and weaving, – a story originating from a fancied resemblance of their rays of light to a weaver's web'[82] while among many of the remaining Finno-Ugrian and other peoples of north Eurasia, they were likened to a sieve.[83]

In relation to Orion himself, classical sources recount his marvellous birth, his hunting exploits accompanied by his dog Sirius, his amorous pursuit of the Pleiades, his rape of Merope, daughter of Oenopion, who took revenge by putting out Orion's eyes, his eyesight being subsequently restored by his travelling towards the sun, and his eventual death at the hands of Artemis, to mention but some of the traditions which attach to him.[84] H. J. Rose characterizes the legend of Orion's persistent pursuit of the Pleiades as 'one of the few stories in all mythology which we may definitely trace to an astronomical source' and he argues concerning the legends surrounding Orion in general that 'no one great poet or group of poets ever put forth a version which imposed itself on the world at large, hence the popular local legends often told no doubt by country folk... remain to us more or less in their original shape'.[85] Interestingly, the constellation Boötes (connected, perhaps, with *bous* /βους),[86] the Bear, Orion, the Hyades, the Pleiades and the Dog 'were the only starry figures mentioned by Homer and Hesiod...'[87]

Orion, Sirius and the Pleiades, then, were perceived as being connected with animal husbandry, particularly the management and herding of cattle or other domesticated animals in mountain pastures, on the one hand, while the image of Orion, on the other, was also that of the passionate hunter whose boast was that he would exterminate all wild beasts. ML 8025, with its setting of transhumance and mountain pastures, and backdrop of abduction and marauding wild-life, mirrors these seemingly contradicting circumstances to quite an extent.

Leisiö, quoting the popular Nordic tradition that the bear was thought to possess the strength of twelve men and the wisdom of ten, goes on to claim that 'the twelve men in the forest' of the ML 8025 rescue message is nothing less than a metaphor for the bear and avers that 'the purpose of the story and the adjoining song seems to be in the protection against the peril of the bear, [along with] the wolf the worst enemy of the cattle.'[88] The origins of this interpretation are first traced, then vehemently opposed by af Klintberg who rejects the notion of 'twelve men' functioning as a kenning for 'the bear'; he roundly declares that 'more than one hundred Swedish and Norwegian versions of the legend bear unambiguous witness to the fact that the primary meaning of 'twelve men in the forest' is twelve robbers.[89] It may be ventured, perhaps, that the evidence adduced here has rendered it a tad more difficult to lend credence to af Klintberg's case against the 'bear' interpretation.

Doubts about the correctness of seeing a single bear metamorphose into twelve robbers, however, are ultimately dispelled, I believe, by a widening of the focus on this animal to take account of the extraordinary story of the Bear Wife. Various Nordic cultures yield accounts in which vivid expression is given to the nature of the intimate relationship between a human female and a male bear as the exposition of the relevance of the story of the Bear Wife to the celebration of the festival of Brigit has shown.[90]

We may also invoke an account given by Saxo Grammaticus as further corroboration of the validity of postulating an equation between the bear and twelve 'villains'. His story concerns a group of Norwegians – all brothers and twelve in number – who, in opposition to Halvdan, the King of Sweden, engaged in wholesale killing and pillaging before being subdued eventually. Saxo goes on to say that the names of five of the brothers had been forgotten, but that the remaining seven were called Gerbjørn, Gunbjørn, Arnbjørn, Stenbjørn, Esbjørn, Thorbjørn and Bjørn – all of which names, of course, contain the element *bjørn* meaning 'bear'.[91] Interestingly, the latter brother and chief among them, Bjørn, was said to have possessed a huge, fierce and terrible dog, a veritable beast of prey most dangerous to humans, which on its own and on numerous occasions had disposed of twelve men. This dog was said to have once been the favourite dog of Offote, the giant, and to have guarded his cattle when they were put to graze.[92] It would seem possible that the common source of inspiration behind ML 8025 (given that such can be presumed to have existed in the first place) must have included elements and ingredients of the bear cult that was once prevalent over much of Europe.[93]

The complement of the robber band in the Kilkenny/Tipperary version quoted at the outset was stated to be eleven (...*go dtáinig aoinne déag ar a gcuaird chugham*). This probably represents an approximation of the arithmetic inherent in the remaining Irish versions in which the final line of the message could easily be construed as indicating the raiding party (including the dog) also to have been eleven in number (*'Ceathrar, cúigear, cú agus buachaill'* – 'Four, five, a hound and a boy'). Leaving aside other possible permutations by which the total human personnel of the Irish versions could be rounded up to twelve (say, by counting the girl in the booley and her brother along with the nine men and a boy) we may simply note that the *'Ceathrar, cúigear'* ('Four, five' [= nine]) combination is mirrored in the account given in the *Life of St Brigit* by Cogitosus 'Of the Nine Very Wicked Men Vowing Bloodshed'[94] and, by the same token, in the following anecdote from the same source, we may, perhaps, detect an echo of the popular estimation of the strength of the bear as being equivalent to that of twelve men:

> There was a very strong man, in fact the strongest of men, Lugaid, whose bodily strength was so great that he could perform the work of twelve men by himself in one day whenever he wished and likewise could eat food enough to feed twelve men. Just as he could do their work on his own, so also he could match several men by eating the same amount of food as they. He implored her [Brigit] to beg the Lord almighty for him to moderate his gluttony which made him devour excessive food without losing the pristine strength of his body on that account... And so, Brigit blessed him and prayed for him to

the Lord and thereafter he continued to enjoy the same strength as before, doing the task of twelve workmen, as he used to previously, while being satisfied with the food of one man.[95]

* * *

By way of summarizing the outcome of this investigation of the content of the rescue messages in the Irish and Nordic versions of ML 8025, perhaps, our probings may be claimed to indicate that, at the very least, there are grounds for believing their wording to contain a good deal more than meets the eye at first glance. The possibility of substantiating an interpretation other than that which satisfies scholars while leaving doubts in the minds of the storytellers may also be said to have hoven into view: in essence this entails looking upon the rescue message, not as a simple straightforward S.O.S., but rather as an invocation or charm. This is the kind of existence it may have maintained down through the ages, previous to and independent of the legend format now familiar to us, being thus a formula – to borrow Solheim's description of charms used as protection against bears and other wild animals – which must be as old as transhumance itself.[96]

This examination of ML 8025 has exposed something of the intricate nature of the legend type itself as well as the background of the tale field to which it belongs. The existence of a complex skein of relationships within and between the Irish and the Scandinavian as well as other branches of European folk tradition upon which an earlier common tradition endowed with elements of the very oldest stratum of European culture may have exercised a bearing has also been exposed. And through the tenacity with which oral art survived in an isolated corner of Ireland, we may have been lucky enough to catch a whiff of ancient gods and goddesses and savour something of the ageless ingenuity of man.

Notes to Chapter 4

1 Hyde 1895 (114-5).
2 Christiansen 1958.
3 For a discussion of these legend types cf. Ó Catháin 1991 (145-159). ML 8025 has been described by one of those who collected it in this part of Mayo as being 'known generally throughout the locality' (NFC 1242:316).
4 Aarne & Thompson (340).
5 Wildhaber (233-56). For a review of Swedish 'robber' tale types (including ML 8025), cf. Tillhagen 1975 (713-725).
6 Wildhaber (234ff.)
7 Wildhaber (249).
8 The only versions not already available in print at that juncture were the two Mayo versions recorded by me in the 1970s and the nineteenth-century Prim Mss. version.
9 These are NFC 1230:251-54, NFC Tape SÓC 37/1) and NFC Tape SÓC 100/1 (all in Irish), the latter appearing in English translation in Ó Catháin 1991(153-5). The earliest of the seven Mayo versions – also in Irish – can be found in NFC S130:225-6, being part of the Schools' Manuscripts Collection made by pupils of Porturlin N.S. in 1937-8. Next in line is an Ediphone recording made on 1.6.1939 by full-time collector Liam Mac Coistealbha from Micheál Ó Corrdhuibh (Michael Corduff) of Rossport (transcribed in NFC 625:465-8) and subsequently published in *Béaloideas* 16 (1939), 269-70 (not *Béaloideas* 14 as stated in Ó Catháin 1991, 156). The same Michael Corduff also contributed three further versions – NFC 1242:314-6; NFC 1243:13-5; and NFC1461:79-82 – all rendered by him in English out of the local Irish-language tradition (in which connection cf. Ó Catháin 1991, 148). The remaining Mayo version which is quoted here in English translation (NFC 713:286-9) was contributed by Tomás a Búrca who collected it on 12.10.1940. The only other Connacht version – also in Irish – stems from county Galway where it was collected in 1931 (NFC 62: 218-9) from Micheál Mac Donnchadha (Páidín) of Cárna by Seán Mac Giollarnáth and later published by him in *Béaloideas* 10 (1940), 31-2. The last of the eleven Irish versions to be mentioned here is in English (apart from the verse recue message) and is quoted above; it is contained in the Prim Papers (NFC) and was collected in the period 1864-70. It is, therefore, the oldest Irish version of the legend known to us. The verse and the accompanying explanation of it are given here as published in Ó hÓgáin 1981 (99-100).
10 '*na mbó seo*' is the reading given in Ó hÓgáin 1981 (99); Dr Ó hÓgáin informs me that he would now wish to emend this to '*na buaile seo*'.
11 NFC 713:286-9. This and other translations here from the Irish are by me unless otherwise stated. The Irish-speaking communities of Portacloy and Stonefield (where Peadar Bairéad lived) are separated by less than a kilometre of wild mountain bogland in which lies a place called *An tSí Ruaidh* – the location of Peadar's tellings of ML 8025. Áine Ní Chabhail told the collector that she had heard this story from old people of the

locality. The special atmosphere and extraordinary intimacy of its narrative style may be due to the fact that the storyteller, being a woman, felt a special empathy with the subject matter of the story.

12   This line, which is found in all other Mayo versions and which is missing here has been supplied by me on the basis that its omission is likely to have been either a slip of the tongue on the part of the informant or a slip of the pen by the collector.

13   These are quoted by Wildhaber (246) as being 117 in number.

14   Parts of the verse rendered in italics here and in the other Nordic versions quoted below indicate what are generally taken to be nonsense words (but cf. in this context, p.161 above).

15   Christiansen 1958 (215-6). The stratagem adopted by the girl in climbing a tree to blow her horn (sometimes breaking the branches off behind her as she made her ascent) which is a feature of Nordic versions of the legend is here adverted to in the last line of this verse.

16   af Klintberg (242). According to Tillhagen 1975 (722) – who also notes the existence of Danish versions of this type – there are 57 versions of this legend; Wildhaber (248) makes reference to two Estonian versions as do Aarne & Thompson, *loc.cit.*

17   Christiansen 1958 (215).

18   af Klintberg (242). Solheim (286) also singles out the rescue message in verse as being the essential core element of this story remarking that it has been known in Norway from at least the middle of the sixteenth century. Wildhaber (247) states that the earliest Norwegian version of this legend type dates from 1743.

19   af Klintberg (242). The oldest Swedish version known to us dates from 1600-1601. For an English translation of a Norwegian version, cf. Simpson 1988 (58-9).

20   Moberg's (93) observation that 'everywhere in Europe the people on the dairy-farms [= booleys] were and still are men, whereas in Scandinavia – according to folk tradition – they were mainly women' , is of relevance here insofar as it further validates the propriety of bracketing Irish and Scandinavian versions of ML 8025.

21   Wildhaber (248).

22   Leisiö (7-9); cf. also Wildhaber *passim* and af Klintberg (244).

23   Leisiö (12). The punctuation and spelling have been slightly altered by me. The reference to the 'bull' here referred to here may be of significance in the context of my remarks on p. 162ff.

24   For an account of this practice in late eighteenth-century Ireland, cf. 'Ireland Sixty Years Ago', *The Dublin University Magazine*, No. 121, Vol. 21, 737-742.

25   Cf. Ó Catháin 1991 (152-6). Cf. also *ibid.* Chapter 1, Note 47.

26   Ó Danachair 1983-4 (39). Ó Danachair notes that the practice of transhumance was 'very common in Ireland up to the nineteenth century... and memories or traditions of it are known from no less than twenty-five of the thirty-two counties [of Ireland].' It seems unlikely, however that Irish transhumance – even in its heyday – could match the intensity with which this custom was practised in Norway where, according to Solheim

(396), throughout that country in the year 1907 no less than 44,000 sites were in active use. The widespread persistence of the practice there long into this century, as Professor Bo Almqvist has pointed out to me, has probably contributed in no small measure to the comparative abundance of Norwegian versions of ML 8025 as compared with their relative rarity in Ireland.

27 For example, Peadar Bairéad's tellings are set in a place called *An tSí Ruaidh*, a spot frequently referred to as being full of fairies *(sí)*. Whereas many Irish booley sites lay within easy daily reach of the homestead, in the Nordic context, the summer pastures might lie a distance of thirty or forty kilometres or more away.

28 Ó Danachair 1983-4 (39). Solheim (229-287) devotes an entire chapter (V) to this topic.

29 Ó Moghráin 1943 [1944], (161-172) and cf. also Ó Moghráin 1944 [1945], (45-52). Séamus Ó Duilearga provides us with the following account of an Achill booley in a diary entry entitled *Some notes on my travels for 1941*, under the date June 15 (published here by kind permission of Mrs. Caitríona Miles):

'Seán Mac Pháidín of Dooagh, a lame cobbler, came with me to the west side of Sliabh Mór and from there we walked on the old track at the foot of the hill to a spot immediately above McDowell's Hotel. We visited a number of houses which are still used as *buaile* houses during the month of June. Most of these are owned by the people in Dooagh who keep them in repair and others are taken by people from Duniver and The Valley *(Tón an tSean-bhaile)*. We visited two of these latter houses and in an instant I was back 1000 years – that is precisely how I felt. The house was small – a single room about 20 feet in length and about 7-10 feet in height. Inside were four grown up girls lying on a *sráideog* or palliasse on the floor, and an old woman seated on a large block of bog-deal beside a primitive fire-place consisting of a stone placed about 2 feet from the gable on which the fire was made; at the back of this and on two sides of the fire-place were other stones (four in all incl. hearthstone) about 6-8 inches in height. Room spotless. At back a small hand churn and a number of wooden vessels containing milk and cream. Old woman from Duniver – spoke Irish to us. She told us that they hire the house for a month (June) and come here with the cattle which graze on the slopes of Sliabh Mór, milk them and make butter, the butter and cream and milk being sent down to their homes in Duniver a couple of times a week in *pardógaí* or side-baskets on horseback. The old-time *buaile* in Erris and elsewhere could not have differed much from what I saw today. Closer by was a stream and in a ferny and mossy recess on the track was a well. As we left a tall and very beautiful young girl came out to the well for water – she completed the picture of the *buaile* which I think I shall always remember...'

30 Ó Moghráin 1944 [1945], (51-2).
31 Ó Danachair 1983-4 (39).
32 NFC Tape SÓC 37/1. Peadar Bairéad's telling of this story on this occasion,

was followed immediately by a rendering by him of ML 8025, the first time I had heard him tell it. In Sámi tradition, wolves were thought of as being 'the shaman's most powerful helping animals' and the shaman was believed to be capable 'of both metamorphosing into a wolf and transforming dead beings into werewolves so as to bring harm to people and damage their possessions' (Pentikäinen, 133).

33 This is a fairly common proverbial saying meaning to be entirely deprived of any option or resource. From Armagh, Ua Muirgheasa 1907 (182-3), cites *'Gan Mághnus gan Tadhg'* 'Without Manus or without Teig – without either Codlin or Short'.

34 Peadar Bairéad actually said *táilliúr* 'tailor', but as is apparent from the context clearly meant to say *fíodóir* 'weaver'.

35 The action is located by him and other storytellers of the district in a townland called *'Leacht Murch'* [*anglice* Laughtmurrogh] and an attempted explanation of the name (i.e. 'the [death-] cairn *(leacht)* of *Murch*' forms part of the narrative. Examples of such stories can be found in NFC 528: 402-4; NFC 1230:197-203; NFC S130:205; NFC S139: 51-2 and 400-3.

36 J.F. Campbell 1890 (2. 110-2). I am indebted to my colleague, Dr Seosamh Watson, who has provided me with a version which he collected in Easter Ross as recently as 1983.

37 Cf. Hull & Taylor (21, No. 156).

38 For a fuller account of the above and other stories of rapparees, cf. Ó Catháin 1982 (7-21).

39 O'Dowd (288-9). Séamus Ó Duilearga adds a note saying that he has 'a version of this story from Ballycroy, Erris' and he further directs the reader to Seán Mac Giollarnáth's version of ML 8025 published in this same volume (p. 31-2).

40 Solheim (281-5).

41 It appears that singing also had a similar role to play in some of the Norwegian versions (Christiansen 1958, 216).42

42 The environmental circumstances pertaining to Norway and the western coastal and other upland areas of Ireland differ radically; the former boasts abundant afforestation extending even to quite high levels of altitude, while the latter can be bare of trees to the point where it was once reported that a native of Erris – where most of the Irish versions of ML 8025 have been collected – on seeing 'for the first time in his life a tree, fell down and worshipped it as something super-earthly' (O[tway], 259).

Trees, or rather the stage of growth and the size of the leaves of various kinds of trees, played a specific role in Norwegian transhumance in helping to determine the timing of the transfer of cattle to distant summer pastures in as much as the likelihood of there being sufficient grazing for the animals in the mountains was measured by the level of growth achieved by tree leaves at lower levels (Solheim, 20). These ecological factors undoubtedly account for some of the obvious differences between Irish and Norwegian versions of ML 8025, particularly the 'safe refuge in a tree' motif which, in view of the arguments adduced here, it might now be possible to classify as a secondary development and, in the context of explicating the mechanics of conveying the rescue message, which may be accounted a not altogether necessary requirement, not to mention one which ultimately tends to complicate rather than clarify the issue. In other words, the question of 'buying time', which also enters into Irish versions of ML 8025 but in much less dramatic form, has here become entangled with the artifice of confusing the opposition by means of music and song. These disparate devices actually constitute the distinction between two separate types according to Solheim (285).

43 Cf. Erixon (31-64). and Moberg (53-61). Moberg (55-6) casts severe doubt, however, upon the possibility of anyone being able to play on a horn a rescue message as complicated as that of ML 8025, but notes that this instrument lent itself to being employed with great effect as a megaphone by which means the amplified words of the rescue message – sung or spoken – could be broadcast over a considerable distance. I am grateful to Dr Dáithí Ó hÓgáin for the following reference which serves to illustrate that Irish tradition can also lay claim to similar skills of communication: 'There are two Norman castles on the river Funshion in the neighbourhood of Kilworth – one of them at Cloghleagh on the north bank, near the village, and the other in Ballyhindon on the south bank, about a half-mile further west. There were a number of prisoners in each castle, and one of each group was a piper. The pipers were so skilled that they could send each other messages through their music. The piper yonder sent the question to the piper here: *'Conas 'táthaoi [conas 'táthaoi, conas 'táthaoi istigh ansan?'* 'How are ye [how are ye, how are ye in there?' Back came the answer *'Táimid [is táimid go huireasbhach. Níl greim le n-ithe againn, níl braon den uisce againn. Tá trí thriúr dár muintir tar éis bháis ó inné!'* 'We are, and we are, and we are in deprivation. We haven't a bite to eat, we haven't a drop of water. Three times three of our people have died since yesterday! …' (Ó hÓgáin 1994 [258-9]) and for the verse and musical notation: 203).

Trumpets and other such wind instruments were widely used to scare away wild animals, especially bears (cf. Solheim, 261ff.) and Moberg 94). Moberg *(loc.cit.)* in noting that 'the inarticulate sounds of the pipe (lur) and the horn were supposed to frighten away the wolf and the bear, whereas melodical instruments and call song attracted them' describes the "background of this idea among Swedish country people' as being 'an old conception of the importance of the cry and the megaphone instruments as magical means of incantation'. The primary purpose of horns and trumpets as a means of scaring off wild animals which posed a threat to farm stock is revealed by names such as *björnlur/varglur* 'bear-horn/wolf-horn' and *björnskrämmare/vargskrämmare* 'bear-frightener /wolf-frightener' (Moberg, 53). The differing effect on bears of melodical instruments on the one hand and megaphone instruments on the other is aptly illustrated in an account by Å. Campbell 1948 (156-7) of a young Lapland goat-herd who, Campbell tells us, carried a horn made of pine bound with bark and a whistle made of *Angelica archangelica*: during the mating season for bears, on coming across their spoor or otherwise detecting their presence, he blew his horn in order to frighten them off; on occasions when bears were known to be in the vicinity he dared not play his whistle because of the attraction which its music held for them. Cf. p. 68 above.

44 One Finnish version offers the rather lame excuse that the shepherd boy's playing was so beautiful that that 'the robbers did not understand what he played' (Leisiö, 9).
45 NFC 1461:82. Cf. NFC 770:51-3, for an account from this same part of County Mayo of the *ex tempore* composition of verses to the tune of *Is óró mhíle grá* a practice indulged in by women in order to pass the time while spinning. Cf also in this context, Ó Catháin 1991 (152-3, including notes 13 and 14).
46 Ó Catháin 1991 (149-151).
47 Lucas 1989 (65). The text in *Trí Bior-ghaoithe an Bháis. Séathrún Kéitinn do sgríobh* (Bergin [ed], lines 4102-4107, p. 129) reads as follows (words relevant to booley etc. in roman):
'*Is trés an nguais se do bheith i gcionn an duine fhoráileas Críost ar na daoinibh* imirce na haithrighe *do bheith urlamh inimtheachta aca, ré dtriall a* buailteachas *na beatha so gus an* sean-bhaile *síordhaidhe, maille ré* ceasaibh *agus ré* cliabhaibh *crábhaidh agus caon-duthrachta do bheith líonta go luchtmhar do lón an lóir-ghníomha dhlighidh do dhéanamh...*'
48 Lucas 1989 (65).
49 Ó Moghráin 1944 [1945], (48).
50 This word occurs as *erg* in Old Norse (de Vries, 104), a borrowing from Irish discussed by Ó Moghráin 1944 [1945], (47-8). For remarks on *airge* and the later usage *buaile*, cf. Ó Moghráin, *loc.cit.* and also Lucas 1989 (63-6).
51 Ó Moghráin 1944 [1945], (49-50).
52 Cf. p. 9-11 above. For a brief account of her various *vitae*, cf. Connolly (5-10) and sources quoted there.
53 Connolly (6).
54 Connolly (7).
55 Murphy (lxviii).
56 Graves (1. 75).
57 *Loc.cit.* MacBain 1885 (101), calls St Brigit, 'the canonised fire-goddess, the Vesta of the heathen Gaels'.
58 *New Larousse Encylopedia of Mythology* (204). Graves (1. 74-5) observes that when drunken Priapus 'once tried to violate her at a rustic feast attended by the gods... an ass brayed aloud, Hestia awoke, screamed to find Priapus about to straddle her and sent him running off in comic terror.'
59 *Loc.cit.*
60 Cf. Chapter 3 above.
61 Murphy (lxviii). The word *aed* is cognate with Latin *aedis* 'hearth, house' (cf. Vendryes (A-19 - A-20).
62 Murphy (lxviii).
63 Murphy (lxvii).
64 Cf., for example, the Swedish version quoted above (p. 121) and Christiansen 1958 (216-21).
65 The etymology of this name is unclear. It has been connected *inter alia* with *logi* 'fire' and with *Loptr*, a name of doubtful meaning associated with a west Nordic divinity which in turn may have to do with the word *lypta* – '*der hochgewachsene*' (de Vries, 365, 366). Rooth (*KL* 10. 683), regards the myths portraying Loki as a fire spirit as being among his most important primary characteristics.

66 Moberg (86-7).
67 These and their connections with Brigit are treated on p. 150ff.
68 af Klintberg (242-3).
69 Graham notes (75), that in Achill this movement 'to the summer pastures was usually made in May, from the first to the twelfth according to the weather and custom, and the return was at the end of October in time for Hallowe'en.' Ó Danachair 1983-4 (40) draws attention to the fact that 'in Irish writings of the seventh to twelfth centuries' the Irish system of summer pasture was already 'familiar in all its essentials', including 'the removal of milking stock to distant pastures usually in mountains about May Day, houses or huts on the pastures, butter and cheese made there by the womenfolk and return to the homestead about November Day.' The constellation [Orion] is a weather sign in many parts of the world, rising near dawn at the beginning of summer and in the early evening as winter approaches the morning rising of the Pleiades which commonly brought in fine weather, occurred about the 9th or 11th of May and the setting in Hesiod's time about October 26 or early November cf. *FW* 2. 874-5).
70 This is the name I have heard used in Erris. For traditions about these and other stars, cf. Mac Coisdealbha (166) who confirms the name as applying to the Pleiades in west Mayo. Ó Coistealbha also calls them *'A' Bhualaí Bhodach'* whereas Ó Moghráin's name for them – *'Buailidh na mBodach'* – rather reflects that given by Ó Máille *s.a.* (26) – *Buaile an Bhodaigh* – which he glosses 'Belt of Orion?'. de Bhaldraithe 1959 (498 [sub Orion]) gives *Buaile an Bhodaigh* as does Ó Dónaill, 153, the former in the meaning 'Belt of Orion', the latter *(sub buaile)* as 'nebula in Orion'.
71 Cf. *Béaloideas* 8 (1937), 116.
72 That such a phallic reference would not be out of place is indicated by other usages such as the Sámi word for the North Star, *Boahje-naste*, a borrowing from Finnish *pohjan naula* literally 'North nail' one of a number of forms (others include *alme-navlle* 'heaven's nail' and *batte-navlle* 'pot-nail/peg etc') which advert to the world-tree (cf. Qvigstad 1921, 4-5) with its strong phallic connotations.
73 Blöndal (1. 198).
74 Allen (450).
75 Lid 1923 (ed.), 85. I am grateful to Dr Inger Christensen of Norsk Folkminnesamling (University of Oslo) for this reference. Old Norse *rokkr* may be related to Irish *rucht* 'a tunic, a garment' and also to *rogait* possibly meaning 'distaff' (de Vries, 451; Hellqvist, 2, 840-1; Vendryes (R 39-40 and R-50).
76 Lid 1923 (ed.), (85).
77 Ó Danachair 1983-4 (38) characterises 'the carding and spinning of wool and the knitting of stockings and other garments' as being 'the main secondary task' of the females working in the booley.
78 Allen (392-3).
79 Allen (396).
80 Allen (424).
81 Qvigstad 1921 (7-8).
82 Allen (424).

83 Cf. Chapter 5, Note 228.
84 Graves (1. 151-4).
85 Rose (116, 117).
86 Allen (92).
87 Allen (99).
88 Leisiö (13) where he also intimates that the expression 'twelve men in the forest' (as a metaphor for the bear) does not feature in the Finnish rescue messages. Cf. also Moberg, (86-7) and sources cited there.
89 af Klintberg (243). Professor Bo Almqvist has drawn my attention to the fact that von Sydow 1923b (63) in his review of Ek (27 f.) also voiced strong disagreement with the idea of equating the bear with 'twelve men in the forest'.
90 Cf. pp. 55-57 above. Moberg (21) adverting to Scandinavian traditions concerning the capture of booley-maids *(vallflickor)* by bears, draws attention to the mention by Olaus Magnus (probably in this instance describing conditions without the bounds of Scandinavia, according to Moberg) in Book 18, Chapter 31 of his *Historia de gentibus septentrionalibus* (1555) of bag-pipe playing herds and the fact that they were sometimes carried off by bears.
91 J. Olrik (282-93). I am grateful to Ole Munch-Pedersen for this reference.
92 J. Olrik (283).
93 In contrast with its latter-day confinement to widely separated relict areas such as the Balkans, Iberian peninsula, Ireland and Scandinavia, it appears that the custom of transhumance may have once enjoyed a similar widespread distribution extending across the whole continent of Europe (Moberg 18).
94 Connolly & Picard (20).
95 Connolly & Picard (21). For a discussion of the numbers 9 and 12 in Celtic tradition, cf. the Rees brothers (192-7).
96 Solheim (280). Moberg (70) characterises the style of delivery of cattle-calls used in the context of booleying as high-pitched, strangulated and nasalized. In likening the sound produced to that of a crowing cock, he notes the similarity in usage and meaning between the northern Swedish expression *köka* meaning 'cattle-call' and also 'crow' and the Alpine word *gallen* and he speculates on the possibility of the existence of further connections with north and west Germanic *galan*, a word meaning to render magic formulae, and *galder*, the name for the person by whom such formulae were delivered, the implication being that these were uttered in a falsetto voice not dissimilar in effect to the noise created by a crowing cock. Moberg further speculates (71, 91) that in the practice of disguised-voice singing and cattle-calling with or without megaphone amplification or the use of reed instruments, it may be possible to see in both the Alpine and Scandinavian worlds a reflection of the ancient Germanic and Nordic tradition of chanting magic formulae.

—Chapter 5—

> Weave a circle round him thrice,
> And close your eyes with holy dread,
> For he on honey-dew hath fed,
> And drunk the milk of Paradise.
> —Samuel Coleridge, *Kubla Kahn*

'IN THE WESTERN ISLANDS,' a nineteenth-century Scottish commentator tells us, 'St Columba appeared to have been regarded as the patron of cattle. When a man spoke to a neighbour about the neighbour's cattle, he said – *Gu'n gleidheadh Calum Cille dhuibh iad* ('May St Columba protect them for you'). As a woman left her cattle on the hill-side to graze she waved her hand towards them, saying – *Buachailleachd Dhia 's Chaluim Cille oirbh* ('May the herding and guardianship of God and St Columba be on you'). 'An Eriskay woman,' this source continues, 'used to address her cattle'—

Gu'm ba duinte gach slochd	May each pit be closed
'S gu'm bu reidh gach cnoc;	And each hillock be plain;
Buachailleachd Chalum Chille oirbh,	Columba's herding on ye,
Gus an tig sibh dhachaidh.	Till home ye return.[1]

Another Scottish authority confirms Colm Cille's connections with cattle husbandry and also links his name with that of Brigit and the Virgin Mary in this regard:

Thig, a Mhoire, 's bligh a bhó,	Come, Mary (Virgin), and milk the cow,
Thig, a Bhrìde, 's comraig i,	Come, Bridget, and encompass her,
Thig, a Chaluim Chille chaoimh,	Come, Calum Cille, the beneficient,
Is iadh do dhà laimh mu m'bhoin!	And wind thine arms around my cow.[2]

This verse is described as being a 'secular-superstitious' milking song, 'a croon or a charm combined, intended to soothe the restlessness of a cow that has lost her calf...'[3] In Irish and Scottish Gaelic traditional charms, and in prayers of one kind or another, Mary, Brigit and Colm Cille, rank alongside Colm Cille, Brigit and Pádraig[4] – the 'Triad of the Irish conversion period', who 'stand in the center of Irish medieval hagiography.'[5] An analysis of Carmichael's *Carmina Gadelica* by Hamish Robertson has shown that among the more than score of personal names... that may be associated, more or less safely, with saintly figures of the Irish and Scottish Celtic churches, the 'names of Brìghde, Calum Cille and Pàdruig are those most commonly met with in invocations, though the role of Patrick is considerably diminished compared with the two former in the Scottish context',[6] to which is added:

> Columba and Bride, from the evidence of the Carmina, are the salient figures of the Scottish Gaelic pantheon of saints. They are invoked more frequently and more exclusively than the biblical apostles. They are connected with prayers concerning a wide range of aspects of rural life, protecting cattle, healing disease, blessing the duties of hearth and home. The figures of the two saints seem to accompany and complement each other in the popular imagination, though the characters ascribed to them, especially in the case of Calum Cille, respond but hardly to the image portrayed to us by the Old Irish or Latin Lives. Bride is most definitely connected with the protection of herds and with the healing of the sick in the old sources. Her assumption of these functions in the world of Carmina Gadelica is not to be wondered at.[7]

For all that, Robertson still only grudgingly admits the validity of Colm Cille's folk credentials which, he concludes, really rest upon the capacity of 'popular imagination' to elaborate upon 'a historical image that became progressively lost from memory.' A not dissimilar assessment is implicit in James Kenney's depiction of Colm Cille as 'a clear-cut historical personality' standing out 'against a background wherein his associates in sanctity, including the legend-encrusted Patrick and the half-mythical Brigit, move as shadows in a land of twilight.'

These appraisals take scant cognizance of the nature of the rich body of lore and legend which surrounds the person of Colm Cille in Irish and Scottish folk tradition and as a result the saint tends to emerge diminished as a folklore figure from them. The experienced Donegal folklore collector, Seán Ó hEochaidh (Fig. 32) almost overwhelmed by the sheer vivacity of folk memories of the saint and his doings (abundantly available until recent times in his native county) paints an entirely different picture, however.[8]

As in the Scottish material, we find here ample evidence of Colm Cille's connections with cattle – a phenomenon, of course, which also features in his various Lives. In this connection, the following accounts are of particular interest, dealing as they do with the saint's miraculous capacity to restore dead or dying animals (cows) to life, collocating him in this context with two separate figures, one of them a contemporary saint, known in modern folk tradition as Aodh Mhic Bricne, and the other a local Glencolmcille woman who went by the name of *An Chailleach Dhubh* 'The Black Hag'. The first of these stories goes as follows:

> When Colm Cille was in Glen[colmcille] he went out to Comhar na dTrí Searc to meet up with Aodh Mhic Bricne for a chat. 'You are thriving well,' said Aodh Mhic Bricne. 'Indeed, I'm not,' said he. 'You are,' said Aodh, 'for I can see it in your face. You must be getting some kind of milk food to eat,' said he. 'I am not,' said Colm Cille. When he got back home he asked the woman of the house was she putting anything in the bread. She said she had been putting a mixture of milk and water in it. He flew into a temper then on account of the white food he was getting.
>
> She had a cow and he killed it so that she could put no more milk in the bread. They buried the cow and after it had been buried some time, he was full of regret for what he had done and they disinterred the cow – which by that time was nothing but bones – and they reassembled all the bones they could find except the knee bone. This was missing and the cow [which he restored to life] was lame as a result. He ordained that from that day to this a special quality of all lame cows would be that they would always yield an extra supply of milk. And it is just so.⁹

Rather typically, as far as the folk tradition is concerned, this account highlights not only Colm Cille's power but also other somewhat less favourable sides of his personality – his famous short-temper and general irascibility and his penchant for swift and vindictive retribution.¹⁰ The following account was taken down by Ó hEochaidh at the very beginning of his long collecting career.¹¹ Having heard it retold many times in the intervening period, Ó hÉochaidh briefed Joseph Szövérrfy about it in 1953 and he, in turn, subsequently published the following version of it, in which the role played by Aodh Mhic Bricne's housekeeper is taken on by a trio of nuns known locally as the Holy Women:

> Another tradition tells us that the Holy Women had a very good cow. This cow was so lactiferous that not only did she give sufficient milk to supply the little nunnery, but she also supplied enough to keep the poor of the district. After a few years, the cow died, and the Holy Women were broken hearted. According to the tradition, these women once went to meet St Columcille, who was at this time in Glencolumcille, in order to discuss certain problems with him which were troubling them. The place where they met is said to be Curraoin na dTrí Searc on the Glen road, about five miles north of Teelin. When they discussed all their important matters, they told St Columcille about their cow, and he was so touched by their grief, that he came back with them to Teelin, and got some men to dig up the place where the cow was buried. He put the bones together, and prayed over them until he restored their cow to life.[12]

Szövérrfy highlights an important issue in suggesting that the various similar miracles described by Manus O'Donnell in *Betha Colaim Cille*, his sixteenth-century Life of Colm Cille,[13] may have exercised some influence on this story. He adverts in particular to 'the story of the cow of the Saint which was lost and found, that of the ox restored…[and] the episode of the warrior who eats the ox reserved for the reapers. At St Columba's prayer, the flesh re-covers the bones, in order to ensure proper food for the reapers coming back to take the meal.'[14] It is by no means certain, however, that literary influence should necessarily be credited with holding complete sway in this instance as I hope further discussion here of this and related themes will show.

A further episode in which Colm Cille's miraculous powers are also brought to bear in a similar context introduces another female figure by the name of *An Chailleach Dhubh* ('The Black Hag'). This account, which renders interesting details of the health-restoring techniques employed by the saint, also draws attention to yet another side of Colm Cille's complex character, namely his compassionate nature. It goes as follows:

> About the same, time there was another woman in Glen[colmcille] called the Black Hag. She had a very good cow which was capable of keeping the children of three or four townlands in the vicinity supplied with milk. Colm Cille was going around and he saw the Black Hag sitting there crying. He asked her why she was so sad. 'Oh,' said she, 'my cow is dying of glanders and I weep not for her or

for myself but for the poor children that will go hungry.'

Colm Cille took pity on her and he pulled a piece of string from his pocket and made a few knots in it. Then he donned his stole and while he was working the charm, he loosed the knots and this is what he said:

'A charm made by Colm Cille
   For the only cow of the Black Hag
A foot on the sea and a foot on land
Loose knot and cure the glanders.'

Colm Cille cured the cow and saved the children's food-supply.[15]

In drawing preliminary conclusions from the range of Scottish and Irish traditions about Colm Cille that have been adduced hitherto, it will be expedient to lay particular stress upon the following points: he is invoked as a protector of cattle (and, by extension, the milk supply) which he has the power to restore to health or even raise from the dead, as the occasion demands; he is associated with certain female figures – in Scotland his name is linked with that of Brigit and Mary, in Ireland, he consorts with a dim figure called the 'Black Hag', a religious threesome rejoicing in the designation 'The Holy Women' and the anonymous housekeeper of another local saint who together with the Holy Women, will now become the focus of further attention.

* * *

The 'Aodh Mhic Bricne' of Donegal folk tradition is mentioned in early sources such as the *Martyrology of Tallaght* where – as Aedh meic Bricc – we find him listed under various dates (28 February, 4 May, 30 July) and where his 'true' feastday is given as 10 November. The *Martyrology of Donegal* has this to say of him:

> Aodh mac Bric, mic Corbmaic, mic Cremhthainn, mic Fiachach, from whom are the Cinel Fiachach, was born in Cilláir of Meath…
> AEDH son of Breac, Bishop, of Cill-Air, in Meath, and of Sliabh Liag, in Tir-Boghaine, in Cinel-Conaill. He was of the race of Fiachaidh, son of Niall of the Nine Hostages. The age of Christ when he sent his spirit to heaven was 588.[16]

Kenney[17] records that 'Aedh, son of Brecc' was known as '*sui-liag*, the 'master-physician' and opines that, apart his being of the royal

Uí Néill line and his reputed sanctity, his fame rested upon an extraordinary ability to cure headaches, which accomplishment is noted, as it happens, in a fragmentary *Life of Brigit*.[18] His *Life*, as T. F. O'Rahilly tells us, 'credits him with various solar powers, such as flying through the air in his chariot, travelling in a chariot with a single wheel, and warding off a deluge of rain from a cornfield,' features which O'Rahilly concludes invest him 'with the attributes of his name-sake, the pagan sun-god [*Aed* = 'fire'].'[19] Kenney, in sober summation, labels him one of the few Irish saints, 'the basis of whose fame is personal and general, rather than monastic.'[20]

John O'Donovan, on his visit to south west Donegal in October 1835 on Ordnance Survey business, was well placed to gain some insight into what constituted the saint's 'personal' fame when privileged to sample at first hand some of the local memories of him. His barely concealed contempt for the oral tradition almost came between him and that prospect, however, as is revealed by the tone of his comments:

> On the summit of the gloomy Mountain of Slieve Leag [Figs. 29 & 30] are yet shewn the ruins of the little cell of Aodh Mac Bric, whom tradition styles *Aodh na Bricna* (or Hughy Breaky)[21] and a holy well blessed by him. A most solemn *turas* was performed here in the memory of the last generation, but he liveth not now who could point out all the hallowed spots to be visited and prayed at, so that it has been abandoned as a station of pilgrimage to the rapid oblivion (forgetfulness) of the name and fame of the good and solitary Aidus.[22]

O'Donovan's predictions were somewhat premature, however, for almost a century to the day later, the saint's name was still alive on the lips of local people, one of whom, Máire Ní Dhonnagáin, recounted that:

> the old people [used to say] – that they [the Holy Women] were related, closely related – sisters even – of Saint Ó Bricne and that they used to go up Slieve League to visit him in the summer-time and that he used to come down to keep them company in the winter-time. And they used to say that they [the Holy Women] were related to Colm Cille and that all the saints, indeed, at the time were related to one another. But I cannot say if that is true or not.[23]

Chapter 5   181

Figs. 29 & 30:
Views of *Sliabh Liag* (Slieve League), Teelin, County Donegal.

In *Betha Colaim Cille*, reference is also made to a trio of women identified as *Ógacht* ('Virginity'), *Egna* ('Wisdom') and *Fáidhedóracht* ('Prophecy'). How these three became symbolic 'wives' of Colm Cille, is related thus:

> And when the angel has departed from Columcille, anon there appeared three maidens that were passing young and beautiful... as he had never looked on before, and each maiden clasped her hands about his neck and they gave him three kisses. The lover of chastity, to wit, Columcille, turned a wry face and an ill visage upon these maidens, and he put from him their kisses corrupt and unclean, for he thought it was for sin they came to him. Then the maidens inquired of him if he knew who they were, since he was not taking from them kisses nor their love. Columcille said that he knew them not, and they said it was their own father that had given them in wedlock to Columcille and that three sisters they were to each other. Then inquired Columcille who it was that was father to them; and they said it was the Lord Jesus Christ, Creator of Heaven and Earth, that was their father. Saith Columcille: 'Right noble is your father; tell me your names'. 'Virginity and Wisdom and Prophecy are our names', they say, 'and we shall be three wives to cherish thee till thy death and we shall foster and keep love for thee without change for ever.' And then Columcille said: 'I give glory and great thanks to Almighty God that hath joined and received me in wedlock with his own three noble daughters and I but a poor lowly bondslave...'[24]

The basis of this story, we are told, is the following passage in the *Old Irish Life*, the oldest common exemplar of which 'was probably at least as old as the eleventh century ...'[25]

> Then Columcille offered himself to the Lord of the Elements and he begged three boons of him, to wit, chastity, and wisdom, and pilgrimage. This three were fully granted to him.[26]

It seems reasonable to suppose – as Szövérrfy suggests – that the 'chastity', 'wisdom' and 'pilgrimage' of the earlier text find approximate matches in the personages of O'Donnell's *Ógacht*, *Egna* and *Fáidhedóracht*. Szövérrfy has no hesitation in speedily connecting these three figures in turn with the three Holy Women of Teelin folk tradition, who, as we have seen, were said to be sisters of Colm Cille (and Aodh Mhic Bricne) and whose names are given as *Ciall*, *Tuigse* and *Náire*, translated respectively by Szövérffy and others as 'Sense'. 'Understanding' and 'Modesty'. He regards the two sets of names as being 'equally symbolic and allegorical'[27] concluding in short that 'the hagiographical allegory and the popular tradition of the three legendary sisters of Columcille in Teelin are basically identical.'[28]

Three possible explanations for the linkage between *Ógacht*, *Egna* and *Fáidhedóracht*, on the one hand and *Ciall*, *Tuigse* and *Náire* on the other, are put forward by him: '(i) ...the written record by Manus O'Donnell was the source of the Teelin oral tradition; (ii) ...the Teelin local legend (in some form) was the model for Manus O'Donnell's allegory; (iii) ...they were based on a third (common) source, referring to the same basic tradition and echoing it in two different forms...'[29] Szövérffy concludes unequivocally, however, that what we witness here is simply 'the transformation of a hagiographical episode into twentieth century folklore...'[30] and that latter-day tradition 'was exclusively based on the vision described by Manus O'Donnell...'[31]

Two problems remain for him to address, the first of these being the issue of the unseemly *ménage* of Colm Cille and three maidens 'passing young and beautiful' and its subsequent translation into the innocuous combination of the saint plus a triad of 'morally neutral sisters'.[32] Szövérffy's assertion that 'the story must have reached the folk through some sermon at an unspecified age', the preacher on that occasion having sidestepped the delicate issue of polygamy by transmuting wedlock bands to kinship bonds, this being supposedly the sort of affiliation which satisfied 'the popular taste much better than the literary allegory'[33] is unconvincing. Of even greater moment, however, is the question as to how the three Holy Women 'became associated with the St Columba tradition in Teelin'[34] in the first place and here Szövérffy confesses that he finds himself more or less at a loss as far as finding an adequate explanation is concerned: 'It is not very easy to answer this question,' he states, 'as no survey has been made of this problem, and this legend is preserved only in local folklore without records of historical or hagiographical character.'[35]

The solution to this problem lies in rejecting Szövérffy's preferred option as expounded above (1), electing instead to pursue his suggestion of a possible common source from which both traditions might be descended (3). Ironically, this will entail the elevation of the self-same 'local folklore' to a position of parity of importance as we turn to deliberating upon some basic elements of this naming complex and examine more closely the body of lore associated with it.

* * *

In Donegal, as in most other parts of Ireland, there is no shortage of holy wells and the parish of Glencolmcille is fairly typical in this regard in boasting at least three of them – one of which, not unexpectedly, happens to be named after St Colm Cille himself. Two other wells are of particular interest in the present context. One of these, Énrí Ó Muirgheasa tells us is:

> *Tobar na mBan Naomh* or 'The Well of the Holy Women' at Teelin. The *turus* is still made on the 23rd June 'Bonfire Night'. Often if this night is fine the pilgrims sit up all night at the well until daylight. Stations are also made on the 29th June, probably because it is a Church holiday. The 'Holy Women' are called locally *Ciall, Tuigse,* and *Náire* (Sense, Understanding and Modesty) and are said to have been three sisters (some deny, however, that they were sisters) who were reared at Rann na Cille, beside the well, and who became nuns, and blessed this well. Two of them are buried at *Roilig na mBan,* 'The Graveyard of the Women' also near the well, and the third is buried west of Teelin Bay in Dúinín, but there is no *roilig* there now. But another tradition says one of the trio is buried in Cladach na gCaorach. Stations used to be made at both Dúinín and Cladach na gCaorach, but not in the present generation. The station on Bonfire Night suggests that it was originally a pagan sanctuary, christianised by early missionaries.
>
> Fishermen sailing out from Teelin Bay to fish in the open sea lower their sails by way of salute on passing Tobar na mBan Naomh, take off their caps, and ask the blessing and help of the holy women.
>
> An almost similar custom is observed by fishermen on the North-West coast of County Mayo, who, when passing under a jutting cliff known as the Cailleach Crom, salute it bareheaded three times in occult terms, at the same time striking the water with the flat of their oars.[36]

Whatever the nature of the 'occult terms' of the Mayo salutation may have been, it would appear that the Donegal equivalent took

Fig. 31: *Tobar na mBan Naomh* ('The Well of the Holy Women'), Teelin, County Donegal.

Fig. 32: Folklore collector Seán Ó hEochaidh at *Tobar na mBan Naomh* ('The Well of the Holy Women').

the form of a pious aspiration – *Faoi choimrí Dé agus na mBan Naomh sinn go bpillimid arís!* ('May we be under the protection of God and the Holy Women till we return!')[37] – customarily uttered in the following circumstances:

> When the fishermen of Teelin are going out to fish they have a long-standing custom of raising their oars clear of the water as they pass the end of the pier and saying three *Ave Marias* so that God, the Virgin Mary and 'the Holy Women' whose well and pilgrimage round is located up behind the pier) may grant them a safe return and save them from any loss or harm on the ocean. This is a lovely custom which until a few years ago no fisherman passing beyond the pier dared ignore. In the old days, any one refusing to participate in it would not be allowed to fish. Alas, I fear there are some young fishermen nowadays who do not subscribe to this pleasant tradition, though many of them do still follow the example of the older generation.[38]

Ó Muirgheasa also notes the existence of another well called *Tobar na Córach*, 'The Well of the Fair Wind' hard by *Tobar na mBan Naomh*, and alludes to the possibility that this may have been the real object of the local fishermen's reverence (Figs. 31 & 32).[39] It is probably best, however, to view them as operating in tandem, just as local tradition implies:

> Just behind *Tobar na mBan-Naomh*, there's a little well called *Tobar na Córach*. In the old days, if a vessel was harbour-bound for a long while, someone associated with it would clean out this well in order for them to get a fair wind and that's how it got its name. Tradition, however, says that someone belonging to them would die when that was done and that the wind followed the day after. John Anna, the husband of the last woman to clean the well had been nine weeks [harbour bound] in Sligo when she cleaned it. He got a fair wind the next day, but they say a little girl of hers died after that and no one dared clean it since. But it's still there in combination with *Tobar na mBan-Naomh*.[40]

Though it has been the scene of Christian devotion for thirteen centuries *Tobar na mBan Naomh*, Ó Muirgheasa concludes, is essentially a 'christianised pagan sanctuary.'[41] As such it fits comfortably within a widely documented pattern of well-worship incorporating the conjunction of wells and holy women.⁴² Here Szövérrfy has been at pains to draw a parallel between the *Matrae* and *Matrones*, fate goddesses such as *Moirai*, *Parcae* and the Norns, various groups of Christian saints and what he terms 'characters of fairy mythology and other supernatural beings in folklore areas.'⁴³ Bearing this in mind, it will be politic to take a closer look at the nomenclature of the female figures within the two groupings with which we have been concerned hitherto – to wit *Ógacht*, *Egna* and *Fáidhedóracht* of *Betha Choluim Cille* and *Ciall*, *Tuigse* and *Náire* of Teelin folk tradition.

The rough and ready match which Szövérrfy's *Egna* ('Wisdom') and *Fáidhedóracht* ('Prophecy') and *Ógacht* ('Virginity'), find in the *ecna* ('Wisdom'), *ailithri* ('Pilgrimage') and *oighi* ('Virginity') of the *Old Irish Life*, on the one hand,⁴⁴ and in *Ciall* ('Sense'), *Tuigse* ('Understanding') and *Náire* ('Modesty') on the other may be represented as follows:

ecna	*ailithri*	*oighi*
Egna	*Fáidhedóracht*	*Ógacht*
Ciall	*Tuigse*	*Náire*

While there is a fairly exact vertical correspondence within the first *(ecna, Egna, Ciall)* and final *(oighi, Ógacht, Náire)* groupings, the middle set – 'Pilgrimage', 'Prophecy' and 'Understanding' – would appear more difficult to reconcile. 'Pilgrimage' and 'Prophecy' are not, of course, synonymous, though both relate smoothly enough to Colm Cille's role and reputation as exile and seer respectively. *Tuigse* ('Understanding'), however, seems totally out of step with this pair and perilously close in meaning to *Ciall* ('Sense'), the first element in that particular sequence, to boot. Szövérrfy acknowledges the seeming tautological dilemma inherent in the names *Ciall* and *Tuigse* by listing them under one heading thus reducing the trio 'Sense', 'Understanding' and 'Modesty' to a duo – 'Virtue and Wisdom', as he has it.⁴⁵

This is an unnecessary expedient, however, for a closer scrutiny of the name *Tuigse* exposes other possibilities which render irrelevant the threat of any bothersome concordance of meaning. While Middle Irish *tuicse*, the verbal noun of *do-ucci* means 'understanding, perceiving, realizing',⁴⁶ this form could also be taken to be the participle of the verb *do-goa* 'to choose', giving the meaning 'chosen, elect, acceptable'.⁴⁷ Given that *tuicse* in the latter meaning can be related to *Tuigse* – holy woman of Teelin – then not only does this serve to create a clear distinction between herself and *Ciall*, but it introduces into the overall equation a fascinating new component with far-reaching implications.

The concept of choice and the act of choosing bear directly upon the idea of seeking to define the future, either by a process of prophecy as symbolized by *Fáidhedóracht*, spiritual wife of Colm Cille, or, in the manner of fate goddesses, by spinning the thread of destiny for newcomers to the world. In this regard, the Norns of Norse mythology and Scandinavian folklore generate a range of material with many interesting Irish parallels. Most immediately arresting are the names of the individual Norns and the fact that these seem to stand in a pattern of relationship which closely follows the disposition of *Ciall*, *Tuigse* and *Náire*, the Holy Women of Teelin, as outlined above.

The traditional estimation of the role of goddesses of Fate centred around the notion of a tripartite division of human existence in terms of a beginning, middle and end which in turn was related to the deployment of past, present and future on the temporal plane.[48] With respect to the three Norns – *Urð*, *Verðandi* and *Skuld* – Jacob Grimm lent this idea the following application:

> In the[se] three proper names it is impossible to mistake the forms of verbal nouns or adjectives: *Urðr* is taken from the pret. pl. of *verða* (*varð*, *urðum*), 'to become', *Verðandi* is the pres. part. of the same word, and *Skuld* the past part of *skula*, shall, the auxiliary by which the future tense is formed. Hence we have what was, what is, and what shall be, or the past, present, and future, very aptly designated, and a Fate presiding over each.[49]

Verða 'to become', which derives from the Indo-European root **u̯ert-* 'turn, spin, rotate' being the parent verb of both *Urðr* and *Verðandi*, sets these two apart from *Skuld* which carries the 'force of obligation or necessity' and which enjoys a different origin; consequently, it is probably best translated as 'Necessity' in other words 'what is of necessity' or 'what *shall* be'.[50] This representation of a forward-looking aspect of present state is complemented by the semantically related *Urðr* and *Verðandi*, which convey the meaning of 'becoming', expressing other aspects of present state or, as Bauschatz puts it:

Chapter 5   189

If we divide the influence of the Norns among the three, their names suggest that they define what we normally think of as the total range of verbal action: Urth reflects actions made manifest, brought to a full clear, observable fruition; they have 'become'; they are accomplished. Verthandi clearly reflects the actually occurring process of all that Urth eventually expresses. The two Norns are closely linked, with the influence of Verthandi flowing directly to Urth. As actions pass from Verthandi to Urth, they move from 'becoming' to 'become'. As Skuld is involved with necessary or obligatory action, she stands slightly apart from the other two Norns.[51]

On this basis, there would seem to be a *prima facie* case for seeing a parallel between the deployment of the Holy Women of Teelin and the three Norns into their respective *Ciall/Tuigse* + *Náire* and *Urð/Verðandi* + *Skuld* configurations. The agents relevant to the initial determination of fate (*Ciall/Tuigse* and *Urð/Verðandi*) and its contingent corollary (*Náire/Skuld*)[52] encapsulate a similar correspondence between both sets of names at a deeper level, some further ramifications of which phenomenon we shall now seek to unravel.

*   *   *

In Old Norse literature, *Urð*, the personification of fate is pictured as a female figure seated under the world tree *(Yggdrasill)* by a well *(Urðarbrunnr)*[53] from the vicinity of which she and her sister Norns, Verðandi and Skuld, were said to have emerged. They are generally referred to in the plural, though sometimes only Urð, whose name is also used as a word for 'death', is mentioned.[54] Yggdrasill was also known as *Mímameiðr*,[55] the tree or post of Mími, and one of its three roots was said to extend into the well of Mímir *(Mímisbrunnr)* which is described as being *fullr af vísindum* 'full of wisdom',[56] another into the well of Urðr and the third into the well *Hvergelmir*.[57] According to some commentators, these three add up to one and the same thing – 'the well of fate, and hence the source of wisdom'.[58] Bruce Lincoln comes to a similar conclusion about two of the wells, *Hvergelmir* and *Mímisbrunnr*, and, following de Vries, speculates that the etymology of the initial element of the latter *(Mímir)*, 'may be a re-duplicated form of the... Proto-Indo-European... verb **(s)mer-*, 'to think, recall, reflect, worry over...' He further suggests that this 'as a nominal form... would best rendered as 'memory' and the personified being Mímir, 'a wise giant, patron of memory' might thus be compared to the Celtic goddess Rosmerta, patroness of memory, whose name is also derived from Proto-Indo-European *(s)mer-'.[59]

Similarly, according to Simpson, the various images of Mímir, whether as giant guardian of a well of wisdom or the oracular severed head preserved by Óðinn and resorted to by him for information about other times and other worlds, are capable of being resolved into one, namely that of the severed head which 'still magically alive, is inside the well at the root of Yggdrasill' where its major function is 'to be both the source and the guardian of wisdom, especially magical, chthonic and prophetic wisdom.'[60] Óðinn appeared under many guises and took many names, among them some which refer to his being blind or one-eyed. One of these – *Hárr* – is 'said to derive from *Haiha-hariR* (the One-eyed Hero) and to be related to Gothic *haihs* (one-eyed) and ultimately to Latin *caecus*'.[61] The loss of Óðinn's eye was due to his having promised it to Mímisbrunnr 'in order to gain a drink, and by extension, wisdom'.[62] In Gylfaginning, this is described in the following terms:

> But under the root that runs towards the frost-giants is Mímir's Well, in which wisdom and understanding are hidden, and he whose well it is is called Mímir. He is full of knowledge for he drinks from the well out of the horn Gjallarhorn. All-Father came there and asked to have a drink from the well, but he did not get it until he had given his eye as a pledge. So it says in the *Vǫluspá*:
> > I know well, Óðinn,
> > where you hid your eye
> > in that famous
> > well of Mímir
> > Every morning
> > Mímir drinks mead
> > from Val-Father's pledge.
>
> Then Óðinn rides to Mímir's Well and takes counsel from Mímir for himself and his host. Then the ash Yggdrasill trembles...[63]

Simpson warns that while the concealment of Óðinn's eye in the well 'has often been interpreted as being on one level a nature-myth symbolizing the dipping of the setting sun in the ocean, and on another, a myth of the winning of wisdom by sacrificial torments... it cannot be dissociated from the practice, amply attested over a wide area of Europe and at many periods, of offering sacrifices to sacred wells by casting objects or victims into them. Thus,' she adds, 'Adam of Bremen speaks of the sacrifices held at the well beneath the sacred tree at Uppsala, and of a living man being cast into it. Such sacrifices,' she observes, 'would accord well with a belief in an Otherworld deity dwelling in the depths of a well.'[64] Simpson's observation that the 'decapitation of the head, its preservation, its association with a well and its prophesy and otherworld knowledge are all features which recur in Celtic tradition and belief'[65] is further elaborated upon by Anne Ross who in reference to the cult of the human head in general, notes it as being –

> ...a persistent theme throughout all aspects of Celtic life, spiritual and temporal, and the symbol of the severed head may be regarded as the most typical and universal of their religious attitudes. The Celts seem truly to have venerated a 'god head' and they imbued the *'tête coupée'* with all the qualities and powers most admired and desired by them – fertility, prophecy, hospitality, wisdom and healing.[66]

Elsewhere, Ross tells us that 'the human head, especially in conjunction with a pillar-stone or a sacred spring' was for the Celts, the 'most highly significant sexual symbol of all.'[67] Of the utmost relevance here too is the discussion above of the association between the head and the phallus and the phallus and the eye.[68]

An interesting attribute of Urðarbrunnr is that its sacred powers are so strong that it is capable of changing the colour of all things submerged in it to the purest white[69] and Gylfaginning tells us that the Norns who dwell by it –

> take water of the well every day, and with it that clay which lies about the well, and sprinkle it over the Ash [Yggdrasill], to the end that its limbs shall not wither nor rot; for that water is so holy that all things which come there into the well become as white as the film which lies within the egg shell...[70]

The tree itself, bathed with revitalizing liquid from the well, in turn sends this liquid *(aurr)* as dew upon the earth. In this dew the honey-bees are born:

> That dew which falls from it onto the earth is called by men honeydew, and thereon are bees nourished.⁷¹

The white liquid which drips down the tree has been interpreted as cosmic seed, a heavenly sperma which fertilizes the world a parallel to which is suggested by the blood that drips into the well from the ritually slaughtered Óðinn, hanging head downwards on the cosmic tree.⁷² Within the context of *hieros gamos*, the 'genitalia of the female earth' ⁷³ is depicted cosmicly by this body of liquid while the cosmic tree, acting as the connecting axis between a masculine heaven and a feminine earth, is supremely phallic in nature.⁷⁴

Óðinn's sperm Fleck sees not only as 'the source of his own ritual rebirth', but as an ingredient of the well with two separate functions namely as 'the poet's mead and ... [as] *Valföðrs veð*, the cosmic father's pledge of fertility to rejuvenate the universe after each cyclical *ragnarök*.' ⁷⁵ He continues:

> As the mead, it shares its place in the fountain with other sources of numinous knowledge: the norns, the *völva* to whom Óðinn turns for information, and Mímr's head. As *Valföðrs veð*, Óðinn's sperm is parallel to Kvasir's blood and Mímr's head; it is that part of his physical being which lives on after the victim's death in sacrifice...⁷⁶

If, however, the issue of Óðinn's eye in the well, is seen against the background of the severed head, eye and phallus complex as outlined above,⁷⁷ the possibility of finding a different interpretation begins to emerge. This approach requires that *Valföðrs veð* be equated with Óðinn's eye which in turn is seen as symbolizing a phallus and, by extension, the sperm of Óðinn deposited in the well. Vindication of the role of the phallus in this regard makes it unnecessary to seek a symbolic source of Óðinn's sperm in the blood dripping from his spear wound and its functioning can be incorporated naturally into the circular process of generation and regeneration central to Óðinn's self-sacrifice.

* * *

Considerable emphasis has already been placed upon the fact that the celebration of the festival of Brigit is riddled with similar sexual imagery and symbolism and ultimately its *raison d'être* is underpinned by this same process of seeking to secure the best prospects for the survival and future continuation of the species. Apart from the timing of the arrival of new life, the supply of milk to help sustain it during its early stages was a major preoccupation. It is not surprising that the ideal of an ever ready source and endless supply of this commodity at a time of scarcity should have been associated with Brigit and her cow: as one person put it – 'St Brigid's Cow was supposed to be white and never ran… dry.'[78] It was said the Brigit herself would not drink milk other than the milk of a white cow.[79]

Irish folk tradition sometimes identified Brigit's cow as the famous *Glas Ghoibhneann*[80] taken as meaning, 'the grey of Goibhniu', a cow whose inexhaustible supply of milk finally dried up when she was mischievously milked into a sieve.[81] Otherwise, the *Glas Ghoibhneann* was credited with being a fairy cow which had emerged from the sea and/or derived her enormous milking capacity from licking an object at or near the shore. A number of these motifs is combined in the following charmingly anachronistic version of this legend:

> There was a cow at Faughart called St Brigid's cow. No one was to put a small vessel under her to milk this cow in. This cow used walk each day from Faughart to Narrow Water (Omeath) and lick a barrel that was there in the water and return again to Faughart.
>
> One day a poor woman at Faughart had no milk for her tea and she went to St Brigid's cow with a pint tin to get a drop of milk. She got it. Either that day or the following day, the cow took her calf and journeyed to Narrow Water. They jumped into the water beside the barrel and made down Carlingford Lough. Now there are two big rocks out in the sea at Whitestown which are called the Cow and Calf.
>
> It is said in this story that the barrel is the one in which St Patrick came to Ireland.[82]

The motif of the marvellous supply of milk produced by licking an object at or near the shore is also linked with Colm Cille: Donegal folk tradition, for example, records the instance of stupendous milk production by a cow which persisted in licking a coffin cast ashore and half buried in the sand; in it was the corpse of Colm Cille which had miraculously drifted back to Ireland following his death in Iona.⁸³

In Snorri Sturluson's account of the origin of the Norse gods, melting rime is described as having taken the shape of a cow called Auðhumla. She nourished with her milk the man Ymir who had already emerged from the same source.⁸⁴ Auðhumla received sustenance in turn from the salty blocks of rime which as a result of her licking eventually assumed the shape of a man. This was how Búri, whose son Bor had three children, one of whom was Óðinn, was created.⁸⁵

Here we enter the realm of creation myth, in which two of the key players in the Nordic context are the primeval bovine Auðhumla and the first man, Ymir. The latter name derives from a Proto-Germanic form which can be traced back to Proto-Indo-European *Ym[mi]yós, 'a term intimately related to P-I-E *yemo- 'twin' corresponding *inter alia* to Middle Irish *emuin*, Latin *geminus* and Avestan *yəma*, all meaning 'twin'.⁸⁶

Lincoln postulates the existence of two differing versions of the original P-I-E creation myth, one Indo-Iranian, the other European, and registers a strong claim for the authenticity of the role fulfilled by Auðhumla which he regards as 'one of the most important elements for interpretation of the myth in its two differing forms.'⁸⁷ An essential component of the creation myth is human and animal sacrifice, a practice frequent among the Indo-Europeans of the fifth and fourth millenia, subsequently giving way to animal sacrifice only and later reducing to vegetable or liquid offerings.⁸⁸ Traces of the early form of sacrifice continued to manifest themselves in various parts of the Indo-European world – in sources such as Adam of Bremen's account of the well beneath the sacred tree of Uppsala into which victims were hurled alive and, perhaps, also indirectly and much less dramatically, in the surrender of a human life which was accounted part and parcel of the successful invocation in Teelin of the power vested in *Tobar na Córach*.

Auðhumla, the extraordinary milker, bears a name inviting a number of interpretations. According to de Vries, its constituent elements probably derive from *auðr* and *humla*, the former in the meaning 'riches, wealth', being a word which in turn is possibly derived semasiologically from *auðr* meaning 'fate, death, Norn'; this latter auðr is from the Indo-European *audh-* which is ultimately connected with the root *au- 'to weave'.⁸⁹ More favoured by de Vries, however, is the possibility of seeing *auðr* 'riches, wealth', as being associated with *auð*, a prefix probably meaning 'light, easy, swift' or the like, which is possibly related to the Indo-European root *awi- (Sanscrit *avi-* 'favourable', *ávati* 'be helpful, happy', Greek 'Εu 'well', Latin *avere* 'be healthy') and to be compared with the Gaulish proper name *Avicantus* and the Old Irish verb *con-oí* 'protects, guards, keep'.⁹⁰

A somewhat less tortuous history appears to lie behind the second element of the name, with *humla* being derived from *humala-, *humula- with which English 'humble' and Scots *homyll* 'hornless', as well as German *hummel* 'a bumble-bee' are to be compared. *Auðhumla* could thereby be taken to mean 'the (milk)-rich, hornless cow'.⁹¹

Hornless cows were believed to be good milkers in Nordic tradition⁹² as they were in Ireland and in times of scarcity – say, in early spring-time – it was said with respect to horned cattle, that the milk had 'gone up into their horns'.⁹³ It will be profitable to remind ourselves here that, as we have seen above, a prolific milk supply was also a feature associated with lame cows.⁹⁴ In this context, perhaps, it may not be amiss to recall the want of a bone which resulted in the lameness of the cow whose skeleton was reassembled and restored to life by Colm Cille and to suggest that this deficiency may be directly compared with the lack referred to in Auðhumla, namely the absence of horns.

The latter element of Auðhumla's name appears to derive from the Indo-European root *qem- in the meaning 'to buzz' (cf. English 'hum') a root which also carries the meaning 'to press/pinch together' (cf. English 'hem [in]').⁹⁵ The meanings 'hornless (of certain animals)' and 'to cover' are among those applied to a similar-sounding root *kem- (cf. English 'hind' and Latin *camisia* 'shirt' [a borrowing from Gaulish]) and here too belongs Old Norse *hamask*, 'to behave like a werewolf or berserker, to appear in animal disguise'.⁹⁶ The range of meanings yielded by these roots and their associated motifs and symbolic substance provide ample scope for observation of the phenomenon of matching thematic and etymological ambiguity noted above.⁹⁷ Thus we see the notion of riches or plenty (= 'milk-rich') sitting cheek by jowl with weaving and fate (= Norns), on the one hand and hornlessness or lack of sting (= castrated drone)⁹⁸ with buzzing (= bees, honey and bears), on the other.⁹⁹

Auðhumla's many-sided nature is replete with possibilities for comparison with the Irish material at different levels and some of these have already been the subject of discussion. In any event, the likely identity of her Irish counterpart already hinted at is not solely dependent upon the evidence adduced here. However, the full import of the *Glas Ghoibhneann's* role and what her double-barrelled name may signify is a topic which must needs await a more comprehensive treatment and assessment elsewhere.[100] Suffice it to say at this stage that she symbolizes the promise of an abundant supply of milk and that through her association with Brigit[101] whom she was said to accompany as she made the rounds on the eve of her feast[102] she plays her part in the process of recreation and regeneration and thereby earns the right to take her place alongside the life-determining bovine of Nordic mythology.[103]

This excursion has carried us far back in time and a long way from the humble holy wells of Teelin. With the aid of the Nordic parallels and analogues inspired by the Irish and Scottish material we have added some important new elements to a mounting body of comparative material and, perhaps, from this vantage point, begun to sight new vistas which beckon us even further.

* * *

As with many other features of the festival held to honour Brigit, particulars of the ceremonial behaviour outlined above also find interesting echoes in the Nordic area, in this instance within the general context of childbirth and with specific reference to the institution of the *barselgillen* ('childbirth feasts') or *kvinnogillen* ('women's feasts') which, in that region, once formed a central part of the ceremony and celebration attending the safe delivery of a child into the world. Before proceeding to a closer examination of this institution, we may note the following reflection of it in Irish tradition:

> If the issue was only pending and the crucial hour had not arrived, the midwife gave instruction for the sweeping of the floor and the laying of fresh clean straw thereon, if these things had not been already done. The expectant mother was transferred from the kitchen bed, which was her usual sleeping place, to the straw-littered floor. She put on her husband's sleeved waistcoat or 'báinín' which was an

outside flannel garment worn by men in those days. As the great event drew near, the husband stood at his wife's back and placed his hands on her shoulders, while she was in a kneeling position on the floor. With words of faith, hope, and encouragement, he buoyed and morally supported her during her ordeal, the midwife, or in her absence, her substitute being simultaneously engaged in the great task of bringing a new life to the world – the long story of mankind... During the regime of the old midwife which presumably stretched back to the mists of antiquity, after the woman had given birth to her child, she was accommodated to a bed on the floor, near or beside the kitchen fire. In Irish the bed was called *'leaba thalúna'* ('ground bed'). In this bed the woman was obliged to remain for nine days, and was then transferred to the 'high bed' or *'leaba ard'*, her normal sleeping place, where she had to stay for about three weeks, and then she was allowed to get up and resume her household duties. During her post-birth detention in bed, she was fed on oatmeal gruel, milk, toast bread and tea. She was also given occasional sips of whiskey for the alleviation of pains and aches... When a child was born all the neighbouring women and distant relatives came to visit the lying-in woman and took her presents of loaf-bread, tea, sugar, butter etc. During the convalescent period, the house was replete with the choice viands brought by the visitors and the family enjoyed their share of the good things – and the lion's share at that, because the sick woman, being on a special diet, she did not consume much of the contributed food stuffs. When that short season of full and plenty was over, the household had once again to revert to its erstwhile austerity...[104]

An unexpected source of information describing the more elaborate working out of this custom in the Nordic context occurs in a Latin manuscript dating to c.1350, written by an English Franciscan during the latter part of the thirteenth century. The author, a friar who had been associated periodically with the Franciscan communities in Cork and Dublin, reported a Danish-born confrère as having recounted that:

> ...in Denmark, the land of his birth, it is the custom for women in childbed to be visited by women of the neighbourhood, to help them and cheer them up with dancing and licentious songs. Thus it happened once that some women who had gathered for a feast intending to conduct themselves with customary tumult according to

> the wicked habits of the country, got a bundle of straw and having fashioned it into the shape of a man with straw arms, fitted him with a belt and a hat and called him Boui; thereafter they began to dance, two of the women holding him between them as they skipped and sang, and, as was the custom, they turned towards him between the verses with lewd gestures, saying – 'Sing along, Boui, sing along, Boui; why are you silent?' There and then, the devil, who held these wretched women in his power, replied – 'I shall sing!' and he screeched (not, of course, the bundle of straw, but the devil within it) emitting such a horrible sound that some of them fell down as if dead and others were so struck with fear and dread as to lie ill long after and almost not recover...[105]

This corresponds in many details with accounts of the *'konebarsel'* or *'kvindegilde'* in modern Danish folk tradition. These parties took place shortly after the birth of a child and began with the assembly of the womenfolk of the place who then proceeded to drink themselves merry following which they often tumbled out onto the street and into the houses of the locality making all sorts of mischief, forcing every man they met along the way to join in their dance, sometimes ripping off his trousers or, in latter times, simply forcing him to remove his hat.[106] Alternatively, a passing male might be dragged into the *'barselhus'* ('party house'), be debagged and forced to drink and dance with the women. In some cases, the man would be dragged around by the genitals to the wild screeches of the women. On other occasions, a passing male might be treated to the sight of women, their skirts raised high 'behaving worse than animals'.[107] Such lack of decorum was not a constant feature of this festivity, nor did the menfolk always suffer total exclusion or humiliation as the following account reveals:

> The women turned up to the *Konebarsel* about two o'clock and got coffee and cakes; later in the afternoon they partook of sandwiches with beer and snaps. Still later in the evening, the men appeared, but they were not allowed in until the women had gone home. Those men who came too early would stand at the corner of the house and grab the women for a quick swing around as, more or less tipsy, they made their appearance at the door. The men were subsequently treated to coffee and sandwiches following which it was a case of toasting and singing till clear daylight. This custom continued up to the [First] World War.[108]

Chapter 5

In Latvia, the worship of Laima, the birth-giving goddess, was commemorated up to the early years of this century in a sauna ritual described by Gimbutas as taking the following form:

> This [ritual] was presided over by the grandmother of the family. It was a celebration of birth which included an offering to the Goddess, followed by a feast. A hen was sacrificed when the grandmother killed it with a wooden ladle. Four or five weeks after the birth, another offering and feast was given in which only women participated. Upon seeing the young mother approaching, participants exclaimed; 'The Bear is coming.'[109]

It is not unreasonable to suggest that, while they do not agree in all respects, these revels, the doings of the *banal Bride* and the Irish-style social gathering and female assembly outlined above should be treated conjointly, nor to purport that they depict aspects of a common celebratory body of tradition with pragmatic relations to the domain of childbirth, on the one hand and symbolical associations with the fundamentals of procreation on the other.

Straw images are known from other festival contexts (Harvest and Christmas) in Denmark as elsewhere, but – as noted by the Olrik brothers – Boui, the medieval straw man, has been replaced by a living person in modern times.[110] Møller's suggestion[111] that the straw image may actually have been an individual – perhaps even the husband of the woman in question – dressed in straw finds numerous parallels elsewhere, not least in the person of Jack Straw, one of the characters of Irish Christmas Mummers' plays, whose exotic straw-clad presence is of the utmost relevance to their Life-Death-Resurrection theme[112] and in the Strawboys, the masked and straw-costumed well-wishers who graced with their presence the house-parties of Irish country weddings.[113] Within the Nordic context, the Olriks did not baulk at identifying a possible ancient phallic element in the wild dance with Boui and in the crude gestures which attended it, relating this to the famous account by Adam of Bremen of the court at Uppsala where at weddings the ithyphallic image of Fricco (Frö)[114] was displayed and offerings made to the accompaniment of numerous obscene songs.[115]

A further phallic reference may be discerned in the Danish custom of deputizing a young girl to do the rounds, for the purpose of issuing invitations to the childbirth feast, armed with a stick or branch from which the bark had been stripped. This she was to keep hidden underneath her apron until she had an opportunity to secretly deposit it with a household where a child was greatly desired or a birth was shortly to take place. It was believed that the next child to come into the world in that locality would be born in that particular house.[116]

With this we may compare Carmichael's description of the preparation of the bed of honour for Brigit on the eve of her feast. He tells us that having made an oblong basket in which 'a choice sheaf of oats' fashioned into the form of a woman is placed and decorated, one of the women of the house, standing on the step of the open doorway, bids Brigit to enter and take her place in the bed which has been prepared for her. Carmichael continues:

> The women then place the ikon of Bride with great ceremony in the bed they have so carefully prepared for it. They place a straight white wand (the bark being peeled of) beside the figure. This wand is variously called *'slatag Bride'*, the little rod of Bride, *'slachdan Bride'*, the little wand of Bride and *'barrag Bride'*, the birch of Bride. A similar rod was given to the kings of Ireland at their coronation, and to the Lords of the Isles at their instatement.[117]

We read also of the matter of peeled rods in one of the *Lives of Brigit* :

> Brigit went to Bishop Mél, that he might come and mark out her city for her. When they came thereafter to the place in which Kildare stands to-day, that was the time that Ailill, son of Dunlang, chanced to be coming, with a hundred loads of peeled rods, over the midst of Kildare. Then maidens came from Brigit to ask for some of the rods, and refusal was given to them. The horses were (straightaway) struck down under their horseloads to the ground. Then stakes and wattles were taken from them, and they arose not until Ailill had offered the hundred horseloads to Brigit. And therewith was built Saint Brigit's great house in Kildare, and it is Ailill that fed the wrights and paid them their wages.[118]

The modest communal feasting by the members of the *banal Bride* and the frugal festive meal which is the centrepiece of the Irish celebration of Brigit on the eve of her feastday[119] find a counterpart in the Nordic observance of serving the postparturient woman a special (first) meal of porridge, the ingredients for which had sometimes been donated by her female friends and neighbours who also joined in the repast.[120] This went by various names in the Scandinavian languages, the most interesting of these being the likes of Faroese *Nornagreytur*, and Norwegian *Nornegraut*, both meaning 'Norn-porridge'.[121] The evocative title of this meal, in which we see a reminder of the Irish custom of giving oatmeal gruel to the mother after her child is born in order to safeguard her against fairy abduction,[122] is generally believed to harbour a reference to the fate-spinning Norns who, as is seen from the Eddic poems, established a connection with the infant child at the moment of delivery:[123]

> In *Fáfnismál* it is told of Norns 'who help in distress and deliver children from the mother's womb'... In the first *Helgakviða* it is described how the norns come to Helgi's birth in Brálund: It was night in the house, norns were coming to create life and fortune for the hero. They decided that Helgi who was to be born, should be the leading man. They steadily twisted the threads of destiny, etc.[124]

The various Nordic words for 'porridge' ultimately derive from a root **ghreu-* which also yields English 'great, grits' and basically conveys the notion of something coarse-grained.[125] Here too belongs Swedish *gryt* 'stony ground' (Icelandic *grjót*, 'gravel, a sandy beach' with special reference to the hides of badgers and other such animals. According to Wessén,[126] the same root also yields Modern Icelandic *grúi* meaning 'a swarm of insects'; the related root **greut-* yields English 'curds', Irish *gruth* 'curds'.[127]

It is appropriate that the badger, one of the creatures (along with the hedgehog) whose reappearance in spring signals the onset of a new season,[128] should gain mention here. One of the Irish names for the badger is *brocc*, meaning 'the grey one';[129] the Old Irish personal name *Tadg* also meaning 'badger' is cognate with German *dachs*, and goes back to a Celtic root **tazgos*, which may in turn underline common Germanic **thahsaz*.[130] Our interest, however, centres in the fact that, *brocc* and *Tadg* provide us with a pair of names closely paralleling the *milchobur, math(gamhain)/Art* arrangement with respect to the bear, the significance of which has been discussed by me above.[131] *Tadg* also occurs in the meaning 'poet'[132] and most interestingly of all for us, perhaps, in the Modern Irish expressions, *Lá Thadhg na dTadhgann* 'Tibb's Eve' (literally, 'The Day of *Tadhg* of the *Tadhgs*')[133] and *Tadhg an Gheimhridh* (literally '*Tadhg* of the winter' (or 'Tim the Winter'), the name applied to the hunk of meat partaken of at Shrovetide and then 'hung on a spike in the kitchen for the duration of Lent.'[134]

Returning to the subject of porridge, the Irish word *brothchán*, 'broth, pottage, soup, gruel' is formed on *bruth*, meaning, *inter alia*, 'boiling heat, fiery glow, fury excitement fervour, valour, nap of cloth', on the one hand and '(glowing) mass, lump, charge of metal, boiling, brewing (= measure of ale)', on the other.[135] According to Vendryes[136] *bruth* goes back to **bhru-to-* and is thereby comparable to Latin *de-frutum*, *vin cuit*, 'new wine boiled down, mead'. From this, the possibility arises of seeing a connection between the transformation, as it were, of coarse-grained meal to porridge by boiling, or (representing an opposite process) of smooth milk to lumpy curds, by coagulation, and the conversion of other substances to ale or mead. Interestingly enough, while the various *Lives of Brigit* make no reference to the former process, strong emphasis is laid on the latter in accounts which detail how Brigit transformed water to mead[137] and water to ale.[138] On one occasion, Brigit was also said to have turned water into milk 'between the two Easters' i.e. between Easter Sunday and Low Sunday[139] and, as the following passage tells us, the transformation of water to ale was said to have taken place at the same time of year, a little earlier again in the springtime:

> Low Sunday approached. 'I do not think it pleasant *now**,' said Brigit to her maidens, 'not to have ale on Low Sunday for the bishop who will preach and say Mass'. As she said that, two maidens went to the water to bring in water, with a large vat with them for that purpose, and Brigit was not aware of this. When they were coming back again, Brigit saw them. *'Thanks be to God'*, said Brigit, *'God has sent us beer for our bishop*.'* The nuns are frightened at that: 'May God help us O maiden. Though I have said something stupid, I have not said anything evil, O nuns.' 'The water which has been brought inside, because thou has blest it, God did what you asked and *at once** it was turned into ale with the smell of wine from it and better ale has never been set to brew in the whole world.' The one vat was sufficient for the guests and the bishop.[140] *[* originally in Latin]*

The custom of placing three splinters or pegs in the 'Norns' Porridge' – an action believed to be intimately connected with the luck of the new-born provides us with a further reminder of the Norns.[141] This pattern is repeated in Sámi tradition where three pegs, one white, one black and a third with three rings carved in it, were put in the 'Sarakka-porridge' which the mother together with her married female friends ate immediately following the birth of her child. When the porridge had been consumed, these pegs were left under the threshold for three nights, the belief being that if the black one disappeared, the mother of the child would die soon, whereas both mother and child would survive if it was the white one which happened to go missing.[142] Listed among the 'Questions to put to the Sámi concerning their idolatry', drawn up by Henric Forbus of Torneo (Finland) in 1727, is the query – 'Have you eaten Saraca's porridge after the birth? N.B. This is usually done in honour of Saraca who not only helped the birth pains, but also formed the body in the womb.'[143] The same clerical commentator provides an interesting alternative arrangement for the 'lottery pegs', as Bäckman calls them:[144] when the child was a boy, instead of three pegs, a little bow, broken in three pieces – shaft, stock and arrow – was put in the porridge, each subsequently ascribed its own special significance as it fell into the spoon of the person supping the porridge. Of even greater moment, however, was the custom of hanging the bow afterwards on the child's cradle 'so that he should become in time a good shot.'[145] The sun, whom the Sámi people regarded as the mother of all living creatures, following the consumption of what they called 'Beiwe's (i.e. the Sun's) porridge' was also begged on bended knee to give them a 'happy milking summer' and otherwise bless their reindeer herds.[146]

The following version of a Sámi creation myth which was documented by the Christian missionary Jens Kildal in his treatise 'Afguderiets dempelse' ['The suppression of idolatry'] helps us to place Sarakka in the wider context of other Sámi divinities:[147]

> Maylmen radien ['The Ruler of the World'] is the chief god of Lapps, and at the child's birth he sends down a soul to Madderakka ['The Earth Mother'] which she gives to her daughters Sarakka, Juxakka and Uxakka, who live together under the ground beneath the floor of the Lapps' tent. Sarakka then causes flesh to grow around the soul in the womb, and if one offers to her there will be a good delivery; similarly,

if offered to, she causes (easier) menstruation. Juxakka's function is to change girls into boys within the mother's womb; but she must receive a good offering if she is to allow herself to arrange this, since when she changes female children into males she gives the child to her own enemy, and to that of her mother and sisters, Leybolmaj, who is the god of the hunt, and to whose service the child belongs when it grows up ... Uxakka will, when offered to watch at the door and take care of the child when it has been born, and when in time it begins to walk protect it against harm and falling.[148]

Sarakka, by far the most popular of the Sámi divinities,[149] was then one of the four Sámi female deities who constituted a distinct and homogeneous group known as the *Akkas* (Fig. 18). Information drawn from the accounts of missionaries concerning their abode and tutelary roles, and suggestions as to how their names should be interpreted is summarized by Louise Bäckman as follows:

> The dwelling-places of the goddesses are connected with the living-house of the people: *Madder-Akka* dwells under the floor of the *kåta*, hut, *Sarakka* in the neighbourhood of the hearth under the floor and *Juksakka* and *Uksakka* near the entrance... *akka*, the last component of the names, means old woman, and in some dialects also wife. *Madder-* is origin, root, earth. In present-day Saamian usage *'madder-akka'* means ancestress or sometimes great-grandmother. Moreover, the floor-area alongside the inside-walls of the *kåta* ['hut, tent'] is called *'madder'* in all Saami dialects, *Sar-* in *Sarakka* is probably derived from the verb *'saaret'*, which means to separate, to split, to divide. The goddess separates the child from the mother's uterus. *Jukse-* means a bow and *Ukse-* is door, entrance. It is also said that the word *'Saragads'* or *'Sarak'* was used as *nomen appellativum* instead of 'Creator' and this being was believed to be an active component in the creation of the world and was said to be a male god... *Madder-Akka* and *Sarakka* guarded the women during their menstrual periods and pregnancy, and without the assistance of the goddesses a child could not be successfully delivered. Furthermore. the goddesses mentioned also gave fertility to animals and they received offerings for that reason too. The sacrificial gifts consisted of food and drink, and animals as well. It will also be said that the cult of the four female deities, with the exception of that of *Sarakka*, was practised by women only, not men.[150]

Bäckman regards *Madder-Akka* as being a 'variant of the Great Mother... and in this respect the First Mother'[151] and her 'first daughter', *Sarakka*, whom she judges to be 'nearer to the people', she describes as holding many traits in common with the Mother Fire whose cult was one of the best preserved of the North Eurasian pantheon.[152] Bäckman's overall conclusion is that 'the *akkas* in their role as goddesses connected with birth can also be seen as an archaic element in the religious belief of the Saamis'.[153]

Recent scholarly opinion, therefore, has moved sharply away from the concept that the old religion of the Sámi derived mostly from Scandinavian sources, with the *akkas* being seen as a reflection of various household spirits or of the Norns. With regard to the *akkas*, this shift has led to the conclusion that the prerequisites for their 'coming into existence and further development... are to be found in the Lapp religion itself.'[154] Rather than regarding the Sámi customs which attended the birth of a child as being more or less a carbon copy of those prevailing among the Germanic population of Scandinavia, the feeling now is that these should rather be thought of as sharing various similarities with both the Scandinavians and the peoples of northern and central Eurasia.[155] In other words, as Ränk puts it – 'The functional differentiation of the Norwegian Lapp deities of birth need not be connected with the narrow pattern of the three Norns but...[rather] the multiplication of these spirits is the result of development on a broader historical basis.'[156] Regarding the many common characteristics between Sámi religion and that of the so-called Altaic peoples in general, Ränk believes that 'these prove clearly and convincingly that some essential details in the Lapp religion which hitherto were considered to be of purely Scandinavian (North Germanic) origin, are as much or even more closely related to those among peoples living further east, whose way of life and spiritual conceptions are closer to the Lapps than those of the North Germanic peoples.'[157] Furthermore, he urges that 'in all comparisons between Lapp and North Germanic religions [we] are fully entitled to ask whether these religions are not originally related to one another and whether there exist in the North Germanic religions ancient strata not absolutely without Arctic influences.'[158] To the distinctive configuration of the *Ciall/Tuigse + Náire* and the *Urð/Verðandi + Skuld* groupings, it may not be inappropriate to suggest the addition at this point of the *Juksakka/Uksakka + Sarakka* complex.

More and more emphasis has come to be placed on the relevance of the ecological circumstances that dominated the development of Sámi and other circumpolar cultures and which were instrumental in shaping their systems of religious beliefs. It will be useful to remember at this juncture too that, apart from the development of a similar expression of shamanism in the North Eurasian hemisphere, one of the distinguishing features of arctic and sub-arctic cultures was the emergence of a highly sophisticated complex of bear-ceremonialism,[159] various reflexes of which it has proved possible to trace in Scandinavian folklore and early Norse literature as well as in Irish and Scottish Gaelic tradition. We recall too that Óðinn shows a number of traits reminiscent of shamanism: *óðr*, for example, the basis of his name simply means 'master of ecstasy';[160] and Adam of Bremen consolidates the correctness of this etymology by saying of him – '*Wodan, id est furor*'[161] – thus confirming Bucholz's conviction that he should be regarded as 'the celestial prototype of a terrestrial shaman.'[162] Bucholz also suggests that, apart from the figure of Óðinn, one can find shamanistic elements distributed within what he dubs 'the ensemble of pagan Scandinavian traditions' in two further areas, viz. 'the mythical universe (layers and world tree) and magic, poetry and warfare' and wonders if all of these might not go back to the pre-Teutonic indigenous populations (precursors of the Lapps?) or to 'Eastern' contacts and influences at any time up to that of the Varangian expeditions into a Russia that was then more inhabited by Finno-Ugric than by Slavonic tribes.'[163]

Not unconnected with shamanistic activity is the phenomenon of *Arctic Hysteria*, a nervous disorder met with in 'almost all inhabited places of the Arctic',[164] and whose chief symptoms have been listed as including *inter alia*, fits, unconscious state, susceptibility to hypnotic suggestion temporary gift of second sight, singing while asleep, utterances of erotic expression and cramps of the vagina.[165] An extreme form of *Arctic Hysteria* occurs in northern and north eastern Siberia where it has been observed to be most prevalent among females who are especially susceptible to it at the menarche, during pregnancy and at the climacteric and where men, particularly young men who are preparing to become shamans, also fall prey to it.[166] The onset of this disorder arises from a number of circumstances, the most important of which would appear to relate to the geographical environment and the severity of the climate with its long cold dark winters and short summers. A nineteenth-century Polish political exile captured something of the implacable harshness of these conditions when he wrote:

> Days and nights go, weeks and months pass and the severe cold does not weaken, does not diminish in its severity. The man accustomed to another, more mild winter is tormented by that constant struggle with that never weakening enemy which the winter represents. But the strength is exhausted, the man seeing that he is left alone in this struggle collapses and his nervous system is shattered. His soul craves sunshine, warmth, day and light, and craves as only a dying person can. Not only would he give his possessions, but even life itself, all his blood for a sun-ray, but the sun is far and disappears in the West farther and farther.[167]

Novakovsky synchronizes his affirmation of 'a striking and close connection'[168] between the distribution of *Arctic Hysteria* and the character of the Siberian climate with the following observation:

> The first summer days coincide with an outburst of amorous instincts. We can suppose a close connection between the surrounding nature and not only the sexual life, but also the sex anomalies. Hysteria is very frequently accompanied by a heightened sexuality, and hence it can be supposed that the instincts which have been dormant during the period of darkness come out with all their force on the arrival of spring. But meeting with a weakened nervous system they often produce those abnormalities which are seen in hysteria. Thus the secret of such sexual anomalies becomes clear only after a relationship between sexual life and the surrounding nature is established.[169]

The culture of the high North of Europe and adjacent domains harbours further connective nodes relating to Brigit and her festival which are worthy of mention. The first of these has to do with the assignment of special positions to the goddesses of birth within the Sámi tent and particularly their close links with the door or door-area.[170] As Ränk explains, this is an issue bound up with a strict demarcation between male and female areas, the door area pertaining to the women and the rear area or 'poshjo' belonging to the men:

> The rear area of the tent, poshjo, is markedly connected with the economy of the men, hunting and fishing and preparation of food. Hunting implements, hunting clothes, but also meat and fish to be prepared for food were stored there... The above food supplies could not be brought into the tent through the ordinary front door and for this purpose there existed a special opening in the rear wall... In the door area, on the other hand, we meet with functions and objects which were to be attended to by the women... When we look at the distribution of places in a Lapp tent, it is remarkable how the sitting and sleeping places of men are gravitating towards the poshjo and those of women and children towards the door... At the border of poshjo, behind the hearth there even lay a special boundary stone... which was to remind the women how far they were to step in the poshjo area. However the rear door door did not serve the economy of the men only but a clearly ritual moment was connected with it too. First of all this door was used by hunters, particularly when going to or coming from a bearhunt. The rear door was moreover used when the men went to pray or sacrifice in the sacred places. The magic drum could only be taken in or out through the rear door. Women were strictly forbidden to make use of this door.[171]

On the other hand, the door area was generally:

> ...the traditional place for the cult of the deities of birth... There the Sar-akka porridge was put on account of childbirth and there the deities of birth generally received their libations. This observation is, moreover, accompanied by another characteristic feature, viz. that the Lapp women were obliged to move into the door area temporarily under critical periods when the deities of birth had ceased to be particularly active. First of all this change of place was undertaken during childbirth, when the woman left her ordinary sleeping and sitting place for a certain time and moved to the left side of the door. A similar change of place also occurred during menstruation periods... Thus it can be said that there were two polar cult places in the Lapp tent: that of the men in the poshjo and that of the women at the opposite end of the room, in the door area. A certain parallelism between these places is obvious: men are connected with the poshjo and the rear door by their hunting and particularly the cult connected with it, women with the door area by their special circumstances during which the deities of birth had cause to be particularly active.[172]

This schism of the sexes underpins what Ränk identifies as 'an ancient antagonism' between woman and man, the hunter, a tension which is translated, he argues, into 'the worlds of the deities' where, for example, Leib-olmai[173] was said to despise 'all women, the entire female sex'; it is this 'translation' reflex, Ränk supposes, which provides 'the key for the understanding of contradictory features in primitive religious conception.'[174]

The characteristics of the Sámi birth goddesses were mirrored in the cultures of other North Eurasian hunters and reindeer nomads as well as among the cattle-breeding peoples living to the south of these, on the border of the Siberian forests and steppes.[175] There they were believed to be spirits connected with the earth and associated with the dead or the souls of the ancestors; their original function was medical in nature, with obstetrics, including the parturition of animals, and menstruation being very much in the picture.[176] One of these groups, the Samoyedes, the nearest Eastern neighbours of the Sámi, has 'an absolute counterpart of the female deity of birth living underground, to whom they like the Lapps sacrificed a dog, burying it in the ground in front of the door of the tent in order to facilitate childbirth.'[177] Further east again, among the Yakut, we meet with *Ajysyt*, a female deity 'who in account of her ambiguity and versatility is very much like the Lapp and Ob-Ugrian deities of birth.'[178] Her function and the ceremonies associated with her are described by Ränk as follows:

> ...in ancient times images of *Ajysyt* were made and... her cult was connected with the time of childbirth... dolls were made from multicoloured rags and personifying *Ajysyt* were kept above the bed of the married couple... These images were obviously worshipped in the interests of the fertility of the women more particularly in order to get male children. The cult in honour of *Ajysyt* which took place under and after childbirth is very remarkable in several respects. It was celebrated in a closed circle of women, and the men had absolutely no access to it... in ancient times it was customary among the well-to-do Yakuts that pregnant women made a pledge to sacrifice to *Ajysyt* an animal which was killed during childbirth. The heart, liver, spleen and peritoneum were cooked and served to *Ajysyt* on a special table in the room of the childbirth, as *Ajysyt* was supposed personally to attend the childbed and stand at the head of the lying-in woman. If *Ajysyt* did not come, the woman and the child both died... During

the act of birth the midwife cast butter to *Ajysyt* on the hearth, saying: 'We thank you *Ajysyt* for what you have given and ask for it even in the future!' [For] three days the house was closed for men. Women, however, visited the lying-in woman during that time and ate together sitting at the hearth. The special ritual food for the occasion was butter in three dishes, one of which was reserved for *Ajysyt*, one for the midwife and one for the female visitors. When three days had passed from the birth, the midwife took from the floor the straw on which the lying-in woman had lain, and took it together with the birth refuse into the forest to the top of a tall tree. *Ajysyt* was believed to leave the house with this ceremony.[179]

Finally, among the Turkish peoples of the Altai-Sayan Mountains and to some extent also among the Mongols, there is a group of deities going by the name – *'Emegender'* or the like, a word derived from a root meaning '(old) woman, grandmother, ancestress' – whose main task was to assist in childbirth.[180] These deities were represented by wooden images, small stuffed rag dolls or even drawings on cloth and were given coloured glass pearls as eyes, the belief being that these would induce the same eye colour in the child due to be born (Fig. 33). A woman would receive these *Emegender* dolls before marriage and carry them with her to her new home; without them, she did not dare to give birth, because she might die and her child could be born blind. These dolls were also procured by women who were childless or who had experienced stillbirths, infant mortality and the like.[181]

Attention has already been fixed on the concept of liminality immanent in the celebration of the festival of Brigit where as we have seen heavy emphasis is placed on ceremonial entry, the doorway being the scene of a variety of solemn occasions and other formalities sometimes involving both sexes, as in Ireland, or alternatively, as in Scotland, the sole prerogative of the women.[182] It goes without saying, of course, that this does not warrant the supposition of a direct cultural-historical connection linking these phenomena or the many other cultural manifestations adverted to here which have been drawn from widely different language backgrounds and physical environments. On the other hand, we may justifiably permit ourselves to concur with Ränk's perception of the existence of 'an interesting parallelism which is probably a result of the differentiation process of the spirits of birth under influence of higher forms of religion.'[183]

Chapter 5

Fig. 33: *Emegender* dolls – Siberian fertility deities.

* * *

The use of the hallucinogenic mushroom, *Amanita muscaria* or fly-agaric, by a number of Siberian peoples has been known for many centuries;[184] its consumption served purposes as diverse as aiding communication with supernatural forces, divining the future and diagnosing illnesses on the one hand, or boosting the festive spirit of family occasions, such as weddings, on the other.[185] Most significantly, within the realm of ecstatic shamanism in northern Eurasia, this plant was widely invoked as a divine inebriant.[186]

The Uralic and Palaeosiberian languages share a common expression for it (Ob-Ugrian *panx*), a word which is also attested in a variety of ancient Indo-European languages being cognate, for example, with Greek σφόγγος/*sphóngos*, Latin *fungus*, proto-Slavic **goHba* and Old High German *swamb*.[187] While the direction of the borrowing remains unclear, the antiquity of fly-agaric as a hallucinogen and its utilization in shamanistic practice in northern Eurasia and elsewhere is well established.[188]

Its identification with *soma* – the mysterious sacred psychotropic plant of ancient India which is described in the Rigveda as having no leaves, no flower, no roots and no fruit, which is red in colour and whose unmixed juice yellow or brown when combined with milk and water and also sometimes barley, curds or honey, is capable of producing intoxication *(máda)*, visions and a sense of strength and expansion – has been regarded by some commentators as 'perfectly accounted for'[189] and a 'scholarly triumph'[190] which has 'set right almost three thousand years of ignorance about the 'plant of immortality''.[191] *Soma*, which is a word derived from the Indo-European root *su*, meaning 'to press' and literally meaning 'the pressed one',[192] is the name applied to an intoxicating drink, to the plant from which it was squeezed and to one of the most important of the Hindu gods; by some accounts, the god Soma was the creator of the world and chief of all the gods, by others his domain extended over the stars, all kinds of healing, barren women and motherless children, plants, priests and, of course, intoxication.

The fly-agaric, as Wasson tells us, is apt to be found in 'the fall of the year, hard by a birch or pine' and 'the season in the temperate zone,' he continues:

...lasts two or at most three weeks, with the climax coming in the middle week. The fly-agaric emerges as a little white ball, like cotton wool. It swells rapidly and bursts its white garment, the fragments of the envelope remaining as patches on the brilliant red skin underneath. At first the patches almost cover the skin, but as the cap expands they are reduced in relative size and finally are nothing more than islands on the surface. In fact, under certain conditions, especially as a result of rain, they are washed off altogether and the fly-agaric then shines without blemish as a resplendent scarlet mushroom. When the plant is gathered it soon loses its lustre and takes on a rather dull chesnut hue... When the fly-agaric is crushed and the juice milked out, the liquor comes forth a tawny yellow.[193]

Wasson believes the fly-agaric's cap to have suggested an udder to the Rigveda poets and likewise the stalk or stipe to have been likened by them to a teat[194] and, in this context, he also identifies various poetic references to the 'single eye', the mainstay of the sky and the navel.[195]

Wasson also draws attention to the 'intimate and all pervasive ties' that link Soma to Agni, the god of fire and he notes that hymns 'addressed to Soma, sometimes call him Agni.'[196] He further proposes the existence of a 'peculiar relationship... in primitive man's mentality between the mushroom world and thunder-storms' where 'the flame-like plant, child of the thunder-bolt, possesses inebriating qualities that harmonize with its celestial appearance.'[197] Ingalls in commenting upon this aspect of Wasson's conclusions is driven to add:

...I am keenly aware of a qualitative difference between the Soma hymns and certain other hymns of the Rigveda. The two poles seem to me to be the Soma hymns and the Agni hymns. The two gods represent the two great roads between this world and the other world... they are the great channels of communication between the human and the divine: the sacred fire and the sacred drink... [representing] two sorts of religious expression and religious feeling, one built about the hearth fire, with a daily ritual: calm, reflective, almost rational; the other built about the Soma experience which was never regularized into the calender, which was always an extraordinary event, exciting, immediate, transcending the logic of space and time.[198]

A further connection with fire is manifest in the widespread use of *Fomes fomentarius*, a shelf fungus, most commonly found on birch; dried and used as punk tinder, this has been located in association with hearth punk tinder stones in excavations dating at least to Mesolithic times.[199] Toadstools, according to folk tradition, were produced by thunder, and punk-fungus, or touchwood timber, was credited with the same celestial origin and also believed to contain hidden fire.[200] The most common host of punk fungus is also pre-eminently the tree of Siberian shamanism and living in mycorrhizal intimacy with the birch (sometime also with the pine and occasionally the fir) we also find the fly-agaric.[201] Wasson describes this combination of birch, punk and fly-agaric as 'nature's triangle', fly-agaric holding 'the place of honour in this Trinity',[202] and adds:

> Some will find it astonishing that the Siberian peoples observed and understood, according to their lights, the *mycorrhizal* relationship, only rediscovered by mycologists in 1885. For the tribesmen the roots of the birch tapped the lake of the Waters of Life and filled to overflowing with tawny yellow milk the breasts of the fly-agaric. The noble stance of the superb birch befitted its rôle as host and divine guardian… the fly-agaric and punk are primary in the hold of the birch on the souls of the natives and it must follow as night the day that the whiteness of the birch is in most fitting and wonderful harmony with its supernal attributes.[203]

Most of the points raised by Wasson which have been mentioned above also seem to sit in such 'fitting and wonderful harmony' with the central issues and various other elements associated with the festival of Brigit that it is something of an anticlimax to hear Wasson declare that, while in the territories of the 'Slavs and Lithuanians, and the Mediterranean littoral from Majorca and Catalonia to Provence and including apparently the whole of the *langue d'oc* area of France… wild mushrooms are considered friends,'[204] the Germanic and Celtic peoples 'are infected with a virulent mycophobia, coming down from pre-history'.[205] With regard to the Germanic peoples, the testimony of Saxo Grammaticus in describing the military campaign waged in Sweden in the tenth century by Hadding the Dane may be admitted as a rough guide to their tastes in bygone days:

...After the spring thaw, Hadding returned to Sweden and there spent five years in warfare. By reason of this lengthy campaign, his soldiers, having consumed all their provisions, were reduced virtually to starvation, and resorted to forest mushrooms to satisfy their hunger. Finally under pressure of extreme necessity they ate their horses, and in the end they satisfied themselves with the carcasses of dogs. Even worse they did not scruple to eat human limbs.[206]

Danish *paddehat* ('toad's hat'), Dutch *paddestoel* ('toad's stool'), Frisian *poddehûd* 'toad's hide'), Welsh *caws llyfant* ('toad's cheese'), Breton *kabell tousec* ('toad's cap') and Irish *bolg loscainn* ('frog's pouch') together with English 'toadstool' (and a choice of dialect words such as toadcheese, taddecheese, toad's bread, toad's cap, toadskep and toad's meat) are among the many disparaging appellations applied to wild mushrooms, constituting what Wasson calls a 'citadel of the 'toadstool", which describes an arc 'embracing the shores of the North and Irish Seas' and stretching as far as Biscay.[207] Within this area and, unlike some parts of the continent where names such as these also denote fly-agaric, the term toadstool etc has no specific meaning. It tends rather to be applied in a general way to wild mushrooms and is essentially a term which comes 'freighted with evil',[208] to use Wasson's phrase, a circumstance which he believes arises from Celtic custom and belief:

> I suggest that the 'toadstool' was originally the fly-agaric in the Celtic world: that the 'toadstool' in its shamanic rôle had aroused such awe and fear and adoration that it came under a powerful tabu, perhaps like the Vogul tabu where the shamans and their apprentices alone could eat of it and others did so under pain of death; that people hesitated to pronounce the very name of this mushroom, so that in time it became nameless and the name it formerly carried hovered thereafter ambiguously over the whole fungal tribe so that all the mushroom fell under the same floating *tabu*. This *tabu* was a pagan injunction belonging to the Celtic world. The shamanic use of the fly-agaric disappeared in time, perhaps long before the Christian dispensation. But in any case the fly-agaric could expect no quarter from the missionaries, for whom toad and toadstool were alike the Enemy... Today we are dealing with a deep-seated emotional attitude born in a *tabu* long forgotten.[209]

'How strange it is', Wasson muses, that in vernacular English the 'most spectacular, the most potent, mushroom lacks a name' and that no mention of the 'fly' – other than in the bookish designation 'fly-agaric' is to be detected.[210] In German, on the other hand, we find the words *Fliegenpilz* and *Fliegenschwamm* ('fly mushroom') while in Russian and French the mushroom is popularly known as the 'fly-killer' (*mukhomor* and *tue-mouche*, respectively), names owing their origin to the mistaken belief that the juice of this mushroom was insecticidal.[211] Among the evidence adduced by Wasson in support of the notion that the fly, like the mushroom, was believed to be divinely possessed, is the case of Loki who in Nordic mythology assumes 'the appearance of a fly to enter the tightly closed apartment of the sleeping goddess Freya. He pricks her and when she starts, deftly detaches her necklace and steals it. Whatever that fly was,' concludes Wasson, 'no one thought of it as a housefly, for the housefly does not bite.'[212]

Honey, 'the old Indo-European sweet',[213] which was in general use until the introduction of sugar, was the substance from which the 'oldest IE intoxicating drink, the 'mead'[214] was made. Within the Germanic language group, with the exception of Gothic, the word for honey is expressed by a new coinage (Old Norse *hunang*, Old English *hunig* and the like) which derives from its yellow colour; otherwise, as Buck tells us, 'the words for honey belong to one of two inherited groups' – Indo-European **melit-* 'honey' (yielding Latin *mel*, Irish *mil* etc.) and Indo-European **medhŭ-* 'honey, mead' (yielding Lithuanian *medus*, Old Church Slavonic *medu*, Sanscrit *madhu-* and the like).[215] Buck concludes that familiarity 'with the bee in the IE period, if not proved by the partial European agreement in words for 'bee' is clearly shown by the more complete agreement in the words for 'honey' and 'mead'.[216]

According to Hamp,[217] *maksika-* the Sanscrit word for 'bee' is likely to be Finno-Ugrian in origin; Collinder, on the other hand, believed the borrowing to have occurred in the opposite direction – with Finnish *mehi-* in *mehiläinen* 'bee', Mordvin *meks*, Hungarian *méh* etc. standing alongside the likes of *maksa-* 'fly', *maksika-*, *maksika* 'fly, bee' (Sanscrit), and an Indo-European provenance being similarly attributable to Finnish *mesi, mete,* Mordvin *med'* and Hungarian *méz* – meaning 'honey' – with which Sanskrit *madhu-* is to be compared.[218]

Vendryes derives Irish *bech* 'bee' from a root **bheko-* and he also draws attention to a possible Gaulish form **beko-* or **biko* with unaspirated initial.²¹⁹ Scottish Gaelic *beacan* 'bee'²²⁰ also belongs here as do the Irish expressions *beacán* 'mushroom' and *beacán bearaigh* 'toadstool' (where *beacán* ('bee/mushroom') is qualified by an adjective meaning 'pointed' *(bearach/biorach)*.²²¹ Regardless of its putative point of origin whether Finno-Ugrian or Indo-European, it is clear that, *pace* Wasson, we are now in a position to claim not one but two words for 'toadstool' in Irish; Wasson's *bolg loscainn* 'frog pouch' may now assume the by now familiar mantle of a Noa name and our *beacán bearaigh* provides us with a native name for fly-agaric which forges a range of highly significant associations and also begs a number of interesting questions.

On the basis of the references to bees, honeydew, mead etc, noted earlier in connection with Óðinn, Mímir and Yggdrasill as also the connections with fire which Thórr, and to some extent Loki have been shown to have, we may be able to discern the outline of a fly-agaric syndrome in the Nordic context.²²² It is not my intention to dwell upon this matter further here, however, but rather to focus briefly on what further clues as to the extent of this phenomenon may be located within the body of Irish tradition, taking the axiom *Oíche Fhéile Bríde Bric*²²³ – *Lá Fhéile Bríde Bán* ('The Eve of Brigit's Feast, Speckled – The Day of Brigit's Feast, White') as the point of departure.

To the best of my knowledge, no explanation has been vouchsafed hitherto as to why the two halves of Brigit's feastday should be colour-coded into 'speckled' and 'white'.²²⁴ I suggest that consideration of some role or other in the festival of Brigit for the fly-agaric with its startling contrasting colours so well described by Wasson, may well point us in the direction of the solution to this conundrum. A further pennyweight of evidence in support of this proposition may be won from the name of the individual with whom Brigit (in her triadic persona of *Ciall, Tuigse* and *Náire*) was associated, namely Aed meic Brecc – the flying *sui-liag* ('master-physician') of Sliabh Liag in Teelin, County Donegal; his patronymic – son of Brecc – sports the qualifying element *(breac/ Brecc)* applied to the eve of Brigit's feastday and his name – *Aed* – means 'fire'.²²⁵

The tawny yellow liquid of the fly-agaric and the golden honey of the bee both share a common association with milk; in the expression 'milk and honey', the felicitous combination of these products has been commemorated since antiquity in a variety of ways, for example, in the disposition of *Auðhumla*, the prodigious milk-producer and the bee/honey complex associated with *Óðinn, Yggdrasill* and *Mímir*.²²⁶ The Greeks described the food of the infant Zeus on Crete as curds and honey while, In India, milk and honey formed a part of the most valued offerings to the gods; here the milk was often mixed with *soma*, the lacteal element sometimes being sour. Similarly, honey was used as an offering; sometimes mixed with *soma*, sometimes with milk, while in the early Church, the newly baptized were given milk and honey to taste by way of symbolizing their regeneration through baptism.²²⁷

Likewise, we see traces of an ancient symbiosis between milk and fly-agaric in a custom attaching to the Hungarian *táltos* or the *tudós-pásztor* ('knowledgable shepherd') – a modern-day reflection of that people's once powerful fly-agaric consuming shamans: having slept for days and 'disappeared from the visible world', the *táltos* frequently appeared at doorsteps asking for milk; this motif, as Hoppál tells us 'often ignored as a curiosity, seems to make sense when collaborated with the evidence of modern pharmacology, which confirmed that milk is a powerful detoxicant to counteract the impact of fly agaric.' ²²⁸ We may well wonder whether some such consideration lies behind Aed meic Brecc's chaffing of Colm Cille about the excellence of his physical condition, a circumstance which arose from the adulteration of his daily sustenance with watered down milk.²²⁹ Fascinating as it would be to dwell upon the implications of this line of thinking, it would be inappropriate to pursue further investigation of these points at this juncture as, inevitably, this would carry us far beyond the scope of the present exercise.

Colm Cille faces us with one final challenge, however, namely that adumbrated by the legend describing how he succeeded in calling back to life from its assembled bones the cow which his female housekeeper, as the story has it, held in such secret conceit.²³⁰ A reminder of this rebirth from the bones, as it were, occurs in the traditional prayer of parturient women to Brigit, beseeching her in their hour of need *'An gein a thoir bho'n chnaimh'* – 'The conception to bring from the bone'.²³¹ The motif of birth from a bone or bones, best known perhaps from the biblical context,²³² is manifested in creation myth²³³ and also in folk custom and belief under many different guises as in German tradition, for example, where we find another intriguing formulation, namely, *'Der Storch hat die Mutter ins bein gebissen'*.²³⁴

However, it is probably within the framework of Nordic and North Eurasian bear cult that the most compatible context in which to place Colm Cille's vaunted capacity to restore cattle to life is ultimately to be located. We may allow Chapter 44 of *Gylfaginning* in Snorri's *Edda* to set the scene for us in this respect:

> ...Thór-the-charioteer was on a journey with his goats and in his chariot, and with him the god Loki, when they came one evening to a farmer's where they got lodgings for the night. During the evening Thór took the goats and slaughtered them, then had them skinned and put into a cauldron. When they were cooked, Thór and his companion sat down to supper and Thór invited the farmer and his wife and children to the meal. The farmer's son was called Thjálfi and his daughter Röskva. Thór spread the skins out away from the fire, and told the farmer and his household to throw the bones on to the skins. Thjálfi, the farmer's son took firm hold of a thigh-bone of one of the goats and split it with his knife, breaking it off for the marrow. Thór stayed there that night, and just before daybreak got up and dressed, took the hammer Mjöllnir, raised it and consecrated the goatskins. Then the goats stood up. One of them was lame of a hind leg; Thór noticed that and declared that the farmer and his household had done something silly with the bones; he knew that a thigh bone was broken.[235]

This account (which goes on to describe how the household having thrown themselves at his mercy were forced to surrender their children to Thórr as his bondservants) forms the basis of an extensive analysis of this general theme by von Sydow in whose opinion it is not Nordic but rather Celtic in origin.[236] However, Ulf Drobin sees this episode, as revealing 'an unmistakable connection with the so called 'animal ceremonialism' among many hunter tribes', and, rejecting the notion that it must have emerged from within the Celtic area, he suggests instead that it is just as likely to have been around for quite some time in the Nordic world.[237]

Throughout Northern Europe and Northern Eurasia, there was a widespread custom of preserving or burying single bones or even whole skeletons of game animals, such as the bear;[238] according to local tradition, these might be buried, placed on trees or platforms, or simply laid out on the surface of the ground (with or without cover) and occasionally some of the soft parts (flesh or hide) might also be preserved with the bones. Noteworthy also was the frequently referred to prohibition on breaking or otherwise damaging the bones of the animals in question.[239] Further elucidation of the most relevant aspects of these customs from our point of view is provided by Fjellström's description of the burial rites for bears which prevailed among the southern Sámi people:

> Just as none of the bear's bones is ever broken or damaged, so also do they forbear to throw away the bones as they would those of other creatures, but rather gather them all together forgetting not even the tiniest of them and thus preserve them in this manner. A hole the same length as the bear is made at the place where it had been cooked, following which a fine soft bed of birch twigs is prepared in the hole and on this all the bones and knuckles are laid arranged in precisely the same order as in a live bear. The patch of skin which had been cut from the bear's nose and which was worn by the person who had flayed the skull was then replaced in the proper spot it formerly occupied; so also the skin with the aforementioned bear's tail is also put in its proper place: first, however they remove the brass rings and chain links which had been put there by the women, to whom these are not returned but rather kept for use as a decoration or helping medium in connection with the magic drum. The rod wrapped in alder bark which had been positioned under the bear's nose while it was being flayed, was now also placed by its nose. Finally the hole is completely clad with timber cut to the same size as the hole and then covered with pine branches so that no wild animal might disturb or damage the bones.[240]

From other sources we learn that the birch rod to which the bear's tail had been fixed and which had been solemnly wrapped in linen was used for the purpose of stringing the back bones together in the proper sequence.[241] Following its burial, the bear was addressed in a friendly manner and encouraged to inform other bears with the utmost alacrity about the honour paid it so that these might not be afraid or make undue resistance when trapped or cornered.[242]

As Fjellström implies, this behaviour seems to be chiefly motivated by the desire to ensure future luck in hunting and to ameliorate the threat to hunters from animals of the same species, but there is also evidence to show, as Paulson points out, that 'the killed animal is not only supposed to continue in life in some simple, unspecified form, but is also believed to be revived or resurrected. Such beliefs among the Lapps', he continues, 'included the "slow resurrection" of the killed bear, or "new bears" or "new birds" to be formed of the bones of the killed animals. Elsewhere it is said that an animal will resume its life if its bones are properly and correctly preserved (Yukagirs)'.[243]

Nevertheless, continued existence rather than revival in the strictest sense seems to have been the keynote as far as the perception of the whole process by those who practised it is concerned for, Paulson concludes, 'in the primitive imagination, dead animals, as well as men, are always doubly present, as corpses and as surviving souls or spirits... and [thus] the belief in an animal's soul surviving, and representing it after death, had important consequences in the evolution of hunting and religious rites among primitive peoples.'[244]

At a later stage of human development, rather than being the quarry of the hunter (like the bear, even down to our own day), certain animals (for example, cows) were destined instead to become the cherished possession of house and home. Such creatures presented a soft target and frequently stood in need of protection from the ravages of wild animals.

This problem is addressed directly in the numerous prayerful invocations of Colm Cille, Brigit and other figures aimed at helping to secure the safety of various domesticated creatures.[245] These prayers or charms could be regarded as reflecting the development of a new phase in religious thinking linked with the emergence of an agricultural economy.

Obviously the stories which credit Colm Cille with the power to revive a deceased bovine from the bones do not concern themselves with matters pertaining immediately to the hunt; however, granted that there is substance to the argument favouring a definite role for northern European and northern Eurasian culture and tradition in the analysis and assessment of the body of material pertaining to Brigit and related matters, Colmcille's facility in exercising this particular function may well be considered to harbour echoes from an earlier era, represented, for example, in the bear cult as it was practised until relatively recently by the Sámi people and their neighbours.

* * *

The story of Brigit and her festival is relatively straightforward; reflections and ramifications of it in the folk record in respect of other Irish saints (such as Colm Cille)[246] less so. Less immediate again are the myriad ways in which elements of it are manifested in various more or less contemporary folklore sources in neighbouring traditions and language cultures across Europe, and also to an extent in antiquity. The most powerful attestation stems from the Gaelic-speaking Highlands and Islands of Scotland and from Scandinavia, where in the latter case, the Irish and Scottish materials provide a new vantage point from which aspects of Nordic (including Sámi and Finnish) folk tradition can be viewed.

Among the features identified as common to both Irish and Scottish Gaelic traditions by Alexander Carmichael in his comparison of the *Brídeog* custom in Ireland and the Scottish 'Bride maiden band' called *Banal Bríde* are the fashioning and decorating of a doll figure in the likeness of a woman which is then carried with ceremony from house to house on St Brigit's Eve and the receipt of small gifts, including donations of food (butter, cheese, eggs *inter alia*), by the members of the *Brídeog* or *Banal Bríde*.[247] In Ireland, a churn staff, topped perhaps with a turnip head and surrounded by a straw-stuffed white garment constituted the actual *brídeog* or doll figure (literally 'a bride' or 'little Brigit') while in Scotland, the basic ingredient used in the manufacture of the image of Brigit was a corn sheaf. According to Irish custom, either or both sexes might participate and mixed groups as well as all-male and all-female groups were in evidence.[248] To judge by Carmichael's description, however, the latter assortment appears to be the norm in Scotland, a circumstance probably emphasized by the use of the word *banal* in the name of the 'maiden-band', given that this word may be assumed to contain the elements *ban* + *dál* and thus giving the meaning 'a meeting of women'[249]; this interpretation is lent substance, as we shall shortly see, by the existence of certain customs both within and without the domain of Gaelic culture directly and indirectly related to the body of tradition surrounding Brigit and her feast.

The subsequent sharing out of the spoils gathered by the circumambulating bands, in the form of a 'feast', is recorded as forming a part of the proceedings in Ireland,[250] though Carmichael in this respect here concentrates solely on the Scottish material, which in this particular regard is more absorbing in any case. His account tells us that:

> Having made the round of the place the girls go to a house to make the *'feis Bríde'*, Bride feast. They bar the door and secure the windows of the house and set Bride where she may see and be seen of all. Presently the young men of the community come humbly asking permission to honour Bride. After some parleying they are admitted and make obeisance to her. Much dancing and singing, fun and frolic, are indulged in by the young men and maidens during the night. As the grey dawn of the Day of Bride breaks they form a circle and sing the hymn of *'Bríde bhoidheach muime chorr Chriosda'*, Beauteous Bride, choice foster-mother of Christ. They then distribute *'fuidheal na feisde'*, the fragments of the feast – practically the whole, for they have partaken very sparingly, in order to have the more to give – among the poor women of the place.[251]

In the Christian context, Brigit's manifold fertility associations culminate in her being cast in the role of companion or midwife to the Virgin Mary[252] or figuratively presented as the actual mother of Christ;[253] at a more mundane level, they extend to her being called upon to succour women in childbed, either symbolically through the placing of the *Brat Bríde* on the person of the woman concerned[254] or, what amounts in effect to the same thing, by inviting her to attend in spirit at the birth. The mechanics of the latter event are described by Carmichael as follows:

> When a woman is in labour, the midwife or the woman next her in importance goes to the door of the house, and standing on the *'fad-buinn'*, sole-sod, door-step, with her hands on the jambs, softly beseeches Bride to come:
>
> | | |
> |---|---|
> | *Bhríde! Bhríde! thig a steach,* | Bride! Bride! come in, |
> | *Tha do bheatha deanta,* | Thy welcome is truly made, |
> | *Tabhair cobhair dha na bhean,* | Give thou relief to the woman, |
> | *'S tabh an gein dh'an Triana* | And give the conception to the Trinity. |
>
> When things go well, it indicates that Bride is present and is friendly to the family; and when they go ill, that she is absent and offended. Following the action of Bride at the birth of Christ, the aid-woman dedicates the child to the Trinity by letting three drops of cold clear water fall on the tablet of his forehead.[255]

And similarly, the mother-to-be might turn to Brigit and appeal directly to her in the following prayer:

Mar a gheineadh Criosd am Moire	As Christ was conceived of Mary
Coimhliont air gach laimh,	Full perfect on every hand,
Cobhair thusa mise, mhoime,	Assist thou me, foster-mother,
An gein a thoir bho 'n chnaimh;	The conception to bring from the bone;
'S mar a chomhn thu Oigh an t-solais,	And as thou didst aid the Virgin of joy,
Gun or, gun odh, gun ni,	Without gold, without corn, without kine,
Comhn orm-sa, 's mor m'othrais,	Aid thou me, great is my sickness,
Comhn orm a Bhride!	Aid me, O Bride![256]

Fig. 34: St Brigid's Well, Clondalkin, County Dublin.

Notes to Chapter 5

1 MacKenzie (169).
2 MacBain 1890-1 (233). MacBain credits Alexander Carmichael as his source.
3 *Loc.cit. CG* 4. 46-7 cites what is designated a cattle-driving song entitled *Buachailleachd Chaluim Cille* 'Calum Cill''s Herding' which contains the following verse:
   Sìth Caluim dhuibh san ionailt, The peace of Columba be yours in the grazing,
   Sìth Bhrighde dhuibh san ionailt, The peace of Brigit be yours in the grazing,
   Sìth Mhoire dhuibh san ionailt, The peace of Mary be yours in the grazing,
   'S bhur tilleadh dachaidh anaglainn. And may you return home safe-guarded.
   Cf. *CG* 4. 40-1 for another example in which the invocation extends to embrace Saint Michael and includes a range of Gaelic notables such as Maol Odhrain, Maol Oighe, Maol Domhnaich, Maol Ruibhe, Fionn mac Cumhaill, Cormac and Conn.
4 Cf. for example, Ó Laoghaire (1, 76, 220, 236, 242, 253).
5 Szövérrfy 1988 (3).
7 Robertson (249).
6 *Loc.cit.*
8 Cf., for example, Ó hEochaidh 1963 (33-50). So well-beloved of Donegal people was the memory of Colm Cille that they frequently referred to him simply as 'Colm' (cf. Ó Catháin 1985, 72-7).
9 NFC 142:1697-8. This and other translations here from the Irish are by me unless stated otherwise. This was noted by Seán Ó hEochaidh from Máire Ní Bheirn (68) of Málainn Bhig, Glencolmcille on 1.1.1935. This version corresponds in all essential details with the retelling of this story by Seán himself in Ó hEochaidh (1963, 43).
10 Ó hEochaidh 1963 (45-6) and An tAth.Colmcille (10).
11 For a detailed account of the initial stages of this career, cf. Ó Catháin 1989 (49-85).
12 Szövérrfy 1955 (115 = Ó hEochaidh's version [1963, 43]) where monks are substituted for nuns. A comprehensive treatment including numerous references to Irish, Welsh and other variants of this legend type can be found in von Sydow 1910 (65-104).
13 For *Betha Colaim Cille* texts and translations, cf. Kenney (442).
14 Szövérrfy 1955 (121-2). Elsewhere, Szövérrfy 1956-7, (124) adds: 'I am inclined to see in this incident the echo of two different group (sic) of traditions: (1) the marvellous cow giving plenty of milk – a motif common to many Irish tales – and (2) two stories in *Betha Colaim Cille*, the resuscitation of an ox and the tale of the bones re-covered by flesh at Columcille's prayer.'
15 Ó hEochaidh 1963 (44: translated from the Irish). The Finnish words *sampa, sammas, sampaat* denote 'disease of the mucuous membranes of the mouth of a child, glands of chin in swollen state, a disease of horses' and these are related to the word *sampa*, meaning 'fungus, foam', also found in compounds such as *maansampa* 'puffball' and *puunsampa* 'white fungus

the size of a pinpoint on birch, on alder, on willow' (Hajdú in *Diószegi* [ed.],155), in which connection, cf. Note 210 below.
16   O'Donovan (xli, 303).
17   Kenney (393).
18   *Loc.cit.* He is invoked in a prayer against headache – what Kenney (393-4) calls 'a riming, jingling Latin hymn which is at least as old as the eighth, and might be of the seventh century.' His *Life* – compiled according to Kenney (393) 'at a late date, probably the twelfth century, and not in Aed's own community' – consisted 'of matter taken over quite freely from secular sources or from the common stock of hagiographic material' replete with anecdotes 'which convey interesting information; e.g. as to ploughing; as to the building of those earthen ramparts that surrounded most monasteries and well-to-do residences; as to hallucinations caused by druids *(loc.cit.).*' From O'Brien (128) we learn that 'During the time between the two Easters, Brigit suffered greatly from headache. 'That does not matter', said Mel, 'when we shall go to visit our first settlement with the men of Teffia. Brigit and her maidens shall go with us; there is a wonderful physician with the men of Meath, namely Aed mac Bricc; he shall heal you…' The springtime occurrence of this event – 'between the two Easters' i.e. between Low Sunday and Easter Sunday is worthy of note; cf., also in this connection, p. 171-2.
19   O'Rahilly 1957 (472).
20   Kenney (393).
21   Elsewhere he dubs him 'the Right Revd. Hughy Breaky', Ordnance Survey Letters, Donegal, October 23, 1835, Typescript 131.
22   Ordnance Survey Letters, Donegal, written at Kilcar, October 20th 1835, Typescript, 125. Cf. also Ó hEochaidh 1989 (41).
23   NFC 140:201-2 (translation from the Irish). This item was collected by Seán Ó hEochaidh. These remarks concerning the removal of the Holy Women to Slieve League for the summer are strongly reminiscent of the practice of transhumance and highly relevant to the subject matter of Chapter 4 above.
24   Szövérrfy 1988 (24).
25   Kenney (434).
26   Stokes (173).
27   Szövérrfy 1956-7 (123).
28   Szövérrfy 1955 (119).
29   Szövérrfy 1955 (113).
30   Szövérrfy 1988 (24).
31   Szövérrfy 1955 (121).
32   Szövérrfy 1988 (25).
33   Szövérrfy 1955 (121).
34   Szövérrfy 1955 (116).
35   *Loc.cit.*
36   Ó Muirgheasa 1936 (148-9). Cf. also Ó Muirgheasa 1937 (247). J. O'Donovan (Ordnance Survey Letters: Mayo. 1. Typescript 104) documents more or less the same tradition in respect of Inishglora – off the North Mayo coast – telling us that 'ships when sailing by it, lower

their top sails in honour of St Brendan'. The *'Cailleach C[h]rom'* referred to by Ó Muirgheasa is, in fact, a sea stack (cf. Ó Catháin 1975, 217-20) and the 'jutting cliff' which he mentions is, in all probability, the *Lúnasa* site described by MacNeill (1962, 189-91) called *An Dúna* situated near Portacloy.'Three rocks at the foot of the Dúna', MacNeill tells us, '… are known as *'Trí Cailleachaí Thón a' Dúna'* (the Three Hags at the end of the Dún) and are believed to be three women under a spell of transformation by a witch' (Cf. Ó Cathain 1975, 212-27).
Tobar na mBan Naomh and its three holy women are discussed in Sveinsson (170-1). Szövérrfy 1955 (118) notes the existence of other wells with similar names: *'Tobar na n-Ingen* or *Fons Puellarum* in Munster; *Tobar na secht mBannaomh* (The Well of the Seven Holy Women) on the West side of the Hill of Doon near Bunowen Castle County Galway and a similar one East of Rinvile Castle on Killary Bay'. J. L. Campbell (1978) mentions the site of a Columban nunnery in Canna known as *Sgorr nam Ban Naomh*. A *Reilig na mBan* or 'Graveyard of the Women' is also to be found at Carrickmore, County Tyrone, a place which also boasts a number of connections with Colm Cille (e.g. Colmcille's Bed, Colm Cille's Chair and Colm Cille's Well). According to local tradition, a certain women accused Colm Cille of committing some crime or other; when she died, he ordered that she be taken from the church for burial and laid to rest where the ringing of the church bell could no longer be heard, a spot called *Reilig na mBan* where many women but no men have ever been buried (Ó Máirtín, 66-7).
37 Ó hEochaidh 1944 [1945], (131).
38 *Loc.cit*. Translation from the Irish. Elsewhere, Ó hEochaidh 1963 (40) adds: 'It is said that when he [Colm Cille] was in Glencolmcille that he used to visit his sisters in Teelin (*Ciall, Tuigse* and *Náire*) and that as he sailed into the harbour he would lower his peak-sail thrice at their well in honour of the Trinity – a custom followed by the fishermen of Teelin until recently.'Translated from the Irish.
39 Ó Muirgheasa 1936 (149).
40 NFC 140:206 (translation from the Irish). This item was collected by Seán Ó hEochaidh. Further information on this subject is given by him in *Watson* (ed.), 41-2. The word *cóir*, an oblique form of which is contained in the name *Tobar na Córach* has been taken here as the equivalent of *cóir gaoithe* meaning 'fair wind'. The word *cóir* also means 'rightness, justness, propriety', and, most aptly in view of the above-mentioned tradition of a death arising from supplicants having recourse to this well, 'claim, due, tribute' (*DIL* C, 314). Plummer (1. cli) having noted that some 'fountains on being drained ensure a favourable wind' proceeds to refer to a well on the northern coast of Inishmurray (County Sligo) called *'Tobar na Cobhrach'* i.e. 'Well of Assistance' concerning which he observes: 'When the islanders are too long detained on the island by tempestuous weather, they drain this well into the sea and repeat certain prayers.'
41 Ó Muirgheasa 1936 (149).
42 Szövérrfy 1955 (116ff).
43 *Loc.cit*. For an extensive treatment of this theme, cf. Drinkuth.

44 Stokes (265).
45 Szövérrfy 1955 (117).
46 *DIL* to-tu, 354.
47 *Loc.cit.* Cf. also Vendryes (T-167). *Teinm as in teinm laída* 'a divinatory incantation used by the *'filid'* [poets] was taken by native glossators to mean 'illuminating...understanding: *teinm laeda i. teinm taithnim 7 teinm tuicsi'* (*DIL* T-tnúthaigid, 118). For further discussion of this matter, cf. Ford (69-74).
48 Bauschatz (59-61).
49 Stallybrass (405).
50 Bauschatz (64, 66).
51 Bauschatz (67). Cf. also in this context, Polomé 1989 (88-9).
52 *Náire* is derived from an adjective *nár*, meaning 'modest' and also 'noble, magnanimous, honourable' (*DIL* N-O-P ,13; cf. also Vendryes (N-3) and O'Rahilly 1950 (368).
53 *EOR* 5. 293.
54 *KL* 12. 348.
55 Turville-Petre 1964 (279).
56 Gylfaginning 8. 15: F. Jónsson (1931), 22).
57 Cf., for example, Turville-Petre, *loc.cit.*
58 *Loc.cit.*
59 Lincoln 1982 (27). Lincoln is careful to point out, however, that serious etymological difficulties render it 'premature to accept an interpetation of Mímir as 'memory', however much comparative mythology points in favor of such a reading.' Cf. Chapter 1, Note 127.
60 Simpson 1962-5 (50-1).
61 Turville-Petre 1964 (62).
62 Bauschatz (77).
63 Gylfaginning *loc.cit.* – translation quoted in Simpson 1962-5 (41).
64 Simpson 1962-5 (51). Concerning drowning as a form of sacrifice among northern peoples, cf. Turville-Petre 1969 (248-9).
65 Simpson 1962-5 (41).
66 Ross 1967 (126).
67 Ross, in *Rawson* (ed.), 86.
68 Cf. p. 94ff.
69 Gylfaginning 8. 23 : Jónsson (1931), 24).
70 Brodeur (30).
71 *Loc.Cit.*
72 Fleck (401, 411).
73 Fleck (401).
74 Fleck (400, 401).
75 Fleck (411).
76 Fleck (412).
77 Cf. p. 94ff. The arguments advanced by me here in this context are in large measure in line with Carey's suggestion (217) that 'instances in Irish literature of one-eyedness, one-handedness and one-footedness occurring in magical and supernatural contexts, and the pervasiveness of the conception of inspiration as a drink...belong to a single complex of

ideas, in which the semi-personified water of knowledge, associated with hazel-nuts and salmon, springs from a source identified with an eye and becomes a river identified with a single arm or leg'.

78 NFC 901: 115 (information supplied in July 1942 by Brighid Bean Uí Chadhla [64], Bodyke, County Clare).
79 NFC 900: 41.
80 Cf., for example, NFC 25:537-8. Campanile (237-47) has a number of interesting observations to make concerning the colour *glas*, which, in the combination *cú glas*, he takes to mean 'blue'; the expression *cú glas* meaning 'blue wolf' he regards as being 'a very ancient metaphor [meaning 'stranger' – specifically from the Irish point of view, a woad-painted Briton] which Old Irish shares with Germanic, Hittite and Old Indian and which surely goes back to I.E. culture' (246), 'wolf' in this context basically designating 'the stranger or the man banished from his people' (245). Cf. also Pollak (161-205) and Lehmann (73-9) who states that: 'Light gray is *glas*, related to *líath* much as *gel* is related to *bán* and *finn*, that is light and shining gray. But it is also the usual term for light green and light blue. The usage with this term suggests that to the Irish, the brilliance rather than the hue was of primary importance. *Glas* is used of eyes, of the sea, of frost, clouds, mist, and then of foliage, often the tips of branches, but including yew and watercress, hazel and oak. It is used of fields and streams and of horses. In compounds with other colors it signifies pale. Except that nothing that we would call yellow or red may be termed *glas*, the word may be applied to any light color of the blue, green or gray range – high brilliance, and medium low or low saturation (75).'
81 Ó hÓgáin 1990 (240-1).
82 NFC 906:16-7. This was collected by Éibhlís Bean Uí Mhathghamhna from Tomás Ó Domhnaill (70) of Omeath, County Louth in May 1942.
83 Cf., for example, Ó Catháin 1985 (11-2). Across Donegal Bay, directly opposite Teelin (and Glencolmcille), lies Killala, in the vicinity of which traditions about St Cuimín held sway, many of them resembling or even identical to those pertaining to Colm Cille. Of particular interest is the story of a cow which having licked a stone near the shore, subsequently began to deliver a copious supply of milk; its owner broke open the stone and inside found a child which he reared and who grew up to be St Cuimín (cf., NFC 195:470-5).
84 For the importance of heat as a creative principle in combination with ice, cf. Polomé 1986 in Brogyanyi & Krömmelbein (eds.), 474-6).
85 Turville-Petre 1964 (275).
86 Lincoln 1975 (29). Cf. also Lincoln 1981 (69-95). Polomé 1986 (486) while agreeing with Lincoln that Auðhumla represents the primeval bovine, doubts, however, that she was originally part of the cosmogonic sacrifice and proposes instead a cyclical scheme for the emergence of primal beings in Germanic tradition with Ymir who engenders the *giants* and is slaughtered by the sons of Bor, providing 'the constituents of the *cosmos*, Buri who is licked out of the ice by Auðhumla and begets Burr, begetting the 'first *gods*' and Ask and Embla –originally pieces of wood which drifted ashore – 'given *life* and human *features* by a triad of gods led by Óðinn' becoming 'the ancestors of mankind' (483). It is tempting

to associate the drifting logs which turned into Ask and Embla with the drifting coffin which carried Colm Cille's body back to Ireland.
87 Lincoln 1975 (142).
88 Lincoln 1975 (144).
89 de Vries,18. Polomé 1974 (114) compares *auðr* 'fate, death' (actually what is woven by the 'Norns') with Lithuanian *áudzu áusti* ('to weave') and Latvian *audi* ('fabrics'). Gimbutas 1985 (19-25) explains the name of *Austeja*, the bee goddess of Baltic mythology, as being connected with the verb *austi*, *austyti* 'to weave'; *Austeja* is described by Gimbutas as being 'the protectress of married women [who] promoted growth and increase. She cared for the multiplication of the beehive and the human family' and offerings 'were made to her in a jumping motion whilst pouring them upward to the ceiling or into the air' (24).
90 de Vries, 18. Cf. also Vendryes (O-2).
91 Cf. *KL* 1. 279.
92 *Loc.cit.*
93 Cf. p. 10 above.
94 Cf. pp. 54, 177 above.
95 Walde & Pokorny (1. 388-9).
96 Walde & Pokorny (1. 385-6).
97 Cf. pp. 120-121 above.
98 Cf. pp. 188 ff. above.
99 The significance of these and other elements is discussed above (cf. p. 100 ff above). Intriguingly, Aurgelmir, the initial element of whose name, *aur-*, is taken to refer to the 'sandy slime where water and land meet, and also applies to the honey dew that drips down from the cosmic tree' (Polomé 1986, 477) is one of two other names enjoyed by Ymir. For a comprehensive review of the correlation between milk and honey in classical and other sources, cf. Usener (177-95).
100 Cf. Ó hÓgáin 1990 (240-1) and references cited there. The initial element of her name presumably refers to her colour (*Glas* = 'white' [literally, 'grey, blue']) while the remaining element would seem to impute ownership (*Goibhneann* ['of Goibhniu']).
101 Though not mentioning the *Glas Ghoibhneann* by name, passages in the '*Lives*' such as the following, point unambiguously towards Brigit's connections with a prodigious milker: '1. Here is a deed which, among the rest of her miracles, seems amazing and worthy of admiration. 2. As bishops had arrived and were staying with her and since she had no food to give them, God's manifold power came to her aid, abundantly as usual, according as her needs demanded. So she milked one and the same cow three times in one day, contrary to normal practice. 3. And what it normally took three of the best cows to produce, she, by an extraordinary turn of events, obtained from her one cow' (Connolly & Picard, 15).
102 Cf. pp. 10-11 above and also NFC 25:537-8.
103 She may also be compared with Laima, one of the goddesses of Baltic mythology, characterized according to Latvian tradition as 'Fate, the birth-giver and determiner of the life-thread, short or long, good or bad' (Gimbutas 1985, 20). Gimbutas describes the 'Latvian 'Cow Laima' also

known as 'the Old Shepherdess of Cows' as possessing 'an inexhaustible source of milk in her magic spring (or three springs). She appears in cow stalls at calving time as a black snake, black bug, or as a black or white hen... She is invoked for good pastures and the easy birth of calves. The association with pastures, cows and calves links this archaic aspect of the Goddess with that of the pre-Greek Hera (21).'

104 NFC 1340:418-30 *(passim)*. Cf. also in this connection, Ó Catháin 1994 (103-5).
105 J. & A. Olrik (175-6). The exhortation 'Sing along Boui, sing along, Boui; why are you silent?' is offered as a translation of the *'Canta Boui, canta Boui. quid faceret?'* of the Latin text with *taceret* (though still inappropriate as to person) fitting the sense of the narrative better. Axel Olrik identifies *Bovi* with *Bous*, according to Saxo (*Gesta Danorum* III, 82) the son of Rinda who conceived him from Óðinn (*KL* 14. 326 and Wikman 1917 (43-9).
106 J. & A. Olrik (176).
107 Møller (306).
108 Møller (303).
109 Gimbutas 1985 (20-1). Gimbutas is of the opinion that the formula 'The Bear is coming' may stem 'from prehistory when it was believed that the Birth-giving Goddess assumed the shape of a bear.' She points out that 'Artemis, the Birth-giving Goddess of pre-Indo-European origin, was worshipped in ancient Greece by young girls who dressed as bears' and would see the importance of the 'female bear in cult' extending back to the neolithic and upper palaeolithic era and her origins as having been 'an ancestress, a tribal mother' (21).
110 J. & A. Olrik (176). The straw bears of continental European tradition were not known in Ireland. In England, however, the Tuesday following Plough Monday (the first Monday after Twelfth Day) was called Straw Bear Tuesday after the custom of leading around a man swathed completely in straw who danced in front of people's houses in return for money (Wright & Lones [eds]., 104-5).
111 Møller (309).
112 Gailey 1969 (74-5).
113 Gailey 1966, while acknowledging the probability of two types of folk-play in Ulster tradition, one of which belonged in all probability to an older stratum of tradition incorporating a native *ludus* in which Jack Straw would have figured, also suggests the existence of a connection between the Strawboys and the Christmas Mummers and does not rule out the possibility that Jack Straw may have been adopted into the folk play from the latter source (154). The Jack Straw rhyme of the mummers' plays – which also occurs as a riddle in which the answer is 'Lightning' (or, according to Gailey 1969, 49, 'a moth or a maggot') – takes the following form:
'Here comes I, Jack Straw//Such a man you never saw//
Through a rock, through a reel//Through an old spinning wheel//
Through a bag of pepper//Through a miller's hopper//
Through a sheep's shank bone//Such a man was never known!'
Snippets of self-description which Jack Straw's utterances sometimes provide further enhance his image as a fertility figure, e.g. 'My mother was

straw, my father was straw//And I was reared in a barn of straw' (Gailey 1969, 75); and, more explicitly, 'Here comes I, Jack Straw//With a stick in me hand ready to draw//I had fourteen childer born in the one night and not two in the one townland' (Glassie, 82).
114 *KL* 4. 618.
115 J. & A. Olrik (176).
116 Møller (295). Cf. also, Wikman 1917 (49 -58).
117 *CG* 1.168.
118 Stokes (194). According to Rose (104), 'the ritual of Hera included fetching her statue out of her temple, once a year, carrying it down to the shore and there hiding it under withies and setting cakes before it'. According to Solheim (230-1), Norwegian herds were not supposed to make use of a stick or crook from which the bark had been removed as this was thought to attract wolves and bears, the rationale behind this being the notion that just as the stick had been stripped of its bark, so also the herd could be stripped of his cattle, the 'flayed' stick providing a further reminder of the bear and the wolf, the two most dangerous predators.
119 Cf. p. 22ff. above.
120 *KL* 1. 363.
121 *Loc.cit.* Cf. also Møller (290-1) and Hagberg (1944).
122 S. Ó Súilleabháin 1977 (44).
123 Lid 1946 (18-9).
124 Lid 1946 (19). Among the pronouncements concerning them in the Eddic poems are – 'No one lives to the evening after the Norns' decree'; 'The judgement of the Norns meets you close to the coast' (i.e. even in shallow water one may drown); 'No man can stand against the word of Urð'. For a discussion of these and other aspects of the Norns, cf. Motz (174-5) and also Hallberg in *Brogyanyi & Krömmelbein* (eds.), 220, 244.
125 Walde & Pokorny (2. 648).
126 Cf. Hellqvist, 305.
127 Walde & Pokorny (2. 649).
128 Cf. NFC 902:95 and NFC 904:95 (re badgers) and NFC 902:233 (re hedgehogs). Cf. Chapter 2, Notes 93 and 140.
129 For a discussion of this and various other aspects and interpretations of the name, cf. Pokorny 1959 (108-9); Wagner 1953b (92-3); and Heiermeier (1. 137-58).
130 Cf. Mac an Bhaird (150-55). For other associations and connections, particularly in continental Celtic, cf. Koch (101-18) and especially, Ellis Evans (263-5, 378) – for which reference I am grateful to my colleague, Professor Próinséas Ní Chatháin.
131 Cf. pp. 50 & 74 (note 2) above.
132 Cf. Vendryes (T-5, T-6) and *DIL* T-tnúthaigid, 11.
133 Dinneen, 619.
134 S. Ó Súilleabháin 1977 (68).
135 *DIL* B, 216-7.
136 Vendryes (B-106).
137 Ó hAodha (34).
138 O'Brien (28).

139 O'Brien (127). Cf. also note 18 above.
140 O'Brien (128). Words in italics are translated from the Latin. The style and tone of this account is remarkably close to what one would expect in a folk narrative source.
141 Hagberg 1944 (23).
142 Bäckman 1984 (32).
143 H. Grundström 1956 (204).
144 Bäckman 1984 (33).
145 H. Grundström 1956 (204-5). In the Munster counties, Cork, Limerick and Tipperary, a St Brigit's Cross of the 'wheel type' was known. This type, called in Irish *Bogha Bríde* ('Brigit's Bow', consisted of a cross enclosed by a circle or ellipse (J. C. O'Sullivan 1973 (76). Cf. also Danaher 1972 (34). For a wide-ranging discussion of the symbolism of bow and arrow, especially the erotic implications, cf. Dundes (327-60); this article includes an extensive bibliography. Austerlitz in *Hoppál* (ed.), 232) further develops Roman Jakobson's suggestions that the Nivkh word *qas* '(shaman's) drum' is etymologically connected with a verbal root *xa-* meaning 'to shoot', the 'underlying assumption [here being] that, in order to establish contact with the other world, the shaman must propel himself ... into the other world' thus making it possible to compare the bow-and-arrow ('the hunter's principle piece of equipment' with the shaman's drum (and drumstick).
146 *KL* 16. 411. Animal offerings to the sun made by the Sámi and other north-Eurasian and circumpolar peoples specified that the animal should be coloured white and of the female sex (*KL*.16. 410). The North Star was sometimes called in Sámi *batte-navlle*, literally 'the pot-peg/nail/rivet' (Qvigstad 1921, 5). Cf. Chapter 4, Note 73.
147 Cf. *Nordnorske Samlinger* 5, Oslo 1945.
148 Quoted in Ränk (11-2).
149 H. Grundström 1956 (203).
150 Bäckman 1984 (32-3). Another derivation of Sarakka appears to lie behind Ernst Manker's description of her ('Seite Cult and Drum Magic of the Lapps', in Diószegi (ed.), 30, as *sar-akka* 'the old woman of spinning, who dwelt under the fireplace, spinning threads of sinew and assisting births, as well as the fawning of reindeer'. Manker (89-98), also contains an account of the '*Akkas*'.
151 Bäckman 1984 (33).
152 Bäckman 1984 (37-8). Cf. also Nahodil, in *Diószegi* (ed.), 459-77).
153 Bäckman 1984 (38).
154 Ränk (79). Cf. also Hultkrantz 1983 (27-28), who while noting the important changes in the history of Sámi religion involving the incorporation of figures from Scandinavian religion into their religious pantheon – an event he suggests 'probably happened at the same time as Scandinavian stockraising became the model for reindeer breeding, perhaps almost two thousand years ago' – concludes that even with the advent of full nomadism, 'the old hunting and fishing religion' remained dominant. For a useful summary of the nature of the relationship between the Sami and other peoples, cf. Nesheim (95-104).
155 Bäckman 1984 (38) and Ränk (74). Cf. also Weiser-Aall (20, 86 n. 47).
156 Ränk (75).

157 Ränk (10).
158 *Loc.cit.*
159 Cf. Bäckman 1984 (33-4) and Bäckman in *Hultkrantz & Vorren* (eds.),143-62) and Bäckman 1987a (172-3).
160 Bucholz (428).
161 Bucholz (429).
162 Bucholz (435).
163 Bucholz (429).
164 Novakovsky (118). Cf. also Christiansen 1953 (19-92), and for a recent assessment of various concepts of shamanism and, particularly a discussion of its hysterical or hysteroid traits, Hultkrantz 1978 in *Diószegi & Hoppál* (eds.), 27-58 (49-51); for a useful review and bibliography of this subject, cf. Voigt in *Diószegi & Hoppál* (eds.), 59-79.
165 Novakovsky (116).
166 Novakovsky (119, 126).
167 Quoted in Novakovsky (124).
168 Novakovsky (122).
169 Novakovsky (125).
170 Ränk (35-6).
171 Ränk (37-8). For comparative material in Finnish tradition, cf. A. Vilkuna (22-35 [re birth and menstruation] and 100-6 [re bear ceremonialism]).
172 Ränk (39-40).
173 Cf. p. 118, and Chapter 3 Note 187 above.
174 Ränk (43).
175 Ränk (48).
176 *Loc.cit.*
177 Ränk (50).
178 Ränk (56).
179 Ränk (58-9). According to Irish tradition, the afterbirth of a cow was not buried (the belief being that this might cause the calf to die) but placed in a tree and allowed to be feasted upon by the birds of the air or wither away in wind and weather.
180 Ränk (61-3, 65).
181 Ränk (64-5). The making of (male and female) straw dolls at Christmas (*lussekäringar, halmgubbar, halmgummor* etc.) as also dressing in straw was a feature of Christmas and other winter-tide celebrations in many parts of Sweden; in some places, a sheaf of straw called *Jungfru Maria sänghalm* ('The Virgin Mary's bed-straw') was placed by the wall on Christmas Eve for the servants and the younger members of the household to sleep on and the straw doll was regarded as symbolizing the Christ child. Interestingly, the eyes of these Swedish straw dolls also seem to have been of special significance for they were often poked out (Cf. Hagberg 1921, 33-47 and Campbell & Nyman, 109-19). Celander 1920 (168-76) argues strongly for a connection between the custom of making a special sheaf of straw at Christmas, ostensibly for the consumption of birds but actually dedicated as an offering to Óðinn's horses.
182 For a discussion of the concept of 'the safe *inside* and the dangerous *outside*', with 'the door as a boundary between the two' in the context of the 'ethnocentricity of the I-E community', cf. Polomé 1984 (162).

183 Ränk (59). Maringer (71) has no hesitation in suggesting that some ice-age hunters 'held beliefs similar to those that underlie the bear cult as practised by modern primitives'. I am grateful to my colleague Dr Dáithí Ó hÓgáin for this reference.
184 Wasson (10), in summing up its distribution states that our 'earliest eye-witness account of its use is by a Pole, Adam Kamanienski, in 1658, among the Ostyak of the Irtysh River (tributary of the Ob), an Ugrian people of the Finno-Ugrian family. Today we know its use is common to the Ostyak and their kin the Vogul, the Ket of the Yenisei Valley, the Samoyed peoples (who together with the Finno-Ugrians make up the Uralic group), and three sister tribes, unrelated linguistically to the others, on the north Pacific Coast, the Chukchi, the Koryak, and the Kamchadal. Responsible observers have reported that the Yukagir, who survive in Siberia in tiny communities near the Arctic Ocean, and the Inari Lapps in Finland, preserve oral traditions of having consumed the fly-agaric in times past, though they no longer do so.' Cf. also Wasson, (151-63).
185 de Rios (16, 18).
186 Wasson (172).
187 Wasson (164-5, 168-70).
188 Wasson (68). The etymologically related names for the fly-agaric in the different Finno-Ugrian languages are listed in Balázs in *Diószegi* (ed.), 56-8. Cf. also Note 15 above.
189 Ingalls (188). The history of the search for Soma is traced by Wendy D. O'Flaherty in Wasson (95-147).
190 La Barre (371).
191 Kramrisch (266). Cf. also Lévi-Strauss 1970b (11), who offering qualified support, declares – *'L'ouvrage de M. Wasson établit, de façon à notre avis convaicante, que parmi toutes les candidatures à représenter le Soma, celle d'Amanita muscaria es de loin la plus possible'.*
192 Wasson (62).
193 Wasson (35-6).
194 Wasson (43,44).
195 Wasson (46-51).
196 Wasson (39).
197 Wasson (39-40).
198 Ingalls (19).
199 La Barre (369).
200 Wasson (212) suggests that punk 'captured men' emotions' in far northern climes because 'it was only a ready fire that made life livable' there and that just as fly-agaric provided 'fire for the soul', punk provided 'fire for the body', but, he notes *(loc.cit.)* that punk also exercised no small 'mystic role': '... among many primitive peoples the procreation of fire is analagous to the sexual act. In French punk is *amadou*, a word that goes back to Latin *amare*, and in English a 'punk' until only a few centuries ago was the harlot who sparked her lover into flame. The parallel 'spunk' has to this day the scabrous meaning of 'semen', and 'spark" a different grade of the same word, carries various erotic meanings'. *Spongcaíbell* meaning 'spark of tinder' has as its latter element the word *aíbell* or *oíbell* meaning 'spark' but also carrying

the meaning 'heat' as in *bóu a n-aibiull* '*vaches en chaleur*', both of which Vendryes (O-15) believes may derive from the root **eis-* signifying 'well-being, energy, etc' as proposed by O'Rahilly 1946 (6). The word applies not only to the heat of animals in the breeding season, but also the gadding of cattle in sultry weather.

201 Wasson (212).
202 Wasson (216).
203 Wasson (216-7).
204 Wasson (180).
205 Wasson (181).
206 Saxo, Gesta Danorum, I:vii:7 (quoted in Wasson [184]).
207 Wasson (186).
208 Wasson (187).
209 Wasson (191).
210 Wasson (190, 194).
211 Wasson (194).
212 Wasson (195). The names of certain kinds of '*muchomor*' have strong sexual overtones e.g Polish *Muchomor mglejarka* (lit. 'foggy' *muchomor*), *Amanita Vaginata; Muchomor sromotnokowy* (where *srom-* means 'vagina') *Amanita Phalloides; Sromotnik bezwstydny* (where *bezwstydny* means 'shameless') *Phallus Impudicus*. The latter when young are egg-shaped, later producing a rotten-smelling olive-green slime which attracts flies who disseminate the spores. I am grateful to Ewa Loumbée-McCabe for this information.
213 Buck, 384.
214 *Loc.cit.*
215 *Loc.cit.* 225
216 Buck, 192.
217 Hamp 1971 (184-7).
218 Collinder 1974 in *Mayrhofer et al.* (365). Wagner's argument 1960 (81-4) in favour of associating the Irish dialect form *meach*, 'bee"with Sanscrit *maksa-* was opposed by Hamp *(loc.cit.)* who preferred to see the occurrence of initial *m-* in this case as a modern development.
219 Vendryes (B 24-5).
220 Dwelly, 79.
221 Ó Dónaill, 92. *Buíocán* is the word used for mushrooms in the Irish of Erris, County Mayo, while 'dog's *bocáns*' is a Leitrim name applied to toadstools.
222 As far as I know, nothing less oblique than Loki's transformation into a stinging insect has yet been adduced as an equivalent to the Irish *beacán bearaigh*.
223 Another common saying in which a version of this phrase occurs is:
    '*Aoche Fhéil' Bríde Brice*
    Buin a' mhaol don feircín,
    Buin a' chluas don toirtín,
    'S tóir a sháith don dailtín' (Ó Tuathail [192])
    ['The Eve of Speckled Brigit's Feast
    Slice the top off the firkin of butter
    Break a corner off the loaf (of bread)
    And give the child its fill']

224 The notion of colour-coding would seem to be embedded in designations such as *Lá Bealtaine Buí* ('Yellow May Day') and *Domhnach Chrom Dubh* ('*Lúnasa* Day' – literally, 'The Sunday of Crom Dubh' [where '*Dubh*' means 'black']) applied to two of the remaining Quarter Days. *Samhain*, the fourth of these days, appears to be the exception unless the connected Feast of St Martin (11th November) with its ritual slaughter element and the scattering of animal blood may be regarded as symbolizing the colour red.
225 Cf. pp. 60-61, 172 Note 61, and pp. 222-228.
226 Cf. p.217 above. Old High German *miluh*, Gothic *miluks*, Old Norse *mjölk* etc derive from a disyllabic root **meleg-* which can be broken down into the elements **mel +a +eg*, where **mel* may actually mean 'honey' (Bonfante in Mayrhofer *et al.*, [79, note 9]).
227 *EORE* 8. 635-7.
228 Hoppál in *Hoppál* (ed.), 434-5. A notable feature of the *táltos* tradition was the use of a (leather) sieve as a substitute for the drum formerly used in magic and healing rituals *(op.cit.*, 437). In Hungarian, the Pleiades (cf. pp. 162ff., 173[note 69] above) are sometimes called *szitáslyuk* 'sieve-hole' (*szita* 'a sieve' being a word of Slavic origin), embodying a concept which has a widespread distribution among the Finno-Ugrian various north-Eurasian peoples (Mándoki in Diószegi [ed.], 485-7).
229 Cf. pp. 177, 202, 212 above.
230 Cf. pp. 177-178 above.
231 Cf. p. 224 above.
232 *Genesis* 2:23:2 where the description 'bone of my bones' is used in connection with the creation of Eve. The frequent ascription of sensation to bones in the Old Testament is likely to 'spring from their inherent vitality, and of the quasi-consciousness diffused through them and the whole body...' (*EORE* 2, 791), a notion which would also seem likely to be reflected in the veneration of relics of the saints.
233 Cf., for example, Norse mythology where we learn how the 'sons of Bor took the body of Ymir to Ginnungagap and proceeded to build the world from it: from his flesh they made the earth, encompassed by the ocean, made with the blood from his wounds; from his bones, they fashioned the mountains, using the broken ones and his teeth for rocks and pebbles; from his skull, they made the sky, placing it over the earth, with its four sides supported each by a dwarf, and in the midst of it, they put sparks and flying embers from Muspell to lighten up the heavens and illuminate the earth... Other parts of Ymir's body served to create the clouds (= his brains [and] the trees (= his hair)...' (Polomé 1986 in *Brogyanyi & Krömmelbein* [eds.] 472). For a number of highly important observations relevant to this subject, cf. Lincoln 1977 (247-640).
234 *HDA* 1. 1010.
235 Young (69-70). Missing parts seem to have been a feature of animal burials in the far distant past, for example, an upper palaeolithic reindeer burial at the Aurignacian settlement of Malta in the Irkutsk province of Siberia revealed bones arranged in anatomical order and undamaged but with the hind part of the animals missing (Maringer, 64-5).
236 von Sydow 1910 (65-104).

237 Drobin (21). For a further contribution to this debate, cf. Wikander (90-9).
238 Paulson 1968 in *Diószegi* (ed.), 452; cf. also Paulson 1959 (270-93). For a treatment of this theme in the context of the folktale, cf. Röhrich (120-1) – for which reference I am grateful to Dr Miceál Ross.
239 Paulson 1968 (452-3).
240 Fjellström 1981 (30-1). My translation from the Swedish.
241 Holmberg 1987 (46).
242 *Loc. cit.*
243 Paulson 1968 (453). This is summed up by Alekseenko (in *Diószegi* [ed.], 188-9) as follows: 'The closing phase of the festival (farewell to the bear's image and bones) is a brilliant manifestation of the idea of the rebirth of the slain animal, which characterizes all hunting peoples of Siberia and which can be traced back to the magic rite of reviving the animal. This idea applied to all wild game (elk, wild reindeer etc.) and was connected with man's striving to secure his food for later times. This also explains why the Ket observe the taboo prohibiting the cutting of the bones of the bear, the custom of cooking of the flesh in one kettle, of placing in a chest bits of the tongue, the penis and the gall of the bear together with the cedar-twig ring and 'ribs', glue and copper to 'solder' and 'glue' the bones of its body. The scenes of imitating the bear, calling the beasts and asking for well-being, all mirror elements of the ancient magic of hunting.'
244 Paulson 1968 (456).
245 Cf., for example, *CG* 1. 272-83 and *CG* 4. 43-53.
246 Further information about this saint and his affiliations to Brigit, together with discussion of additional Nordic themes, can be found in S. Ó Catháin: 'Fetter and Foot. Some Links in a Chain of Celtic-Nordic Cultural Connections,' *Arv. Nordic Yearbook of Folklore*, Vol. 55 (1999), pp. 143-69.
247 *CG* 1. 166-7.
248 Cf. p. 18ff. above.
249 The compound *ban-dál* is listed in *DIL* D-degóir, 44, and its existence is also acknowledged by MacBain (1911, 29, 273) who glosses it as 'an assembly of ladies' but prefers, however, to see *banal* (and *pannal*) 'a troop, gang, a band or company' derived from English 'band'. My thanks are due to my colleague Dr Seosamh Watson for this suggestion.
250 Cf. pp. 10-11 above.
251 *CG* 1. 167. Gailey 1969 (86) notes the similarity between these customs and various features of the Irish mumming tradition.
252 Cf. pp. 93.
253 Cf. p. 27 above.
254 Cf. Chapter 1, Note 19 p. 25 above.
255 *CG* 1. 166.
256 *CG* 1. 176-7.

REFERENCES

AARNE, A. & THOMPSON, S. 1973 *The Types of the Folktale, FF Communications* 184, Helsinki.
AF KLINTBERG, B. 1990 'Några sägner i Bureus' "Sumlen",' *Inte bara Visor. Studier kring folklig diktning och musik tillägnade Bengt R. Jonsson den 19 mars 1990. Skrifter utgivna av svensk visarkiv* 11, Stockholm.
ALEKSEENKO, E.A. 1968 'The Cult of the Bear among the Ket [Yenesei Ostyaks]', in *Diószegi* (ed), 175-91.
ALLEN, R.H. 1963 *Star Names. Their Lore and Meaning*, New York.
ALMQVIST, B. 1991 'Björnens natur. Folkloristiska och filologiska bidrag till tolkningen av två fornisländska textställen', *Saga och Sed. Kungl. Gustav Adolfs Akadamiens Årsbok* (1991) 93-102.
ANDREWS, Elizabeth 1992 'Rush and Straw Crosses; Ancient Emblems of Sun Worship', *Man* 22, No. 34 (1922), 49-52.
ANISIMOV, A.F. 1963 'Cosmological Concepts of the Peoples of the North', *Studies in Siberian Shamanism. Arctic Institute of North America. Anthropology of the North. Translations from Russian Sources* No. 4, ed. H.N. Michael, Toronto 1963, 157-229.
AQUILINA, J. 1961 *Maltese meterological and agricultural proverbs*, s.l. 1961.
ARENDT, Josephine 1986 'Role of the pineal gland and melatonin in seasonal reproductive function in mammals', *Oxford Review of Reproductive Biology* 8 (1986), 266-320.
ARMSTRONG, E.A. 1958 *The Folklore of Birds. An Inquiry into the Origin and Distribution of some Magico-Religious Traditions*, London.
AUSTERLITZ, R. 1984 'On the vocabulary of Nivkh Shamanism: The Etymon qas ('Drum") and Related Questions' in *Hoppál* (ed.) 231-9.
BACKMAN, E.L. 1947 *Jungfru Maria Nyckelpiga*, Stockholm.
BÄCKMAN, Louise 1982 'Female – Divine and Human. A Study of the Position of the Woman in Religion and Society in Northern Eurasia', in *Hultkrantz & Vorren* (eds.), 143-62.
– 1984 'The Akkas. A study of four goddesses in the religion of the Saamis Lapps)', *Current Progress in the Methodology of the Science of Religions*, ed. W. Tyloch, Warsaw 1984, 31-9.
– 1987a 'Akkah', *EOR* 1, 172-3.
– 1987b 'Saami Religion', *EOR* 12, 497-9.
BALÁZS, J. 1968 'The Hungarian Shaman's Technique of Trance Induction', in *Diószegi* (ed.), 53-75.
BARBEAU, M. 1946 'Bear Mother', *Journal of American Folklore* 59 (1946), 1-12.
BARNS, T. 'Trees and Plants', *EORE* 12, 448-57.
BAUSCHATZ,P.C.1975'Urth'sWell', *Journal of Indo-European Studies* 3/1 (1975),53-86.
BELMONT, Nicole 1983 'Myth and Folklore in Connection with AT 403 and 713', *Journal of Folklore Research* 20, 2/3 (1983), 185-96.
BENET, Sula 1975 'Early Diffusion and Folk-Uses of Hemp', in *Cannabis and Culture*, ed.Vera Rubin, The Hague & Paris 1975.
BERGIN, O. (ed.) 1931 *Trí Biorghaoithe an Bháis. Séathrún Kéitinn do sgríobh*, Dublin & London.
BEST, R.I., & LAWLOR, H.J. (eds.) 1931 *The Martyrology of Tallaght*, London.

239

BJÖRNSSON, Á. 1980 *Icelandic Feasts and Holidays. Celebrations Past and Present. Iceland Review History Series*, Reykjavík.
BLACK, R.I. 1985 'The Gaelic calendar months: some meanings and derivations', *Shadow* 2/1 1985, 3-13.
BLEIBTREU-EHRENBER Gisela 1970 'Homosexualität und Transvestition im Schamanismus,' *Anthropos* 65 (1970), 189-227.
BLÖNDAL, S. 1920-4 *Islandsk-Dansk Ordbog*, Reykjavík 1920-24. 2 vols.
BØ, O., 1974 *Vår norske jul*, Oslo (2nd ed.).
BØ, O. 1980 'Bjørnen i folkedikting og folketru', *Norveg* 23 (1980), 89-99.
BOLLE, K.W. 1987 'Hieros gamos', in *EOR* 6, 317-21.
BOBER, Phyllis F. 1951 'Cernunnos: Origin and Transformation of a Celtic Divinity,' *American Journal of Archaeology* 55 (1951), 13-51.
BONFANTE, G. 1974 'Das Problem des Weines und die linguistische Paläontologie', in *Mayrhofer et al.*(eds.), 85-90.
BREWER, E.C. 1895 *Dictionary of Phrase and Fable*, London.
BRODEUR, A.G. 1929 *The prose edda by Snorri Sturluson*, New York.
BROGYANYI, B. & KROMMELBEIN, T. (eds.), 1986 *German Dialects. Linguistic and Philological Investigations*, Amsterdam & Philadelphia.
BRØNDEGAARD, V.J. 1979 *Folk og Flora, Dansk Etnobotanik*, Copenhagen. 4 vols.
BRUFORD, A. 1983 '"Deirdire" and Alexander Carmichael's Treatment of Oral Sources', *Scottish Gaelic Studies* 14/1 (1983), 1-24.
BUCHOLZ, P. 1984 Odin: Celtic and Siberian Affinities of a Germanic deity', *The Mankind Quarterly* 24/4 (1984), 427-37.
BUCK, C.D. 1949 *A Dictionary of Selected Synonyms in the Principal Indo-European Languages*, Chicago & London.
BUTTERWORTH, E.A.S. 1970 *The Tree at the Navel of the Earth*, Berlin.
BYRNE, F.J. 1973 *Irish Kings and High-Kings*, London.
CAMERON, J. 1900 *The Gaelic Names of Plants*, Glasgow.
CAMPANILE, E. 1979 'Meaning and Prehistory of Old Irish *Cú Glas*', *The Journal of Indo-European Studies* 7/1 & 2 (1979), 237-47.
CAMPBELL, Å. 1948 *Från Vildmark till Bygd. Skrifter utgivna genom Landsmåls och Folkminnesarkivet i Uppsala*. Ser. B:5. Uddevalla & København 1948.
 – & NYMAN, Åsa (eds.) 1976 *Atlas över svensk Folkkultur* 2. Uppsala 1976.
 – & NYMAN, Åsa (eds.) 1976 'Traditioner knutna till Lucia-dagen, 13 december', 109-19.
CAMPBELL, J.F. 1860 *Popular Tales of the West Highlands*. 1. Edinburgh. 4 vols.
CAMPBELL, J.F. 1891 *Popular Tales of the West Highlands. New Edition*. 2. Paisley & London. 4 vols.
CAMPBELL, J.L. 1958-61 'Two Notes on Early Irish Lyrics (Murphy)', *Éigse* 9 (1958-61), 75-6.
 – 1978 Notes on Hamish Robertson's "Studies in Carmichael's Carmina Gadelica",' *Scottish Gaelic Studies* 13/1 (1978), 1-17.
CAMPBELL, L. 1990 'Indo-European and Uralic Tree Names', *Diachronica* 7/2 (1990), 149-80.
CARDONA, G., HOENIGSWALD, H.M., SENN, A. (eds.) 1970 *Indo-European and Indo-Europeans. Papers presented at the Third Indo-European Conference at the University of Pennsylvania*, Philadelphia.
CAREY, J. 1983 'Irish Parallels to the Myth of Odin's Eye', *Folklore* 94 (1983) 214-8.

CARMICHAEL, A. 1928-71 *Carmina Gadelica*, Edinburgh & London. 6 vols.
CELANDER, H. 1920 'Julskärve och Odinskult', *Rig* 3 (1920), 168-76.
- 1931 'Om Eldborgs skål som eldoffer och orakel', *Folkminnen och Folktankar*, 18 (1931), 61-82.
- 1944 'Barfotaspringningen vid vårdagsjämningstiden', *Folkminnen och Folktankar*, 31 (1944), 12-26,49-74,85-138.
- 1950 'Månadsnamnen Thorre-Góe-Gø(j)a och Torsmånad och därtill anknuten kalendertradition', *Arv* 6 (1950), 1-28.
CHANDOR, C.A.B. 1976 *The Attic Festivals of Demeter and their relation to the Agricultural Year* (Xerox University Microfilms). Ann Arbor (Mich.).
CHARLES-EDWARDS, T. & KELLY, F. 1983 *Bechbretha. Early Irish Law Series* 1. Dublin.
CHICHLO, B. 'Tunguz Religion', *EOR* 15, 83-6.
CHRIST, Carol P. 'Virgin Goddess', in *EOR* 15, 276-9.
CHRISTIANSEN, R. Th. 1953 'Ecstasy and Arctic religion', *Studia Septentronalia* 4 (1953), 19-92.
- 1958 *The Migratory Legends. FF Communications* 175, Helsinki 1958.
COFFEY, J.E. 1989 'The *Drunnur* – A Faroese Wedding Custom', *Arv* 45 (1989), 7-16.
COLLINDER, B. 1953 *Lapparna. En bok om Samefolkets forntid och nutid*, Stockholm.
- 1955 *Fenno-Ugric Vocabulary. An Etymological Dictionary of the Uralic Language*, Stockholm.
- 1965 'Birkarlar och lappar', *Namn och Bygd* 53 (1965), 1-21.
- 1974 'Indo-Uralisch - oder gar Nostratisch', in *Mayrhofer et al.* (eds.), 363-75.
COLMCILLE, An tAth. 1963 'An Dá Cholmcille', *Irisleabhar Muighe Nuadhat* 1963, 8-21.
CONNOLLY, S. 1987 'Cogitosus's Life of St Brigit. Content and Value', *Journal of the Royal Society of Antiquaries of Ireland* 117 (1987), 5-10.
- 1987 & Picard, J.M. 'Cogitosus: Life of Saint Brigit,' *JRSI* 117 (1987), 5-27.
CORSO, R. 1955 *L'Orso della Candelora, FF Communications* 153, Helsinki 1955.
COSI, D.M. 1987 'Castration' *EOR* 3, 109-12.
COURTNEY, M.A. 1973 *Cornish Feasts and Folk-Lore*. Reprinted from the 1890 edition, Wakefield.
CROSS, T. P. 1952 *Motif-Index of Early Irish Literature*, Bloomington, Indiana.
CUSHING, G.F. 1977 'The bear in Ob-Ugrian folklore', *Folklore* 88/2 (1977), 146-49.
DANAHER K. 1972 *The Year in Ireland*, Cork.
DANVIR, Karin 1943 *Folktraditioner kring vårdagjämningen med särskild hänsyn till kontinentala traditioner. Meddelanden från Lund universitets folkminnesarkiv* 1, Lund 1943.
- 1975 (as Karin Johansson) *Då allt var jemnskiftad*, Stockholm.
DE BHALDRAITHE, T. *English-Irish Dictionary*, Baile Átha Cliath.
- 1991 'Varia IV... 2, clapar ', *Ériu* 42 (1991), 147-8.
DELANEY, J.G. 1992 'Two Holy Wells in County Roscommon. Their Relation to the Festival of Lughnasa,' *Journal of the County Roscommon Historical and Archaeological Society* 4 (1992), 56-9.
DELARUE, P. 1959 'Le conte de "Brigitte, la maman qui m'a pas fait, mais m'a nourri",' *Fabula* 2/3 (1959), 254-64.

DELLA VOLPE, Angela 1990 'From the Hearth to the Creation of
   Boundaries', *Journal of Indo-European Studies*, 18 (1990), 157-84.
DE RIOS, Marlene Dobkin 1976 *The Wilderness of the Mind: Sacred Plants
   in Cross-Cultural Perspective*. Sage Research Papers in the Social Sciences
   90-039, Beverly Hills & London 1976.
DE VRIES, J. 1958 'Die "Tierverehrung in Gallien",' *Saga och Sed. Kungl.
   Gustav Adolfs Årsbok* 5 (1958) 48-62.
- 1961a *Altnordisches etymologisches Wörterbuch*, Leiden.
- 1961b *Keltische Religion*, Stuttgart.
DE VRIES, A. 1974 *Dictionary of Symbols and Imagery*, Amsterdam & London.
DIL = *Contributions to a Dictionary of the Irish Language*, Dublin 1913-76.
DINNEEN, P.S. 1927 *Foclóir Gaedhilge agus Béarla. An Irish-English
   Dictionary*, Dublin.
DIÓSZEGI, V. (ed.) 1968 *Popular Beliefs and Folklore Tradition in Siberia.
   Indiana University Publications. Ural and Altaic Series* 57, Bloomington &
   The Hague 1968.
- 1979 & HOPPÁL, M. (eds.), *Shamanism in Siberia. Bibliotheca Uralica*. 1.
   Budapest 1978.
DOHERTY, C. 1985 'The Monastic Town in Medieval Ireland', *The Comparative History of Urban Origins in Non-Roman Europe etc*. eds. H.B. Clarke
   & Anngret Simms, BAR International Series 255, Oxford 1985, 45-75.
DOKKEN, E.H. 1954 *Bjørnen. Om Bjørn, Bjørnejakter og Bjørnejegere*, Oslo.
DRINKUTH, R. 1934 'Die drei Frauen in Deutschland in Sage, Märchen
   und christlichen Kult', *Hessische Blätter für Volkskunde* 32 (1933), 109-54,
   33 (1934), 1-77.
DROBIN, U. 1968 'Myth and Epical Motifs in the Loki-Research', *Temenos*
   3 (1968), 19-39.
DUNDES, A. 1991 'The1991 Archer Taylor Lecture. The Apple Shot: Interpreting the legend of William Tell', *Western Folklore* 50/4 (1991), 327-60.
DWELLY, E. *The Illustrated Gaelic Dictionary*. Fleet (Hants.), 1918. 3 vols.
DYRENKOVA, N.P. 1930 'Bear Worship among Turkish Tribes of Siberia',
   Proceedings of the Twenty-Third International Congress of Americanists, 411-440.
EB = *The Encyclopaedia Brittanica*, Eleventh Edition 1911.
EDSMAN, C.-M. 1953 'Studier i jägarens forkristna religion: finska
   björnjaktsriter. Tillika ett bidrag till frågan om kyrkan och folklig tro och
   sed', *Kyrkohistorisk Årsskrift* 53 (1953), 48-106.
- 1956 'The Story of the Bear-Wife in Nordic Tradition', *Ethnos* 1-2, 36-56.
- 1987 'Bears,' *EOR* 2, 86-9.
EJDESTAM, J. 1940 'Piskning med ris vid årshögtider', *Folkminnen och
   Folktankar* 27 (1940), 52-81.
- 1971 'Piskning med ris. Sed vid påsk och jul' in *Campbell & Nyman*, 105-6.
EK, S. 1922 'Bohusländska vallvisor', in D. Arill (ed.) *Bohusländska folkminnen*,
   Uddevalla 1922, 23-53.
ELDER, G.R. '1987 'Phallus', *EOR* 11, 263-9.
ELIADE, M. & Sullivan, L.E. 1987 'Earth', *EOR* 4, 534-41.
ELLIS EVANS, D. 1967 *Gaulish Personal Names. A Study of some Continental
   Celtic Formations*, Oxford.
EMENEAU, M.B. 1948 'Taboo on animal names', *Language* 24 (1948), 56-63.

ENÄJÄRVI-HAAVIO, Elsa 1954 *The Finnish Shrovetide, FF Communications* 146, Helsinki 1954.
EOR = *Encyclopaedia of Religion* (ed. M. Eliade), Vols. 1-16 (1987), New York.
EORE = *Encyclopaedia of Religion and Ethics* (ed. J. Hastings), Vols. 1-13 (1908-26), Edinburgh.
ERIXON, S. 1937 'Folklig telegrafering', *Svensk Kulturbilder. Ny Följd*, Stockholm 1937.
ESKERÖD, A. N:n. 1847 'Julhalmen och fruktbarhetsteorierna. En granskning och en tolkning', *Rig* 30/1 (1947), 16-41.
– 1965 *Årets Fester*, Halmstad.
EVANS, E.E. 1967 *Irish Folk Ways*, London. Fourth Impression.
FEILBERG, H.F. 1891 '"Making Weather" in Denmark' *Folk-Lore* 2 (1891), 133.
– 1899 Ilden-Arnen-Hjemmet *Aarbog for Dansk Kulturhistorie 1899* 36-75.
FISHER, Nora 1934 'The last Irish wolf', *Irish Naturalists' Journal* 17 (1934), 41.
FJELLSTRÖM, P. 1981 *Kort berättelse om Lapparnas Björna-fänge samt Deras der wid brukade widskeppelser, Stockholm 1775*. Facsimile edition published with biography & commentary by Louise Bäckman in *Norrländska Skrifter*, 5 (1981).
FJELLSTRÖM, Phebe 1971 'Nordic and Eurasian Elements in Lapp Culture', *Anthropos* 66 (1971), 535-49.
FLECK, J. 1971 'Óðinn's self-sacrifice - a new interpretation. II: The Ritual Landscape', *Scandinavian Studies* 43/4 (1971), 385-413.
FLINT, Valerie, I.J. 1991 *The Rise of Magic in Early Medieval Europe*, Oxford.
FORD, P.K. 1974 'The Well of Nechtan and "La Gloire Lumineuse"', in *Larsen*, (ed.), 69-74.
FRIEDRICH, P. 1970 *Proto-Indo-European Trees*, Chicago.
FRIMANNSLUND, RIGMOR 1949 'Skikk og tro ved friing og bryllup', *Nordisk Kultur* 20, Stockholm etc.1949, 41-87.
FW = Funk and Wagnalls *Dictionary of Folklore Mythology and Legend*. New York 1950, ed. Maria Leach. 2 vols.
GAILEY, A. 1966 'The Folk-Play in Ireland', *Studia Hibernica* 6 (1966) 113-54.
– 1968 'Straw Costume in Irish Folk Customs', *Folk Life* 6 (1968), 84-93.
– 1969 *Irish Folk Drama*, Cork.
– 1972 The Last Sheaf in the North of Ireland', *Ulster Folklife* 28 (1972), 1-33.
– & Ó hÓGÁIN, D. [1982] *Gold Under the Furze. Studies in Folk Tradition Presented to Caoimhín Ó Danachair*, Dublin.
GASKI, H. 1985 'Bjørnen forstrå ikke metaforer. Om samiske navn på "villmarksgubben",' *Ottar* 5 (1985), 20-3.
GIMBUTAS, Marija 1974 *The Gods and Goddesses of Old Europe 7000-3500 BC. Myths Legends and Cult Images*, London 1974.
– 1989 *The Language of the Goddess*, London.
– 1985 'Pre-Indo-European Goddesses in Baltic Mythology', *The Mankind Quarterly* 1985, 19-25.
– 1987 ' Prehistoric Religions: Old Europe', *EOR* 11, 506-15.
GLADSTONE, R.J. & WAKELEY, C.P.G. 1940 *The Pineal Organ*, London.
GLASSIE, H. 1976 *All Silver and No Brass*, Dublin.
GOJMERAC, W.J. 1980 *Bees, Beekeeping, Honey and Pollination*, Westport (Conn.)
GPC = *Geiriadur Prifysgol Cymru*, Caerdydd, (1950-).
GRAHAM, Jean M. 1953 'Transhumance in Ireland', *The Advancement of Science* 10 (1953), 74-9.

GRANBERG, E. 1931 'Är björnen vår fruktbarhetsgud? Några reflektioner', *Festskrift för Carl J.E. Hasselberg på hans 75=årsdag XVI. V.MCMXXXI*, Östersund, 45-52.
- 1941 'Björnsud. Några anteckningar om en härjedalsk folksed', *Folkminnen och Folktankar* 28 (1941), 23-35.
GRANBERG, G. 1935 *Skogsrået i yngre nordisk folktradition*. *Skrifter utgivna av Gustav Adolfs Akadamien för folklivsforskning* 83, Uppsala 1935.
GRAVES, R. 1960 *The Greek Myths* 1. Penguin Revised Edition. 2 vols.
GREEN, Miranda 1989 *Symbol & Image in Celtic Religious Art*, London & New York.
- 1992 *Animals in Celtic Life and Myth*, London & New York.
GRUNDSTRÖM, H. 1953 *Lulelapsk Ordsbok 1, Skrifter utgivna genom Landsmåls- och Folkminnesarkivet i Uppsala. Ser. C: 1*. Uppsala & København 1953.
- 1956 'Sarakkagröt-nornegröt-barselgröt-lystenbit', Some parallels', *Arctica. Studia Ethnographica Upsaliensia* 11 (1956), 203-7.
GUYONVAR'CH, C-J. 1967 'Notes d'Étymologie et de Lexicographie Gauloises et Celtiques XXIX', *Celticum* 16 (1967), 215-38.
HAGBERG, Louise 1913 'Matsmässan i Gagnet. På spaningsfärd efter en gammal folksed', *Fataburen* 1913, 9-16.
- 1921 'Julhalm och Juldockor', *Rig* 4 (1921), 33-47.
- 1944 'Seder och tro vid märkestillfällena i barnets liv', *Nordisk Kultur* 20. *Livets Högtider*, Stockholm etc. 1949, 14-40.
HAJDÚ, P. 1968 'The Classification of Samoyed Shamans', in *Diószegi* (ed.), 147-73.
HALL, J. 1813 *Tour though Ireland*, Vol. 1, London. 2 Vols.
HALLBERG, P. 1986 'Elements of Myth in the Heroic Lays of the Poetic Edda', in *Brogyanyi & Krommelbein* (eds.) 213-47.
HALLOWELL, A.I. 1926 'Bear ceremonialism in the northern hemisphere', *American Anthropologist* (New Series), 28/1 (1926), 1-175.
HALLSTRÖM, G. 1921 ' "Halmstaffan". En julsed från Björkö, Adelsö socken, Uppland. Meddelande och rekonstruktion', *Etnologiska Studier tillägnade Nils Edvard Hammarstedt 19 3/3/ 21. Föreningen för svensk kulturhistoria* 2, Stockholm 1921, 227-31.
HAMMARSTEDT, N.E. 1913 'Bröllops- och fastlagsbjörn', *Fataburen* 13, 1-9.
- 1929 'Vår- och bröllopsbjörn' in *Wikman & Andersson* (eds.), 1-15.
- 1915 'När vänder björnen sig i idet ?', *Fataburen* 15, 227-35.
HAMMERICH, L.L. 1970 'Irland og Kontinentet i middelalderen, *Saga och Sed. Kungl. Gustav Adolfs Akadamiens Årsbok*, Uppsala 1970, 25-40.
HAMP, E. P. 1971 'Varia III ... 2. The "bee" in Irish, Indo-European, and Uralic', *Ériu* 22 (1971), 194-7.
- 1978 'Varia II' *Ériu* 29 (1978), 149-54.
- 1979 'Indo-European g^{wen}-H,' *Zeitschrift für vergleichende Sprachforschung [Kuhns Zeitschrift]*, 93/1 (1979), 1-7.
- 1979/80 'imbolc, óimelc', *Studia Celtica* 14/15 (1979/80), 106-13.
- 1986 'Varia ...5. *brigantinos*', *Études Celtiques* 23 (1986), 47-51.
HARRISON, A. 1988 'Tricksters and Entertainers in the Irish Tradition', in *MacLennan* (ed.), 293-317.
HARTING, J.E. 1880 *British animals extinct within historic times with some account of British wild white cattle*, London.
HDA = *Handwörterbuch des Deutschen Aberglaubens* (eds. E. Hoffmann-Krayer, & H. Bächtold-Stäubli, Vols 1-10 (1927- 42), Berlin & Leipzig.

HEIERMEIER, Anne 1955 *Indogermanische Etymologien des Keltischen.*
 Arbeiten aus dem Institut für Keltologie und Irlandkunde an der Universität Würzburg 1. Würzburg 1955.
HELLQVIST, E. 1929 *Svensk Etymologisk Ordbok*, Lund 1929. 2 Vols.
HENDERSON, J. 1975 *The Maculate Muse. Obscene Language in Attic Comedy*, New Haven and London.
HEUSLER, A. 1969 'Die Gedichte vom Völsi, eine altnordische Bekehrungsanekdote', in A. Heusler, *Kleine Schriften*, 2, Berlin 1969, 372-87.
HERITY, M. 1989 'The Antiquity of *An Turas* [the Pilgrimage Round] in Ireland', *Lateinische Kultur im VIII Jahrhundert, Traube Gedenkschrift*, ed. A. Lehner & W. Berschin, St. Ottilien 1989, 95-143.
HICKEN, N. 1980 *Irish Nature*, Dublin.
HOGAN, F.E. 1900 *Luibhleabhrán. Irish and Scottish Gaelic Names of Herbs, Plants, Trees Etc.*, Dublin.
HOLMBERG, U. 1914 'Lapps', *EORE*, 7, 798-800.
 – 1987 *Lapparnas Religion (Lappalaisten uskonto, 1915), Uppsala Multiethnic Papers* 10 (1987).
HOLMER, N.M. 1942 *The Irish Language in Rathlin Island, Co. Antrim. Royal Irish Academy Todd Lecture Series* 18, Dublin 1942.
HONKO L. 1990 'Mute Brides and Bridegrooms', *Inte Bara Visor. Studier kring folklig diktning och musik tillägnade Bengt R. Jonsson den 19 mars 1990. Skrifter utgivna av svenskt visarkiv*, 11, Stockholm 1990, 117-31.
HONKO, L. TIMONEN, S., BRANCH, M., BOSLEY, K. 1993 *The Great Bear: A Thematic Anthology of Oral Poetry in the Finno-Ugrian Languages. Finnish Literature Society Editions*, 533, Helsinki 1993.
HOPPÁL, M. (ed.) 1984 *Shamanism in Eurasia*, Göttingen 1984. 2 vols.
 – 1984 'Traces of Shamanism in Hungarian Folk Beliefs', in *Hoppál* (ed.) Part Two, 430-49.
HORWOOD, A.R., & FITCH, J.N. *A New British Flora, British Wild Flowers in their Natural Haunts,* London s.a.
HULL V. & TAYLOR, A. 1955 *A Collection of Irish Riddles. Folklore Studies* 6, Berkeley & Los Angeles.
HULTKRANTZ, Å. 1978 'Ecological and Phenomological Aspects of Shamanism', in *Diószegi & Hoppál* (eds.), 27-58.
 – 1982 'Reindeer Nomadism and the Religion of the Saamis,' *Arv* 39 (1983), 11-28.
 – & VORREN, Ø. (eds.) 1982 *The Hunters. Their Culture and Way of Life. Tromsø Museum Skrifter* 18 (1982).
 – (ed.) 1961 *The Supernatural Owners of Nature. Nordic symposium on the religious conceptions of ruling spirits (genii loci, genii speciei) and allied concepts. Acta Universitatis Stockholmiensis/Stockholm Studies in Comparative Religion* 1, Stockholm 1961.
HYDE, D. 1895 *Abhráin Grádh Chonnacht or Love Songs of Connacht*, Dublin.
 – 1899 *A Literary History of Ireland*, London.
INGALLS H.H. 1971 'Remarks on Mr Wasson's "Soma",' *Journal of the American Oriental Society* 91/2 (1971), 188-91.
JACQUART, Danielle & THOMASSET, Claude 1988 *Sexuality and Medicine in the Middle Ages*, Cambridge & Oxford.

JACOBSEN, Grethe 1984 'Pregnancy and Childbirth in the Medieval North: A Topology of Sources and a Preliminary Study', *Scandinavian Journal of History* 9 (1984), 91-11.
JAKOBSEN, J. 1928 *An Etymological Dictionary of the Norn Language in Shetland*, London and Copenhagen.
JAMES, E.O. 1959 *The Cult of the Mother-Goddess. An Archaeological and Documentary Study*, London.
JÓNSSON, F. (ed.) 1893-1900 *Heimskringla*, København.
- (ed.) 1931 *Edda Snorra Sturlusonar*, København.
JÓNSSON, G. (ed.) 1950 *Fornaldar Sögur Norðurlanda* 1, Reyjkjavík.
JOSEPH, H.S. 1972 'Völsa Thattr: A Literary Remnant of a Phallic Cult', *Folklore* 83 (1972), 245-52.
KELLY, F. 1970 'The Old-Irish Tree-List', *Celtica* 11 (1970), 107-24.
KENNEY, J.F. 1979 *The Sources for the Early History of Ireland. An Introduction and Guide*, Dublin.
KIRBY, W.F. (trans.) 1985 *Kalevala, The Land of Heroes*, London & Dover, New Hampshire.
KL = *Kulturhistoriskt lexikon för nordisk medeltid*, Malmö etc. 1-21 (1956-77).
KLEIN, E. 1926 '"Dyngbröllopet" vid Haneberg', *Folkminnen och Folktankar* 13 (1926), 1-14.
KNOTT, Eleanor 1920 [1922] *The Bardic Poems of Tadhg Dall Ó Huiginn* (1550-1591) 1. *Irish Texts Society* 22 (1920 [1922]).
KOCH, J.T. 1992 'Gallo-Brittonic Tasc(i)ouanos "Badger-slayer" and the reflex of Indo-European g^{wh},' *Journal of Celtic Linguistics* 1 (1992), 101-18.
KRAMRISCH, Stella 1972 'Review of Wasson's "Soma",' *Artibus Asiae* 34/2-3 (1972), 263-7.
LA BARRE, W. 1970 'Review of Wasson's "Soma",' *American Anthropologist* 72 (1970), 368-73.
LADURIE, Le Roy 1979 *Carnival in Romans. A People's Uprising at Romans 1579-1580*. Penguin Books 1979.
LANE, T. O'N. 1916 *Larger English-Irish Dictionary*, London, Dublin & Belfast.
LANKFORD, G.E. 1980 'Pleistocene Animals in Folk Memory,' *Journal of American Folklore* 93, No. 369 (1980), 293-304.
LARSEN, G.J. (ed.) 1974 *Myth in Indo-European Antiquity*, Berkeley, Los Angeles & London.
LAURENT, D. 1982 'Brigitte, accoucheuse de la Vierge. Présentation d'un dossier', *Le Monde Alpin et Rhodanien*, 1-4 (1982), 73-9.
LEEM, K. 1767 *Beskrivelse over Finmarkens Lappar*, København.
LEEMING, D.A. 1987 'Virgin Birth', *EOR* 15 271-6.
LEHMANN, R.P.M. 1966 'Color Usage in Irish', *Studies in Language, Literature, and Culture of the Middle Ages and Later*, Austin, 73-9.
LEISIÖ, T. 1985 'Turu luru, turu luru ! Myth and Reality in a Finnish Folk Tale', *Musiikin suunta* 1 (1985), 6-14.
LEWIS, C.T. & SHORT, C. 1975 *A Latin Dictionary*, Oxford.
LÉVI-STRAUSS, C. 1969 *The Raw and the Cooked. Introduction to a Science of Mythology*: 1, Harper Torchbook Edition, New York.
- 1970 'Les Champignons dans la Culture', *L'Homme* 10/1 (1970), 5-16.

LID, N. 1923 (ed.) Joh. Th. Storaker, 'Rummet i den Norske Folketro', *Norsk Folkeminnelag* 8 (1923).
- 1926 'Ein samisk skikk ved bjørnefesten', *Maal og Minne* 1926, 202.
- 1928 'Goa, Sporysj, Jumis og Cailleach', *Nordiskt Folkminne. Studier tillägnade C.W. von Sydow 19 21/12 28*, Halmstad 1928, 199-206.
- 1928 (ed.) 'Joh. Th. Storaker, Naturrigerne i den norske folketro' (Storakers samlinger IV), *Norsk Folkeminnelag* 18 (1928).
- 1946 'Light-mother and Earth-mother', *Studia Norwegica* 41 1/4 (1946), 1-20.
LINCOLN, B. 1975 'The Indo-European Creation Myth, *History of Religions* 15 (1975), 121-45.
- 1977 'Death and Resurrection in Indo-European Thought', *The Journal of Indo-European Studies* 5/1 (1977), 247-64.
- 1981 *Priests, Warriors and Cattle*, Berkeley etc.
- 1982 'Waters of Memory, Waters of Forgetfulness', *Fabula* 23 (1982), 19-31.
LITHBERG, N. 1932 '"Dyngkalaset". Ett inlägg i en gammal diskussion', *Folkminnen och Folktankar* 19 (1932), 24-32.
LIUNGMAN, W. 1961 'Das Rå und der Herr der Tiere' in *Hultkrantz* (ed.), 72-90.
LOCKWOOD, W.B. 1961 *The Faroese Bird Names*, København.
- 1966 Linguistic Taboo in Manx and Anglo-Manx *The Journal of the Manx Museum* 7, No. 82 (1966), 29-32.
- 1978 'Chr. Matras' studies on the Gaelic element in Faroese: conclusions and results', *Scottish Gaelic Studies* 13/1 (1978), 112-26.
LORENZEN, P. 1930 *Jakt og vildt i Dansk folketro* 1, København.
LÖVKRONA, Inger 1978 ' "The Pregnant Frog and the Farmer's Wife", Childbirth in the Middle Ages as Shown through a Legend,' *Arv* 45 (1989), 73-124.
LUCAS, A.T. 1963 'The sacred trees of Ireland', *Journal of the Cork Historical and Archaeological Society* 68 (1963), 16-54.
- 1965 'Washing and bathing in ancient Ireland,' *JRSAI* 95 (1965), 65-114.
- 1989 *Cattle in Ancient Ireland*, Kilkenny 1989.
LUNDMARK, B. 1982 *Bæi'vi Mánno Nástit. Sol- och månkult samt astrala och celesta föreställningar bland samerna. Acta Bothniensia Occidentalis. Skrifter i västerbotnisk kulturhistoria* 5, Umeå 1982.
LURKER, M. 1987 *Dictionary of Gods and Goddesses, Devils and Demons*, London & New York.
Mac AN BHAIRD, A. 1980 'Varia II. Tadhg mac Céin and the badgers', *Ériu* 31 (1980), 150- 55.
MacAONGHAIS, I. 1989 'Baird is Bleidirean', in *Watson* (ed.), 94-110.
MacBAIN, A. 1885 *Celtic Mythology and Religion*, Inverness.
- 1890-1 'Gaelic Incantations', *Transactions of the Gaelic Society of Inverness* 17 (1890-1), 222-66.
- 1911 *An Etymological Dictionary of the Gaelic Language*, Stirling.
Mac CANA P. 1970 *Celtic Mythology*, London.
- 1988 'Placenames and Mythology in Irish Tradition: Places, Pilgrimages and Things', in *MacLennan* (ed.), 319-41.
- 1987 'Celtic Religion', *EOR* 3 (1987), 148-66.
Mac COISDEALBHA, L. 1943 [1944] 'Seanchas ó Iorras', *Béaloideas* 13 1943 [1944], 172-237.

McCONE, K. 1982 'Bríd Chill Dara', *Léachtaí Cholm Cille (Na Mná sa Litríocht)* 12, Maigh Nuad 1982, 30-92.
— 1984 'Aided Cheltchair maic Uthechair: Hounds, Heroes and Hospitallers in Early Irish Myth and Story', *Ériu* 35 (1984), 1-30.
— 1985 'Varia II... 2. OIr. Olc, Luch- and IE *$w\underset{.}{l}k^wos$, *$lúk^wos$ "wolf",' *Ériu* 36 (1985), 169-76.
— 1987 'Hund, Wolf und Krieger bei den Indogermanen', *Studien zum Indogermanen Wortschatz* (ed. W. Meid), Innsbruck 1987, 101-54.
— 1990 *Pagan Past and Christian Present. Maynooth Monographs* 3, Maynooth 1990.
MacCURDY, E. 1953-9 'Carmina Gadelica, *Transactions of the Gaelic Society of Inverness* 42 (1953-9), 240-56.
MacKENZIE, W. 1891-2 'Gaelic Incantations, Charms and Blessings of the Hebrides', *Transactions of the Gaelic Society of Inverness* 18 (1891-2), 97-182.
MacKINLAY, J.M. 1893 *Folklore of Scottish Lochs and Springs*, Glasgow.
MacLAGAN, R.C. 1895 'Notes on folklore objects collected in Argyleshire', *Folk-Lore* 6/2 (1895), 144-61.
McLAUGHLIN(CONBOY), Noeleen 1986 *Old, New, Borrowed and Blue. A Classification of some Irish Marriage Customs*, unpublished M.A. Thesis (1986) in the Department of Irish Folklore, UCD.
MacLENNAN, G.W. (ed.) 1988 *Proceedings of the First North American Congress of Celtic Studies*, Ottawa.
MacLEOD BANKS, Marjorie 1939 *British Weather Customs. Scotland 2 (Publications of the Folk-Lore Society* 104), London.
— 1946 *British Calendar Customs. Orkney and Shetland (Publications of the Folk-Lore Society* 112). London.
McMANUS, H. 1863 *Sketches of the Irish Highlands*, London.
McMILLAN, Nora F. 1971 'More "last Irish wolves"', *Irish Naturalists' Journal*, 17 (1971), 103.
MacNEILL, E. 1919 *Phases of Irish History*, Dublin.
MacNEILL Máire 1962 *The Festival of Lughnasa. A Study of the Survival of the Celtic Festival of the Beginning of Harvest*, Oxford 1962.
— 1981 (trans.) *Seán Ó Conaill's Book*, Dublin.
MacQUEEN, J. 1985 *Numerology. Theory and outline history of a literary mode*, Edinburgh.
MAHON, Bríd 1991 *Land of Milk and Honey, The Story of Traditional Irish Food and Drink*, Dublin.
MALONE, K. 1960 'Bonnyclabber', *Celtica* 5 (1960), 142.
MÁNDOKI, L. 1968 'Two Asiatic Sidereal Names, in Diószegi (ed.), 485-98.
MANKER, E. 1950 *Die Lappische Zaubertrommel. Eine ethnologische Monographie. II Die Trommel als Urkunde geistigen Lebens. Nordiska Museet, Acta Lapponica* 6, Uppsala 1950.
MARGLIN, Frédérique M. 1987a 'Yoni', *EOR* 15, 530-55.
— 1987b 'Hierodouleia', *EOR* 6, 309-13.
MARINGER, J. 1960 *The Gods of Prehistoric Man*, London.
MARKEY, T. 1988 'The Celto-Germanic 'dog/wolf'-Champion. *Nowele* 11 (1988), 3-30.
MARSTRANDER, C.J.S. 1910 'Hibernica', *Zeitschrift für celtische Philologie* 7 (1910), 357-418.

References & Bibliography 249

MARSTRANDER, C.J.S. 1915 *Bidrag til det Norske Sprogs Historie i Irland* (*Videnskapsselskapets Skrifter. II Hist.-Filos. Klasse. No. 5*). Kristiania.

MARTIN, M. 1716 *A Description of the Western Islands of Scotland*, London.

MASON, T.H. 1945 'St. Brigid's Crosses,' *JRSAI* 75 (1945), 160-6.

MATTHIESSEN, C.C. 1945 'Hesten i Nordisk myte og kult', *Danske veterinærhistorisk Aarbog* 12 (1945), 9-89.

MAYRHOFER, M. et al. (eds.) 1974 *Antiquitates Indogermanicae. Studien zur Indogermanischen Altertumskunde und zur Sprach- und Kulturgeschichte der indogermanischen Völker. Gedenkschrift für Hermann Güntert. Innsbrucker Beiträge zur Sprachwissenschaft* 12, Innsbruck 1974.

MESLIN, M. 1987 'Eye', *EOR* 5, 236-9.

MEYER, K. 1894 *Anecdota Oxoniensia. Hibernica Minora*, Oxford.

MITCHELL F. 1986 *The Shell Guide to reading the Irish Landscape (incorporating The Irish Landscape)*, Dublin 1986.

MOBERG, C-A. 1955 'Om vallåtar. En studie i de svenska fäbodarnas musikaliska organisation', *Svensk Tidskrift för Musikforskning* 37 (1955), 7-95.

MOE, M. 1925 'Hellenske og Norske Folketraditioner', *Moltke Moes Samlede Skrifter 1, Instituttet for sammenlignende kulturforskning, Serie B; Skrifter 1*, Oslo 1925, 23-82.

MOFFAT, C.B. 1937-8 'The mammals of Ireland', *Proceedings of the Royal Irish Academy* 44 B (1937-8), 61-128.

MÖLLER, J.S. 1940 'Moder og barn i Dansk folkoverlevering. Fra svangerskab til daab og kirkegang', *Danmarks Folkeminder* 48 (1940).

MOTZ, Lotte 1980 'Sister in the Cave: the stature and function of the female figures of the *Eddas*', *Arkiv för nordisk Filologi* 95 (1980), 168-82.

MURPHY, G. 1941 [1953] *Duanaire Finn, Part 3, Irish Texts Society* 43 1941 [1953].

MUSURILLO, H. 1961 *Symbol and Myth in Ancient Poetry*, New York 1961.

MYSTERUD, I. 1980 Bjørn og bjørneforskning', *Norveg* 23 (1980), 101-20.

NAGY, G. 1974 'Perkunas and Perun ' in *Mayrhofer et al.*(eds.),113-31.

NAGY, J.F. 1985 *The Wisdom of the Outlaw. The Boyhood Deeds of Finn in Gaelic Narrative Tradition*, Berkeley, Los Angeles & London.

– 1990 'The Herons of Druim Ceat Revisiting, and Revisited', *Celtica* 21 (1990), 368-76.

NAHODIL, O. 1968 'Mother Cult in Siberia', in *Diószegi* (ed.), 459-77.

NESHEIM, A. 1979 'Cultural Contact of the Lapps with their Neighbours', *Fenno-Ugrica Suecana* 2 (1979), 95-104.

– *New Larousse Encyclopaedia of Mythology, London 1972. New Ed. 4th Imp.*

NICOLSON, A. 1951 *Gaelic Proverbs*, Glasgow.

NILSSON, M.P:n. 1921 'Kråknedandet' in *Etnologiska Studier tillägnade Nils Edvard Hammarstedt* 19 3/3 21, 48-51, Stockholm.

– 1936 *Årets Folkliga Fester*, Stockholm. Second edition.

– 1938 'Julen' in *Årets Högtider* in *Nordisk Kultur*, Oslo 1938, 26-8.

NORDSETH, P. 1980 'Ketilbjørn og Arinbjørn,' *Namn och Bygd* 68 (1980), 76-85.

NORLANDER-UNSGAARD, Siv 1983 'On gesture and posture, movements and motion in the Saami bear ceremonialism', *Arv* 39 (1983), 189-99.

– 1987 'On Time-reckoning in Old Saami Culture', *Saami Religion. Scripti Instituti Donneriani Aboensis*, ed. T. Ahlbäck, Åbo 1987, 81-93.

NOVAKOVSKY, S. 1924 'Arctic or Siberian Hysteria as a Reflex of the Geographic Environment', *Ecology* 5/2 (1924), 113-27.
O'BRIEN, M.A. 1938 *The Old Irish Life of St. Brigit*. *Irish Historical Studies* 1/2 (1938), 121-34.
Ó CATHÁIN, S. 1975 'An tOsnádúr agus an Tíreolaíocht i Logainmneacha Mhaigh Eo', *Hereditas. Essays and Studies presented to Professor Séamus Ó Duilearga*, eds. B. Almqvist, B. Mac Aodha and G. Mac Eoin, Dublin 1975 (*Béaloideas* 39-41 [1971-3]).
– 1980 *The Bedside Book of Irish Folklore*, Dublin & Cork.
– 1982 *Irish Life and Lore*, Dublin & Cork.
– 1985 *Uair a Chloig Chois Teallaigh/An Hour by the Hearth*, Dublin.
– 1989 'Printíseacht Phroifisiúnta Sheáin Uí Eochaidh Lúnasa 1935 - Eanáir 1936', in *Watson*, (ed.) 1989b, 49-85.
– 1991 'Tricking the Fairy Suitor (ML 6000). A Rare Peripheral Relic?', *Béaloideas* 59 (1991), 145-59.
–1994 'Research Opportunities in the Department of Irish Folklore at University College Dublin. New Departures; Old Directions', *Proceedings of the Third Symposium of Societas Celtologica Nordica held in Oslo 1-2 November 1991. Acta Universitatis Upsaliensis. Studia Celtica Upsaliensia* 1 (1994), 87-114.
Ó CATHASAIGH, T. 1977 *The heroic biography of Cormac mac Airt*, Dublin.
Ó CONCHEANAINN, T. 1966/7 'Ainmneacha Éideimhne', *Dinnseanchas* 2 (1966/7), 15-9.
O'CONNOR, Anne 1991 *Child Murderess and Dead Child Traditions. A ComparativeStudy*, *FF Communications* 249, Helsinki 1991.
Ó CORRÁIN, D., BREATNACH, L., McCONE, K. (eds.) 1989 *Sages, Saints and Storytellers. Celtic Studies in Honour of Professor James Carney. Maynooth Monographs* 2, Maynooth 1989.
Ó CRÓINÍN, D. 1980 *Seanachas Amhlaoibh Í Luínse. Scríbhinní Béaloidis* 5, Baile Átha Cliath.
Ó DANACHAIR, C. 1958 'Holy Well Legends in Ireland', *Saga och Sed. Kungl. Gustav Adolfs Akademiens Årsbok*, 1958, 35-42.
– 1959 'The Quarter Days in Irish Tradition', *Arv* 15 (1959), 47-55.
– 1965 [1967] 'Distribution patterns in Irish folk tradition', *Béaloideas* 33 (1965 [1967]), 97-113.
– 1983-4 'Summer Pastures in Ireland', *Folk-Life* 22 (1983-4), 36-41.
– 1983-4 (trans.) 'Summer pasture in Donegal' (Niall Ó Dubhthaigh), *Folk-Life* 22 (1983-4), 42-54.
Ó DÓNAILL, N. (ed.) 1977, *Foclóir Gaeilge-Béarla*, Baile Átha Cliath.
O'DONOVAN, J. (ed.) 1864 *The Martyrology of Donegal. A Calendar of the Saints of Ireland*, Dublin 1864.
Ó DUILEARGA, S. 1948 *Leabhar Sheáin Í Chonaill*, Dublin.
O'DOWD, J.D. 1940 'Stories about wolves', *Béaloideas* 10 (1940), 288-9.
Ó hAODHA, D. 1978 *Bethu Brigte*, Dublin.
Ó hEOCHAIDH, S. 1943 'Buailteachas i dTír Chonaill', *Béaloideas* 13 (1943), 130-58.
– 1944 [1945] 'Beannachtaí agus Abairtí Ócáide', *Béaloideas* 14 (1944 [1945]), 130-55.
– 1963 'Colm Cille sa tSeanchas', *Irisleabhar Muighe Nuadhat* 1963, 33-50.
– 1989 'Folach Éireann' in *Watson* (ed.) 1989b, 31-48.

O'HANLON, J. s.a. *Lives of the Irish Saints etc*, Dublin etc. 8 vols.
Ó hÓGÁIN, D. 1981 *Duanaire Thiobraid Árann*, Baile Átha Cliath.
– 1990 *Myth, Legend and Romance. An Encyclopaedia of Irish Tradition*, London 1990.
– 1994 with DEASY, Marian & uí ÓGÁIN, Ríonach, *Binneas thar Meon. A collection of songs and airs made by Liam de Noraidh in east Munster*, Baile Átha Cliath 1994.
Ó LAOGHAIRE, D. 1975 *Ár bPaidreacha Dúchais. Cnuasach de Phaidreacha agus de B[h]eannachtaí Ár Sinsear*, Baile Átha Cliath.
OLRIK, A. 1903 'Sigvard den digre. En vikingesaga fra de danske i Nordengland'. *Arkiv för nordisk filologi* 19 (1903), 199-203.
– 1910 'Wettermachen und Neujahrsmond im Norden', *Zeitschrift des Vereins für Volkskunde* 20 (1910), 57-61.
– & ELLEKILDE, H. 1926-51 *Nordens Gudeverden*, København, Vols 1 & 2.
OLRIK, J. (trans.) 1925 *Sakses Danesaga. Oldtid og ældste middelalder*, København.
– & A. OLRIK 1907 'Kvindegilde i middelaldern. En gråmunks vidnesbyrd fra 13de århr.', *Danske Studier* 1907, 175-6.
Ó MÁILLE, T.S. 1948 & 1952 *Sean fhocla Chonnacht*, Baile Átha Cliath. 2 Vols.
– s.a. *An Béal Beo*, Baile Átha Cliath.
Ó MÁIRTÍN, S. 1963 'Traidisiúin Áitúla i dTaobh Cholmcille', *Irisleabhar Muighe Nuadhat* 1963, 66-7.
O'MEARA, J. *The First Version of the Topography of Ireland by Giraldus Cambrensis*, Dundalk 1951.
Ó MOGHRÁIN, P. 1943 [1944] 'Some Mayo traditions of the buaile', *Béaloideas* 13 (1943 [1944]), 161-72.
– 1944 [1945] 'More notes on the *buaile*,' *Béaloideas* 14 (1944 [1945]), 45-52.
Ó MURCHÚ, L.P. 1982 *Cúirt an Mheonoíche*, Baile Átha Cliath.
Ó MUIRGHEASA, É. 1936 'The holy wells of Donegal', *Béaloideas* 6 (1936), 143-62.
– 1937a 'Features Common to Irish, Welsh, and Manx Folklore', *Béaloideas* 7/2, (1937), 168-79.
– 1937b (as Henry Morris) 'Corrigenda', *Béaloideas* 7/2 (1937), 247.
ONIANS, R.B. 1951 *The Origins of European Thought about the body, the mind, the soul, the world, time and fate. New interpretation of Greek, Roman and kindred evidence, also of some basic Jewish and Christian beliefs*, Cambridge.
ONIONS, C. T.(ed.) 1952 *The Shorter Oxford English Dictionary*, Oxford. Third Edition. 2 vols.
O'RAHILLY, T.F. 1931 'Etymological Notes III', *Scottish Gaelic Studies*, 3 (1931), 52-72.
– 1946 'Ir. *AOBH, AOIBHEALL*, etc., W. UFEL, UWEL, GAUL ESUS' *Ériu* 14 (1946), 1-6.
– 1950 'Varia II', *Celtica* 1 (1950), 328-86.
– 1957 *Early Irish History and Mythology*, Dublin 1957.
ORDÉUS, Valdis 1962 *Traditioner omkring tjugondag Knut. En kartkommentar*. Unpublished student essay (Uppsats för tre betyg, ht. 62, Uppsala University).
– 1975 ' "Eldborgs skål" in Wales', *Arv* 31 (1975), 151-5.
Ó RIAIN, P. 1978 'Traces of Lug in early Irish hagiographical tradition', *Zeitschrift für celtische Philologie*, 36 (1978), 39-55.

Ó SÚILLEABHÁIN, S. 1942 *A Handbook of Irish Folklore*, Dublin 1942.
- 1967 *Irish Wake Amusements*, Dublin & Cork.
- 1977 *Irish Folk Custom and Belief/Nósanna agus Piseoga na nGael*, Cork, 2nd ed.
- & CHRISTIANSEN, R.Th. 1967 *The Types of the Irish Folktale. FF Communications* 188, Helsinki.
Ó SÚILLEABHÁIN, S.C. 1977 *Lá Fhéile Bríde*, Baile Átha Cliath 1977. Pamphlet.
- [1982] 'An Crios Bríde', in *Gailey & Ó hÓgáin* (eds.), 242-53.
O'SULLIVAN, J.C. 1963 'St. Brigid's Crosses, *Folk Life* 11 (1963), 60-81.
Ó TUATHAIL, É. 1933 *Sgéalta Mhuintir Luinigh. Munterloney Folk-Tales*, Dublin.
O[TWAY], C. 1841 *Sketches in Erris and Tyrawley*, Dublin.
PATERSON, T.G.F. 1945-8 'Brigid's Crosses in County Armagh', *County Louth Archaeological Journal* 11 (1945-8), 15-20.
PATON, C.I. 1939 *Manx Calendar Customs (Publications of the Folk-Lore Society* 110 [1939]), London.
PAULSON, I. 1959 'Die Tierknochen im Jagdritual der nordeurasischen Völker', *Zeitschrift für Ethnologie* 134 (1959), 270-93.
- 1968 'The Preservation of Animal Bones in the Hunting Rites of Some North-Eurasian Peoples', in *Diószegi* (ed.), 451-7.
PECK, A.L. 1943 *Aristotle. Generation of Animals*. The Loeb Classical Library. London & Cambridge (Mass.)
PEDERSEN, H. 1909 *Vergleichende Grammatik der keltischen Sprachen*, Göttingen. 2 vols.
PENTIKÄINEN, J. 1984 'The Sámi Shaman – Mediator between Man and Universe', in *Hoppál* (ed.), 125-48.
PICARD J.-M. 1989 'The Strange Death of Guaire mac Áedáin', in *Ó Corráin et al.* (eds.), 367-75.
PIZARRO, J.M. 1976-7 'Transformations of the Bear's son Tale in the Sagas of the Hrafnistumenn,' *Arv* 32-3 (1976-7), 263-81.
PLUMMER, C. 1910 *Vitae Sanctorum Hiberniae* 1. Oxford. 2 vols.
POKORNY, J. 1927 'Das nicht-Indogernmanische Substrat im Irischen', *Zeitschrift für celtische Philologie* 16 (1927), 95-144.
- 1958 'Some further notes on Old Irish derc "berry",' *The Journal of Celtic Studies* 3 (1958), 25.
- 1959 *Indogermanisches etymologisches Wörterbuch*, Bern & München.
POLLAK, Johanna 1958/9 'Beiträge zur Verwendung der Fareben in der älteren irischen Literatur', *Zeitschrift für celtische Philologie* 27 (1958/9), 161-205.
POLOMÉ, E. (ed.) 1969 *Old Norse Literature and Mythology. A Symposium*, Austin & London.
- 1970 'Germanic and Regional Indo-European (Lexicography and Culture)', in *Cardona et al.* (eds), 55-72.
- 1974 'Notes on the Germano-Baltic Lexical Correspondences: A critique on Čemodanov's isoglosses', *The Journal of Indo-European Studies* 2/1 (1974), 101-16.
- 1984 'The Gods of the Indo-Europeans', *The Mankind Quarterly* 21, 151-64.
- 1986 'The Non-Indo-European Component of the Germanic Lexicon', in *O-ope-ro-si. Festschrift für Ernst Risch zum 75. Geburtsdag*. Berlin & New York, 101-16.
- 1989 *Essays on Germanic Religion (Journal of Indo-European Studies Monograph Number Six)*, 661-77.

PRESTON, J. 1987 'Goddess Worship: An Overview', *EOR* 6, 35-45.
QVIGSTAD, J. 1901 'Lappiske Plantenavne', *Nyt Magazin f. Naturvidenskab*, 39/4 (1901), 303-26.
– 1921 'Lappiske Stjernenavne, *Tromsø Museums Årsh[e]fter* 44/3(1921), 3-10.
– 1927 *Lappiske eventyr og sagn*. 1. Oslo. 4 vols.
RAHNER, H. 1957 *Greek Myths and Christian Mystery*, London.
RÄNK, G. 1955 'Lapp Female Deities of the Madder-Akka Group', *Studia Septentronalia* 6 (1955), 7-79.
RAWSON, P. 1973 'Early History of Sexual Art' in *Rawson* (ed.), 1-76.
RAWSON, P. (ed.) 1973 *Primitive Erotic Art*, London.
REES, A. & B. 1961 *Celtic Heritage*, London.
REICHBORN-KJENNERUD 1923 'Lægeradene i den eldre Edda', *Maal og Minne* 1923, 1-57.
REITER, R.J. 1973 'Comparative physiology: pineal gland: pineal gland', *Annual Review of Physiology* 35 (1973), 305-28.
– 1981a 'Seasonal aspects of reproduction in a hibernating rodent: photoperiodic and pineal effects', *Survival in the Cold. Hibernation and Other Adaptations*, eds. X.J. Musacchia & L. Jansky), New York 1981, 1-11.
– 1981b 'The Mammalian Pineal Gland; Structure and Function', *American Journal of Anatomy* 162 (1981), 267-313.
RHEEN, S. 1987 En kortt relation om Lapparnes Lefwarne och Sedher, wijd-Skiepellser, sampt i många Stycken Grofwe Wildfarellser. *Bidrag till kännedom om de svenska landsmålen ock svenskt folkliv* 17/1,1897.
RIES, J. 'Cross', *EOR* 4, 155-66.
ROBERTSON, H. 1971 'Studies in Carmichael's "Carmina Gadelica"', *Scottish Gaelic Studies* 12/1 (1971), 220-65.
ROHDE, E.S. 1922 'The Folk-Lore of Herbals', *Folk-Lore* 33 (1922), 243-64.
RÖHRICH, L. 1959 'Europäische Wildgeistersagen', *Rheinisches Jahrbuch für Volkskunde* 10 (1959), 79-161.
ROOTH, Anna-Birgitta 1961 'The Conception of "Rulers" in the South of Sweden', in *Hultkrantz* (ed.),112-22.
ROSE, H.J. 1928 *A Handbook of Greek Mythology*, London.
ROSS, Anne 1960 Esus et les trois 'grues' *Études Celtiques* 9 (1960), 405-38.
– 1967 *Pagan Celtic Britain. Studies in Iconography and Tradition*. London and New York.
– 1973 'Celtic and Northern Art', in *Rawson* (ed.), 77-106.
– 1976 *The Folklore of the Scottish Highlands*, London.
RUTTLEDGE, R.F. 1966 *Ireland's Birds*, London.
RYNNE, E. 1972 'Celtic stone idols in Ireland', *The Iron Age in Irish Sea Province: CBA Research Report* 9 (1972), 79-98.
– 1987 'A Pagan Celtic Background for Sheela-na-Gigs ?', *Figures from the Past. Studies on Figurative Art in Christian Ireland in Honour of Helen M. Roe*, ed. E. Rynne, Dublin 1987, 189-202.
SCHARFF, R.F. 1907 *European Animals: their geological history and geographical distribution*, London.
– 1915 'On the Irish names of mammals', *The Irish Naturalist* March, 45-53.
SCHRÖDER, F.R. 1927 'Ein altirischer Krönungsritus und das indogermanische Rossopfer', *Zeitschrift für celtische Philologie* 16 (1927), 310-2.

SCOULER, J. 1838 'Notice of animals which have disappeared from Ireland during the period of authentic history,' *Journal of the Geological Society of Dublin* 1(1838), 224-8.
SIMON, Erika 1983 *Festivals of Attica. An Archaeological Commentary*, Madison, Wisc.
SIMPSON, Jacqueline 1962-5 'Mímir: Two Myths or One ?', *Saga-Book* 16. (1962-5) 41-53.
– 1988 *Scandinavian Folktales*. Penguin Folklore Library, London etc.
SKEAT, W.W. 1910 *An Etymological Dictionary of the English Language*, Oxford.
SLOTKIN, E.M. 1990 'Noínden; its semantic range', *Celtic Language, Celtic Culture. A Festschrift for Eric P. Hamp*, Van Nuys, California, 139-49.
SMAL-STOCKI, R. 1950 'Taboos on animal names in Ukrainian', *Language* 26 (1950), 489-93.
SOLHEIM, S. 1952 *Norsk Sætertradisjon. Instituttet for sammanlignende kulturforskning, Serie B: Skrifter* 47, Oslo etc 1952.
STALLYBRASS, J.S. (trans.) 1900 *Teutonic Mythology*, 1. London.
STOKES, W. 1890 *Lives of Saints from the Book of the Dean of Lismore*, Oxford.
SVEINSSON, E.Ól. 1948 'Ferðathaettir frá Írlandi', *Skírnir* 122 (1948), 155-84.
SVENSSON, S. 1942 'Tor med sitt långa skägg" in *Bygd och Yttervärld. Studier över förhållandet mellan nyheter och tradition. Nordiska Museets Handlingar* 15, 122-40, Stockholm.
SWAHN, J.-Ö. 1953 *The Tale of Cupid and Psyche*, Lund.
SZÖVÉRRFY, J. 1955 'The Well of the Holy Women: Some St. Columba Traditions in the West of Ireland', *Journal of American Folklore*, 68/268 (1955), 111-22.
– 1956-7 ' Manus O'Donnell and Irish Folk Tradition ', *Éigse* 8 (1956-7), 108-32.
– 1988 'Some Stages of the St. Columba Traditions in the Middle Ages', *Medieval Notes and Extracts from the Archives for Medieval Poetry. 7. Publications of the Archives for Medieval Poetry: Second Series*. Boston/Randolph, Mass., 1988, 1-28.
THOMPSON, F.G. 1964-6 'The Folklore Elements in "Carmina Gadelica"', *Transactions of the Gaelic Society of Inverness* 44 (1964-6), 226-55.
THOMPSON, W. 1850 *The Natural History of Ireland*, London.
TILLHAGEN, C.-H. 1858 *Folklig Läkekonst*, Stockholm 1958.
– 1975 'Die schwedischen Räubersagen', Miscellanea Prof.Em. Dr. K.C. Peeters, ed. W. van Nespen, Antwerpen.
– 1978 Fåglarna i folktron, Stockholm.
TRAYNOR, M. 1953 *The English Dialect of Donegal*. A Glossary, Dublin.
TSCHERNJETZOW, V.N. 1974 'Bärenfest bei den Ob-Ugriern, *Acta Ethnographica Academiae Scientarium Hungaricae* 23/2-4 (1974), 285-319.
TURVILLE-PETRE, E.O.G. 1964 *Myth and Religion of the North. The Religion of Ancient Scandinavia*, London.
– 1969 'Fertility of Beast and Soil in Old Norse Literature' in *Polomé* (ed.) 1969, 244-64.
UA MUIRGHEASA, É. 1907 *Seanfhocla Uladh*, Baile Átha Cliath.
USENER, H. 1902 'Milch und Honig', *Rheinisches Museum für Philologie* 1902, 177-95.

VAN WIJNGAARDEN-BAKKER, Louise H. 1974 'The Animal Remains from the Beaker Settlement of Newgrange, Co. Meath: First Report', *Proceedings of the Royal Irish Academy*, 74 C 11 (1974), 313-83.
VENDRYES, J. *Lexique étymologigues de l'Irlandais ancien*, Dublin & Paris 1959-81.
VERMASEREN, M.J. 1977 *Cybele and Attis: The Myth and the Cult*, London.
VILKUNA, A. 1965 'Das Verhalten der Finnen in "heiligen" (Pyhä) Situationen', *FF Communications* 164, Helsinki 1965.
VILKUNA, K. 1969 *Finnische Brauchtum im Jahreslauf, FF Communications* 206, Helsinki 1969, 47-61.
VOIGT, V. 1978 'Shamanism in North Eurasia as a Scope of Ethnology', in *Diószegi & Hoppál* (eds.), 59-79.
VON SYDOW, C.-W. 1910 'Tors Färd till Utgård', *Danske Studier* 1910, 65-104.
– 1923a 'Beowulf och Bjarki', *Studier i nordisk filologi* 14 (1923), 1-46.
– 1923b Review, *Folkminnen och Folktankar* 10 (1923), 62-4.
WAGNER, H. 1953a 'Zum Manx-Wort für Feuer', *Lexis* 3 (1953), 133-4.
– 1953b 'Varia', *Zeitschrift für celtische Philologie* 24 1/2 (1953), 92-3.
– 1960 'Zum Wort für "Biene" im Irischen', *Zeitschrift für vergleichende Sprachforschung [Kuhns Zeitschrift]* 76 (1960), 81-4.
– 1964 Zur Bezeichnung des Kranichs im Keltischen *Zeitschrift für celtische Philologie* 29 (1964), 301-4.
– 1972 'Beiträge in Erinnerung om Julius Pokorny', *Zeitschrift für celtische Philologie* 32 (1972), 1-89.
– & Keller, H.-E. 1957 'It. *mattra, mastra*, prov. *mastra*, altfranz. *maistrel*, ir. *maistred*,' *Zeitschrift für romanische Philologie* 73 (1957), 277-301.
WAKEMAN, W.F. 1879 'On certain wells situate in the North-West of Ireland etc.,' *JRSAI* 15. Fourth Series, 1879-1882, 365-84.
WALDE, A. & POKORNY, J. 1930 & 1927, *Vergleichendes Wörterbuch der indogermanischen Sprachen*, Berlin & Leipzig. 2 vols.
WARDE FOWLER, W. 1925 *The Roman Festivals of the Period of the Republic*, London.
WASSON, R.G. (with a section by Wendy Doniger O'Flaherty) 1968 *Soma: Divine Mushroom of Immortality. Ethno-mycological Studies* 1, New York & The Hague.
WATKINS, C. 1962 'Varia'II', *Ériu* 19 (1962), 114-8.
WATSON, A. 1981 'The King, The Poet and the Sacred Tree', *Études Celtique* 18 (1981), 165- 80.
WATSON, J.K. 1981 *Bee-keeping in Ireland. A History*, Dublin.
WATSON, S. (ed.) 1989a *Féilscríbhinn Thomáis de Bhaldraithe*, Baile Átha Cliath.
– (ed.) 1989b *Oidhreacht Ghleann Cholm Cille*, [Baile Átha Cliath].
WATSON, W.J. 1926 *The History of the Celtic Place-Names of Scotland*, Edinburgh & London.
WEBSTER, G. 1988 *The British Celts and their Gods Under Rome*, London.
WEISER-AALL, Lily 1968 *Svangerskap og Fødsel i Nyere Norsk Tradition. En kildekritisk studie. Småskrifter fra Norsk Etnologisk Gransking. Norsk Folkemuseum* 6-7, Oslo 1968.
WENTWORTH, H. & FLEXNER, S.B. (eds.) 1967 *The Dictionary of American Slang*, Toronto.
WESSMAN, V.E.V. 1919 &1917 'Folktro om björnens vintervila', *Hembygden* 7 (1916), 104-5 and 8 (1917), 71-2.

WIKANDER, S. 1950 'Tors bockar och patriarkernas kalv', *Arv* 6 (1950), 90-9.
WIKMAN, K.Rob.V. 1917 'Tabu- och orenhetsbegrepp i nordgermansk folktro om könen', *Folkloristiska och Etnografiska Studier* 2 (1917), 43-9.
– 1929 'Eldborgs skål', in *Wikman & Andersson* (eds.), 198-214.
– 1943 'Vårens almanacka. Orientering, teorier, kritik', *Budkavlen* 22, 1-46.
– & ANDERSSON, S. (eds.) 1929 *Studier och uppsatser tillägnade Otto Andersson på hans femtioårsdag den 27 april 1929*, Åbo.
WILDHABER, R. 1975 'AaTh 958 "Der Hilferuf des Hirten",' *Fabula* 16, 233-56.
WILLETTS, R.F. 1962 *Cretan Cults and Festivals*, London.
WILLIAMS, N.J.A. 1989 'Some Irish plant names,' in *Ó Corráin et al.* (eds.), 449-62.
– 1993, *Díolaim Luibheanna*, Baile Átha Cliath.
WINSTON, M.L. 1987 *The Biology of the Honey Bee*, Cambridge (Mass.) & London.
WRIGHT, A.R. & LONES, T.E. (eds.) 1938 *British Calendar Customs. England* 2, London.
WRIGHT, J. *The English Dialect Dictionary*, Oxford etc., 1898-1905. 6 vols.
YOUNG, Jean I. 1951 *The Prose Edda of Snorri Sturluson. Tales from Norse Mythology*, Cambridge.

ABBREVIATIONS

CG	Carmina Gadelica
DIL	Dictionary of the Irish Language
EB	Encyclopaedia Britannica
EOR	Encyclopedia of Religion
EORE	Encyclopaedia of Religion and Ethics
FW	Funk and Wagnalls Standard Dictionary of Folklore, Mythology and Legend
HDA	Handwörterbuch des Deutschen Aberglaubens
IFC	Irish Folklore Collection
JRSAI	Journal of the Royal Society of Antiquaries of Ireland
KL	Kulturhistoriskt lexikon för nordisk medeltid

Fig. 35 *(opposite)*: Irish Folklore Commission Questionnaire of 1942

Irish Folklore Commission.   **January, 1942**

The Feast of St. Brigid

The Feast of St. Brigid is one of the most important festivals of the Irish year, and with both the Saint and her festival are associated a rich body of ancient custom and belief, prayer, proverb and legend. It is hoped that this questionnaire will help to remind you and the old people in your district of much of this important cultural and literary heritage and that this first systematic attempt to gather the lore of Brigid of the Gaedheal may be successful. We rely upon you to do all that you can to record what is still available, and to send it to us as soon as it is convenient to you. Bíonn an rath ar an mbeagán - Every little helps.

----------oOo----------

1. Write down any traditional stories available locally which tell of incidents in St. Brigid's life. (a) Stories about St. Brigid and the Blessed Virgin. (b) Stories about St. Brigid's association with St. Patrick, Colmcille or other saints. (c) Miracles attributed to St. Brigid. Prayers to St. Brigid, or prayers in which the Saint is mentioned.

2. How was (is) the Feast of St. Brigid observed locally? (a) How was (is) the Eve (vigil) of the Feast observed? If a decorated figure (brídeog) was (or is) carried in procession from house to house, describe the figure and the custom in as much detail as possible. What songs or rhymes were used on that occasion? Write down local stories and accounts of the procession. Is there any local explanation of the origin of the custom? Was a sheaf or a cake placed on the doorstep on St. Brigid's Eve? Why? Describe the ceremony. (b) How was (is) St. Brigid's Day observed locally? Did people work? Was work or action of a particular kind traditionally forbidden on that day? Why? Give details. Were special prayers said on the Feast or on its vigil? What were they?

3. Are crosses made locally at the Feast of St. Brigid? If so, describe how they are made, when, by whom, material used, where and how installed. Can you draw a sketch of St. Brigid's Crosses made locally or send a Cross to the Folklore Commission? Similarly for St. Brigid's ribbon, belt, (girdle, crios) and cloak (brat). Describe their use.

4. Write down any local lore about the following in so far as they are associated with the Feast of St. Brigid: (a) the weather; (b) the tides; (c) birds and animals; (d) agricultural work; (e) fishing; (f) prosperity and fertility. How was St. Brigid's Feast compared or related with other festivals. (e.g., St. Patrick's Day) in local tradition? Stories about this. Is St. Brigid associated in any way with cows or with milk?

5. Are any local wells, churches, or graveyards dedicated to St. Brigid? Does the name Brigid (or any form of it) occur in local place-names? Are girls named after the Saint in your district? What form does the name take locally (Brigid, Bride, Brighid, Brighde etc.)?

------------oOo------------

INDEX OF NAMES

This Index contains proper names – all other indexed words are in the Index of Subjects; 'n' denotes an endnotes page; & English alphabet order is applied for letters: å, ä, ö, ø, æ, ð, þ

A

a Búrca, T. 146, 167n
Adam of Bremen 191, 194, 199, 206
Adonis 131n
Aed(h) 160, 161, 179, 226n
Aed mac Fidaig (Fidga) 160
Aedh meic Bricc 179
Aidus 180
Aodh (Hugh) 6, 73, 145, 146, 147, 155, 161, 163
Aodh Mhic Bricne (Saint Ó Bricne) 177, 179, 180, 182
Aodh na Bricna (Hughy Breaky) 180, 226n
af Klintberg, B. 148, 150, 161, 164, 168n, 173n, 174n, 239, 253
Agni 163, 213
Ailill (son of Dunlang) 200
Ailis (daughter of Hugh O'Neill) 4
Ajysyt 209, 210
Akka(s) 30, 204, 205, 233n, 239
'All Father' 190
Almqvist, Bo xv, xvi, 34n, 85n, 169n, 174n 239, 250
Antigonos of Karystos 98
Aphrodite 114, 136n
Arduinna 74n
Arethas of Caesarea 139n
Aristotle 97, 98, 100, 129n, 141n, 252
Árnason, Jón 69
Arnbjørn 165
Art 50, 73
Artemis x, 36n, 41n, 74n, 99, 163, 231n
Artigenos 50
Ashtart 114
Ask 229n
Astarte 114
Attis 84n, 85n, 102, 131n, 255
Auðhumla 194-196, 217, 229n
Aurgelmir 230n
Austeja 138n, 230n
Avicantus 195

B

Backman, E.L. 79n, 239
Bäckman, L. 119, 140n, 203-205, 233n, 234n, 239, 243
Bairéad, P. 145, 150, 151, 167n, 169n, 170n
Bauschatz, P. 188, 228n, 239
Beorn Beresun 57
Beowulf 131n, 255
Bera 57, 58
Bjarkarimur 57
Bjarki 57, 58, 131n, 255
Björn 57 *[See* björn *in Subject Index]*
Bodb 139n
Bǫðvar Bjarki 57, 58, 131n, 255
Bor 194, 229n, 237n
Boui 198, 199, 231n
Brigit /Brigid /Brigitte
  viii-xiii, 1-11, 13-18, 20-28, 30-33,
  34n-37n, 39n-44n, 46n-48n, 49, 50,
  63, 64, 66, 68, 71-73, 76n, 86n, 88n,
  89, 91, 93-97, 103-106, 109, 113, 114,
  116, 118, 124-126, 128n, 129n, 134n,
  140n, 159, 160, 162, 164, 165, 172n,
  173n, 175, 176, 179, 180, 193, 196,
  200, 202, 207, 210, 214, 217, 218,
  221-224, 225n, 226n, 230n, 236n,
  238n, 241, 246, 249, 250, 252, 257
  Bríd /Bride /Bríde
    1, 3, 6-10, 15, 17, 20-22, 26,
    27, 30, 33, 34n-38n, 40n-42n,
    44n-46n, 63, 64, 67, 71-73, 77n,
    87n, 89-92, 103-105, 109, 110,
    112-114, 124, 135n, 176, 199,
    200, 217, 222-224, 233n, 236n,
    248, 252, 257
  Bridget /Brìghde /Briid
    4, 9-11, 22, 34n, 39n, 71, 175, 176, 257
Broccán 159
Bucholz, P. 206, 234n, 240
Búri 194, 229n

Index of Names

C

Carmichael, A. 14, 15, 40n-42n, 63, 64, 67, 68, 71, 87n, 89-92, 103-105, 112, 114, 132n, 135n, 143n, 176, 200, 222, 223, 225n, 240, 241, 253
Celander, Hilding 81n, 88n, 109, 122, 123, 125, 134n, 135n, 142n, 143n, 234n, 241
Cernunnos 30, 31, 47n, 48n, 240
Chichlo, B. 120, 141n, 241
Christ 15, 41n, 73, 93, 100, 112, 159, 179, 182, 223, 224, 234
  [Carol Christ 241]
Christiansen, R.Th. 132n, 144, 147, 148, 150, 167n, 168n, 170n, 172n, 173n, 234n, 241, 252
Ciall, Tuigse, & Náire 183, 184, 187-189, 205, 217, 227n
Cogitosus 159, 165, 241
Collinder, Björn 67, 81n 85n, 103, 131, 216, 236n, 241
Colm Cille (Columba) viii, 2, 46n, 128n, 175-180, 182-184, 187, 188, 193-195, 218, 219, 221, 222, 225n, 227n, 229n, 230n, 250
Conamhail Conriucht 50
Conn 73, 225n
Corduff, M. 36n, 41n, 167n
Cormac /Cor(b)mac mac Airt 13, 49, 50, 96, 179, 225n, 250
Cormac mac Cuillenáin ix, 96
Cremhthann 179
Crobh Dhearg ('Red Claw') 95, 96
Cybele x, 76n, 84n, 85n 101, 255

D

Dagda 96
Danaher, K. 35n, 41n-43n, 46n, 81n, 113, 136n, 138n, 233n, 241
  See also Ó Danachair, C.
Demeter 118, 139n, 241
de Vries, A. & J. 39n, 44n, 46n-48n, 75n, 80n, 82n, 87n, 130n, 131n, 133n, 134n, 136n, 137n, 139n, 143n, 172n, 173n, 189, 194, 195, 230n, 242
Dinneen, P.S. 110, 127n, 128n, 131n, 133n-136n, 232n, 242

Dionysos 140n
Drobin, Ulf 219, 238n, 242
Dugall 73
Dwelly, E. 61, 67, 86n, 133n, 236n, 242

E

Edsman, C.-M. 57, 58, 76n-80n, 82n, 242
Eiche 94
Eldborg 123, 125, 241, 251, 256
Elgfróði 58
Embla 229n, 230n
Esbjörn 165
Esus 107, 108, 134n, 251, 253
Evans, E.E. 40n, 114, 130n, 136n, 232n, 343
Eve 237n

F

Feilberg, H.F. 69, 87n, 143n, 243
Fenrir 85n
Fiacail mac Conchinn 160
Fiachach 179
Fionn mac Cumhaill 160, 225n
Fjellström, Pehr 119
Fjörgyn 121
Fleck, Jere 192, 228n, 243
Forbus, Henric 203
Freya 76n, 216
Fricco (Frö) 199
Frigg 76n, 162

G

Gerbjörn 165
Gervasius of Tilbury 137n
Gimbutas, Marija 44n, 48n, 75n, 99, 100, 114, 130n-132n, 136n, 138n, 199, 230n, 231n, 243
Giraldus Cambrensis 82n, 93, 98, 137n, 141n, 251
Glas Ghoibhneann 37n, 193, 196, 230n
Góa 70, 72, 88n, 109, 134n, 247
Goibhniu 193, 230n
Green, M. 244
Grimm, J. 188
Gunbjörn 165

H

Hadding the Dane 214, 215
Halvdan 164
Hamp, E. 13, 14, 39n, 44n, 49, 50, 75n, 76n, 88n, 102, 131n, 132n, 138n, 216, 236n, 244, 254
Hárr 190
Heiermeier, A. 88n, 102, 131n, 232n, 245
Helgi 210
Henry, J. 153 (Henry Molly: 127n)
Hera x, 47n 231n, 232n
Hercynia 121
Hermes 118, 139n
Hesiod 106, 163, 173n
Hestia (Vesta) x, 160, 172n
Holmberg, U. 119, 140n, 238n, 245
Homer 163
Hoppál, M. 218, 233n, 234n, 237n, 239, 242, 245, 252, 255
Hringr 57
Hvít 57

I

Ikarios 140n
Ingalls, D. 213, 235n, 245
Ivor 67, 68, 103, 104

J

Jack Straw 199, 231n, 232n
Jacobsen, J. 41, 61, 246
Jemmel 126
John Anna 186
Juksakka 204, 205
Juno x, 14, 15, 40n, 47n

K

Kamanienski, A. 235n
Keating, G. 158
Kenney, J. viii, 88n, 128n, 129n, 176, 179, 180, 225n, 226n, 246
Kildal, Jens 203
Kore 139
Kvasir 192

L

Laima 75n 199, 230n
Lasair, Inghean Bhuidhe, & Latiaran 94-96
Lawless, R. 146
Leib-olmai 119, 209
Leisiö, T. 150, 164, 168n, 172n, 174n, 246
Lid, N. 85n, 88n, 173n, 232n, 247
Lockwood, W.B. 61, 81n, 105, 106, 127n, 133n, 134n, 247
Loki 161, 172n, 216, 217, 219, 236n, 242
Loptr 172n
'Lord of the Elements' 182
Lucan 84n
Lucas, A.T. 10, 11, 37n, 38, 47n, 48n, 142n, 158, 172n, 247
Lugaid 165
Lugh 3, 27, 43n, 47n, 48n
Luperci 52

M

Mac Aonghais, I. 61, 81n, 247
Mac Cana, Proinsias 30, 39n, 42n, 47n, 48n, 74n, 85n, 247
Mac Donnchadha (Páidín), M. 167n
McDonnell, R. (Earl of Antrim) 4
Macha 139n
Mac Giollarnátha, S. 167n, 170n
MacLeod, Banks 133n, 135n, 248
Macleod (Major) 63, 64, 67
Mac Mathúna / Ó Mathúna 50
MacNeill, E. 2, 43n, 248
MacNeill, M. 2-4, 12, 27, 33, 34n, 37n, 38n, 43n, 48n, 78n, 89, 93-96, 127n, 129n, 227n, 248
Mac Pháidín, S. 169n
Madderakka 203, 204
Maol Domhnaich, Maol Odhrain, Maol Oighe, Maol Ruibhe 225n
Marstrander, C. 103, 131n, 138n, 248, 249
Martin, Martin 71, 88n, 249
Matras, Christian 61, 248
Matugenos 50
Maylmen radien 203
Mel 94, 200, 226n

Index of Names 261

Mercurius Artaios 49
Merope 163
Mími /Mímir 189, 190, 217, 218, 228n, 254
Mithras /Mithraic 30, 99
Moberg, C.-A. 161, 168n, 171n, 173n, 174n, 249
Möller, J.S. 249
Moore, J. 146
Mórrígan 139n
Mubenaimo 126
Murphy, G. 160, 172n, 240, 249

N

Nagy, G. & J.F. 81n, 120, 121, 128n, 141n, 249
Niall of the Nine Hostages 179
Ní Bheirn, M. 225n
Ní Chabhail, Á. 146, 150, 155, 167n
Ní Dhonnagáin, M. 180
Novakovsky, S. 207, 234n, 250

O

Ó Cathasaigh, T. 49, 50, 74n, 76n, 250
Ó Corrdhuibh, M. 167n
  See also Corduff, M.
Ó Danachair, C. xiii, 34n, 35n, 38n, 39n, 41n, 150, 151, 168n, 169n, 173n, 243, 250 *See also* Danagher, K.
Óðinn 190, 192, 194, 217, 218, 229n, 231n, 234n, 243
Ó Domhnaill, A. & T. 6, 229n
Ó Dónaill, N. 110, 136n, 173n, 236n, 250
O'Donnell, M. 178, 182, 183, 254
O'Donovan, J. 180, 226n, 250
Ó Duilearga, S. xiii-xv, 78n, 169n, 170n, 250
Oenopion 163
Offote 165
Ógacht, Egna & Fáidhedóracht 182, 183, 187
Ó hEochaidh, S. 4, 39n, 176, 177, 185(*illus.*), 225n-227n, 250
Ó hÓgáin, D. 88n, 146, 167n, 171n, 229n, 230n, 235n, 243, 251, 252
Olaf Haraldsson 60
Olaus Magnus 174n
Olc Aiche 50
Olrik, A. & J. 57, 69, 79n, 85n, 86n, 88n, 109, 174n, 199, 231n, 232n, 251
Ó Moghráin, P. 151, 159, 169n, 172n, 173n, 251
Ó(/Ua) Muirgheasa, Énrí 34n, 170n, 184, 186, 226n, 227n, 251, 254
Ó Murchadh, M. 151-153
O'Rahilly, T.F. 102, 131n, 180, 226n, 228n, 236n, 251
Ordéus, Valdis 81n, 235n, 239
Orion 162-164, 173n
Ó Sírín, M. 145
Ó Súilleabháin, S. & S.C. xiii, xv-xvii, 14, 39n-43n, 81n, 128n, 132n-134n, 232n, 252
Ouranos 131n
Ovid 101

P

Pan 118, 139n
Pashupati 30
Paulson, I. 220, 221, 238n, 252
Pedersen, H. 115, 131n, 134n, 137n, 138n, 174n, 252
Perkunas 121, 249n
Piarun 121
Pliny 52, 78n, 85n
Plutarch 99, 134n
Pokorny, J. 37n, 44n, 50, 72, 74n-76n, 82n, 134n, 137n-139n, 230n, 232n, 252, 255
Pontoppidan 55
Priapus 81n, 118, 172n

R

Ränk, G. 205, 207, 209, 210, 233n-235n, 253
Rinda 231n
Robertson, H. 40n, 176, 225n, 240, 253
Romulus & Remus 52
Röskva 219
Rosmerta 47n, 190
Ross, A. & M. 35n, 39n, 43, 47, 76n, 80n, 87n, 106, 120, 130n, 134n, 137n-139n, 141n, 170n, 191, 228n, 238n, 253

S

Saints (individual) –
  Aed(h) meic Bricc *(etc.)* *See above*
  Brendan 43, 46
  Brigit /Bríd *(etc.)* *See above*
  Colm Cille *(etc.)* *See above*
  Cuimín 229n
  Gobnait 46, 97
  Gregory 106, 109
  Knut 81n, 86n, 124, 125, 251
  Latiaran 94-96
  Martin 2, 85n, 237n
  Mary (Saint) 35n
  Matthew 59, 80n
  Mel 94, 200, 226n
  Michael 37n, 225n
  Olaf 45n, 60
  St Patrick /Pádraig /Pàdruig –
    viii, 27, 34n, 38n, 51, 76n, 94, 109, 135n, 175, 176, 193
Saints (in general) 2, 35n, 43n, 94, 180, 187, 237n, 250, 251, 254
  See Saints' Days *in Subjects Index*
Sarakka 126, 203-205, 233n, 244
Satan /'Mubenaimo' 53, 77n, 125, 126
Simpson, J. 168n, 190, 191, 228n, 254
Sirius 163, 164
Siva 28, 30, 139n
Snorri 45n, 85n, 194, 219, 240, 256
Solheim, S. 45n, 77n, 142n, 155, 166, 168n-171n, 174n, 232n, 254
Solinus 98
Soma 212, 213, 235n, 245, 246
Stenbjörn 165
Sturluson Snorri 45n, 85n, 194, 240, 246, 256
Sucellos 134
Suibhne Geilt 85n
Szövérrfy, J. 177, 178, 182, 183, 187, 225n-228n, 254

T

Tad(h)g 170, 201, 202
Tammuz 131
Thjálfi 219
Thompson, S. 40n, 133n, 144, 167n, 168n, 239, 254
Thorbjörn 142
Thórr /Thorra- /Thorre /Thorri /Þorri x, 69, 70, 88n, 109, 121-123, 126, 139n, 142n, 161, 217, 241
Tiernan, J. 154
Tolmie, J. 63
Trinity 72, 214, 223, 227n

U

Uí Chadhla, B. 229n
Uí Mhathghamhna, É. 229n
Uí Néill 180
Ux-, Uksakka 204, 205

V

Väinämöinen 40n, 87n
Vendryes, J. 74n, 75n, 103, 116, 128n, 132n, 133n, 138n, 139n, 172n, 173n, 202, 216, 228n, 230n, 232n, 236n, 255
von Sydow, C.-W. xv, 79n, 174n, 219, 225n, 237n, 247, 255
Vincent de Beauvais 54
Virgil 99, 129n
Virgin Mary 1, 3, 7, 15, 20, 37n, 40n, 43n, 52, 73, 76n, 77n, 79n, 91-93, 99, 100, 124, 125, 135n, 143n, 162, 175, 179, 186, 223, 224, 225n, 234n

W

Wakeman, W.F. 30, 46n, 47n, 255
Wasson, G. 212-217, 235n, 236n, 245, 246, 255
Watson, J.K. /S. /W.J. 38n, 48n, 81n, 130n, 132n, 170n, 227n, 238n, 247, 250, 255
Wildhaber, R. 144, 145, 149, 150, 167n, 168n, 256
William of Auvergne 54
Wodan 206

Y

Ymir 194, 229, 230n, 237n

Z

Zeus 84n, 218

INDEX OF SUBJECTS

Translations in square brackets; *Texts in italics*; 'n' = endnotes page;
& English alphabet order is applied for letters: å, ä, ö, ø, æ, ð, þ.
(*Note:* Proper names are indexed in the separate Index of Names)

A

abduction 150, 154, 164, 201
acorn 115, 117, 118, 139n
afterbirth 8, 99, 234n
agricultural activity 9, 33, 44n, 46n
 47n 107, 114, 221, 239, 241, 257
aingeal /aile [angel /fire] 37n, 127n
airge [summer pasture] 159, 172n
ale (offering) 123, 124, 142n, 202
amanita muscaria (fly-agaric) 212, 235n, 236n
amatorium virus 52
angel/s 37n, 91, 92, 124, 127n, 182
angelica 28, 29(*illus.*), 44n, 45n, 128n, 171n
animal husbandry 162, 164, 175
Annunciation 86n
arctic hysteria 206, 207, 250n
arctos /arkteia [bear] 75n
art /arth [bear] 49, 74n 201
arum 140n
ashes /embers 1, 90-93, 96, 122-124, 127n, 139, 142n, 237n
Aśva Medha (sacrifice) 62, 82n
aurr [honeydew] 192

B

badger 85n, 86n, 102, 201, 232n, 246, 247
bairenn /baireann [rock] 116
bairneach [barnacle] 115, 116, 138n
banal Bríde 41n, 42n, 112, 199, 200, 222, 238n
bark (peeled) 72, 90, 99, 119, 141, 171n, 200, 220, 232n *See:* tree/s
barnacle 115, 116, 137n
barren /-ness 7, 8, 14, 33, 35n, 48n, 99, 212
barselgillen [childbirth feasts] /barselhus [childbirth party house] 196, 198, 244

beach /bech /beth [bee] 98, 102, 130n, 216, 241   *See:* bee
Bealtaine viii, 34n, 37n, 38n, 89, 237n
bear x, xi, 2, 38n, 49-62, 64-68, 70, 72, 74n-80n, 82n-88n, 93, 101-104, 107, 118-120, 122, 130n, 131n, 134n, 139n-142n, 149, 162-166, 171n, 174n, 195, 199, 201, 206, 208, 219-221, 231n, 232n, 234n, 235n, 238n, 239, 241, 242, 244, 245, 249, 252
bechbretha [bee judgment] 98
bee 50, 74n-76n, 97-104, 115, 116, 129n-131n, 138n, 140n, 141n, 192, 195, 216-218, 230,236n, 243, 244, 255, 256   *See:* beach /bech
beehive 74n, 97-100, 138n, 141n, 230n
beetle 24(implement), 100(insect)
bell 141n, 148, 149
bernache [barnacle] 116
Bern /*Berne Glosses* 50, 74n, 84n
berserker 81n, 195
Betha Colam Cille 178, 182, 187, 225n
bethir [bear] 74n
Bethu Brigte 27, 250
betrothal 58
biocosmic (rhythms /clock) 66
bird
 bird/s (individual) –
  barnacle goose 115
  Bridein ['bird of Bride'] 105
  cockerel 87n, 90, 143n
  crane 106-110, 128n, 132n, 134n, 135n
  crossbill 87n
  crow 8, 106, 124, 132n-135n, 174n
  cuckoo 86n, 132n, 136n
  goose 115, 116, 137n
  hen 8, 43n, 88n
  heron 106, 109, 128n, 132n, 134n, 249

jackdaw 8
oystercatcher ['giolla Bríde']
    105-107, 109, 110, 132n, 133n
raven 106, 119, 139n
sandpiper [gobadán] 110, 132n,
    136n
seagull 105
stonechat 86n
stork 128n
swallow 86n
wren (& wrenboys) 48n, 106, 132n
bird/s (in general) –
    xi, 2, 8, 13, 76n, 84n, 85n,
    105-107, 109, 110, 112, 116,
    128n, 133n, 135n-137n, 221, 234,
    239, 247, 253
birth /rebirth xii, 7, 8, 10, 13, 14, 16,
    33, 35n, 36n, 38n, 39n, 42n, 46n,
    48n, 65, 66, 72, 76n, 77n, 79n, 84n,
    99, 115, 126, 163, 192, 196-201, 203,
    205, 207-210, 218, 223, 230n, 231n,
    233n, 234n, 238n, 246, 247
björn /bjørn 49, 75n, 77n, 131n, 142n,
    165, 171n, 240, 242, 243, 247, 249
bone 40n, 60, 75n, 86n, 177, 178, 195,
    218-221, 224, 225n, 231n, 237n,
    238n, 252
bonfire /bonfire night 92, 93, 184
booley /-ing 13, 38n, 144-147,
    149-151, 155, 159-163, 165, 168n,
    169n, 172n-174n
'borrowing days' 135n
bous 163, 231n
bow (and arrow) 203, 204, 233
brass (rings, chains) 56, 60, 220, 243
brat (/bratach /cochall /ribín) Bríde
    6-8, 17, 26, 35n, 77n, 223
Brehon Laws 158
bride /bridegroom 45n, 46n, 52, 58,
    80, 222, 245
brídeog(a) /banal Bride /biddies
    /biddy boys
    1, 18, 19(*illus.*), 20, 21, 28, 30, 41n,
    42n, 45n, 46n, 48n, 112, 114, 199,
    200, 222, 238n
Brigantiae /-inos ix, 244
Britain ix, 75n, 98, 135n, 253
    England 231n, 251, 256

brocc [badger] 201
Broccan's Hymn 159
brothchán /bruth [broth] 202, 82n
buarach tháil (prayer) 11, 37n
bucrania 134n
bull 12, 13, 98-100, 107, 108, 130n,
    133n, 149, 168n
burial 220, 227, 237n
butter 3, 18, 22, 24, 28, 37n, 41n, 42n,
    45n, 47n, 112, 127n 159, 169, 173n,
    197, 210, 222, 236n
butterfly 130n
byre /byre-women 26, 46n, 162, 163

C
cailleach [hag] 3, 39n, 71, 184, 227n,
    247
calf 7, 8, 10-12, 38n, 50, 72, 74n, 79n,
    99, 175, 193, 234n *See:* cow; deer
candle 10, 11, 15, 30-32, 99, 109
Candlemas 39n, 52, 85n, 86n, 99,
    109, 123, 133n
Carmina Gadelica 40n, 176, 240, 241,
    278, 253, 254, 256
castration 84n, 85n, 101, 131n, 241
Cath Finntragha 158
cattle 12, 26, 34n, 68, 76n, 77n, 97,
    99, 143n, 148, 149, 151, 159, 164, 165,
    169n, 170n, 174n, 175-177, 179, 195,
    209, 219, 225n, 232n, 236n, 244, 247
    See also: cow; ox
Celt /Celtic ix-xi, 31, 32, 34n, 39n,
    41n, 47n, 49, 50, 61, 74n, 78n, 88n,
    93, 102, 103, 106-108, 115-118, 120,
    121, 123, 130n, 132n, 134n, 138n,
    139n, 174n, 176, 190, 191, 201, 214,
    215, 219, 232n, 238n, 240, 242, 244,
    246-255
charm/s 11, 37n, 76n, 112, 143n, 152,
    166, 175n, 179, 221, 248
chastity 99, 182
Chelei (tribe) 141n
childbirth *See:* birth
childlessness 4, 210
Christian /-ity viii, ix, 20, 27, 30, 31,
    33, 36n, 43n, 48n, 51, 53, 60, 77n, 88n,
    94, 95, 97-99, 125, 131n, 159, 184,
    186, 187, 203, 215, 223, 248, 251, 253

Index of Subjects

Christmas 10, 22, 122-125, 199, 231n, 234n
Chukchi (tribe) 235n
churn /churning 20, 22, 28, 29, 37n, 38n, 42n, 44n, 45n, 47n, 127n, 128n, 159, 169n, 222
clothes 6, 18, 20, 24, 36n, 42n, 81n, 96, 208
coffin 194, 230n
conception 12, 115, 135n, 142n, 218, 223, 224
cone 66, 84n, 119
Cormac's Glossary 13, 96
Cornwall /Cornish 115, 116, 138n, 241
courtship 58, 78n, 150(by capture)
cow xi, 2, 7, 8, 10-13, 17, 37n, 38n, 45n, 46n, 77n, 78n, 88n, 99, 134n, 135n, 138n, 142n, 144, 145, 147-149, 175, 177-179, 193(Brigit's), 194, 195, 218, 221, 225n, 229n-231n, 234n, 257
See also: cattle; ox
cradle 71, 89, 146, 147, 203
'creation myth' 44n, 194, 203, 204, 247
Crios Bríde 20, 21(*illus.*), 42n, 252
cross (*incl.* Brigit's, & sign of) 1, 17, 20, 23(*illus.*), 24-26, 30-33, 39n, 85n, 99, 113, 114, 116, 119, 141n, 233n, 239, 249, 252, 253, 257
curds 201, 202, 212, 218

D

Daigh Bhríde (well) 4, 5(*illus.*), 129n
dancing /pantomime 41n, 45n, 59, 63, 74n, 75n, 79n, 83n, 84n, 87n, 134n, 197-199, 223, 231n
dea Artio 49, 51, 74n, 75n
dealbh Bride (ikon) 72, 112
death 38n, 40n, 58, 75n, 78n, 84n, 85n, 99, 106, 114, 130n, 131n, 152, 160, 163, 170n, 182n, 189, 192, 194, 199, 215, 221, 227n, 230n, 247, 252
deer /doe /fawn /reindeer 45n, 83n, 88n, 130n, 141n, 163n, 203, 209, 233n, 237n, 238n, 245

deities /divinities 14, 28, 30, 31, 44n, 49, 51, 74n, 76n, 114-117, 120, 126, 134n, 139n, 142n, 172n, 191, 203, 209, 212-214, 216, 239, 240, 255
See also: gods /goddesses
Denmark 68, 69, 85n, 122, 162, 197, 199, 243
Danish 45n, 55, 81n, 109, 124, 168n, 197-199, 215
dew /honeydew 146, 175, 192, 217, 230n
divination 142n, 212, 228n
dog 52-54, 58, 75n, 77n, 78n, 81n, 93, 103, 119, 130n, 131n, 148, 149, 151-153, 161, 163, 165, 209, 215n, 236n, 248
doll 20, 28, 81n, 112, 114, 137n, 209-211, 222, 234n
door 17, 30, 41n, 52, 61, 69, 72, 76, 93, 112, 113, 126, 152, 198, 200, 204, 207-210, 223, 234n
doorstep /threshold 10, 63, 64, 203, 218, 223
'drinking health' 123-126, 142n
drone 99-103, 115, 130n, 195n
dronn /drunnur [rump] 60-62, 241n
drum 33, 53, 77n, 84n, 119, 128n, 208, 220, 233n, 237n, 239
dubluachair [midwinter] 27
dunghill 78n, 79n, 85n

E

Easter 67, 170n(Easter Ross), 202, 226
ecna, ailithri, oighi 187
Eddic poems 201, 232n
egg/s 8, 42n, 82n, 100, 132n, 140n, 191, 222
emegender deities /dolls 210, 211
Eocene 129n
Epiphany 123
erotic/a 39, 60, 138n, 206, 233n, 235n, 253
essênes 99
Evenki (tribe) 83n, 120
eye/s 1, 15, 18, 28, 34n, 39n, 44n, 56, 71, 72, 80n, 87n, 91, 112, 114, 118-120, 135n-137n, 139n, 141n, 159, 163, 166, 175, 190-192, 211, 213n, 228n, 229n, 234n, 240, 249

F

faechóg [periwinkle] 115, 116
fáel [wolf] 36n
Fáfnísmál 201
fairy /fairies 11, 53, 73, 144, 150, 157, 160, 161, 169, 187, 193, 201, 250
Faroe/s /-se 60, 61, 105-107, 123, 201, 241, 247
fat 52, 60, 76, 88, 120, 137
fate 3, 32, 33, 35n, 48n, 102, 106, 187-189, 194, 195, 210, 230n, 251
Feast *See:* Festival; Saint's Days
February [/'Mí na Féile Bríde'] viii, ix, xvii, 4, 6, 8, 10, 34n, 36n, 38n-40n, 52, 59, 69-71, 76n, 85n, 86n, 88n, 89, 94, 95, 109, 123, 134n, 136n, 142n, 179
Félire Oengusso 98
female 6, 16, 20, 28, 35n, 38n, 57, 58, 69, 78-80, 83, 84, 95, 99, 114, 117, 124-126, 136n, 140n, 141n, 143n, 148-150, 155, 162, 164, 173n, 178, 179, 187, 189, 192, 199, 201, 203, 204, 206, 207, 209, 210, 218, 222, 231n, 233n, 234n, 239, 249, 253
fénnidi 62, 81n
fertility /infertility 2-4, 9, 12, 13, 26, 30, 39n-42n, 44n, 46n-48n, 49, 50, 52, 54, 65, 66, 80n, 82n, 84n, 92, 104, 114, 115, 117, 118, 120, 122, 126, 131n, 134n, 136n-139n, 141n, 142n, 191, 192, 204, 209, 211, 223, 231n, 254
Festival
  Festival of Brigit –
    viii-xiii, xvii, 3, 13, 14, 22, 24, 27, 30, 33, 40n, 41n, 48n, 89, 114, 164, 193, 196, 207, 210, 214, 217, 222, 257
  Festival/s (in general) –
    xvii, 2, 4, 34n, 39n, 57, 58, 60, 76n, 79n-81n, 83n, 93, 118, 120, 123, 129n, 134n, 139n, 140n, 142n, 199, 238, 241, 248, 254-256
Finland 62, 144, 203, 235n
  Finnish 40n, 42n, 55, 58, 76n, 79n-81n, 85n, 86n, 103, 135n, 149, 150, 163, 172n-174n, 216, 222, 225n, 234n, 243, 245, 246
fire /fireside /bonfire viii, xii, 1, 3, 22, 24, 63, 73, 76n, 89-94, 96, 118, 120-126, 127n, 128n, 139n, 140n, 142n, 143n, 152, 159-161, 163, 169n, 172n, 180, 184, 197, 205, 213, 214, 217, 219, 233n, 235n *See also:* flame
fishermen 106, 133n, 184, 186, 227n
flame 15, 73, 93, 94, 160, 163, 213, 235n
Flateyjárbok 60, 70
flax /linen 59, 60, 62, 75n, 80n, 81n, 220
floor 15, 16, 22, 24, 91, 92, 123, 169n, 196, 197, 203, 204, 210
fly-agaric *See:* amanita muscaria
foich [wasp] 102, 115, 116
fomes fomentarius (fungus) 214
food 9, 14, 22, 31, 36n, 39n, 45n, 79n, 84n, 100, 101, 113, 140n-142n, 147, 159, 165, 166, 177-179, 197, 204, 208, 210, 218, 222, 230n, 238n, 248
forest 2, 59, 74n, 76n, 84n, 87n, 141n, 148, 149, 164, 174n, 209, 210, 215
  forest maiden 53, 77n
fox 52, 77n, 79n
France /French 58, 116, 214, 216, 235n
fuadach [kidnapping] 145, 157
furrow 38n, 47n, 92, 94

G

gadhar /gagar /gagarr [dog /hound] 103, 131n *See:* dog
Gael /Gaelic /Gaedhilge 15, 28, 37n, 38n, 40n, 46n, 50, 54, 61, 62, 68, 70, 72, 86n, 90, 91, 93, 105, 107, 124, 125, 127n, 135n, 161, 175, 176, 206, 217, 222, 225n, 240, 242, 245, 247-249, 251-254
galder [spell-caster] 174n
Galium verum [bedstraw] 76n
Galli 84n
gamhain [calf] 38n, 49, 50, 72
gamhnach ['stripper' cow] 12, 38n
Germanic /Germany 49, 50, 78n, 107, 125, 131n, 138n, 139n, 174n, 194, 201, 205, 214, 216, 229n, 240, 248, 252

Index of Subjects 267

Gesta Danorum 57, 231n, 236n
gift/s 41n, 42n, 97, 112, 204, 206, 222
Giolla Bríde [oyster-catcher] 105, 110
Gjallarhorn (horn) 190
glanders 178, 179
Gleipnir (fetter) 85n
goat 130n, 171n, 219
god /goddess viii, ix, xii, 3, 4, 7, 14,
  17, 27, 28, 30, 32, 33, 35n, 39n, 40n,
  43n-45n, 47n, 48n, 51, 53, 57, 74n-77n,
  81n, 84n, 85n, 88n, 91, 92, 95-97, 100,
  104-106, 114, 118, 121-124, 126, 130n,
  134n, 136n-140n, 152, 160, 162, 163,
  166, 172n, 175, 180, 182, 186-188, 190,
  191, 194, 199, 202-205, 207, 209, 212,
  213, 216, 218, 219, 229n-231n, 239,
  241, 243, 246-248, 252, 253, 255
  See also: deities /divinities
Good Friday 99
grace (general) 60, 63, 91, 124, 127n
  grace (after meals) 41
grandmother 152, 153, 199, 204, 210
Greek /Greece 30, 36n, 49, 66,
  74n, 97, 106, 131n, 195, 212, 218,
  231(Greece), 244, 251, 253
groundhog 85n, 86n
Gylfaginning 190, 191, 219, 228n

H

Hallowe'en viii, 38n(hallowmass), 173n
Haloa festival 118, 139n, 140n
harrow head-dress 15, 30
harvest viii, 3, 4, 12, 38n, 39n, 70, 71,
  80n, 95, 142n, 199, 248
head 6, 7, 15, 16, 18, 30, 32, 34n, 39n,
  64, 67, 68, 77n, 87n, 93, 99, 105,
  107, 117, 118, 120, 121, 123, 134n,
  137n-139n, 141n, 161, 190-192, 222
healing 3, 4, 96, 176, 191, 212, 237n
heart 6, 112, 114, 119, 122, 142, 209
hearth 1, 89-92, 120, 123-126, 127n,
  128n, 142n, 160, 169n, 172n, 176,
  204, 208, 210, 213, 214, 242, 250
Hebrides /-ean 67, 68, 248
hedgehog 86n, 130n, 201, 232n
Helgakviða 201
herding 148, 164, 175, 225n
  See also: booley

hermaphrodites 115, 137n
hibernation 65, 66, 68, 84n, 140n,
  141n, 253
hieros gamos 81n, 192, 240
Highlands 91, 112, 222, 240, 248, 253
holy well/s xii, xiii, 4, 5, 27, 35n, 37n,
  46n, 94, 129n, 180, 184, 196, 241,
  250, 251, 257
  well/s (general) 30, 31, 34n,
  47n, 73, 185-187, 189-192, 194,
  196, 224, 227, 239, 241, 243,
  250, 254, 255
Holy Woman (= Brigit) viii, 6, 7, 18,
  33, 71, 188
  Holy Women 95, 96, 177-180,
  182-189, 226n, 227n, 254
honey 49, 50, 74n-76n, 97, 98, 100-
  102, 116, 129n, 131n, 141n, 175, 192,
  195, 212, 216-218, 230n, 237n, 243,
  248, 256
horn 10, 30, 31, 35n, 47n, 48n,
  68, 88n, 99, 100, 130n, 134n,
  138n, 147, 149, 154, 168n, 171n,
  190(Gjallarhorn), 195
horse 52, 60, 61, 81n, 82, 169n, 200,
  215, 225n, 229n, 234n,
Hrólfs Saga Kraka 57
hunter /hunting 55-60, 65, 68, 70,
  74n, 77n, 79n, 83n, 87n, 97, 102, 103,
  119, 120, 131n, 138n, 140n-142n,
  163, 164, 204, 208, 209, 219-221,
  233n, 235n, 238n, 245, 252
Hvergelmir (well) 189
Hyades (star) 163

I

Iceland 45, 57, 68-70, 122, 123, 240
  Icelandic xi, 41n, 69, 70, 109,
  134, 162, 163, 201, 240
Imbolc (óimelc) viii, 13, 34n, 39n, 244
incarnation 130
incense 90, 93, 104, 128n
India 79n, 136n, 163, 212, 218, 229n
Indo-European 14, 28, 49, 50, 72,
  74n, 85n, 102, 120, 121, 128n, 130n,
  138n, 139n, 188-190, 194, 195 212,
  216, 217, 231n, 239, 240, 242-244,
  246, 247, 252

International Tale Type (AT–) 54, 78n, 132n, 144, 149, 150, 239, 242
Ireland viii-xvi, 1, 2, 4, 9, 17, 33, 34n, 35n, 39n, 47n, 48n, 49, 50, 53, 54, 62, 68, 72, 74n-76n, 81n, 86n, 88n, 89, 90, 98, 99, 105-107, 109, 113-115, 124, 130n, 133n, 135n-137n, 142n, 144, 145, 147, 150, 151, 154, 162, 166, 168n-170n, 174n, 179, 184, 193-195, 200, 210, 222, 230n, 231n, 240, 242-247, 249-251, 253-256
Irish viii, ix, xi-xvi, 1, 2, 4, 8, 12, 15, 16, 18, 27, 28, 33, 34n-47n, 49, 50, 53, 54, 62-64, 71, 72, 74, 76n-78n, 81n, 85n-88n, 90, 91, 93, 96, 98, 99, 102-104, 110, 112-116, 118, 128n, 132n, 133n, 136n-138n, 140n, 142n, 143n, 145-147, 150, 151, 153-155, 157-163, 165, 166, 167n-173n, 175, 176, 179, 180, 182, 187, 188, 193-197, 199-202 206, 215-217, 222, 225n-229n, 233n, 234n, 236n, 238n, 240-257

J

January viii, xvii, 3, 10, 18, 69, 70, 81n, 86n, 122-124, 130n, 134n, 135n, 139n, 142n

K

Kalevala 40n, 68, 76n, 246
Ket (tribe) 235n, 239n, 142n
kidnap 144, 146, 147, 153, 155-157
Kildare viii, xii(abbess), 33, 48n, 200
knot/s 40n, 179
konebarsel [childbirth feast] 198
Koryak (tribe) 235n
kråknedandet 135n, 249
kvinna /kvinnogillen /kvindegilde [women's feasts] 88n, 134n, 196, 198, 251

L

Lady Day 109
lamb 26, 39n
lame /-ness 169, 177, 195, 219
Lapland /Lapp/s 62, 119, 171n, 203, 205, 206, 208, 209, 221, 233n, 235n, 239, 243, 245, 249, 253

'leaba Bríde' 24, 71, 72, 89, 90, 112
Lent 59, 123, 137n, 202
lightning 99, 231n
liminality 46n, 110, 210
limpet 105, 114
linga 28
Lives of Brigit viii, 128n, 200, 202
'Lord of the Animals' 30, 140n
love potions 159
luachair [rushes] 27, 43n
lullaby 35n, 148, 155-157
Lúnasa viii, ix, 1-4, 27, 30, 34n, 37n, 93, 94, 128n, 227n, 237n, 250
lye 93, 122, 142n

M

mac tíre [wolf] 53
madadh/madra [dog]/madar alla [wolf] 54, 103, 131n, 151
male 28, 32, 38n-41n, 44n, 55, 58, 59, 69, 78n, 80n, 81n, 84n, 93, 94, 102, 103, 122, 140n, 141n, 149, 164, 198, 204, 207, 209, 222, 234n
Manx 102, 109, 127n, 247, 251, 252, 255
  Isle of Man xiii, 86n, 109, 142n
marriage (customs) 14, 38n, 40n, 47n, 58, 59, 78n, 84n, 210, 248
Martyrology of Donegal 179, 250
Martyrology of Tallaght 179, 239
math /mathain /mathgamain [bear] 38n, 49, 50, 72, 74n, 103, 201
mating 2, 3, 4, 8, 13, 33, 87n, 100, 101, 120, 131n, 171n
Matrae (goddesses) 187
May Day 173n, 237n
  May Eve 38n, 95
mead 190, 192, 202, 216, 217
melatonin 83n, 239
melissai 99
menarche /menstruation 83n, 204, 206, 208, 209, 234n
Metrical Dindshenchas 61
midwife /-wives 7, 15, 16, 44n, 93, 196, 197, 210, 223
Migratory Legend Type (ML–) 144, 145, 150, 151, 153-155, 157, 158, 160-162, 164-166, 167n-171n, 241

Index of Subjects

milchobur [bear] 49, 50, 74n, 201
milk viii, xi, 3, 8, 10-14, 22, 37n, 38n, 40n, 44n-46n, 52, 79, 85n, 132n, 144, 147, 159, 162, 169n, 173n, 175, 177-179, 193-197, 202, 203, 212-214, 217, 218, 225n, 229n-231n, 248
Mímameiðr (tree) 189
Mímisbrunnr (well) 189, 190
'Mistress of the Animals' 53
Mjöllnir (hammer) 219
Moirai, Parcae (goddesses) 187
Mongols 210
moon 32, 70, 73, 88n, 100, 113, 114, 130n, 135n
mummers 62, 199, 231n
mushrooms 212-217, 236n, 255
music 18, 68, 84n, 87n, 101, 128n, 155, 156, 171n

N

Noa (names) 38n, 50, 53, 67, 72, 74n, 76n, 103, 105-107, 110, 217
Norns (Norse deities) xii, 106, 126, 187-189, 191, 192, 194, 195, 201, 203, 205, 230n, 232n, 246
Norway 37n, 45n, 60, 78n, 80n, 122-126, 133n, 144, 148, 149, 155, 162, 168, 170
   Norse x, 103, 106, 121, 125, 141n, 172n, 173n, 188, 189, 194, 195, 206, 216, 237n, 252, 254, 256
   Norwegian 52-54, 57, 60, 67, 68, 70, 78n, 122, 125, 143n, 147, 155, 161, 164, 168n-170n, 201, 205, 232n, 247

O

oak *See under:* tree/s
oatmeal 197, 201
obscene customs 81n, 82n, 199, 245
offering 31, 36n, 51, 75n, 104, 123, 125, 134n, 142n, 191, 194, 199, 204, 218, 230n, 233n-235n
Orochi (tribe) 120
Ostyaks (tribe) 87n, 235n, 239
oyster-catcher *See under:* bird/s
ox 37n 61, 99, 107, 148, 178, 225n
   See also: cattle; cow

P

paasio [rear entrance] 125
Parcae, Moirae 187
parthenogenesis 100, 115
parturition 12, 65, 209
peat 63, 64, 91, 92, 127n
penis /phallus 28, 37n, 45n, 47n, 59, 60, 81n, 85n, 117, 118, 137n, 139n, 141n, 162, 191, 192, 236n, 238n, 242
periwinkle 114, 115, 134n, 136n
Phoenicians 131n
photoperiod 65, 82n, 83n, 253
pilgrim /-age 4, 34n, 46n, 180, 182, 184, 186, 187, 245, 247
   See also: round; turas
piping 101, 104, 110
Pliocene 53
plough /ploughing 9, 43n, 47n, 80n, 107, 127n, 226n, 231n(Plough Monday)
porridge 201-203, 208
potato 9, 10, 22, 24, 26, 36n, 42n, 44n, 113, 114
'poundies' 22, 24, 44n
prayer 1, 4, 11, 17, 18, 20, 24, 37n, 46n, 77n, 91, 124, 125, 127n, 143n, 175, 176, 178, 218, 221, 224, 225n-227n
pregnancy 4, 7, 8, 44n, 45n, 54, 55, 65, 78n, 79n, 82n, 99, 130n, 138n, 204, 206, 209, 246, 247
primordial (water /beings) 44n, 115
Prim Papers 167n
propagation (crops) 9, 141n
prophecy 58, 96, 117, 120, 182, 187, 188, 190, 191
Prose Edda 131n, 240, 256
puberty 83n
punk tinder 214, 235n
purification 14, 15, 39n, 47n, 93

Q

Quarter Day viii, xvii, 3, 27, 34n, 36n-39n, 237n, 250
queen 45, 57, 63, 104
   queen bee *See:* bee

R

rapparee/s 153, 154, 170n
rescue 50, 131n, 144, 148-150, 153, 155, 157, 158, 161, 162, 164, 166, 168n, 170n, 171n, 174n
rhyme 18, 42n, 45n, 60, 70, 87n, 109, 130n, 134n, 158, 231n
Rigveda 212, 213
Riksha (star) 163
rime 194
robber/s 144-148, 154, 155, 157, 159, 164, 165, 167n, 172n
'round/s' 1, 18, 20, 71, 196, 199
  See: turas
rushes 11, 16, 23, 24, 26, 27, 42n, 43n, 113, 114
rústóg [bear] 49

S

sacrifice 70, 82n, 88n, 131n, 191, 192, 194, 199, 208, 209, 228n, 229n, 243
Sagai (tribe) 119
sail /sailing 184, 226n, 227n
Saints' Days /Feast Days
  Aed meic Bric's Day 197
  Brigit's /Bríd's /Bride's Day viii, ix, xvii, 1-4, 8-10, 13-16, 18, 20, 22, 24, 26, 28, 35n, 36n, 40n-42n, 49, 63, 64, 66, 68, 71, 76n, 86n, 89, 94, 95, 103-105, 113, 116, 135n, 196, 200, 217, 222, 223, 236n, 257
  Gobnait's Day 95
  Gregory's Day 106, 109
  Knut's Day 81n, 86n, 124
  Latiaran Sunday 95
  Martin's Day 2, 237n
  Matthew's Day 59, 80n
  Mel's Day 94
  Michael's Day 37n
  Patrick's Day 38n, 76n, 135n, 257
  See also: Festival
  See also: Saints *in Index of Names*
salmon 94, 229n
salute 58, 184
Samhain viii, 4, 22, 34n, 35n, 89, 90, 158, 160, 237n

Sámi xi, 30, 32, 33, 45n, 53, 55, 57-61, 67, 70, 76n-78n, 81n, 84n, 85n, 88n, 93, 103, 119, 125, 126, 131n, 133n, 163, 170n, 173n, 203-207, 209, 220-222, 233n, 252
Samoyed (tribe) 209, 235n, 244n
sauna (ritual) 199
Saxo Grammaticus 57, 137n, 164, 214, 231n, 236n
Scandinavia/n x, xi, 16, 30, 49, 57, 61, 67, 70, 98, 109, 123-125, 143n, 148, 150, 158, 161, 162, 166, 168n, 174n, 188, 201, 205, 206, 222, 233n, 243, 246, 254
Scotland viii, x, xii, xiii, 36n, 39n, 47n, 54, 60-62, 70-72, 89-91, 105, 107, 109, 114, 124, 135n, 179, 210, 222, 248, 249, 255
  Scottish ix, 28, 40n, 50, 60, 63, 68, 71, 72, 91, 92, 103, 105, 113, 127n, 137n, 153, 175-177, 179, 196, 206, 217, 222, 240, 245, 247, 248, 251, 253
segregation 42n
serpent 63, 64, 67, 68, 103, 104
sex /sexual xii, 13, 28, 37n-40n, 44n, 54, 55, 59, 62, 66, 78n, 84n, 85n, 102, 117-120, 131, 138n-141n, 191, 193n, 207, 235n, 236n, 245, 253
shaman 33, 53, 77n, 84n, 119, 120, 170n, 206, 212, 214, 215, 218, 233n, 234n, 239, 242, 244, 245, 252, 255
sheaf 10, 17, 22, 24, 30, 71, 89, 112, 200, 222, 234n, 243
shell/s 41n, 72, 90, 105, 112, 114-116, 132n, 136n, 137n, 191
shepherd /-ess 140n, 144, 149, 172n, 218, 231n
Shetland 111, 133n, 248
Shortsi (tribe) 119, 141n
Shrove /-tide 62, 80n, 81n, 136n, 202, 243
Siberia 59, 83n, 119, 206, 207, 209, 211, 212, 214, 235n, 237n, 238n, 239, 240, 242, 249, 250
sieve 163, 193, 237n
skogsrå [forest maiden] 53, 244

Index of Subjects

skull 58, 66, 79n, 84n, 118, 120, 134n, 141n, 220, 237n
Soiwe neit (Sámi festival) 60
spin /spinning xi, 24, 32, 35n, 42n, 43n, 46n, 106, 116, 162, 163, 172n, 173n, 188, 201, 231n, 233n
spring (season) viii-xi, 4, 8, 10-13, 36n, 38n, 46n, 48n, 59, 65-67, 70-72, 76n, 80n, 83n, 84n, 89, 95, 101, 106, 107, 109, 117, 135n, 195, 201, 202, 207, 215, 226n
star/s 32, 44n, 112-114, 120, 141n, 162, 163, 173n, 212, 233n, 239
stone 30, 32, 46n, 47n, 51, 72, 75n, 77n, 90, 107, 111, 112, 114, 116-118, 132n, 135n, 136n, 138n, 139n, 169n, 191, 208, 214, 229n, 253
straw 15-18, 20-24, 26, 30, 39n, 42n, 43n, 45n, 76n, 81n, 88n, 89, 112, 114, 196, 198, 199, 210, 222, 231n, 232n, 234n, 239, 243
sun /sunny 32, 70, 72, 73, 76n, 85n, 89, 99, 113, 114, 122, 141n, 144, 163, 180, 191, 203, 207, 233, 239
Sweden xv, xvi, 15, 30, 31, 37n, 60, 70, 76n, 77n, 81n, 86n, 109, 122, 123, 135n, 144, 148, 149, 162, 164, 214, 215, 234n, 253
 Swedish xv, xvi, 45n 55, 58, 59, 76n-79n, 81n, 109, 118, 125, 135n, 148, 164, 167n, 168n, 171n, 172n, 174n, 201, 234n, 238n
swine 78n

T

tad(h)g [badger] .201, 202, 247
 lá Thadhg na dTadhgann ['Tibb's eve'] 202
Tarvos trigaranus 107, 108, 134n
thief /thieves /thieving 49, 75n, 102, 123, 151
threshold *See under:* doorstep
thunder 45n, 121, 141n, 213, 214
Tobar na Córach 186, 194, 227n
Tobar na mBan Naomh 35n, 46n, 184-186, 227n

Topographica Hibernia 98, 137n, 251
trandagen /trankvällen 109
transformation 183, 202, 227n, 236n, 240, 252
transhumance xii, 38n, 144, 150, 155, 156, 164, 166, 168n, 170n, 174n, 226n, 243
 See: booley
transvestism 84n, 240
tree
tree/s (individual) –
 alder 48n, 118, 119, 124, 140n, 220, 226n
 ash 137, 190, 191
 birch 48n, 60, 67, 72, 90, 141n, 200, 212, 214, 220, 226
 fir 84n, 128n, 137n, 214
 oak 32, 38n, 48n, 99, 117, 118, 120, 121, 229n
 pine 58, 66, 68, 84n, 85n, 128n, 171n, 212, 214, 220
 rowan 48n
 spruce 148
 willow /sally 9, 37n, 72, 90, 107, 226n
tree/s (in general) –
 xi, 32, 38n, 47n, 48n, 51, 58, 68, 74n, 79n, 84n, 85n, 99, 107, 110, 115, 118-121, 134n, 137n, 140n, 141n, 148, 155, 156, 168n, 170n, 173n, 189, 191, 192, 194, 206, 210, 214, 219, 230, 234n, 237n, 239, 240, 243, 245-247, 255
troll/s 53, 77n
trumpet 68, 171n
Tunguz (tribe) 120, 141n, 241
turas 46n, 47n, 180, 245
 See also: pilgrimage; 'round/s'
turnip 18, 222

U

Udege (tribe) 141n
'understanding' [ciall /tuigse] 183, 184, 187, 190
Urðrbrunnr (well) 189
úrsóg [bear] 49, 74n

V

valföðrs veð 192
virginity /Vestals xii, 6, 8, 47n, 101, 112, 160, 163, 182, 187, 224, 241
Vogul (tribe) 103, 215, 235n
Völsa Tháttr /Voluspá 60, 121, 190, 246
völva (deity) 192

W

wake games 81n, 128n, 252
Wales 251
   Welsh 49, 115, 116, 123, 138n, 215, 225n, 251n
waralde biri (star) 53, 77n
wasp 97, 102, 115
water xii, 9, 11, 22, 24, 35n, 38n, 44n, 47n, 73, 82n, 84n, 110, 122, 133n, 136n-138n, 147, 151, 169n, 171n, 177, 184, 186, 191, 193, 202, 212, 214, 218, 223, 229n, 230n, 232n, 247
wax 76n, 102, 138n
weave/r /weaving 24, 25, 30, 32, 35n, 48, 115, 116, 132n, 138n, 151-153, 162, 163, 170n, 175, 195, 230n
wedding 55, 58-61, 79n-81n, 199, 212, 241
werewolf 151, 153, 161, 170n, 195
whistle /whistling 67, 68, 87n, 101, 133n, 171n
winter 8, 10, 11, 27, 30, 36n, 50, 52, 65-70, 72, 76n, 81n, 83n, 85n, 86n, 101, 107, 109, 115, 122, 135n, 136n, 139n, 151, 162n, 173n, 180, 202, 207, 234n
wolf 2, 36n, 50, 52-54, 57, 75n-79n, 85n, 86n, 103, 131n, 151-153, 161, 164n, 171n, 195, 229n, 232n, 243, 248
womb 38n, 54, 82n, 201, 203, 204
worship 14, 28, 60, 64, 74n, 87n, 96, 119, 126, 130n, 134n, 160, 170n, 186, 199, 209, 231n, 239, 242, 253

Y

Yakut (tribe) 119, 209, 141n
Yggdrasill (tree) 189-191, 217, 218
Yukagirs (tribe) 221, 235n

Z

zoomorphic deity/ies 49

ACKNOWLEDGMENTS

MY FEELING on re-engaging with *The Festival of Brigit* after so many years was in many ways one of sadness as I happened again and again upon references to deceased friends and colleagues who volunteered much valuable information and advice to me in the course of my research. I remember them with gratitude and also renew my thanks to all those still happily extant who helped in any way with the original publication, most especially Des Donegan and DBA Publications Ltd. The support of University College Dublin through its Library and inter-library loan service is also acknowledged. My best thanks are due to Dr Mary Condron whose constant encouragement persuaded me to rescue the original text – without her intervention, this edition would never have seen the light of day.

The second edition of *The Festival of Brigit* owes much to Sheila Jones and John D. O'Dwyer of Phaeton Publishing Ltd. who agreed to take matters in hand, deploying their good sense, style and expertise to maximum effect in identifying additional illustrations and making judicious suggestions regarding the text, and, in particular, for their patience in coping with the consequences of re-pagination. I thank them for their professional engagement and limitless enthusiasm.

Extracts from the manuscript and photographic holdings of the National Folklore Collection (at Figs. 1, 3, 4, 7, 9, 11, 13, 31, 32, & frontispiece) are by kind permission of the Director, Dr Críostóir Mac Cárthaigh. Permission to publish the following illustrations is also acknowledged:

Figs. 5, 6: National Museum of Ireland;
Fig. 16: Rheinisches Landesmuseum, Bonn;
Figs. 17, 18, 19: Nordiska Museet, Stockholm;
Fig. 20: Bernisches Historisches Museum;
Fig. 21: Dr Peter Harbison;
Fig. 22: Kungl. Gustav Adolfs Akademien, Uppsala;
Figs. 24, 25: Musée de Cluny, Paris.

THE AUTHOR

Dʀ Séamas Ó Cathain, born in Drumquin County Tyrone and educated at Queen's University Belfast, has been Professor of Celtic at QUB, and Professor of Irish Folklore at University College Dublin, and Director of Ireland's National Folklore Collection.

He has edited and authored numerous books on the folklore of Ireland and north-western Europe, including *Uair a Chloig cois Teallaigh /An Hour by the Hearth* (Comhairle Bhéaloideas Éireann: 1985); *The Festival of Brigit* first edition, (DBA Dublin: 1995); *Gaelic Grace Notes* (Novus Press, Oslo: 2014); and his autobiography *Jumping the Border* (Phaeton: 2018) also published in Irish as *De Léim thar Teorainn* (Phaeton: 2020). He is the editor of *Northern Lights: Following Folklore in North-Western Europe* (UCD Press: 2001), and joint editor of *Treasures of the National Folklore Collection / Seoda as Cnuasach Bhéaloideas Éireann* (Four Courts Press: 2010).

He has contributed to folklore programmes on RTÉ and BBC; in the 1980s he has been Vice-President and international jury member of RTÉ's Golden Harp Television Festival; and from 1996 to 2005 was Editor of *Béaloideas*, the Journal of the Folklore of Ireland Society.

His many international distinctions and awards include: Knight (First Class) of the Order of the Lion of Finland in 1986; the Dag Strömbäck Prize of the Royal Gustavus Adolphus Academy, Uppsala, Sweden, in 1994; and the Ruth Michaelis-Jena Ratcliff Prize, Edinburgh, in 1995. He is an honorary member of the Finnish Kalevala Society since 1981; and a member of the Folklore Fellows of the Finnish Academy of Sciences, Helsinki, since 1990. In 2021 he received the Jöran Sahlgren Award of the Royal Gustavus Adolphus Academy for his contributions to Nordic-Celtic cultural connections.

Living in Dublin since 1973, he is married to Maj Magnusson, whom he met in the late 1960s while he was a Lecturer in Celtic Philology and Folklore at the University of Uppsala in Sweden. They have a son Pádraig and a daughter Sorcha.

JUMPING THE BORDER
Autobiography
by Séamas Ó Catháin 210 pages, 80 illustrations

ISBNS (HBK): 9781908420275 (PBK): 9781908420268
(ENGLISH-LANGUAGE EDITION)

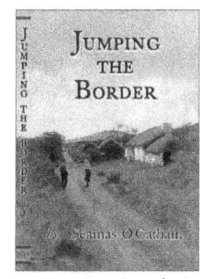

'A timely look at borders here and elsewhere, written in an engaging style. ...Ó Catháin provides fascinating insights ... he got to do research among the Sámi people of Norway and Finland. In this remote area, far from Ireland, he encountered many of the same issues he grew up with in Tyrone. Here, too, was a minority-language community struggling to maintain their identity and language in face of an officialdom determined to assimilate them.' —*Books Ireland magazine*

'The extended descriptions of the people and life of the shrinking Gaeltacht area *Na Cruacha* in Donegal...and the Sámi people high above the Arctic Circle, stand out for their insights into lives and living that few of us might get the chance to glimpse. ...This warm book – a memoir of insights and inspirations...across many borders' —*Béaloideas journal*.

DE LÉIM THAR TEORAINN

'A Gem...' '*Leabhar an-bhreá* Jumping the Border / De Léim thar Teorainn – *bhaineas an-taitneamh as, agus táim cinnte go mbainfidh na léitheoirí sult as.*'
—RTÉ *Raidió na Gaeltachta*

'*Is beag duine nach mbainfeadh taitneamh as an gcuntas beathaisnéise seo ...is blaiseadh iontach é an leabhar seo de shaol eachtrúil.*' —*Iris Comhar*

ISBN (CLÚDACH BOG): 9781908420282
(EAGRÁN GAEILGE)

DE LÉIM THAR TEORAINN
Dírbheathaisnéis
le Séamas Ó Catháin 210 leathanaigh, 80 léaráidí

PHAETON PUBLISHING LTD. DUBLIN WWW·PHAETON·IE

ALSO FROM PHÆTON PUBLISHING

POVERTY IN IRELAND 1837
A Hungarian's View — Szegénység Irlandban
by Baron József EÖTVÖS   216 pages, 70 illustrations, bilingual

ISBNS (HBK): 9781908420206   (PBK): 9781908420213

IRELAND BEFORE THE FAMINE

'An extraordinarily lucid and "modern" account of the desperate conditions and suffering that prevailed in Ireland in the decade preceding the Great Famine...'
—*DUBLIN REVIEW OF BOOKS*

'The Tragedy of the Irish – through Hungarian eyes ...Should be among the recommended readings for the responsible citizens of the European Union...'
—*CENTRAL EUROPEAN POLITICAL SCIENCE REVIEW*

'**One of the Best Irish Books of 2017** – The first thing the book does is demolish the fiction that Irish people were well-fed before the Famine. Ten years before it started they were already half starving in the streets...'
—*IRISH CENTRAL, NEW YORK*

'...acutely accurate...a vivid and gripping tale...totally contradicts the official story of Ireland peddled by its then administrators.'
—*BOOKS IRELAND MAGAZINE*

'Baron József Eötvös was horrified by what he witnessed'—*HISTORY IRELAND*
'A wonderful text...a fascinating insight'—*HUNGARIAN CULTURAL STUDIES, PA.*

PHAETON PUBLISHING LTD. DUBLIN   WWW·PHAETON·IE

CONFIDENT FRENCH from A to Z
—A Dictionary of Niceties and Pitfalls
by Michaël ABECASSIS   208 pages, 125 illustrations

ISBN (PBK): 9781908420183

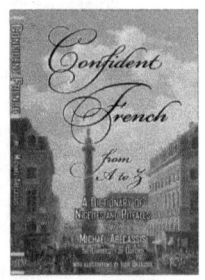

'...This is a lucid, informative and hugely entertaining book of French grammar and usage. ...a concise and illuminating explanation of all aspects of the language – ranging from general grammatical points to idiosyncratic usage of words and phrases, from pronunciation to orthography... This indexed and alphabetically-ordered book, abundant in quotations from authors and examples from everyday French, could be utilised by anyone studying French, but will appeal most to those with intermediate ability or above. It is a delightful book, with numerous illustrations by Igor Bratusek, visualising the content and thus facilitating its internalisation by the reader. This work should be heralded as **a major contribution to the pedagogy of French in our times**.'
—*GENGO NO SEKAI JOURNAL*, TOKYO ['*THE WORLD OF LANGUAGE JOURNAL*']

"Lovers of French will enjoy the latest book by Dr Michaël Abecassis"
—*WADHAM COLLEGE NEWS*, UNIVERSITY OF OXFORD

"An amusing but serious guide to the vagaries of French from a lecturer at the University of Oxford" —*BOOKS IRELAND MAGAZINE*, DUBLIN

ALSO FROM PHÆTON PUBLISHING

BEHIND A GEORGIAN DOOR
—Perfect Rooms, Imperfect Lives
by Artemesia D'ECCA 132 pages, 3 novellas, 6 illustrations

ISBNS (HBK): 9781908420152 (PBK): 9781908420145

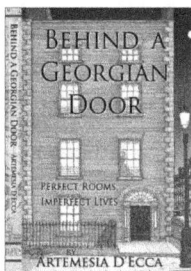

Chosen as '**Book Of The Week**' by *The Lady*:
'...Dublin's Georgian townhouses act as settings, characters and multilayered symbols in three compelling novellas...The houses...described in vivid detail – have biographies as carefully plotted as their inhabitants... from grand colonial residences to desirable flats, meagre bedsits or modern mansions...they chart developments in Ireland's troubled history. Symbols of a violent colonial past, and of modern-day bankers' greed, the houses are beautiful objects that elicit conflicted responses.' —*The Lady* magazine, London

'...firmly rooted in modern day Dublin...The idea behind the book must draw in anyone...who has wondered just what life is like behind those elegant neo-classical doors... Haunting all the stories is the history of the houses in which the action takes place... Dealing with difficult subjects with a light touch and even humour...D'Ecca has imaginatively responded to our curiosity about these old Georgian houses in three domestic dramas. ...wit and charm, but also portrayals of the hardships and cruelties that lie beneath the surface.' —*Midwest Book Review*, U.S.A.

PHAETON PUBLISHING LTD. DUBLIN WWW·PHAETON·IE

FRENCH CINEMA IN CLOSE-UP
—La Vie d'un acteur pour moi
edited by Michaël ABECASSIS with Marcelline BLOCK

452 pages (royal octavo size), 180 illustrations
ISBN (PAPERBACK): 978-1-908420-114
Mini-dictionary of French Cinema Actors

Chosen '**One of the 5 Best Reference Books of 2015 in the Arts**' by *Library Journal*:
'There may be other biographical dictionaries of the French Cinema, but none with such engagingly written biographies as this one. ...The highlights of the dictionary are the hand-drawn caricatures by artists Jenny Batlay, New York, and Igor Bratusek, Sorbonne, that accompany each sketch. Read collectively, the pieces document trends in French cinema and its close connections with the theater.' — *Library Journal*, New York

'...so rich in personal detail that it feels as if the reader is hearing the story from an old friend...its innovative format allows for a vast range of contributors... In linking French cinema to the other arts and to the history of France, the book succeeds in offering everyone who picks it up, from the veteran cinema buff to the merely curious, a chance to learn something new ...succeeds in placing French cinema in general under the magnifying glass, not just its actors...' —*Books Ireland* magazine

'...combines some of the best aspects...of academic study and coffee-table book...' —*Studies in European Cinema* Journal

www.ingramcontent.com/pod-product-compliance
Lightning Source LLC
Chambersburg PA
CBHW031423150426
43191CB00006B/372